Contents

Acknowledgments

As is typical of any endeavor of this scale, we have accumulated numerous debts in preparing this volume. Most important, we wish to thank Teo Ballve, co-editor at the North American Congress on Latin America (NACLA), who played a central role in conceptualizing the volume and who helped us recruit several of the contributors. Absent his input, the book would have turned out quite differently, and less compelling. André Schiffrin encouraged the project from the outset, as did NACLA co-editor Steve Theodore, formerly of The New Press. Moral support was offered throughout by fellow NACListas Christy Thornton and Marisa Maack and by editorial staff at The New Press, particularly Andy Hsiao. Former New Press publisher Colin Robinson was an enthusiastic advocate, and shared useful reflections about the structure of the book. Others on the Press's staff, including Maury Botton and Melissa Richards, assisted ably in the design and packaging of the book. Palgrave Press provided permission for the publication of chapter 2, by Paul W. Drake, an earlier version of which appeared in *Economic Doctrines in Latin America,* edited by Rosemary Thorp and Valpy Fitzgerald and published in 2005. It perhaps goes without saying that our gratitude extends to the chapter authors, all of whom accepted editorial suggestions with good humor and in several instances reworked their contributions repeatedly on tight deadlines.

Latin America After Neoliberalism

1

Turning the Tide?

Eric Hershberg and Fred Rosen

The quest for social justice in Latin America has long had two broad, frequently intertwined dimensions. On the one hand, activists and progressive policy makers have fought against a broad range of inequities within their own societies. In virtually every corner of the Americas, political movements in and out of power have championed the rights of the poor, excluded, and abused, typically incurring the wrath of dominant elites and privileged groups. On the other hand, a commitment to social justice has motivated an overlapping set of political actors to deal with injustices within the broader international system. This international dimension has produced struggles for the right to undertake autonomous national (or regional) development strategies against the predominance of various European powers or, for the past century or so, the United States.

Struggles for justice within Latin American societies have often been associated with one form or another of socialism, the broadening of citizenship, and/or the deepening of democracy. A key example of these struggles over the past century has been the pervasive activism of movements advocating the rights of poor rural workers. This activism has sought, since the Mexican Revolution of 1910–1920, to extend full citizenship, recognition, and a decent standard of living to peasants and landless wageworkers. The fight for social justice within the broader international context, on the other hand, has had more of a nationalistic flavor, typically pursued by leaders who have been able to mobilize national or regional pride. Serious efforts to develop economic institutions and policies independent of (though not necessarily antagonistic to) the United States go back at least to the middle of the last century, then backed by the UN's Economic Commission on Latin America (ECLA), now promoted by the South American member countries of the Common Market of the South (Mercosur). These two struggles—the social and the national—while closely related, have not always easily coexisted. Yet both are implicated in the region's long history of profound and dramatic political and economic transformations. The tectonic shifts that have rocked Latin America repeatedly over the course of its history have stemmed as much from internal dynamics as from the relationship of the region to the broader international system. And they are inextricably linked to the varied, ongoing quests for justice in domestic and international arenas.

At the dawn of the twenty-first century, a fresh wave of progressively in-clined governments has come to office across much of Latin America, backed by organized social actors that have come together to confront some, if by no means all, of the principal obstacles to collective well-being in the re-gion. This wave has gathered its greatest force in the Southern Cone and An-dean regions of South America. Both domestic and international dynamics are very much in play in contemporary Latin America. The focus of this book is on the context in which today's movements for change are operating, the particular challenges they confront, and the distinctive forms that they take in different settings.

By examining the nature of the political moment in Latin America, the vast set of social problems and injustices that afflict peoples across the re-gion, and the broad array of social and political actors who have organized themselves to bring a modicum of justice to the countries of the Americas, the book aims to make sense of ongoing changes at a moment of significant political openings amid unprecedented integration into global economic processes. In so doing, it takes into account both Latin America's shifting re-lationship to the outside world—particularly to the United States—and the evolving economic and demographic landscape of the region itself. Our ob-jective throughout is to explore prospects for development and social justice in the decades ahead. It is our cautious but optimistic premise that after nearly a quarter century of backtracking, the tide may be turning in favor of more inclusive, autonomous, democratic development as we begin the new century.

We take as our point of departure the dramatic shift in development strategy provoked by the international debt crisis that pummeled Latin American economies in the early 1980s. That shift has broadly defined Latin America's past quarter century. Market-oriented economic policies encouraged by the U.S. government and international financial institutions—and accepted enthusiastically by elites across much of the region—have dismantled the region's old, somewhat inclusive institutions of development. But these policies have failed to consolidate a stable alternative development strategy or a recipe for overcoming social injustice. Economic performance has been disappointing almost everywhere except, perhaps, Chile, and even there, already severe indices of inequality have grown worse, independent of trends in economic growth.

Perhaps paradoxically, the negative economic record since the early 1980s has coincided with an unprecedented opening of Latin American political systems. Though often weak, the institutions of electoral democracy exist today almost everywhere in the region. Even more impressive, amid intractable social and economic challenges, a growing array of social actors—including women, peoples of African descent, indigenous peoples, sexual minorities, victims of human rights abuses, the landless, and urban dwellers deprived of the resources necessary for living with dignity—have secured greater access to decision making with regard to countless matters of public life. The combination of persistent economic exclusion and growing political inclusion has been volatile, and is likely to remain so for many years to come.

THE DISCARDED MODEL: IMPORT-SUBSTITUTION INDUSTRIALIZATION

From the end of World War II until the onset of the debt crisis, most Latin American countries had achieved impressive records of economic growth through a process called import-substitution industrialization (ISI), a set of policies that stimulated the emergence of substantial working-class populations in the most advanced economies of the region. ISI was based on the premise that Latin American growth required the development of a strong manufacturing sector, and that such a sector could best be nourished by aggressive national investment (both public and private) accompanied by the temporary creation of high tariff walls to discourage manufactured imports.

Workers and other traditionally low-income groups were able to organize themselves in various ways during this period in efforts to secure greater political voice and to obtain a larger slice of the economic pie. Substantial progress toward greater equality in the distribution of wealth, income, and political participation was achieved by reformist movements of various sorts that emerged along with the rapid urbanization encouraged by ISI policies. Meanwhile, similar advances were pursued by revolutionary governments such as those in Bolivia, Cuba, and Nicaragua. Yet, for the most part, social justice remained an elusive objective. Moreover, periods of relative expansion of democracy alternated with often brutal dictatorships, frequently supported by U.S. assistance, as in Argentina, on and off from 1955 to 1983; Bolivia from 1964 to the early 1980s, followed by a series of quasi dictatorships; Brazil from 1964 to 1989; and, of course, the neoliberal Pinochet dictatorship in Chile from 1973 to 1990 and the many long, personalized dictatorships of Central America and the Caribbean. This uncertain political climate further constrained opportunities for representation and recognition for significant segments of the population.

The old ISI model afforded noteworthy opportunities for upward mobility and also for the sustenance of social solidarities, but the postwar recipe for development was far from perfect, and none of the contributors to this book propose its resuscitation. Based on protection of domestic markets, subsidies for local industry, public investment, and favoritism toward organized producers—who were preponderantly male, white, and urban—it achieved impressive rates of economic growth and constructed incomplete but in some cases ambitious systems for social protection. It was during this period, indeed, that social security, unemployment insurance, health care, and extensive public education became accessible to substantial segments of the region's middle and working classes.

Yet these achievements were woefully partial, and more often than not were bequeathed from the state by authoritarian leaders instead of conquered from below by a mobilized citizenry. Perhaps for this reason, the accomplishments of the system came at considerable cost. Latin America's inequalities remained among the most severe in the world, as social groups that lacked privileged ties to the prevailing political order were typically excluded from the fruits of the industrial boom or the state-building process that endured for several decades.[1] Exclusion was particularly widespread among Latin Americans residing in the countryside, for whom agrarian reform all too often remained an unfulfilled promise—if it was promised at all—as oligarchies, which in some countries remain entrenched to this day, resisted even timid efforts to modernize land-tenure regimes. Nor did the benefits of the inward-oriented model extend to the tens of millions of urban poor who toiled under conditions of informality, frequently residing in teeming shantytowns that sprung up inexorably as entire rural communities migrated to the cities, forced off the land and into urban squalor by the disappearance of agricultural livelihoods.

The highly centralized systems that characterized this period were exclusionary in other respects as well. They typically allowed little space for citizens to articulate their demands autonomously or to forge creative solutions to collective concerns at the national or even the local and community levels. In short, while the development paradigm that was eclipsed with the debt crisis was far from the total failure portrayed by advocates of neoliberal transformation, it was not an effective strategy for empowering subaltern populations, or for constructing social and political citizenship in the broadest, most emancipatory sense of the term.

Given that ISI advanced unequally in different parts of Latin America, the rural-urban distribution of the population varied significantly. In most of Central America, for instance, as well as in the Andean highlands, the majority of the population continued to toil in agriculture, whether in subsistence cultivation or in the harvest of cash crops destined for the world market. By contrast, in such countries as Argentina and Uruguay the overwhelming majority of people and jobs were located in urban settings, in services as well as in industry. In most cases, however, the privileged, overwhelmingly male formal sector depended upon the informal labor relations that persisted across important areas of protected economies. There was a marked tendency for women and indigenous segments of the population to experience inferior work conditions and higher levels of exploitation. The relative prosperity of city dwellers typically owed much to the benefits of subsidies for consumption and artificially low prices awarded to domestic food production.

Another key aspect of the ISI model was its reliance on funds borrowed from abroad, especially toward the end of the period when U.S. and European banks, in an effort to put accumulated "petrodollars" to profitable use, pushed even greater loans on unwary (ofttimes corrupt) Latin American borrowers. Many Latin American countries maintained a constant external debt that, during the many years of relatively stable economic growth, they were able to service on a timely basis. With the simultaneous decline of global commodity prices (slashing the export earnings of most Latin American economies) and rise of global interest rates in the early 1980s, the region's external debt suddenly became unmanageable. The first country to declare a moratorium on its payments was Mexico in 1982. Following Mexico's declaration of its inability to service its debt, the entire continent, in the eyes of developed-country lenders, became uncreditworthy. This was the onset of the debt crisis, which triggered severe economic contraction, widespread hyperinflation, and, in response, the neoliberal restructuring of the ensuing decades.

Inequality, state-level corruption, and subordination to the United States motivated countless popular movements throughout the twentieth century, some reformist, others revolutionary, some urban, and others rural. But ISI was supplanted not as a result of internal conflict but as a consequence of dynamics between Latin American economies and the broader international system. The immediate trigger for the onset of the enormous changes of the past quarter century was the regionwide crisis that followed the Mexican debt moratorium, not the internal contradictions of a development model that distributed prosperity and hardship in persistently cruel ways.

THE IMPOSED MODEL: NEOLIBERALISM

With the debt crisis came the virtual collapse of many of the region's economies and the imposition—sometimes under formally democratic regimes and sometimes under authoritarian rule—of reform packages commonly understood as neoliberalism. Indeed, the current social, political, and economic dynamics of the region were set in motion by the market-based reforms that were designed in the 1980s to impart a measure of fiscal and social discipline to Latin American governments and populations in the wake of that severe economic crisis. The reforms were introduced in the belief that such discipline would build confidence among the private investors—both foreign and domestic—whose self-interested financial activities were seen as necessary to drive the recovery and growth of those collapsed economies. The idea was that significant sums of direct and financial investment could be coaxed out of those investors only if they were reasonably certain that the funds invested in the region would be secure and profitable.

Thus, enforced both by U.S.-dominated international financial institutions and by the absorption of free-market versions of neoclassical economics by local elites, the protection of a secure investment climate quickly became the region's economic and political priority, typically at the expense of social well-being. Since the early 1980s, financial security has replaced social security as a policy goal; social inequality has grown; income has been redistributed upward; and, to lower the costs of doing business, the working poor have deliberately been deprived of economic opportunities and social mobility.

All this has been accomplished by the opening of Latin America's economies to foreign investment and trade by way of the privatization of public activity, deregulation of private activity, and production primarily for export and fiscal austerity—in a word, neoliberalism. This "opening" has stripped the subordinate classes of their old social protections (meager as they may have been) and welcomed them to a new era of social discipline.

The principal objective of the liberalizing reforms was to boost efficiency and jump-start economic growth, without which it seemed that economies in the region could never meet their external obligations. At the same time, however, advocates of structural reform contended that it was only through an opening to the world economy that Latin American countries could generate the efficiencies and employment levels needed to finally address the long-standing problem of poverty and exclusion. The new conventional wisdom

came to be known as the Washington Consensus, a package of policy measures that was advocated by decision makers in virtually every Latin American
country as well as by the international financial institutions (IFIs) that exercised enormous influence over economic policy during this period.[2]

From the 1980s onward, even those analysts who questioned the most
doctrinaire currents of promarket sentiment agreed that there was no alternative to abandoning the ISI framework that had defined Latin American
economies since World War II. The spirit of the times was captured aptly in
the phrase "Unavoidable Restructuring," which served as the title of one of
the best heterodox studies of the era.[3] Of course, no serious observer denied
that the costs of transformation would be painful, or that there would be losers as well as winners in the process of restructuring. Inefficient industries
would be forced to shut down, competition from abroad would squeeze local
producers, and beneficiaries of state largesse would lose long-standing privileges. What was not always acknowledged, however, was that the reforms
would, at least in the short run, redistribute income upward, squeeze the living standards of those who could least afford it, and shred whatever was left
of a social compact between the people and their rulers.

For precisely these reasons, social resistance to restructuring was widespread and, at least on occasion, temporarily successful in delaying if not
avoiding market-oriented reforms. Yet advocates of a shift in the development paradigm were undaunted, arguing that the long-term impact of
greater engagement with the world economy would be increased prosperity
and progress in overcoming Latin America's yawning social divides. Moreover, there seemed to be no alternative. Even when political candidates opposed to restructuring were elected over proponents of liberalization, upon
taking office they routinely applied orthodox policies over the protests of
their erstwhile supporters. This process happened repeatedly in Venezuela,
Ecuador, and Bolivia and played a role in radicalizing the opposition in those
three countries. That this tendency has persisted during the initial years of
the new millennium, alongside the rise to power of such moderately progressive forces as the PT (Workers' Party) government in Brazil and the Socialist
Party in Chile, testifies to the difficulties inherent in breaking out of the pattern installed in the wake of the debt crisis.

LABOR MARKETS AND LABOR DISCIPLINE

As the term "Washington Consensus" implies, the neoliberal reforms were imposed by a set of Washington-based financial and political institutions: the multilateral IFIs as well as a variety of departments and agencies of the U.S. government. As Paul W. Drake and Lars Schoultz make clear in their chapters in this collection, hemispheric domination in the current moment flows from at least two persistent sources of power. On the one hand, the United States has long been determined to maintain its dominant political-economic position within the hemisphere. This determination has not weakened even as challenges to it have ebbed and flowed. On the other hand, alongside U.S. political domination there is a domination of "the markets," frequently presented by promarket ideologues as a kind of domination by nature, or by "reality."

The domination of markets, however, is the domination of those who have preponderant power within those markets. Market power certainly has geographic dimensions, but more important, it has class dimensions. Transnational capital, though frequently headquartered in the United States, exercises class rather than national power. In the Americas, the domination of a capitalist class and the domination of the United States are not always easy to separate, though they have very different dynamics. And, as William Robinson argues in his contribution to this book, that class domination is compatible with a variety of political regimes, and thus has prevailed in times of democracy as well as under dictatorships.

The Washington-directed neoliberal reforms were meant, in part, to discipline the working populations of the Americas. As a result of this imposed discipline, more people are working under conditions of "labor flexibility," without long-term contracts and therefore without the benefits and guarantees (and obligations, of course) that such contracts imply. The proliferation of free-trade zones throughout the Americas and the rise of the maquila industry in Mexico have brought labor flexibility to prominence, but many long-standing formal industries, like construction and cleaning services, make ample use of flexible labor as well.

Formal, long-term, on-the-books employment allows a worker to be

covered by the minimal guarantees of a country's labor laws and allows workers to collectively organize to press for better wages, benefits, and working
conditions. It is the ability to organize, more than anything else, that is
undercut—North and South—by the growing regime of labor flexibility.
This lack of an ability to campaign for formal labor rights and expectations
has, in many settings, destabilized families' connection to community life
and undercut many of the formal rights and obligations that define citizenship. Citizenship, in many cases, has become even more ambiguous as much
of the disciplined, flexible, informal workforce seeks work in other countries
under conditions of uncertain legality and great vulnerability.

Flexible employment is not just about the conditions of work, but also
about a significant change in the culture of social obligations and expectations. Under a regime of flexible labor, every individual is expected to be responsible for his or her own destiny and to anticipate nothing from society as
a whole. Ideologically, flexible labor is accompanied by the belief that this individualist state of affairs is right, natural, and unavoidable. This marks an
enormous cultural change. While many of the grievances confronted by social movements are ancient, it is the neoliberal reforms of the past quarter
century that have sparked so many recent rebellions and protests from
below.

UNFULFILLED PROMISES

By the turn of the twenty-first century, neither advocates nor opponents of
neoliberal reform were satisfied by Latin America's economic performance.
The former had to concede that while inflation had been tamed during the
1990s, initial hopes for improved social welfare had proven unduly optimistic. Moreover, growth rates had declined sharply compared to those
achieved throughout the period of ISI. Whereas during the period from
1950 to 1980 annual growth rates were steady at well over 5 percent, these
figures dropped to 1.0 and 3.2 percent during the 1980s and 1990s, respectively.[4] Given this sluggish growth, it is no surprise that per capita income
stagnated during the 1980s and 1990s while poverty rates remained constant

at over 40 percent of the population. Nor were Latin American economies any less vulnerable than in the past to external shocks, as successive financial crises in Mexico, Brazil, and Argentina provoked contagion effects that undermined stability elsewhere in the region. Portfolio (financial) investors, who typically know very little about their investments beyond which of them are making money at the moment, quickly withdrew their investments from all of Latin America following Mexico's financial crisis of 1994–95, creating what was dubbed the "tequila effect." Subsequent portfolio-investor panics were called "the samba effect" and the "tango effect." For neoliberalism's detractors, this record confirmed expectations that market-oriented reforms imposed over their opposition would yield only greater hardship and continued vulnerability to external forces.

Many of the structures of state-led development that were built during the decades of economic growth that preceded the debt crisis have eroded to the point of near extinction. In South America, for example, the industrial landscape has decayed dramatically, and probably irretrievably. To be sure, the small number of industrial units that survive have boosted productivity to levels hardly imaginable not long ago, but these typically represent mere enclaves, accounting for negligible employment and connecting unevenly, at best, to the broader fabric of economic life. Although industry has performed better in Mexico and in parts of Central America and the Caribbean, dynamism has been concentrated in production of relatively low value-added goods in export-processing zones—the infamous maquilas—that typically afford low wages and limited ties to domestically oriented enterprises.

Thus, as analyzed in a *NACLA Report* in 2003, industrial upgrading remains elusive, and the result is that both the supply of jobs and their quality is inadequate to meet the needs of households and communities throughout the region.[5] Much the same can be said for agricultural production, where again the greatest advances have been achieved in sectors that are oriented to external markets and that provide only limited benefits in terms of employment or demand for domestic enterprises.

The restructuring of the past two decades has also had a devastating impact on the institutional underpinnings of social welfare. Latin America's social security systems and public universities, to cite just two examples outside the narrow realm of economic production, were flawed fundamentally, but they were worthwhile beginnings for societies that imagined a future in which all citizens would share opportunities to improve their lot. The survival of those institutions is now very much in question. They are victims of chronic underfunding and of an ideologically driven crusade to relegate the provision of public goods to the market.

At the beginning of what has been called a post–Washington Consensus era, there are signs that the Washington-based IFIs have come to recognize that their legitimacy was being undermined by the slow disappearance of public goods, public services, and even minimal social well-being. Thus, public expenditures on education and social services have increased substantially in recent years virtually everywhere in Latin America in a trend that has been supported by both the World Bank and the Inter-American Development Bank.[6] And while tax systems remain regressive and raise insufficient amounts of revenue given the range of social and economic needs that states ought to be addressing with urgency, many Latin American governments, with assistance from the IFIs, have substantially raised their administrative capability to collect taxes.

In this regard, as with advances in the efficiency and transparency with which some public services are delivered, not all of the reforms advocated by the IFIs must necessarily be jettisoned in order for a progressive alternative to take hold. Indeed, there are noteworthy instances in which Latin America's peoples are reaping the benefits of administrative reforms aimed at facilitating "good government."[7]

It is possible to build on these gains, but for that to happen at least two decisive shifts are imperative. Above all, policy makers must abandon a fundamentalist faith in markets and in the desirability of economic growth as the be-all and end-all of economic development. Economic policies must be implemented that meet people's needs. This is as urgent as it is straightforward.

Second, and not unrelated, development must be understood as inextricably linked to the construction of democratic societies in which people's needs and preferences are recognized as essential underpinnings of sound public policy. The past decades of Latin American history are replete with examples of market-oriented reforms that were imposed over the objections (or behind the backs) of the citizenry, often by leaders who had been elected to office precisely on the basis of pledges not to enact such measures. Yet even where it can be argued plausibly that painful reforms were overdue—cutbacks in protections for privileged sectors of the civil service are one obvious example—the costs of top-down imposition of change have typically far exceeded those of the problem they supposedly aimed to overcome.

Indeed, whether motivated by their own distance from the everyday lives of the people they govern or by pressures to conform to demands of international investors or officials of multilateral agencies, political leaders throughout Latin America enacted the neoliberal Washington Consensus without regard for public opinion. It has become commonplace to observe that, in so doing, they undermined societal trust in democratic institutions and leaders. But the costs of this exclusionary approach to decision making have run much deeper, and were found throughout the neoliberal period (which in many countries still exists) in the disappearance of the civic engagement, social solidarity, and awareness of collective interests that once characterized Latin American and Caribbean societies.

TURNING THE TIDE?

As suggested at the beginning of this chapter, we may be witnessing the turning of the tide in the importance given to social solidarity, civic engagement, and the quest for social justice, as much within the international arena as in the sphere of domestic relations. For one thing, even in Washington, the so-called Consensus on development seemed to be breaking down, as suggested by the alternative label "Washington Contentious," coined in 2001 by Nancy Birdsall and Augusto de la Torre.[8] More important, across much of South America in particular, the first decade of the new century has brought with it a wave of progressive elected governments that have been increasingly inclined to question economic orthodoxy and to advocate departures from the recipes proposed by free-market advocates. From Argentina and Uruguay to Bolivia and Venezuela, some have begun to contemplate a reversal of controversial privatizations and a partial restoration of barriers to U.S.-

dominated integration that had been torn down during the 1980s and 1990s. And even where steadfast opponents of neoliberalism have not yet come to power, societal opposition has inhibited rulers from moving further down the road of market-oriented reform. Such is the case in countries as distinct from one another as Ecuador and Costa Rica.

Sensing a vulnerability in Washington's current ability to defend its hemispheric influence, brought about, perhaps, by imperial overreach, a number of Latin American states have expressed a strong desire for a greater degree of independence from U.S. dictates. The resurgence of the Common Market of the South (Mercosur); the launching by Venezuela, Argentina, Uruguay, and Cuba of a noncommercial, continent-wide television network (TeleSur); the flexing of Southern muscles in such once-uncontested preserves of U.S. power as the Organization of American States and the Inter-American Development Bank; and the several Caribbean and South American oil-based commercial treaties initiated by Venezuela's Hugo Chávez are all state-level "declarations of independence" from U.S. domination. That the winner of Bolivia's 2005 presidential election could sustain a campaign largely on the basis of a promise to abandon the U.S.-sponsored "War on Drugs" testifies to the degree to which U.S. hegemony has been called into question, as does the electoral strength of presidential candidates opposed by Washington in small countries, such as Nicaragua, and larger ones, such as Mexico.

In this context, the leaders of the countries that make up Mercosur—Argentina, Brazil, Uruguay, Paraguay, and, the most recent member, Venezuela—have positioned themselves as the Latin American leaders who can most credibly organize, support, and protect an independent community of nations south of the Rio Bravo. They have cautiously attempted to cultivate a hemispheric countervailing force to U.S. economic and political power. Most of them would like to build Southern power while maintaining a nonantagonistic relationship with Washington, and in that vein are promoting U.S.-Mercosur negotiations as an alternative to the U.S.-promoted country-by-country negotiations to form a Free Trade Area of the Americas (FTAA). Their hope is that Mercosur, by combining markets and investment potential, will have much greater negotiating strength than each country by itself.

Venezuela's Hugo Chávez is the audacious rebel among these leaders, the self-declared opponent of the Washington Consensus (which he, alone among the South American presidents, refers to as U.S. imperialism), the radical who enlarges political space for everyone else. He has used this position to effectively promote Mercosur's desired regional solidarity. He has conducted a foreign policy based on South-South solidarity, unabashedly embracing the embattled Cuban revolution and even maintaining cordial trade relations with his longtime ideological and geopolitical antagonist President Álvaro Uribe of Colombia. And Chávez has worked closely with Brazil's Luiz Inácio Lula da Silva, Argentina's Néstor Kirchner, Uruguay's Tabaré Vásquez, and even market-friendly leaders like Mexico's Vicente Fox and Chile's Ricardo Lagos in the construction of a prudent political and economic solidarity in the face of U.S. domination.

Accompanying this more-or-less careful state-level dissidence over the years has been a much less cautious series of popular mobilizations. These popular mobilizations are typically aimed not at U.S. power but local elites who generally, these days, happen to be allied with U.S. interests. These mobilizations are also frequently directed against "friendly" governments to give them the backbone they need to withstand the enormous pressures on them to meet the needs of Washington before the needs of their own people. Brazil's Landless Rural Workers Movement (MST), for example, has continued to apply pressure on the Workers Party (PT) government of Lula da Silva to comply with its initial promises of significant land reform. And in Bolivia, from the very first days of Evo Morales's indigenous-rights government, Morales's own coca-growers' (cocaleros) movement has maintained a street presence to press for the legalization of the cultivation and consumption of the coca leaf. Perhaps the most noteworthy aspect of these movements is their social composition. The Andean countries, in particular, have experienced unprecedented mobilization by indigenous peoples whose voices have long been absent from the landscape of national-level politics.

These activists, in and out of government, have made astute use not only of the powerful legitimacy of the social security and solidarity that were undermined by neoliberal reforms, but also of the legitimacy of the representative democracy that has become such a key component of the discourse of

U.S. foreign policy. One of the interesting current responses of the popular movements is their symbolic invasion of the terrain of "democracy promotion," long the property of U.S. discourse. Playing by the democratic rulebook—as in the recent South American moves toward greater independence from U.S. domination—has rendered direct repression and the isolation of dissenting regimes illegitimate (though as we have seen on all too many occasions, not out of the question). This has given democratically elected regimes, and popular movements as well, additional breathing space.

In any case, overcoming the legacy of neoliberal reform will take some time and will require vigorous efforts from civic and social movements as well as from transformation-minded governments. The prospects for achieving greater levels of social justice in the region will hinge on the capabilities of communities to forge integrative projects for development. In other words, it will be essential to elaborate strategies for change that incorporate the abilities and interests—and thus the enthusiasm—of the broadest possible segments of the population. Anything less than that will be insufficient to overcome the heritage of polarization and underdevelopment that predates the neoliberal era but that has grown so severe under its auspices. Identifying a socially driven agenda and politically democratizing modes of decision making are important steps forward, but the realization of democratic aspirations will require prolonged practical and intellectual struggles.

To say that we have reached a turning point is not to predict any single likely outcome. Nor is it to suggest that all of the pressing problems afflicting the peoples of the region will be addressed successfully, or that all of the more-or-less incipient movements for change will see their efforts rewarded. Quite the contrary—in Latin America as in so much of the world, we are witnessing a moment of intense and highly uncertain flux. That very uncertainly signals the degree to which the stakes in the debate over Latin American development strategies are both high and the objects of intense struggle. The processes under way are highly political as well as economic and reveal the often-diverging interests of North and South, not to mention the depth of the chasm separating the forces that wish to safeguard hierarchies and privilege from those who would overturn these in the interest of social justice.

This is also a moment of intellectual struggle between, on the one hand, the defenders of orthodoxy who move in and out of academia, the corporate world, Northern and Southern governments, and the IFIs, and on the other, their critics, who may also inhabit academia, march in the streets, work in communities, or serve in progressive Latin American governments, and who may dream—some of them, at least—that a better world is possible.

THE STRUCTURE OF THE BOOK

This book is divided into three overlapping yet analytically separable sections. We begin with consideration of Latin America's place in the world, particularly vis à vis the United States, whose economic and political preponderance has been a recurring feature of the landscape for the past century. The book then turns to a series of stubborn challenges that confront the peoples of Latin America—and their governments—as they endeavor to achieve a more just social order. The third and concluding section is devoted to analysis of particular social forces that are likely to prove crucial to determining the prospects for progressive change over the coming decade and beyond.

The U.S. presence in the region has encompassed regional economic decision making, as Paul W. Drake contends in chapter 2, as well as persistent efforts to shape the internal politics of Latin American countries. Indeed, time and time again over the past century, the insistence on preserving influence, if not control, over domestic politics in the region has motivated alliances between the United States government and reactionary forces seeking to resist pressures from below for social change. Especially within the past half century, this insistence has produced repeated U.S. confrontations with revolutionary and even reformist movements in the region. The antagonisms these confrontations have generated have typically been framed by U.S. policy makers as matters of national security, as Lars Schoultz explains in chapter 3, and Washington has used that banner to wage covert and sometimes not so covert warfare against its foes: its overthrow of a reformist Guatemalan government in 1954; its invasion of the Dominican Republic in

1965 to prevent the return of an independent, social-democratic regime; its overt support of the Chilean military coup in 1973; its interventions in Central America throughout the 1980s; its ongoing, nearly half-century attempt to isolate and defeat the Cuban Revolution; and, most recently, its persistent attempt to reverse the leftward drift of most of South America.

Aside from Washington's bizarre and persistent obsession with overturning the weakened revolutionary regime headed by Fidel Castro in Cuba, the most tangible evidence of its continuing interventionist leanings are now to be found in the Andean region. Buttressed by the high oil prices of recent years, Venezuelan president Hugo Chávez has had the resources needed both to invest in social policies at home and to act regionally to advance his conviction that there can be a so-called "Bolivarian" alternative to the U.S.-dominated pattern of Hemispheric relations that has prevailed for several generations. Not surprisingly, Chávez's unabashed independence has rankled the Bush administration, which tried to overthrow him in a botched coup d'état in 2002. Washington has generously funded the domestic opposition, and right-wing elements in the United States and elsewhere have gone so far as to advocate his assassination. While rendering some in Washington apoplectic, Chávez's movement has at the same time kindled hopes among many if not all segments of the Latin American left. Whether he will be able to maintain his redistributive agenda in Venezuela and attract enthusiastic support from Latin American and Caribbean governments remains to be seen, as does the degree to which the Venezuelan project can continue to evolve within a democratic institutional framework. There can be no doubt, however, that the Bolivarian agenda will be a central referent for the Latin American left for the foreseeable future.

The Andean region also is the site of the other most prominent example of U.S. intervention: Colombia and Ecuador are the principal theaters for the futile "War on Drugs," though its effects reverberate to neighboring countries as well as to Central America and Mexico, where narcotics-funded criminal networks jeopardize the lives and livelihoods of millions of citizens. As Coletta A. Youngers argues in chapter 4, the drug war is as costly as it is unwinnable, yet it has proven virtually impossible for Andean governments to escape its logic while remaining in the good graces of Washington. For this reason above all others, the Bush administration has responded with grave disapproval to the 2005 electoral triumph of Evo Morales, the charismatic Bolivian indigenous and coca-growers leader who has vowed to reverse that country's policies of coca eradication. Coinciding as it does with powerful social mobilization against neoliberalism, Evo's election has implications that reverberate far beyond Bolivia's borders, even while it carries with it grave risks. The aspirations he embodies may be exceedingly difficult to satisfy in a country in which devastating poverty afflicts the vast majority of the population, which now faces the implacable hostility of the U.S. government, and where elites remain as avaricious as ever.

If the experiences of Venezuela and Bolivia provide hints of the limits of Washington's advocacy of competitive politics, those of the Central American countries reflect the ways in which representative democracy has at times operated to advance U.S. interests. In chapter 5, William Robinson contends that, by favoring the constrained form of electoral democracy called "polyarchy" in such countries as Guatemala and El Salvador, the United States has allied itself with local elites behind a formula for continued exclusionary rule. This is a dramatic development to the extent that the history of the Isthmus during the 1970s and 1980s is largely one of civil conflict pitting popular insurgencies against oligarchic dictatorships in which military forces bankrolled and trained by Washington carried out scorched-earth policies of repression. With the peace accords in El Salvador and Guatemala and the apparent eclipse of Sandinismo in Nicaragua, the ground was cleared for a new model of domination in which neoliberal policies were enacted by elected governments presiding over political systems to which there seemed to be no alternatives. At this writing, despite approval of the Central American Free Trade Agreement (CAFTA) advocated by the Bush administration and Central American elites, cracks may be beginning to emerge in the edifice described by Robinson. Although there is ample reason to question whether today's Sandinismo offers the sort of progressive vision as that which triumphed in the revolution of 1979 and governed for the ensuing decade, the prospect of its return to power in 2006 has motivated Washington, yet again, to backtrack from its stated commitment to respect all "free and fair" electoral outcomes.

Sandinismo was, of course, one of the past century's most dramatic currents of resistance to U.S. domination, continuing a tradition highlighted, perhaps, by the Cuban Revolution but evident in countless movements, big and small, throughout the Americas. Both its aspirations and its failures form part of a long history of revolutionary and reformist politics aimed at both achieving independence from Washington and effecting meaningful social and economic transformation. Stated differently, Sandinismo represents one important episode in the continuing saga of the Latin American left, and remains an important referent for contemporary struggles for justice.

The second part of the book reflects on some of the principal challenges confronting advocates of progressive transformation in Latin America. Perhaps foremost among these is that which we discuss in the first part of this introductory chapter: the need to put forth a development model—or models—conducive to sustaining economic growth while distributing resources and opportunities widely to segments of the population that have long been deprived of both. In this context, chapter 6, by Luis Reygadas, and chapter 7, by Araceli Damian and Julio Boltvinik, deal respectively with the perennial problems of inequality and poverty. Latin America remains the most unequal region on earth, and the distance between the haves and have-nots is, in and of itself, evidence of the distance that remains to be traversed if we are to address problems of injustice. That this inequality coincides with rates of poverty that are as severe as those of a quarter century ago—and that thus affect millions more than at any previous moment in Latin American history—testifies both to the bankruptcy of prevailing development models and to the urgent need for alternatives.

Alongside these fundamentally material (but at the same time eminently political) concerns, numerous other issues stand out as central dimensions of contemporary struggles for justice. One series of issues, which space limitations here preclude our addressing in detail but which nonetheless must be underscored, concerns the unequal distribution of education, health, and environmental resources. Recent decades have witnessed noteworthy advances in access to primary and secondary education, but problems associated with the quality of training have long been overlooked, to the detriment of generations of Latin American youth who find themselves lacking the tools needed to prosper in the increasingly competitive economic environment that has accompanied opening to global markets. Along with the deficiencies in primary and secondary education we find the sorry state of higher education throughout most of the region: more students than ever before are able to access university-level training, but all too often what higher education is available fails to prepare students for meaningful employment.

The situation with health and environmental security is hardly more encouraging. The fragility of ecosystems imperils the livelihoods of rural communities throughout the region and—as demonstrated by the devastating effects of Hurricane Mitch in 1998 and Hurricane Stan in 2005—of those who lack safe housing in urban and rural environments alike. Meanwhile, tens of millions of Latin Americans lack adequate sanitation, access to potable water, and protection from infectious diseases that have long been eradicated in the more prosperous societies of the Global North. Overburdened and underfunded public health and retirement systems are being further hollowed out by the shift in resources toward private health-care provision and pensions. Despite some noteworthy success in extending health coverage to households lacking formal-sector employment, much remains to be done to ensure access to this basic right of citizenship. Meanwhile, the failure to adequately finance existing retirement systems and to extend old-age insurance to millions imperils the welfare of the elderly, who were supposed to have been protected by the existing regime and who are living longer than ever before.

Above and beyond such perennial concerns are others that, at least on the surface, appear to be of relatively recent vintage. As Mark Ungar describes in chapter 8, everyday life in Latin America has become as violent as it is inequitable. Police and judicial institutions are in disarray virtually everywhere in the region, prompting a proliferation of privatized security systems, most of which have begotten further exclusion and violence. Efforts at enlightened reform have been only halfhearted and have lacked sufficient resources or political commitment. The result is a crisis of citizen security of monumental dimensions, and the problem is one that advocates of progressive social change cannot ignore. Forever vulnerable to physical harm, Latin American citizens will neither support nor accept alternative visions that fail to promise a recovery of state protection of public safety: just as truly democratic states require the capability to extract sufficient resources to provide for the public good, they must also have the power to monopolize legitimate instruments of violence.

Yet all too often in Latin America's history, state and para-state monopolies on violence have resulted in campaigns of repression against the citizenry, frequently without discriminating between regime opponents and innocent bystanders. One especially appalling feature of the dictatorships that plagued the region at various moments throughout the twentieth century was their horrifyingly innovative tools of repression. It was in opposition to such savagery that Latin American human rights movements captured the attention of public opinion around the world. The Mothers of the Plaza de Mayo in Buenos Aires were but the most well-known representatives of a phenomenon that was far more widespread than is generally known and that has persisted through the valiant work of human rights advocates seeking to document crimes committed by states and their agents and to hold accountable those who perpetrate abuses.

Alongside the need to find ways to begin to heal the wounds of the victims of these atrocities and their families, a pressing challenge facing Latin American societies today is how best to both acknowledge publicly what occurred and ensure that it never happens again. Katherine Hite explores in chapter 9 some of the principal features of the ongoing debates over memory and commemoration. In so doing she reminds us that the struggle to protect human rights persists long after the dictatorships that violated them have been defeated.

The phenomenon of exile forever marks Latin American societies that suffered under dictatorships during the second half of the past century. Chileans, Uruguayans, Argentines, Guatemalans, and Salvadorans left their countries by the tens of thousands, often never to return. Yet political conditions that compel citizens to go into exile sometimes have coincided with economic circumstances that leave little alternative but to migrate abroad. The relative weight of political and economic factors is sometimes difficult to distinguish, as was evident when Central Americans fled their countries for the United States during the 1980s. But as Judith Adler Hellman considers in

chapter 10, whatever its causes, migration is about dislocation and uprooted-
ness, and about the impossibility of sustaining oneself in one's own land on
one's own terms. Ironically, just as the neoliberal moment made national
boundaries more porous for capital, trade, and investment, it propelled, but
refused to legitimize, cross-border movements of population. The situation
of Latin American migrants, principally in the United States but in Europe
and neighboring Latin American countries as well, extends the realm of justice struggles beyond national and regional borders. In this regard, the struggle for justice for Latin Americans becomes a struggle well beyond the
region's boundaries.

These struggles for justice are the subject of the chapters in the third section of this book. In chapter 11, Carlos M. Vilas sets the stage for this discussion with a critical analysis of the birth and coming to power of a new Latin
American left. This "new left," says Vilas, varies from movement to movement
and country to country, but has in common a pragmatic willingness to work
within many existing global and national structures at the same time that it
challenges those structures to change in ways that increase popular participation and redistribute income downward. This "new left," argues Vilas, is also
sympathetic to the separate "sectoral" struggles of the many oppressed and
disadvantaged groups within society. This is a theme taken up by the final
three chapters of the book.

In chapter 12, Norma Chinchilla and Liesl Haas discuss the advances and
contradictions that are evident in the experience of Latin American women.
Feminism has become a core component of social justice coalitions across
the region at the same time that women have had to fight continually to prevent their demands from being eclipsed by those of class or nation. Transnational and regional coalitions have played an important role in empowering
women's movements as they have for peoples of indigenous and African descent, even while some feminists have justifiably worried whether the focus
on global forums detracts attention from the urgent tasks at hand within
national political systems where a vast amount of work toward women's empowerment—legislative, institutional, and normative—remains to be done.
Similarly, tensions between the collective demands of women and the logic
of individualism embodied in neoliberal formulas for governance affect

women's movements just as they do those for historically repressed racial and ethnic groups.

In chapter 13, Shane Greene turns our attention to the striking advances made in recent years by indigenous-identified movements and by peoples of African descent. Repressed and often silenced for centuries, these communities are increasingly gaining political voice if not yet fulfillment of their historically legitimate demands for full citizenship. Perhaps the most noteworthy changes are those that are sweeping across the Andean region, where indigenous-identified movements have become protagonists on the national political scene in Bolivia and Ecuador and are beginning to negotiate for power in Peru. Yet Greene's analysis of these countries highlights many of the serious pitfalls facing such movements, as well as the ways in which states seek to appropriate ethnic symbols for ends that may be less than emancipatory. Moreover, echoing Chinchilla and Haas's reflections about the challenges facing Latin American women's movements, Greene underscores the contradictory ways in which neoliberalism and international organizations have opened avenues for recognition of cultural diversity while they have at the same time placed constraints on the possibilities of effecting more radical change in relations of power and resources.

Finally, in chapter 14, Mark Anner turns our attention once again to organized labor, the centrality of which we explored in the initial paragraphs of this introduction. Just as organized labor was a central player in ISI, it was (and remains) fundamentally challenged by neoliberalism and must be central to renewed efforts to place people's needs at the forefront of the development agenda. As Anner points to transborder alliances as an important tool in the arsenal available to contemporary labor movements, we see significant overlaps with the perspectives outlined with regard to other social actors considered in this book. Yet with labor as well, transnational alliances cannot substitute for legal and regulatory mechanisms at the national level. Rather, they must complement them.

The need for solidarity across borders is thus one central message of this book. Another is that a viable agenda for social justice must combine an awareness of historic struggles—and the social and intellectual categories used to advance them—with an openness to explore novel ways of framing the world and its opportunities. Ours may be a time, for example, in which Latin America's independence may not require separation from the United States, but rather may benefit from subaltern coalitions spanning both northern and southern regions of the hemisphere. Similarly, a rejection of neoliberalism may not justify dismissal of the potential role of markets, which, rendered accessible to all, may offer opportunities as well as risks to workers and consumers as well as to owners and managers of capital. At the same time, awareness of the dangers inherent in state power may not preclude our commitment to strengthening the state, to developing public institutions that protect the citizenry and create opportunities rather than allow narrow groups to monopolize them.

We live at a moment when democracy matters, but it cannot be reduced strictly to a matter of institutional forms and procedures for selecting among competing candidates for office. Rather, the democracy for which Latin Americans are striving, and for which those working in solidarity must join in conceptualizing and bringing about, is one in which individual and collective interests can be articulated freely and expressed through healthy debates that result in concrete policies entailing institutional change and resource redistribution. Without those substantive democratic changes, the struggles for which are beginning to strengthen, Latin America would face several more centuries of subjugation. The path ahead is a difficult one, pocked with yawning potholes and replete with perplexing forks in the road, but it is one on which there is no choice but to embark. And the chances of reaching a suitable destination look somewhat brighter today than they have for many years. The tide, indeed, may be turning.

2

The Hegemony of U.S. Economic Doctrines in Latin America

Paul W. Drake

INTRODUCTION

The implantation of U.S. neoliberalism in Latin America in the closing decades of the twentieth century resembled the installation of U.S. laissez-faire doctrines in the opening decades of that same century. Both experiences took place when U.S. hegemony was expanding in the hemisphere. Many of the ideas and even some of the transmitters were similar. However, the second period of penetration was more complex, pervasive, and profound. It involved a far greater paradigm shift in Latin America. Whereas the first transfer of economic technology had built upon the previous British promotion of free-market ideas, the second infusion had to roll back decades of Latin American advocacy of government economic intervention. The celerity with which most of the Latin American republics capitulated to that U.S. offensive in the 1980s and 1990s was stunning. However, from the perspective of hegemony theory and history, it looks like the most logical move they could have made.

Hegemony Theory

From the point of view of hegemony theory, the United States, as the dominant economic and military power, has rationally and repeatedly injected its economic doctrines into the Latin American countries. The hegemon has waged this war of ideas to establish, regulate, and maintain a stable and open international economic order commensurate with its policies and interests. Given the paucity of easily enforced international economic laws and regulations, the United States has sought to put in place broad rules of the game that will be accepted, internalized, and obeyed by all the key players. The participants do not always have to adhere to the letter of the law but only to confine their actions within acceptable boundaries. Such conformity has reduced risks for U.S. capitalists venturing abroad and for their counterparts in the recipient countries.

For the Latin American rulers, consumption of the United States's economic model has eased their entry into an international system wherein the United States appears to guarantee some stability and a chance at prosperity. Although sometimes resentful of U.S. arrogance and disproportionate gains, most of them have preferred subordination to anarchy or isolation. Therefore, they have agreed time and again to adopt U.S. institutions and laws, clamp down on inflation, stabilize exchange rates, restrain government spending, open their economies, and respect foreign property and obligations. In return for such good behavior, the United States has provided the collective goods of safeguarding the international flow of capital and commodities.

When the Latin Americans have strayed from the path of virtue, they have been reminded to get back on the straight and narrow by the United States, its agents, and its allies. Once admonished, they have repeatedly vowed to behave better in the future, sometimes by adopting the regimens of foreign advisers, such as the International Monetary Fund (IMF). These accommodations between the hegemon and its underlings have required extensively reiterated bargaining and negotiating over such issues as exchange rates, tariffs, and the rights of foreign investors. Whether independently or through international institutions like the World Trade Organization (WTO), both sides have tried to minimize their costs and maximize their benefits. Even when the hegemon has gained more from this economic version of collective security than have its junior partners, the minions have stayed in the game so long as their long-range benefits seem to exceed their costs. The only other option for the smaller powers has been to defect to an alternative economic regime, which effectively ceased to exist after the end of the Cold War, or to go their own way, which has become impractical after the globalization of capital, production, trade, and neoliberal precepts.

Within the subordinate states, these decisions to collaborate rather than clash with the hegemon have depended on the perceptions of local ruling groups and governing coalitions. Therefore, the United States has sought to shape not only the international arena but also the decision making within the weaker countries. Although willing to use force—including the U.S. Marines and the Central Intelligence Agency—to extract concessions at times, the United States has found it far cheaper to obtain consent through pressure, persuasion, and consensus. The salespersons and intermediaries for U.S. economic doctrines have convinced the Latin Americans to play along and have persuaded the hegemon that its clients are behaving properly, within reasonable limits.[1]

THE HISTORY OF U.S. ECONOMIC DOCTRINES IN LATIN AMERICA

Partial Hegemony, 1890s–1920s

At the end of the nineteenth century, the United States began establishing its political and economic preeminence in Mexico, Central America, and the Caribbean. Following the opening of the Panama Canal and the conclusion of World War I, the Colossus of the North displaced Great Britain in South America as well, bringing the west coast into its orbit in the 1920s and the east coast in the 1940s. After a spate of direct colonization and imperialism in the Caribbean Basin at the turn of the century, the United States opted for the less expensive, controversial, and risky policy of promoting the "open door." Because of its enormous comparative advantages, the United States believed that it could prevail over European and Latin American competitors so long as all the countries in the hemisphere gave it equal access to trade and investment opportunities. The more the Latin Americans adopted U.S. economic ideas, institutions, and practices, the easier that access became. The U.S. demand for openness was generally well received in Latin

America in the prosperous 1920s, as it would be again in the 1980s and 1990s.[2]

From the Spanish-American War until the Great Depression, U.S. trade as well as direct and indirect investment mushroomed in Latin America. U.S. entrepreneurs, bankers, investors, advisers, and government agents prodded Latin America to adopt U.S. economic ideas and organizations to facilitate that commercial interchange. In the Caribbean and Central America, the United States dispatched economists along with troops to install the economic as well as political institutions. In South America, the United States delivered similar economic advice through private agents hired by host countries, the most famous of whom was the "Money Doctor," Edwin W. Kemmerer. From the 1890s through the 1920s, every Latin American country except Argentina and Brazil contracted with U.S. financial consultants.

Throughout the hemisphere, these economists recommended the gold standard, independent central banks, regulated commercial banking, balanced and monitored government budgets, transparent management and accounting of government finances, national comptrollers, effective taxation, prudent and productive public works, streamlined judicial review of business disputes, efficient customs administration, free trade, cautious borrowing and reliable debt servicing, and equal treatment for foreign capitalists. They helped these countries attract foreign loans by combating deficit spending, inflation, and exchange instability. Unlike their counterparts in the 1980s, these fiscal physicians did not have to push deregulation and privatization because the Latin American states were not yet deeply involved in their economies. The Latin Americans imbibed the missionaries' advice mainly to improve their access to foreign loans on reasonable terms.[3]

Hegemony Challenged, 1930s–1970s

The Latin Americans turned against the U.S. open model first in pragmatic response to the international market havoc caused by the Great Depression and World War II and second in intellectual response to their unequal share of world growth after the war. During and following the 1931–33 crash, most Latin American governments scuttled the doctrine promoted by the United

States in the 1920s of the gold standard, autonomous central banks, minimal government, balanced budgets, punctual debt payments, and free trade. They proceeded to junk the gold standard, capture central banks, enlarge currency emissions, expand government intervention, balloon deficit spending, suspend foreign debt payments, install exchange controls, impose import restrictions, and protect national industry. These measures reflected the diminution of U.S. power, the rise of Keynesian statism and protectionism in the United States itself as well as in Western Europe, and the arrival of challengers to U.S. domination, especially Germany.

The economic catastrophe of the 1930s undermined constitutional republics in South and Central America, which were usually replaced by military dictatorships. By contrast, the debt crisis of the 1980s would usher in democracies as well as neoliberal economic policies. In other words, classic liberalism took a beating both economically and politically in the 1930s, while it experienced a resurrection on both fronts in the 1980s. This pattern comports with the broader historical experience with severe external economic shocks, which usually inspire countries to experiment with the opposite of whatever political economy combination existed before.[4]

This inadvertent Keynesianism in the 1930s was rationalized, legitimized, theorized, and institutionalized by the United Nations' Economic Commission for Latin America (ECLA) in the 1940s and 1950s. The doctrine came to be known as "import-substitution industrialization" (ISI) or "structuralism." More radical versions evolved into "dependency theories."[5] What the United States had seen as emergency measures in reaction to the collapse of international trade and finance in the 1930s became, to its dismay, standard Latin American policy from the 1940s to the 1970s.[6]

There was no great mystery as to why the Latin Americans turned away from traditional U.S. economic advice in the 1930s. With the disruption of international trade, they needed to protect domestic industries to produce what they used to import and to conserve foreign exchange. With the interruption of international finance, they naturally suspended debt payments and engaged in deficit spending. There was little incentive to follow free-market doctrine to attract foreign investment, since there was virtually no investment in the offing. Indeed, no massive influx of private indirect foreign capital arrived again until the 1970s, when some Latin Americans began adopting more classical liberal economic policies, reminiscent of the 1920s, in order to obtain and service foreign loans.

If there was a mystery in this period, it was the question of why Latin America hung on to interventionist doctrines so long in the 1950s and 1960s, when U.S. hegemony might have pushed them "back into line." Most U.S. economists and policy makers roundly criticized the ISI strategy and widespread interference with markets. Economists from the U.S. private sector and government, as well as from international agencies like the IMF, urged greater reliance on the private sector. Even though it could extend credits as well as certify creditworthiness to private investors, the IMF and its austerity policies aroused great resistance in Latin America, especially from labor, the left, and nationalists. Despite U.S. strategic and economic domination of the region from the end of World War II through the Cold War, the United States was unable to roll back decisively the ECLA or dependency schools of thought until the 1980s, although a few inroads were made earlier in Chile, Argentina, Uruguay, Peru, and elsewhere.

There were six main reasons for the tenacity of the ISI school of thought. First, the United States itself had succumbed to Keynesianism and moderate government intervention in the economy from the 1930s through the 1970s, when even President Richard Nixon declared that "we're all Keynesians now." Moreover, during the Cold War, the United States exhibited more concern for Latin America's geopolitical and ideological loyalty than for its economic conformity. Second, there were viable alternative models available in the world—whether the European welfare state or socialist options—that lent comfort to the Latin American strategy. Third, foreign capital reached Latin America in the form of public aid and direct investment even without total submission to preferred U.S. policies, and private financial largesse did not reemerge until the 1970s. Fourth, the ECLA formula did produce considerable growth and structural modernization. Fifth, the protectionist policies adopted in the aftermath of the Great Depression had created a coalition of vested interests—industrialists, government bureaucrats, the middle sectors, intellectuals, and organized labor, as well as the institutions committed to these policies—that defended that approach until their dominance was shattered by the stagnation of the model and the destruction of the 1980s debt crisis. Sixth, there was a natural inertia and lag once policies were in place and embedded in institutions, so that no major change was likely in the absence of another disastrous external shock.

In the broad sense of general economic regimes, however, Latin America had not completely broken with U.S. hegemony from the 1940s to the 1970s. Just as it had bowed to the essential tenets of the prevalent free-trade doctrine emanating from Great Britain and thereafter the United States from the 1840s to the 1920s, so had it accompanied the United States and Great Britain in their subsequent conversion to Keynesianism. From the 1930s to the 1970s, Latin America had crafted its own regional version of government macroeconomic intervention, however much at odds with the more restrained U.S. variety. When Keynesianism lost favor in the United States after the oil crisis and stagflation of the 1970s, to be replaced by monetarist and neoliberal concepts, Latin America tagged along once again. In all three eras, Latin America followed the general lead, albeit with its own variations and deviations (especially from the 1930s to the 1970s), of the primary economic power.[7]

Hegemony Entrenched, 1980s–2000s

From the waning years of the Cold War through the dawn of the new millennium, U.S. hegemony in Latin America reached unparalleled heights. In the 1980s, Ronald Reagan reasserted U.S. supremacy after the malaise associated with Vietnam, Watergate, the oil crisis, and the Iranian and Nicaraguan revolutions. In particular, the White House struck back in Central America. President Reagan also reacted to stagflation under President Jimmy Carter by endorsing monetarism, the shrinking of the welfare state, and "the magic of the market." The Latin Americans echoed that change of heart mainly because the international debt crisis left those governments desperate to expand exports and slash expenditures in order to service their external obligations.

Thus, in many ways, the conversion to neoliberalism was like the previous embrace of structuralism. It was a reaction to an externally generated crisis, this time calling for (1) freer trade to expand exports; (2) privatization to reduce government expenditures, to raise revenues, and to attract foreign investment; and (3) further restrictions on government intervention (independent central banks, weakened labor unions, deregulation, etc.) in order to block inflation, maintain exchange stability, and woo foreign capital. Then a series of emergency measures once again hardened into a doctrinal orthodoxy, this time emanating from the north rather than the south. Neoliberalism solidified partly because the United States remained powerful and prosperous enough in the 1980s and 1990s, unlike in the 1930s, to offer Latin America rewards—i.e., investments and trade—in return for obedience to its economic dicta. This cure-all was prescribed not only by the U.S. government but also by most U.S. economists and business leaders, the main multilateral institutions, and many Latin American elites themselves.

THE CAUSES OF THE CONTEMPORARY HEGEMONY OF U.S. NEOLIBERALISM

Basically, there are five possible explanations for the adoption of U.S. economic ideas as policies in Latin America: (1) the economic and political domination of the United States; (2) the economic conditions at the time; (3) the apparent correctness and cogency of the ideas themselves; (4) the power and effectiveness of their transmitters; and (5) their attractiveness to the recipients, especially the state and a winning political coalition. It was a confluence of these factors that made neoliberalism so hard to resist.[8] To overgeneralize, that formula pervaded the hemisphere—and much of the planet—because of the overwhelming dominance of the United States, the debt crisis and subsequent globalization, the perceived superiority of that model to discredited alternatives, the leverage of carriers like the World Bank, and the receptivity of host governments and transnational socioeconomic coalitions.[9]

U.S. Hegemony

From the 1940s through the 1990s, the United States exerted extraordinary political and economic hegemony over Latin America. As the unequivocal power, it set and enforced the basic rules of the political and economic systems, regardless of defiance and defections in various countries and categories. Although its supremacy suffered some setbacks from the 1960s to the 1980s, analysts who interpreted these partial slippages as evidence of long-term U.S. decline in Latin America were mistaken. Instead, from the 1980s into the 2000s, the only remaining superpower vigorously reclaimed its hegemony in the Western Hemisphere as never before. In Panama in 1989 and Haiti in 1994, the United States showed that it was still willing to invade small countries in the Caribbean Basin in the aftermath of the Cold War. As a result of such a resurgence of uninhibited and unquestioned political, economic, and strategic superiority in the region, even more than in the 1920s, most of the Latin American countries fell over themselves to establish better relations with the United States, whether it was Argentina dispatching a ship to the Gulf War or Ecuador adopting the U.S. dollar as its currency.

U.S. economic doctrine became more hegemonic in Latin America when the U.S. economy became more hegemonic. After decreasing from the 1960s to the 1980s, the U.S. share of foreign trade and investments in Latin America climbed from the 1980s to the 1990s, especially in the Caribbean Basin and, above all, in Mexico. While the Soviet alternative vanished, the other two possible external sources of a model or leader for Latin America fell short of expectations. As an economic partner for Latin Americans, the United States overshadowed Asian and European countries in the 1990s, even though they did score significant gains in South America. The more statist East Asian strategy lost its luster with the Japanese recession and the East Asian crisis of the 1990s. At the same time, the main Western European powers, even when they made sizable economic inroads in Latin America, did not offer a starkly different approach from that of the United States, and they were more concerned with Eastern Europe than with the Western Hemisphere. Because of U.S. economic preeminence, exaggerated after the fall of the Soviet Union and fortified by spectacular growth under the two Clinton administrations, U.S. ideas and their U.S. purveyors automatically had more clout than those from less powerful nations. The options for the Latin American republics shriveled as most of them toed the line of neoliberalism.

Economic Conditions

Three economic conditions facilitated the penetration of U.S. neoliberal doctrines: the recession and debt crisis of the early eighties, the concomitant rise of globalization, and the subsequent renewal of growth, however slow and selective, in the nineties.

Economic earthquakes have long opened the way to fresh ideas because they capsize existing orders and beliefs, setting off a frantic search for solutions. What made the concept of free markets so saleable in recent years was its ability to respond to the quadruple crises of the foreign debt, inflation, ISI, and the welfare state. Its other major attraction was its ability to lure foreign capital. The Latin American reproduction of policies copied from U.S. blueprints reduced uncertainties for U.S. investors and traders.

Partly caused by anti-inflationary policies and rising interest rates in the United States, the worldwide recession and the debt crisis devastated Latin America in 1982. Since those debts were owed mainly to U.S. banks, most Latin Americans adopted U.S. formulas to weather the crisis. U.S. economics departments, U.S. economists and their former students, U.S. economic elites, the U.S. government, the Western world establishment, and the international financial institutions espoused a ready-made recipe for a situation well suited to its premises, one requiring the husbanding and redirecting of state resources to meet foreign obligations. The stabilizing response promised to simultaneously curb inflation and honor debts.

Countries desperate for debt relief, fresh foreign capital, and foreign exchange proved unusually receptive to the neoliberal marching orders. Development through export promotion became exceptionally attractive to nations that needed to service their staggering debts by expanding sales abroad. Strapped governments frequently heeded the advice of multilateral institutions because the Latin Americans knew that the approval of these institutions sent positive signals to private investors and to first-world public agencies supplying aid.[10]

After initial belt-tightening and liberalizing failed to stem the debt crisis and reignite growth, the 1985 plan by U.S. Treasury Secretary James Baker called for new loans from the banks and the international agencies. He expected that assistance to be contingent on deeper structural reforms from the Latin Americans to further prune the state and unshackle markets. Then the plan by Treasury Secretary Nicholas Brady in 1989 became the enduring standard for handling the debt crisis. His plan went beyond Baker's in calling for voluntary debt reduction by the banks as well as expanded lending by the multilaterals to countries pursuing structural reforms. The White House linked debt reduction to the further freeing up of domestic markets and foreign trade. Foreign capital began returning to Latin America. These escalating incentives propelled more and more compliance with the principles of neoliberalism. Because these foreign debts malingered and even grew beneath the superficial prosperity of the 1990s, countries remained apprehensive about abandoning neoliberal commandments.

The second economic trend favoring neoliberalism was so-called "globalization." By the 1990s, the world economy had become more interconnected and interdependent than at any time since the 1920s. Countries saw foreign trade and investment soar as a proportion of GNP. Capitalists reorganized production on a global scale. The increasing flow of international goods, services, and capital undercut the effectiveness of market interventions by either governments or labor unions, especially in smaller, poorer countries. As autonomous monetary and fiscal policies became increasingly futile, governments lost power to internationally mobile capital.

To compete or at least survive in the internationalized economy, many countries threw themselves open to global market forces and rode up or down with the world economy. Increasingly susceptible to external currents, most nations had little choice but to heed the demands of international economic elites by curtailing independent policy making, restraining fiscal and monetary practices, deregulating domestic markets, and liberalizing foreign trade and investment rules. As neoliberal reforms accelerated, they became cumulative. The more ground that governments ceded to the marketplace, the less able they were to resist making further concessions to the increasingly powerful domestic and international market forces. Once countries began down the slippery slope of liberalization, deregulation, and privatization, it became very difficult to stop, let alone reverse course. More and more, they were prone to synchronizing their economic institutions and practices with the world standard set largely by the United States.

Given the 1980s–90s sequence of debt crisis followed by globalization, it is easy to see why Latin America generally caved in to U.S. demands for neoliberal policy packages, despite reluctance and resistance in many countries. That widespread compliance was fortified by a third major trend, as renewed growth lent credence to the neoliberal doctrine. After the "lost decade" of the 1980s, the annual average growth rate for Latin America rose over 3 percent in the 1990s. Although that growth was modest and very unevenly distributed, it was enough to fan the flames of hope for neoliberalism, especially when reformed countries like Chile led the way. Equally important, foreign capital returned to the region, partly encouraged by neoliberal transformations. Moreover, extraordinary U.S. economic success in the 1990s made its model increasingly attractive and hegemonic. The recession in Latin America at the end of that decade spawned rising discontent with neoliberalism but not its abandonment.

The Validity of the Ideas

In the 1980s and 1990s, theories supporting market approaches to economic development swept aside emphases on government intervention. This reliance on the private sector became the foundation of what was dubbed "monetarism," "neoliberalism," or the "Washington Consensus." In that last term, "Washington" referred to the U.S. government, economic think tanks, the International Monetary Fund, the World Bank, the Export-Import Bank, and the Inter-American Development Bank. "Consensus" signified agreement about the desirability of macroeconomic discipline, monetary and exchange stability, independent central banks, lean governments, tight budgets, effective taxation, privatization, deregulation, foreign investments, export promotion, and free trade.[11]

It is too soon to know whether neoliberalism became all the rage because, as its proponents would have it, economic science had finally discovered the truth with a capital "T." Although intellectual advances made the model more attractive, the evidence for its success was mixed. Therefore, it seems unlikely that the sudden popularity of U.S. economic ideas in the 1980s and 1990s was mainly a result of their surprisingly self-evident veracity. It seems more plausible that changing conditions rendered long-standing premises more palatable. For over a century, the United States had emphasized the primary role of the private sector in growth and development, both domestically and internationally, albeit with significant intellectual and policy changes within that framework over the decades. The basic litany of monetary and exchange prudence, central bank autonomy, small government, fiscal discipline, broad and efficient taxation, deregulation, private property rights, free markets, free trade, and foreign investment had been the U.S. prescription for other countries for a long time.

The economic wisdom at the time formed part of a larger ideological bundle swathed in liberalism. As they sometimes had been in the past, liberal economics and liberal politics were closely linked in this formulation. This ideology formed part of a resurgent crusade against the Soviet Union and its allies in the 1980s, wherein the Western protagonists called for both economic and political liberalization. Soon alternative regimes found it increasingly daunting to challenge the liberal cannon in light of the recent failures of communism, socialism, social democracy, and populism.[12]

Although neither neoliberal economics nor foreign investors required political democracy for their operation, freer markets and freer politics increasingly coincided in U.S. rhetoric and in Latin American reality in the 1990s. Many analysts came to believe that authoritarianism really offered more uncertainty than did democracy. A dictatorship might make it clearer who was and was not going to rule, but it put few limits on what that ruler could do, including abrupt and arbitrary changes in the rules of the economic game. By contrast, so long as all major contenders agreed on the fundamental economic paradigm, which had not been true in the 1960s and 1970s but was largely true by the 1990s, democracy provided more checks and balances on policy changes. It also supplied improved feedback and flexibility on policy implementation and outcomes, enhanced transparency of decision making, greater reliability and less corruption from the bureaucracy and the judicial system, more openness for foreign economic agents, and insulation from charges of consorting with dictators and torturers. Although democracy and all its tumult presented more instability on the surface than did a dictatorship, underneath all the pulling and hauling it was more sturdy and predictable. Consensus trumped coercion as a guarantor of policy continuity.

Aware of these mutually reinforcing economic and political linkages, more and more U.S. and international opinion leaders—politicians, policy makers, bureaucrats, academics, etc.—promoted the tandem liberalization of markets and politics. According to proponents of neoliberalism, the reduction of the state, invigoration of the private sector, expansion of property ownership, and reliance on market mechanisms established the classic economic prerequisites for an individualistic liberal political system. In short order, the U.S. economic and political models encircled the globe together, with the greatest impact in Europe and Latin America.[13]

The Transmitters of the Doctrines

The transmitters provided information, legitimacy, and leverage for the diffusion of these economic ideas. These authorities helped the Latin American governments choose among competing alternatives, forge a transnational coalition to support the policies, explain and justify the new directions, and receive external funding to facilitate their implementation. In some cases, these messengers also supplied a foreign scapegoat for attacks on the policies. The main broadcasters were government institutions, multilateral agencies, the private sector, and economists.[14]

One of the most graphic examples of the influence of these transmitters occurred when Peru's Alberto Fujimori, between his first election in 1990 and his inauguration as president, switched from being an opponent to an advocate of rapid and drastic structural adjustment. That conversion took place partly through the lobbying of Peruvian economists and businessmen but mainly through Fujimori's visit to the IMF and the governments of the United States and Japan. Overnight, they convinced him to jump from heterodox to orthodox programs.[15]

Government Institutions

From the U.S. government, emissaries promoting neoliberalism fanned out from the Federal Reserve, the Commerce Department, the State Department, the Treasury, the Agency for International Development, and even the presidency. Under President Reagan, the White House mounted an aggressive campaign to enlist all the agencies of the U.S. government, multilateral institutions, and its allies overseas in a crusade to replace statist with market strategies. The dominant spokespersons were Ronald Reagan in the United States and Prime Minister Margaret Thatcher in Great Britain, seconded by many others such as Chancellor Helmut Kohl in Germany. On a much smaller scale, another U.S. promulgator of the Chilean and East Asian export promotion models was the National Bureau of Economic Research. In the 1970s and 1980s, its economists hailed these cases as the triumph of market mechanisms over import-substitution-industrialization.

A key U.S. offensive involved the conclusion of the North American Free Trade Agreement (NAFTA) in 1993 and the continuing promotion of a hemisphere-wide counterpart. NAFTA assured Mexico's commitment to freer markets, and those wishing to compete in the hemisphere felt they had to follow that huge example. The United States made it indelibly clear to the Latin Americans that they had to open their markets—and usually their politics—in order to participate. Thereafter international trade and investment agreements increasingly bound countries to market-friendly policies. Under both the George Bush and Bill Clinton administrations (1988–2000), the United States promoted framework agreements to encourage more market-oriented economies in Latin America in exchange for greater access to the U.S. market. At the first Summit of the Americas in 1994 in Miami, the United States and the Latin Americans pledged to negotiate a hemispheric free-trade area (the Free Trade Area of the Americas, FTAA) by 2005. Summitry continued to promote free trade—at least verbally—at the second conclave in Santiago in 1998. Thereafter, President George W. Bush continued to pursue the same policies. Despite U.S. procrastination on free-trade agreements, these accomplishments and the hopes of more kept most Latin American governments on the approved path of neoliberalism.

Other foreign governments and models reinforced the message from the United States. Along with U.S. examples and preaching, privatization policies in England and Japan provided exemplars for governments drained by fiscal crises. From the mid-eighties onward, Chile became Latin America's paragon of the success of neoliberalism, while Peru under President Alan García became the showcase for the failure of statism and populism. The dismal record of heterodox solutions in Brazil and Argentina, accompanied by the scourge of hyperinflation, rendered the "Washington Consensus" even more alluring. Latin American governments learned from one another how to adopt neoliberalism as well as democracy. Amid the uncertainty of simultaneous liberalization of the economy and polity, it was tempting to imitate nearby success stories.[16]

International Institutions

Key international advocates of the new economic orthodoxy included, with variations, the World Bank, the International Monetary Fund, and the Inter-American Development Bank, all, but especially the first two, heavily influenced by the United States. Nevertheless, as multilateral organizations, their advice was seen as somewhat less tainted by national motives than were similar directives from the U.S. government. After the onset of the debt crisis and the increase in the funds of these prestigious and powerful institutions, their ability to sell neoliberalism to Latin America expanded dramatically, as did their demands for policy reforms.

The World Bank peddled these ideas by promoting the new paradigm, by helping design and implement these policies through "structural adjustment programs," by training local officials, and by conditioning financial assistance on the carrying out of these programs. The International Monetary Fund diffused the same doctrine through its research, publications, courses, missions, and conditional loans. Although the IMF, under pressure from the United States, had been promoting a similar monetarist formula for austerity since the late fifties, mainly to squelch inflation and stabilize the balance of payments, it found states to be more receptive to its entreaties in the wake of the debt crisis. Further enhancing their impact, these multinational institutions could coordinate the participation of foreign lenders and donors in assistance packages. Although neither the World Bank nor the IMF insisted officially on democracy as a condition for loans, their emphasis on "good governance" (transparency, accountability, etc.) from the late eighties onward tilted in favor of democratic regimes.[17] In the 1990s, that propensity for these institutions and official Washington to favor capitalist democracies became more blatant.[18]

According to the World Bank and the IMF, the vast majority of their economic compliance conditions were fully implemented by recipient countries in the 1980s. From the early eighties to the early nineties, every Latin American country except Cuba enacted IMF and World Bank adjustment programs. The Inter-American Development Bank also adopted policy-based lending practices hinged to the ingestion of neoliberal axioms. Another proponent of deregulating and denationalizing economies was the General Agreement on Tariffs and Trade (GATT), which most Latin American countries did not join until the 1980s. Its promotion of free trade and investment forbade members from favoring domestic over foreign producers.

Private Institutions

U.S. and Latin American business leaders and their associations also spread the gospel of neoliberalism. Foreign investors and financiers joined the chorus in favor of liberalization. Enormous banking consortia pressured the Latin American debtors to go along, using threats as well as credits to extract compliance. It was much harder for the Latin Americans to reject this advice in the 1980s than it had been to spurn thousands of atomized bondholders in the 1930s.

Economists

An international "epistemic community" of economists emerged in these decades. Increasingly trained in the United States from the 1960s onward, they shared a common learning experience, a specialized discourse, a fund of knowledge, a storehouse of expertise, a commitment to certain cause-and-effect concepts, and a set of theoretical and normative beliefs. From the 1970s to the 1990s, that training increasingly reflected the trend among U.S. economists, particularly those specializing in international trade and public choice, to prefer untrammeled markets over government activism. Turning against Keynesianism, that universal doctrine left virtually no room for regional, national, or local idiosyncrasies, let alone what used to be called "development economics." As U.S. economics departments stopped producing area specialists, so they turned the rising numbers of economics students from those foreign areas into generalists who believed that "one size fits all." Standard training by U.S. universities was supplemented by U.S. government exchange programs, by visits from U.S. economists, by foreign support for local think tanks, and by socialization in multilateral agencies and multinational corporations.

The commitment of these economists to these universal truths overshadowed nationalistic values. They dazzled politicians and the public with their claims to scientific objectivity and certainty.[19] According to these high priests of modernity, there were hardly any rational alternatives to neoliberal policies. After economists themselves converged on these approaches, they presented a united front to governments. By excluding some fundamental economic issues from the public agenda—such as government ownership of industries or massive redistribution of income and wealth—they made unruly democracies safe for domestic and foreign capital.[20]

The Recipients of the Doctrines

Policy change reflected the influence of not only ideas but also interests and institutions. Whatever the transmission mechanism, neoliberalism was not simply imposed on the Latin Americans, although many leaders realized that they had very limited choices in the economic climate of the 1980s and 1990s. To a significant extent, neoliberalism coincided with what some rulers and their supporters wanted to do anyway. The three decisive recipients were the government, technocrats, and a winning sociopolitical coalition.[21]

Governments

Assuming that the opposition could be cowed, crushed, or co-opted, some governments found neoliberal ideas attractive because they were simple and cheap. In Chile, when one of Pinochet's economists asked one of his generals why they had taken the economists' advice, the general replied, "Because you agreed with each other and gave us simple answers to our questions."[22] These promarket policies were also relatively easy and inexpensive to administer. They required little government action or expertise except to get out of the way of market mechanisms. Neoliberal remedies called for the government to do less, not more, at a time when it had few resources to do anything anyway. Moreover, they promised that their medicine would bring rapid relief by both stanching inflation and attracting external credit.

The reliability and stability provided by turning over economic policymaking to neoliberal technocrats were especially attractive to politicians during democratization, when uncertainty abounded. Civilian leaders were eager to prove that they were at least as skillful as military dictators were at managing the economy. Appealing to advice from exalted experts helped justify belt-tightening to their own citizens. Their audience was not only foreign investors but also domestic capitalists, whom they wanted to coax away from coup coalitions. Many Latin American leaders, even from the left, were using neoliberal policies to placate those groups most prone to authoritarianism while taking for granted those sectors more inclined toward democracy. By winning over or neutralizing the traditional opponents of democracy and by undercutting the traditional proponents of populism and redistribution, neoliberal reforms were intended to stabilize not only the economy but also the polity. They made democracy safe for and from capitalists.

In some cases, the Latin American governments accepted these U.S. rules and regulations with alacrity—for example, signing one "letter of intent" after another with the IMF to slash domestic deficits—because they really had little intention of fully implementing or obeying them. After rubber-stamping recommendations to please foreign investors, host governments sometimes circumvented those promises in order to satisfy domestic political and economic pressures. Despite impressive compliance statistics from the IMF and the World Bank, some of their programs were implemented partially or not at all.

This evasion was scarcely unprecedented, since Latin America has walked a tightrope between external demands and internal expectations for centuries. For example, officials in colonial Spanish America told the Crown in Spain, "I obey but do not execute," to avoid implementing royal decrees unacceptable to local elites. In similar fashion, Brazilians in the nineteenth century labeled behavior mimicking the British in order to propitiate powerful foreigners "for the English to see." In the 1920s, Bolivians called economic legislation concocted more to curry foreign favor than to apply to local citizens "laws for export." By the same token, some of today's Latin American infatuation with neoliberalism may have been more strategic than sincere.

Above all, Latin American governments heeded the advice of U.S. economists and their local protégés because they mollified capitalists. The appointments and pronouncements of these economists sent reassuring market signals to jittery foreign and domestic investors. Restoring investor confidence was particularly essential after the debt crisis of the 1980s. Given the extreme dependence on foreign funders, governments needed technocrats with contacts and influence with their counterparts in Washington and Wall Street more than ever. Technocrats helped politicians establish credible commitments to discipline budgets and meet foreign obligations, thus enhancing their government's reputations for creditworthiness with fluid foreign and domestic capital.[23]

Technocrats

With the rise of technocrats in Latin American politics in the 1980s and 1990s, a convergence took place between them and their U.S. counterparts. A transnational coalition congealed to install and defend free-market economics.[24] This "import substitution" of relying on local economists trained abroad instead of foreigners probably shielded some of these programs from nationalistic attacks. The panegyric in favor of neoliberal economic approaches by multilateral institutions strengthened the hand of these local technocrats steeped in the same tradition.[25]

Many of those international ties were woven in U.S. graduate schools, particularly in economics. Such training had been denounced in the 1960s by Chilean economists Anibal Pinto and Oswaldo Sunkel. They complained that such foreign education indoctrinated Latin American economists with universalistic theories with no adjustment to conditions in their home countries. Nevertheless, the numbers of Latin Americans undergoing graduate training in the United States and Western Europe increased, partly owing to the exile of many Latin American intellectuals during the dictatorships of the 1970s.[26] Other Latin American thinkers and politicians also became enamored of the private sector, including Hernando de Soto and Mario Vargas Llosa in Peru.[27]

After returning home, the foreign-trained economists spread their neoliberal ideas through universities, think tanks, interest associations, consulting firms, the media, political parties, and government agencies. National teams of these professional economists proved most successful at carrying out neoliberal reforms. The most famous example was the "Chicago Boys" in Chile.[28] For another example, trade liberalization only caught on in Colombia at the start of the nineties when a majority of its economists converted to neoclassical doctrines; the economist who was president, Cesar Gaviria, shared their faith; the IMF, World Bank, and U.S. trade negotiators pushed the same concept, and so did domestic exporters.[29]

Sociopolitical Coalitions

U.S. economic theories caught on in Latin America also because powerful local interests profited from these concepts. For ideas to become policies, they had to appeal to a winning coalition of international and domestic political actors. As a result of crises and reforms, domestic groups who benefited from internationalization and openness gained in wealth and power, thereby imposing and consolidating their policy preferences, despite the rearguard resistance of domestic losing sectors.[30] For the steamroller of neoliberalism, the supportive coalition included rising interest groups such as new middle-class entrepreneurs, internationalist businesses, exporters, financiers, and entrepreneurial elements of the informal sector. Some capitalists previously dependent on government protection shifted to more competitive strategies. Privatization multiplied the numbers of supporters. Consumers above the poverty line also benefited from neoliberalism and the importation of foreign goods without high tariff barriers. Foreign capitalists also favored the new policies. Monetarism and neoliberalism provided a rationale for antistatist policies that many conservatives and economic elites had advocated for many years anyway. To a significant extent, the two Latin American groups long most heavily influenced by the United States—the business executives and the military—were won over to neoliberalism. It fit with the business magnates' devotion to capitalism and markets, and it comported with the military's faith in technocracy, order, antisocialism, and antipolitics.

The neoliberal coalition opposed declining interest groups, such as protected and inefficient industrialists and agriculturalists (both mainly producing for domestic markets), government bureaucrats and some other white-collar middle sectors, organized labor, and segments of the unorganized poor. In short, the old ISI coalition lost out. The sudden drainage of resources caused by the debt crisis diminished the possibility of populist or leftist leaders pumping up state redistribution programs. Even those politicians who promised such outmoded solutions on the hustings—for example, Carlos Menem in Argentina—usually surrendered to market realities and neoliberalism once in office.

Wherever the neoliberal program unfolded, its central elements undercut the principal proponent of the previous statist model: organized labor. Unionized workers were also reeling because of the globalization of trade, production, investment, and competition. Especially in the early stages of implementation, neoliberalism's austere fiscal and monetary policies, suppression of inflation, reduction of social services, privatization of public enterprises, unharnessing of markets, restriction of unions, constriction of wages, and loosening of restrictions on hiring and firing workers further eroded the ability of the traditional labor movement to resist this juggernaut. In some cases, growing income inequality and unemployment exacerbated these trends. For example, in Chile, General Augusto Pinochet adopted neoliberal policies that rewarded the groups he wanted to favor (e.g., internationalist capitalists) and punished those he wanted to disfavor (e.g., organized workers and state employees), so that his economic and political agendas dovetailed.[31]

CONCLUSION

It was not surprising that U.S. doctrine prevailed in the hemisphere in the 1980s and 1990s. Multiple factors coincided to favor that outcome: (1) a long history of U.S. hegemony over most of the region most of the time; (2) a resurgence of U.S. hegemony to unprecedented heights; (3) a set of economic conditions that rendered Latin America exceptionally receptive to ideas from its premier creditor, investor, and trader; (4) a coherent policy package well attuned to the economic and political exigencies at the time; (5) a group of potent and luminous transmitters eager and able to sell that package; and (6) a cluster of Latin American governments, technocrats, and social actors inclined to adopt that remedy. By contrast, the forces outside and inside Latin America that might have resisted the neoliberal leviathan were in an unusually weak position.

Indeed, neoliberalism engulfed not only most of Latin America but also vast sections of the entire globe. Consequently, it would have been surprising if Latin America, the region of the world most dependent on the United States, had bucked the tide. Although degrees, patterns, and choices varied among the countries in the hemisphere, the most striking phenomenon was the uniformity of the general trend.

Of the causal factors, which were the most important? The ideas had been around and gaining strength since the early sixties, as seen in the standard potion prescribed by the IMF and in stabilization plans adopted by various authoritarian regimes in the 1960s and 1970s. Like the ideas, the hegemon, transmitters, and recipients were not completely new in the 1980s, although their leverage, status, and coherence had increased significantly. Therefore, it seems that the key variables were the crucial international changes in the 1980s and 1990s. The debt crisis delivered a tremendous shock that made many of the other factors fall into place. That crisis propelled the general turn to neoliberalism, which was accelerated and locked in by the increasingly omnipresent and aggressive hegemony of the United States and its agents, the tidal wave of democratization, the end of the Cold War, the contagion of globalization, and the spurt of renewed growth, all rationalized and legitimized by the evangelists of the new economic orthodoxy.

By the turn of the century, doubters increasingly criticized and resisted the "Washington Consensus," and observers expressed more concern about social inequalities and poverty, as well as environmental and labor degradation. Despite mounting dissatisfaction in Latin America, the essential neoliberal framework remained in place. If the past was any guide, this policy syndrome seemed likely to persist until a comparable conjuncture of powerful international and domestic forces blew it off course.

3

Latin America and the United States

Lars Schoultz

The United States and Latin America are continuously growing closer. The process began almost three centuries ago, when Yankee traders first sailed into Caribbean harbors and exchanged their cargoes of salted cod for barrels of molasses, which they took back to Boston and made into rum. After that, the exchanges grew steadily but generally very slowly; until the 1960s few U.S. citizens outside the Southwest had even seen a *tortilla*, much less realized that they might want to try one. But in recent decades the pace of interaction has been accelerating rapidly. If it continues, in a century or two our heirs might conceive of the difference between the United States and Latin America in much the same way that today's Vermonters look at Alabamans: as somewhat strange in their customs and, frankly, a bit backward, but still members of their set of united states.

What forces are driving this integration? The easy answer is the revolution in transportation and communication, which continues to shrink the distance between us. However, jet aircraft and Internet connections are only facilitating mechanisms; behind these changes in technology are *interests:* there are specific reasons why we are seeking to live in closer contact with our neighbors. This is a chapter about these interests and how they are shaping our future.

THE ECONOMIC IMPERATIVE

The desire to protect and promote U.S. economic interests is by far the most important force driving today's policy toward Latin America. This desire is

not new; it was why the Continental Congress appointed Robert Smith as
the nation's first diplomat to Latin America in 1781: when he was posted to
Havana, his primary assignment was "to assist the American traders with his
advice, and to solicit their affairs with the Spanish Government."[1] Despite
this early start, however, it was only in the final decades of the nineteenth century that the U.S. government formally recognized Latin America's economic importance. Crucial to this recognition was a series of major U.S.
depressions (in 1873–78, 1882–85, and 1893–97), each of which had significant domestic political repercussions, as angry out-of-work voters punished
incumbents and as public figures reacted to their electoral peril by developing various ways to avoid boom-and-bust cycles. The basic problem was then
known as "overproduction," a problem caused largely by increased efficiency: with ever-more-modern U.S. factories producing in record quantities
and domestic consumption growing not nearly as fast, periodic production
cuts—layoffs—were inevitable while inventories were reduced.

Searching for a solution to this problem, U.S. political leaders discovered
Latin America. In 1888, reasoning that the inventory-reducing lulls in production could be shortened or even eliminated by finding additional
consumers, the Cleveland administration issued invitations to the first International Conference of American States, the principal purpose of which was
to promote U.S. exports. The conference formally convened in Washington,
D.C., but then immediately declared a *six-week* recess so that the delegates
could participate in a 6,000-mile railroad excursion to visit factories from
Boston to Omaha. Argentina's Roque Sáenz Peña was correct when he observed that the conference chair, Secretary of State James G. Blaine, "wished
to make Latin America a market."[2]

That is what has occurred, and Latin Americans have generally welcomed
the trade because they, at the same time, have found willing customers in the
United States. What began as Latin America's sale of molasses soon expanded to include the export of agricultural nitrates and then of the raw materials that fed the industrializing U.S. economy, symbolized best, perhaps,
by the nineteenth century's burgeoning demand for copper, which led entrepreneurs such as William Braden and the Guggenheim brothers to search
for deposits from Mexico to Chile. Then oil took over. The United States im-

ported no petroleum until Edward Doheny's first Mexican well entered production in 1904, and in the years leading up to World War I domestic wells continued to produce nearly all that was needed. But demand soon outstripped domestic production, and by 1920 Mexico was producing 24 percent of the world's petroleum and exporting most of it to the United States, where there were over nine million automobiles on the road, up from fewer than two million in 1914.

Everyone wanted to own a car, it seemed, and every one of those vehicles would need gasoline at a time when many experts predicted that U.S. reserves would soon be exhausted. So the Harding administration's secretary of commerce, Herbert Hoover, sat down with the secretary of state, Charles Evans Hughes, and "Mr. Hughes supported a suggestion of mine that the practical thing was to urge our oil companies to acquire oil in South America and elsewhere before the European companies preempted all of it. As a result, a conference of the leading oil producers was called, and such action taken that most of the available oil lands in South America were acquired by Americans."[3] By the time Hoover was elected President in 1928, *hundreds* of U.S. oil companies were drilling in Latin America, dramatically accelerating the integration of the economies of the Western Hemisphere.

It did not hurt that World War I had taken Europeans out of the Latin American market—the shooting began in August 1914, three years before U.S. entry into the conflict, and Latin American consumers, cut off from European suppliers, turned to the only alternative: U.S. exports to Latin America rose from $540 million in 1916 to $1.6 billion in 1920, placing the Yankee foot so firmly in the door that Europe has never been able to recover its prewar preeminence in Latin American markets. Nor did it hurt that in 1913 the new Federal Reserve Act had authorized U.S. banks to open overseas branches for the first time, and when the war broke out, New York's National City Bank was ready to open the first U.S. overseas branch bank—and not in London or Zurich or Amsterdam, but in Buenos Aires. Here, too, wartime dislocations forced European competitors out of many financial markets, and by 1920 National City Bank had fanned out, opening fifty-six branch banks in Latin America, every one of which was dedicated to facilitating trade. New York soon became the finance capital of the world.

As these economic ties were developing, they regularly served U.S. security interests. In 1939, two weeks after Hitler triggered World War II by invading Poland, a worried State Department official urged that Washington focus on "the most difficult task of creating a perpetuating complex as well as a peaceful area of influence," and he assigned the U.S. private sector a central role: "Since trade is a permanent foundation of such influence, the whole series of inter-American economic institutions should be molded toward the simplification of the currencies and customs regulations now in force in the twenty-one republics; they should be attached inseparably to the dollar."[4] That is what had happened by the war's end in 1945.

Today's debates over whether and how to integrate the hemisphere's economies—NAFTA, CAFTA, and the Free Trade Area of the Americas—are best understood as the logical extension of this historical process that began three centuries ago with the simple exchange of molasses for salted cod. This process developed momentum as it grew slowly but steadily into what we now see, in hindsight, as a never-ending search for additional markets for U.S. producers and additional suppliers for U.S. consumers. Yesterday's simple search for industrial raw materials has blossomed into an extraordinarily complex array of economic relationships involving everything from coffee to cocaine and, most recently, to an unprecedented demand for millions and millions of Latin American workers, some to labor at home and some to work in the United States.

Because today's relationships are more complex, they require prolonged negotiations over issues our forebears could never have imagined—the protection of electronic intellectual property rights, for example—but the complexity of the package should not obscure its framework: the economies of North and South America have been merging for centuries, and now the revolution in transportation and communication has accelerated the integration process to speeds that are sometimes astonishing. As the chapters by Professor Anner and by Professor Reygadas suggest, the integration process has costs as well as benefits, creating both winners and losers, and we therefore need to develop mechanisms that distribute the gains and especially the losses more equitably. But while we can tinker with the integration process or perhaps slow it for a season, it has now advanced to the point that no political force can repeal the logic driving it: the United States produces too many goods and services that Latin Americans want to purchase, and Latin America produces too many goods and services (especially blue-collar labor) that find willing purchasers in the United States. In the abstract we can still live without one another, just as Vermonters can live without Alabamans, but in making a million and one daily choices, the hemisphere's billion or so residents have made an informal but now-irrevocable decision not to do so.

PROTECTING U.S. SECURITY

A second major reason for the accelerating integration process is a dramatic shift in U.S. security interests in Latin America. The region is close to the United States, of course, and this physical proximity motivated the first statement of United States policy toward Latin America, the 1811 No-Transfer Resolution, which reflected Washington's concern that Britain might acquire Florida from the Spanish in partial payment for England's help in ousting Napoleon during the Peninsular Wars.[5] It was a statement of U.S. resolve, coming only months before the outbreak of a war with England and reflecting the concern that the English might value Florida both as a base from which to blockade southern ports and as a convenient site to stockpile weapons. In the end Spain did not transfer Florida, and soon the War of 1812 passed into history, but in less than a decade it was replaced by a threat from the monarchial Holy Alliance, intent on squelching republicanism. In 1822 the Alliance authorized France to restore Ferdinand's monarchy in Spain, and Washington, worried that Spain's rebellious colonies were next in line, issued the second statement of U.S. policy, the 1823 Monroe Doctrine. It reflected the same concern as the No-Transfer Resolution: that a powerful adversary might obtain a toehold in Latin America and then use it to threaten U.S. security.

This early security policy was based upon two convictions, both of them realistic and still today easily understandable: first, prudent people keep potential adversaries at arm's length; and, second, weak neighbors are preferable to strong neighbors. A weak Spain and an even weaker set of Latin American republics were not capable of harming U.S. security because, as a U.S. envoy to Colombia reported in the 1820s, the entire region was little more than "twenty millions of people spread over a pathless continent."[6] Let either the Spanish or these twenty million, barely able to govern themselves—let them control the territory within striking distance of the United States. In their hands, Secretary of State James Monroe concluded, "East Florida is itself comparatively nothing, but as a post, in the hands of Great-Britain, it is of the highest importance. Commanding the Gulph of Mexico, and all its waters, including the Mississippi with its branches, and the streams emptying into the Mobile [River], a vast proportion of the most fertile and productive parts of this Union, on which the navigation and commerce so essentially depend, would be subject to its annoyance."[7] Then and now, no one could imagine a Latin American state bottling up U.S. commerce by blockading the Straits of Florida and the Yucatan Channel.

Then this calculus changed. Science marched on, technology-driven advances in warfare led to the nightmare of intercontinental ballistic missiles, and in the course of about 150 years Latin America lost its original significance for U.S. security. By the time of the 1962 Cuban Missile Crisis, President Kennedy would comment that "it doesn't make any difference if you get blown up by an ICBM flying from the Soviet Union or one that was ninety miles away." True, the shorter distances from Cuba gave the Soviets clear tactical advantages—shorter flight time and more accurate targeting—but almost everyone nodded in agreement when Kennedy pointed out that in the missile age "geography doesn't mean that much."[8]

By that time, however, Latin America had acquired a *symbolic* significance that was every bit as powerful as the original and more-concrete "arm's length" logic driving U.S. security policy: by the mid-twentieth century the United States had come to see Latin America as part of its sphere of influence, a site where the United States demonstrated its status as a world power. In hindsight, we should have anticipated this shift from the literal to the symbolic, for it began decades before the Cold War. As one assistant secretary of state explained in the late 1920s when Mexico began to meddle in Nicaragua, a U.S. protectorate since 1912, "we must decide whether we shall tolerate the interference of any other power (i.e., Mexico) in Central American affairs, or insist upon our own dominant position." It was *not* because the United States wanted much of anything from Nicaragua, which was to U.S. officials in the 1920s exactly what East Florida had been to James Monroe a century earlier—"comparatively nothing"—and, of course, it was not that Mexico might use Nicaragua as a base from which to launch an attack upon the United States; rather, it was because "if this Mexican maneuver succeeds it will take many years to recover the ground we shall have lost. The tangible evidence of our influence will have disappeared and *notice will have been conveyed . . . to the rest of the world, that recognition and support by this Government means nothing.*"[9]

The Cold War witnessed the apotheosis of this view of Latin America as a symbol of U.S. resolve, and was captured best by President Ronald Reagan, who, pleading with Congress for funds to maintain U.S. hegemony in El Salvador, explained that "the national security of the Americas is at stake in Central America. If we cannot defend ourselves there, we cannot expect to prevail elsewhere. Our credibility would collapse, our alliances would crumble, and the safety of our homeland would be put in jeopardy."[10] This is the logic that made Central America into a pawn on a global chessboard, part of a game where the goal of both superpowers was to capture its opponents' pieces while protecting its own.

As for U.S. policy toward Latin America itself, Washington's principal Cold War question was tactical: how to counter Moscow's moves. Should the United States attempt to win Latin Americans' hearts and minds with economic aid, or should it use military aid to bolster the domestic strength of Latin Americans who were allied with Washington? The answer was both. Economic aid began modestly under the Mutual Security Act (a telling title) in the early 1950s, expanded dramatically with President Kennedy's Alliance for Progress in the 1960s, and continued to the end of the Cold War with President Reagan's Caribbean Basin Initiative and President George H.W. Bush's Enterprise of the Americas Initiative. At the same time these carrots were being offered, U.S. military aid was providing sticks to bolster friends— some of them reprehensible but dependably anticommunist dictators— while the Central Intelligence Agency undermined indigenous leftists who might turn to the Soviet Union, sponsoring one unsuccessful covert invasion (the Bay of Pigs) and coups that toppled several left-leaning but democratic Latin American governments, from Guatemala's Jacobo Arbenz in the 1950s, to Brazil's João Goulart in the 1960s, to Chile's Salvador Allende in the 1970s. The costs were all justified by the need to protect U.S. security.

Then the Cold War ended and the Soviet Union dissolved. Without a challenge by a rival superpower in the 1990s, many observers expected the U.S. government to curtail the military assistance programs designed to deter a violation of the Monroe Doctrine, just as lamplighters disappeared when streetlights were converted to electricity, but new threats were identified instead, and they had nothing to do with the takeover of Latin America by a non-hemispheric power. Today, the Department of Defense reports, "we face two primary types of threats in the region: an established set of threats," which consists of narcotics traffickers and urban gangs "drawing substantial support from the drug business" and, second, "an emerging threat best described as radical populism" which undermines the nation's interests "by inflaming anti-U.S. sentiment."[11]

Unlike the threat of narcotrafficking and gang violence, the United States has been battling the threat posed by Latin American populists since the 1930s, when Mexican president Lázaro Cárdenas nationalized the U.S.-dominated petroleum industry. Then and now, U.S. officials have generally argued that these populist leaders are being inspired or supported or manipulated by U.S. adversaries; after visiting Mexico on the eve of World War II, for example, Bernard Baruch reported to President Roosevelt that Cárdenas's petroleum nationalization "has been fomented by the representatives of Japan, Italy and Germany."[12]

This interpretation of Latin American populism was especially prominent during and immediately after World War II, when Juan Perón's Argentina adopted an independent foreign policy and encouraged other Latin American governments to follow his lead—Perón "has completely fascised the life of the country," wrote Assistant Secretary of State Adolph Berle, adding that the Argentine leader was attempting "to set up an Argentine-controlled Fascist bloc running as far North as Peru"; in this, Berle warned, the Argentines "are working hand in glove with the Germans."[13] Thus Perón's Argentina became just one more Axis power to defeat, and a hostile policy continued after the surrender of Germany and Japan. Initially elated when Perón was taken prisoner by a rival military group in October 1945, a disappointed U.S. envoy soon reported that Perón had been freed after protests by the blue-collar workers whose welfare he championed and among whom he was obviously immensely popular: "Fascist nature of Perón regime again emphasized by yesterday's events," the embassy cabled Washington. "Manifestations showed excellent organization of hoodlums on Fascist lines like Brown Shirts and Black Shirts."[14] Then when Perón resigned his military commission and became a candidate for election, Washington supported the opposition party, publishing its famous Blue Book to convince Argentine voters that Perón's government "is a partnership of German Nazi interests with a powerful coalition of active Argentine totalitarian elements."[15]

The Argentines' reaction? In the cleanest and most inclusive election in the nation's history, Perón tapped into nationalist sentiment to win an overwhelming victory, and then continued to advocate a "Third Position" in foreign relations. Washington's reaction? With fascism no longer a threat, the assistant secretary of state responsible for the Blue Book adjusted to the times: a month after the election he reported that "the Commies are now actively climbing on the Perón bandwagon."[16]

"Radical populism" in the early twenty-first century is embodied by Hugo Chávez of oil-rich Venezuela, who is replaying, scene by scene, the drama written for Juan Perón. The popular champion of Venezuela's less-privileged citizens, Chávez seems intent not simply upon using Venezuela's oil wealth to improve the lives of the poor, but also upon challenging U.S. hegemony in Latin America, and to Washington's dismay he has demonstrated three times that he is unbeatable at the polls—and he has won his victories despite support of his domestic opposition by the U.S. government-funded National Endowment for Democracy, whose backing of Chávez's opposition in Venezuela's 2004 presidential recall referendum (which Chávez won resoundingly) was only marginally more subtle than that of U.S. policy toward Perón's Argentina. Washington's criticism focuses, first, on allegations that President Chávez is behaving in an authoritarian manner, threatening Venezuelan democracy (a topic beyond the scope of this chapter) and, second, on Venezuela's ties to Fidel Castro's Cuba, which is the best we can muster today as a replacement for Hitler's Germany and Stalin's Soviet Union.

To read recent Defense Department statements about the security threat from Latin America—both the hand-wringing over Chávez's "radical populism" and the effort to convert organized crime syndicates into a terrorist threat—is to marvel not simply at the elasticity of the human imagination, but also at the agility with which programs designed to address one problem (challenges to the Cold War bipolar balance of power) can shift to another. Today's fundamental global security problem is, of course, terrorism, with the Pentagon warning that "terrorists throughout the Southern Command area of responsibility bomb, murder, kidnap, traffic drugs, transfer arms, launder money, and smuggle humans."[17] Should this be called *terrorism?* This volume's chapters on the drug war by Coletta A. Youngers and on crime by Mark Ungar suggest that what the United States identifies today as Latin American "narcoterrorists"[18] are simply yesterday's criminals or, more accurately, organized crime, now conveniently repackaged to make military aid relevant to today's terrorism-obsessed security environment.

Lost in the debate over U.S. drug policy or Washington's indignation over Chavista populism is the most significant aspect of this repackaging process: U.S. security interests in Latin America have been "Latin Americanized." For the first time in history, these interests are no longer conceptualized as keeping a powerful adversary (the British, the Holy Alliance, the Nazis, the Soviets) out of a region that was otherwise considered inert from a security perspective; today, the real or imagined threats are all indigenous. For two centuries Latin Americans have presumably had organized groups who kidnap and murder, deal drugs and launder money, just as we do in the United States, but U.S. policy has *never* considered organized crime a security threat. Today it does. In 2005 the Pentagon warned Congress that Latin America "is the world's most violent region," and it talked about the region in the same way that U.S. law enforcement officials talk about the drug-infested and gang-poisoned neighborhoods of urban America, providing supporting data on criminal behavior such as "27.5 homicides per 100,000 people."[19] We are all in this together, they seem to be saying, and, of course, we are—but only to the extent that we define *security* as freedom from such perils as gang-based drug trafficking, a lamentable feature of urban landscapes North and South. If we do, then Latin America's law enforcement problems have become our security problems, and the Pentagon is correct to argue that we should address them together. In terms of U.S. security concerns, the integration is basically complete.

DOMESTIC POLITICS—APPLYING THE BRAKES?

Today's debates over security policy are remote from the everyday lives of most U.S. citizens. If any aspect of U.S. policy toward Latin America attracts a domestic audience in the post–Cold War and post–9/11 world, it is *economic* issues, and that is where the third force affecting the integration process—domestic politics—is now slowing the integration process. The impact of domestic political considerations was especially evident in the 2005 debate over the Central American Free Trade Agreement (CAFTA), when domestic sugar producers, worried about competition from lower-cost Central American growers, waged a spirited campaign to defeat the agreement. They lost, but only after extracting side agreements that amounted to a victory. To the extent that integration is measured by access to larger amounts of Latin American sugar, CAFTA stopped the integration process.

Once again, this was nothing new. The United States has fought over the domestic implications of trade policy for two centuries, generally over whether to raise or lower the tariff, and, as for sugar, we have been arguing for a century about who should have the right to satisfy the nation's sweet tooth. The squabbling began in 1898, when President McKinley made a major concession to domestic sugar producers in order to gain congressional approval of a declaration of war against Spain; specifically, he agreed to amend his resolution authorizing the war to specify that the United States would not acquire Spanish Cuba. The amendment was offered by Colorado senator Henry Teller, representing the beet sugar industry that had recently developed in the Rocky Mountain states. These producers worried—with good reason—that if Cuba became part of the United States, its duty-free sugar would drive beet producers into bankruptcy.

Then, when the war was over and the island was about to be granted its independence, Cuba's U.S. military governor convinced President Theodore Roosevelt to eliminate the tariff on Cuban sugar in order to give the fledgling republic a solid market for its principal product. That alarmed the head of Utah's Republican Party, who fired off a letter to Secretary of War Elihu Root, the man holding overall responsibility for Cuba's pre-independence government—and, not incidentally, also a close friend of the President and a major figure in Republican party politics:

> Now it is proposed to take the duty off from Cuban sugar through a reciprocity arrangement. If this is done, it will destroy the sugar beet industry in the State of Utah. It was through the prospect of the beet and the erection of the [refining] factories that the Republicans carried the State a year ago. It was this same prospect that carried several cities of the State for the Republican ticket, a month ago. If this duty is taken off, or materially lessened, as is proposed, you can look for a Democratic Senator and a Democratic Congressman from Utah.[20]

The Roosevelt compromise was to cut the sugar tariff by 20 percent for Cuba, but only for Cuba—not enough to damage domestic producers, who in effect determined this part of United States policy toward Latin America.

Today, in a quite different way, every major U.S. politician remains acutely aware of the domestic significance of Cuba, whose 1959 revolution might qualify as the single most important event affecting the integration of the United States and Latin America, not simply because the revolution integrated Cubans into the domestic U.S. political system, but because that integration has opened a pathway for others. The Cuban Revolution did to U.S. politics what Jackie Robinson did to baseball.

It is not simply that the Cuban Revolution triggered the flight of its opponents to U.S. shores—that also was nothing new. Several nineteenth-century secretaries of state could have written what Secretary of State Cordell Hull wrote in 1933: that "not only all of the political leaders of importance, but a great majority of the intellectual leaders of Cuba as well, have been forced to leave the Republic and most of them have taken refuge in the United

States."[21] What was new about the 1959 revolution was (and still is) its duration; four decades after Fidel Castro's triumphal entry into Havana, the 2000 census counted over 1.2 million Cuban Americans, and it is now doubtful that many will return to live in a post-Castro Cuba. Of the 1.2 million, many (40 percent of the total) have not yet become U.S. citizens, many of the native-born (about 30 percent) are still too young to vote, and some of the naturalized Cubans undoubtedly fail to do so, but their numbers are nonetheless of great political significance because they are concentrated in fast-growing Florida, whose twenty-seven electoral votes make it the fourth largest state in the winner-take-all Electoral College. Cuban Americans constitute about 4 percent of Florida's voters, and many of them exchange their votes for a hostile policy toward Castro's Cuba. That is why today's Cuba policy has become *the* textbook example of the integration of domestic politics and U.S. foreign policy. Ask Democratic presidential candidate Al Gore: in 2000, five months after the Clinton administration returned young Elián González to Cuba, he lost Florida (and the White House) by 537 votes.

Cuban exiles had slowly integrated themselves into the U.S. political system during the 1980s, and with the end of the Cold War they were perfectly positioned to move into the policy space being vacated by national security officials. Philip Brenner had been among the first to see this, writing in 1990 that the White House "has delegated Cuba policy to an active congressional group, inspired by domestic lobbies."[22] Indeed, Congress now included its first Cuban American: in 1989, Miami's longtime Democratic representative Claude Pepper had died, and in a special election his seat passed to a Cuban American Republican, Ileana Ros-Lehtinin, who would build her career around increasing the political influence of Miami's Cuban American community. Her campaign was managed by the president's son Jeb, who knew what it would take to fire up her natural constituency: his father needed to visit Miami and, at a Ros-Lehtinin fund-raiser, promise that "there will be no improvement of relations with Cuba."[23]

But winning this commitment from the Republicans was only half the battle for the policy territory yielded by national security officials; what cemented the Cuban American community's control over post–Cold War U.S. policy was its simultaneous capture of the other half—of the Democrats. As the 1990s unfolded, the Democrat most eager to win the Cuban American vote was New Jersey representative (later senator) Robert Torricelli, but he was challenged for that title by a lengthy list of Democratic office seekers, including Florida senator Robert Graham and Miami representative Dante Fascell, who, when asked why the United States should remain hostile toward Cuba while pursuing detente with the Soviet Union, replied as any vote-maximizing politician would: "We do not have 2 million Soviets living in Miami, Florida. . . . That makes a big difference, I want to tell you."[24] Then, in 1992, when President George H.W. Bush balked at legislation proposed by Cuban Americans to tighten the embargo, Democratic challenger Bill Clinton told a group of wealthy Cuban exiles in Miami that the Bush administration "has missed a big opportunity to put the hammer down on Fidel Castro and Cuba." In contrast, he continued, "I have read the Torricelli-Graham bill and I like it." The White House responded promptly to the challenge: when the House Committee on Foreign Affairs met a few weeks later, it had before it a concession letter from President Bush: "I support the action your committee is taking."[25] Then, just before the election, President Bush flew to Miami, where he signed what had come to be known as the Cuban Democracy Act, and eleven days later he carried Florida. President Clinton did the same thing four years after that, signing the anti-Castro Cuban Liberty and Democratic Solidarity (Helms-Burton) Act shortly before the 1996 election. He carried Florida in November, the first Democrat to do so in two decades.

Cuban Americans and U.S. policy toward Cuba are now so tightly integrated that to touch one is to touch the other. As the head of the U.S. Interests Section in Havana recently commented when asked why he was flying so frequently to Miami to meet with Cuban exile leaders, "We have to pay attention to domestic politics."[26] While there is nothing yet quite like the Cuba lobby, the future is obvious: other Hispanic interest groups such as the Mexican American Legal Defense Fund (MALDEF) and the League of United Latin American Citizens (LULAC), which have traditionally focused on the domestic civil rights of Hispanic Americans, are now finding that their constituents also worry about transnational issues such as immigration, drug trafficking, and gang violence that are central to United States policy toward Latin America. Given the Cuban example, it is unrealistic to believe that other Hispanic Americans will continue to sit on the "foreign policy" side-lines.

THE POLITICS OF PREJUDICE

These new Hispanic American participants will not be standing on a wel-come mat as they knock on Washington's foreign policy door. Integration has always been a gradual process: in the late eighteenth century, Vermon-ters joined a confederation that included faraway Alabama and gained access to what little they wanted (a few bales of cotton), but they went decades with-out actually seeing a flesh-and-blood Alabaman. Neither did they see the pro-ducers of the Caribbean molasses that got them through the winter blizzards, and their grandchildren never encountered the Peruvians who mined the ni-trate that fertilized Vermont's rocky fields. Today, in sharp contrast, there is little that can be called incremental or gradual about one central part of the integration process: the Hispanic population of the United States is growing like Topsy: already representing 13 percent of the population in the 2000 census, it expanded from 35 million in 2000 to 39 million in 2002, and is es-timated to reach 103 million by mid-century, at which time Hispanics will make up a quarter of the nation's population.

A few non-Hispanics applaud their communities' growing cultural diver-sity, but only a few; most have a less-positive reaction, and all of us can only marvel at how the tables have turned since the late nineteenth century, when Theodore Roosevelt wrote that "it was inevitable, as well as in the highest de-gree desirable for the good of humanity at large, that the American people should ultimately crowd out the Mexicans from their sparsely populated Northern provinces."[27] Now Roosevelt's "American people" often protest that they are the ones being crowded out.

Giving voice to their concern is Harvard professor Samuel Huntington, who recently wrote that "the single most immediate and most serious chal-lenge to America's traditional identity comes from the immense and contin-uing immigration from Latin America." Why? Because "this reality poses a fundamental question: Will the United States remain a country with a single

national language and a core Anglo-Protestant culture?" Huntington's concern is that the sheer size of today's Latin American immigration is encouraging the creation of isolated enclaves that allow new arrivals to avoid
assimilation into the dominant U.S. culture, perhaps forever. "Continuation
of this large immigration (without improved assimilation) could divide the
United States into a country of two languages and two cultures," he warns,
and while he acknowledges that this "would not necessarily be the end of the
world; it would, however, be the end of the America we have known for more
than three centuries." Commenting on *The Americano Dream,* a new book
about Hispanic immigration by Lionel Sosa, Huntington tells us "there is no
Americano dream. There is only the American dream created by an Anglo-
Protestant society." [28]

Professor Huntington is not a voice crying in the lonely wilderness. In
mid-2005 the problems created by large-scale illegal immigration led the
governors of Arizona and New Mexico to declare states of emergency, giving
them access to funds to beef up law enforcement in their counties bordering
Mexico. "This is an act of desperation," explained New Mexico governor Bill
Richardson. Meanwhile, citizens next door in Arizona took to patrolling
their own border, calling themselves "Minutemen" to recall an earlier era
when civilians were ready on a moment's notice to defend their communities
from attack.

As we enter the twenty-first century, this concern over domestic immigration policy is being reinforced by a second new anxiety: a fear that the economic integration of North and South is facilitating the export of U.S. jobs to
Latin America (and elsewhere, of course), where low wages, docile labor, and
lax environmental standards now encourage U.S. producers to do what May-
tag did in 2004: it closed its refrigerator factory in Galesburg, Illinois, where
wages and benefits averaged $15 an hour, and opened an identical plant in
Reynosa, just south of the Texas-Mexico border, where wages are about $2 an
hour. Meanwhile, in Washington, the concern over job losses has reached
the point that in 2005 the House of Representatives could approve a free
trade agreement with Central America and the Dominican Republic only
after tacitly gutting key provisions and then only by the narrowest of margins—217 to 215—and the task of negotiating a Free Trade Area of the

Americas, scheduled for completion in early 2005, has now been placed on the back burner.

The challenges of large-scale immigration (the Irish and Italians in Northeastern cities, for examples) have traditionally created a significant backlash, and job losses have always been profoundly upsetting to the workers who have pink slips in their hands. But still, it is difficult to examine the issues surrounding today's domestic disputes over integration without sensing that there is something at work that we do not want to say openly but that nonetheless has an important role in determining U.S. policy. To read the congressional debate over the 1993 ratification of the North American Free Trade Agreement, for example, is to encounter a set of *predispositions* that U.S. citizens appear to bring to the consideration of *any* issue of United States policy toward Latin America. At one point in the debate, Democratic representative James Trafficant, who represented a blue-collar Ohio district, stood up on the House floor and complained that "we're going to open up the borders with Mexico. Wow. I predict jobs and investments going to Mexico like Olympic sprinters. In return, we'll get a used Ford pickup truck, two tons of heroin, and three baseball players to be named later."[29] Then Representative Helen Bentley, a Maryland Republican, rose to tell her colleagues about her fact-finding trip to Mexico: "When we were shaking hands with different people there, the Air Force doctor who accompanied us would come up and whisper in our ear to 'make sure you do not touch your face until you wash your hands' to ensure that we could not get some kind of a disease."[30] Are these the kind of people we want growing our vegetables or, worse yet, playing with our children? Do we want even more broken-down Mexican vehicles on our streets—the "jalopies" that originally referred to used cars that had been reconditioned in the Mexican city of Jalapa?

These types of comments are heard so frequently in debates over U.S. policy toward Latin America that the temptation is to dismiss them as simple ethnocentrism—i.e., many people simply prefer to live with their own kind of people or with "assimilated" Hispanics who behave like Anglo-Protestants.

In this Professor Huntington would appear to be a representative of his generation, born in 1927 and reared in a society that openly denigrated Latin Americans. In 1941, when Huntington's generation was entering high school and beginning to become aware of the wider world, public opinion pollsters handed a random sample of his generation's parents a sheet of paper containing nineteen adjectives and asked: "From this list, which words seem to you to describe best the people who live in Central and South America?" Respondents were allowed to select as many of the words as they wished. The results are shown in Figure 3.1.

FIGURE 3.1

What People in the United States Think and Know about
Latin America and Latin Americans

Descriptor	Percent Selecting
1. Dark-skinned	77
2. Quick-tempered	47
3. Emotional	42
Backward	42
Religious	42
6. Lazy	39
7. Ignorant	33
8. Suspicious	30
9. Friendly	28
10. Dirty	27
11. Proud	24
12. Imaginative	21
13. Intelligent	15
Shrewd	15
15. Honest	13
16. Brave	12
Generous	12
18. Progressive	11
19. Efficient	9

Source: Hadley Cantril, confidential memorandum to Mr. Young, "What People in the United States Think and Know about Latin America and Latin Americans," 18 January 1941, 710.11/2686, Record Group 59, National Archives.

Setting aside the adjective "dark-skinned"—it was an error to include a physical feature on a list of eighteen personality characteristics—the terms that U.S. respondents considered positive (efficient, progressive, generous, brave, honest, intelligent, imaginative) are *least* likely to characterize Latin Americans, while the terms that Huntington's Anglo-Protestants considered negative (quick-tempered, backward, lazy, ignorant) are *most* likely to characterize Latin Americans. There is room to quibble about the meaning of vague terms such as "emotional" and "religious," but there is no debating that you have to go halfway down the list to find the first unequivocally positive adjective, "friendly."

This poll was taken long ago, however, and while it may have captured the thinking of the generation that reared Professor Huntington, it was only in 1990 that his generation had its own opportunity to respond to a similar poll, this one much more sophisticated. It asked respondents to rank five ethnic groups (Jews, blacks, Asians, Southern whites, and Hispanics) on six dimensions when compared to "Whites" (see Figure 3.2).

FIGURE 3.2

Images of Groups Compared to Whites

Characteristic	Ethnic Group	Mean
Rich/Poor	Jews	+0.58
	Southern Whites	−0.56
	Asians	−0.77
	Negroes	−1.60
	Hispanics	−1.64
Intelligent/Unintelligent	Jews	+0.15
	Asians	−0.36
	Southern Whites	−0.54
	Negroes	−0.93
	Hispanics	−0.96
Patriotic/Unpatriotic	Southern Whites	−0.31
	Jews	−0.57

(*continued*)

68 LARS SCHOULTZ

FIGURE 3.2 (*continued*)

Images of Groups Compared to Whites

Characteristic	Ethnic Group	Mean
	Negroes	−1.03
	Asians	−1.16
	Hispanics	−1.34
Hardworking/Lazy	Jews	+0.38
	Asians	−0.19
	Southern Whites	−0.52
	Hispanics	−0.99
	Negroes	−1.24
Nonviolent/Violent	Jews	+0.36
	Asians	−0.15
	Southern Whites	−0.23
	Hispanics	−0.75
	Negroes	−1.00
Self-Supporting/Live off Welfare	Jews	+0.40
	Southern Whites	−0.71
	Asians	−0.75
	Hispanics	−1.72
	Negroes	−2.08

Source: Tom W. Smith, "Ethnic Images," *General Social Survey Topical Report Number 19,* National Opinion Research Center, University of Chicago: December 1990.

In Figure 3.2 "whites" have been given a score of zero, and a positive score indicates that the ethnic group being evaluated is "better" than whites—richer, harder working, more patriotic, and so forth. A negative score indicates the opposite. On all six dimensions, Hispanics are at or near the bottom of the barrel. They are the poorest, the least intelligent, and the least patriotic; blacks are slightly—but only slightly—lazier, more violent, and more likely to live off welfare.

This poll does not purport to measure how intelligent (or hardworking or patriotic or violent) Hispanics actually are when compared to other ethnic groups; it is an assessment of *images*—of what a random sample of U.S. citizens believes to be true of Hispanics. Professor Huntington may or may not share these beliefs, but respondents to this poll would clearly agree with the argument he makes. It reflects a strain of thinking that has characterized U.S. society since the early nineteenth century, when Secretary of State John Quincy Adams recommended against recognizing the newly independent nations of Latin America: "There is no community of interests or principles between North and South America," he wrote in his diary. Recalling what he had said to Henry Clay earlier in the day, he added, "arbitrary power, military and ecclesiastical, was stamped upon their education, upon their habits, and upon all their institutions. Civil dissension was infused into all their seminal principles. War and mutual destruction was in every member of their organization, moral, political and physical."[31]

Now, two centuries later, the polls tell us that U.S. citizens believe much the same thing. And it is not simply survey researchers who tell us that U.S. citizens conceive of Hispanics as poor, lazy, ignorant, violent and unpatriotic; negative images of Hispanics pop up everywhere in our daily life, as in 2005 when a San Francisco baseball broadcaster complained about "brain-dead Caribbean hitters"[32] or when *Vanity Fair,* a magazine aimed at middle-class white women between the ages of eighteen and thirty-four, recently published an "Ask Dame Edna" advice column:

Q: I would very much like to learn a foreign language, preferably French or Italian, but every time I mention this, people tell me to learn Spanish instead. They say, "Everyone is going to be speaking Spanish in 10 years. George W. Bush speaks Spanish." Could this be true? Are we all going to have to speak Spanish?

A: Forget Spanish. There's nothing in that language worth reading except *Don Quixote,* and a quick listen to the CD of *Man of La Mancha* will take care of that. There was a poet named García Lorca, but I'd leave him on the intellectual back burner if I were you. As for everyone's speaking it, what twaddle! Who speaks it that you are really desperate to talk to? The help? Your leaf blower? Study French or German, where there are at least a few books worth reading.[33]

Dame Edna is trying to be funny, of course, and perhaps this gaffe reflects nothing more than the fact that she is a he (Barry Humphries) and that humorists occasionally hit sour notes. There are no polls of *Vanity Fair*'s age group, and until there are we will simply have to wonder about the reception of Dame Edna's underlying message by the magazine's readers who are, we need to remember, the children of the respondents in Figure 3.2. Have they learned that they need pay no attention to these people? That Hispanics are here to tidy our gardens?

That, of course, is a defensible position: today's middle-class lifestyle requires an enormous supply of Latin American labor—millions of young women to clean our houses and take care of our children, and an equal number of young men to wash our cars and work on our construction projects. But neither today's public nor today's policy envisions that these overwhelmingly young Hispanic immigrants might become part of the American Dream, despite the mountain of research findings demonstrating that is exactly what these workers are doing—struggling to get ahead. And surely we do not need a research report to tell us that in their off hours these young men and women do what Anglo-Protestants often do: some fall in love, some marry, and some have children. And then their children all go to school, as the law both permits and requires, where some do more than climb up a notch on the occupational ladder—occasionally a Rodríguez meets and marries a Smith. Most of us know it is politically incorrect to voice concern about the wisdom of such nuptials, but who can read Dame Edna or look at Figure 3.2 and not conclude that we are silently thinking more or less as President Woodrow Wilson did in 1915, when he sought to console Edith Bolling Galt after learning that her niece had somehow managed to fall in love with a Panamanian: "It would be bad enough at best to have anyone we love marry into any Central American family, because there is the presumption that the blood is not unmixed; but *proof* of that seems to be lacking in this case."[34]

No doubt we will someday overcome this prejudice, but for now U.S. policy conceives of the young Hispanics who blow our leaves as doing only that, and never coming to think of themselves as "belonging" in the United States; instead, in our fictional world they remain in the shadows as "undocumented workers" or emerge into the sunlight as "guest workers," but with the emphasis on "guest." And since we need so many of them, President George W. Bush, in his 2004 State of the Union address, asked Congress to approve "a new temporary worker program to match willing foreign workers with willing employers, when no Americans can be found to fill the job." In his speech the President placed extra emphasis on the word "temporary" and on his insistence that these foreign workers had to be linked to "willing employers." The mental image U.S. policy seeks to create is of a legion of economically integrated workers picking our fruit but never becoming a part of our community, our united states. They will continue to belong in one of those small countries that lie beneath the United States, and if the demand for their labor dries up during an economic downturn, we will cancel their permission to continue selling their labor and insist that we have no responsibility for the consequences.

So, where are we headed as we enter the twenty-first century? Certainly toward ever more intensive economic integration, probably toward a growing awareness that our security problems are their problems (and vice versa), regrettably toward a continuing battle against the domestic politics of prejudice, and hopefully toward more children from the Rodríguez-Smith marriage.

4

Dangerous Consequences:
The U.S. "War on Drugs" in Latin America

Coletta A. Youngers

U.S.–Latin American relations—long characterized by asymmetrical power relationships and the political tensions inevitably associated with that asymmetry—are presently at a low point. Since the Organization of American States (OAS) and its member countries first rallied around the United States in the wake of the September 11, 2001, terrorist attacks, the United States has squandered the support offered by its southern neighbors. Although there are no terrorist threats to the United States emanating from the region, U.S. policy makers view it through that lens, with the issue of "narcoterrorism" at the top of their hemispheric agenda. Casting issues from radical populism to various types of gang warfare as national security threats has met with resistance by regional leaders, many of whom face deep-rooted economic crisis and growing popular unrest.

Opposition to the war and the subsequent U.S. occupation of Iraq is widespread across the region. Both Chile and Mexico stood up to the United States as the UN Security Council debated the issue and faced Washington's wrath afterward. Many countries have resisted U.S. pressure to sign "Article 98" agreements granting U.S. troops and officials immunity in the International Criminal Court; eleven countries in the region have refused outright and have faced reductions in U.S. economic aid as a result.[1] The administration's saber rattling on Cuba and Venezuela has irked many regional leaders, who have failed to take up the Bush administration's call to isolate Venezuelan president Hugo Chávez. The fissures in U.S.–Latin American relations were most evident, however, in the election for the new OAS secretary general, Chile's José Miguel Insulza. Though Washington eventually threw its weight behind him, he is the first OAS secretary general to be elected who was not Washington's candidate.

Alongside these more recent trends, the so-called "War on Drugs" has long been a point of contention between the United States and the countries bearing the brunt of U.S. policy. Local governments have resisted Washington's militarized approach and have instead called for greater levels of economic assistance and trade benefits to address the poverty and lack of meaningful employment opportunities that lead people to engage in the lowest levels of the illicit drug trade. The U.S. government has used its diplomatic and economic muscle to obtain cooperation with its one-size-fits-all antidrug programs; however, it is facing increasing difficulty in garnering such cooperation on two fronts. First, in the Southern Cone, left-leaning governments have come into office in Brazil, Argentina, Uruguay, and Chile. All benefited at the polls from taking a more critical stance toward Washington and have shown more willingness to stand up to their powerful northern neighbor. Second, political unrest across the Andean countries—due in part to opposition to coca eradication policies—has led governments in Bolivia, Ecuador, and Peru to tread carefully on drug control policies. The recent election of the coca growers' leader Evo Morales as president of Bolivia, initiatives to allow unregulated coca production in Peru, and the Ecuadorian government's objections to fumigation over its border with Colombia all illustrate the widening cracks in U.S. international drug control policy.

Moreover, the arguments of drug policy critics are bolstered by two factors. On the one hand, twenty-five years and $45 billion later, international drug control efforts have failed to lead to any reduction in illicit drugs flowing into the United States; on the contrary, cocaine and heroin are more readily available at cheaper prices than ever before. On the other hand, the dangerous consequences of U.S. drug policy are more and more evident. The War on Drugs strengthens military forces at the expense of civilian authorities, exacerbates human rights problems and undermines civil liberties, further impoverishes poor farmers, harms the environment, and generates social conflict, violence, and political instability. It is fueling conflict within and between countries, and it has brought the U.S. government into a direct role in Colombia's brutal counterinsurgency campaign. In short, the costs of implementing U.S.-backed drug policies are high, particularly in the volatile Andean region.

U.S. INTERNATIONAL DRUG CONTROL POLICY

The Andean countries of Bolivia, Peru, and Colombia are the source of the coca leaf—a traditional and culturally important crop among Andean peasant communities—that is processed into cocaine. Coca leaves are mixed with easily obtainable chemicals and other products to make coca paste, which is then transported to laboratories and processed into powder cocaine. All three countries produce cocaine, though Colombia is the source of over 90 percent of the cocaine that enters the United States, as well as 50 percent of the heroin.[2] A vast and complex network of dealers and transportation routes facilitates the smuggling of these illicit drugs into the United States and other parts of the world. Though virtually all of Central America and the Caribbean are considered "transit" countries, Mexico is the most important route into the United States. Lately, turf wars between rival drug gangs have led to a dramatic escalation in violence in that country.

U.S. international drug control policy is intended to decrease the supply of illicit drugs by eradicating coca production, curbing illicit drug production overseas, and seizing shipments en route. While it was President Nixon who first declared drugs a national security threat, the launching of the Andean Initiative in 1989 by President George H.W. Bush led to a dramatic increase in U.S. involvement in "source" country efforts. Its centerpiece was the empowerment of Latin American military and police forces to carry out counter-drug initiatives, and significant U.S. training and support was provided to those forces willing to collaborate. The Andes quickly replaced Central America as the primary recipient of U.S. security assistance. At the same time, the U.S. Congress designated the U.S. Department of Defense as the "single lead agency" for the detection and monitoring of illicit drugs.

A range of programs were put in place, including crop eradication and alternative development projects targeting small farmers; interdiction of the precursor chemicals used in cocaine and heroin production, as well as the drugs themselves; seizing laboratories; dismantling criminal networks; extradition to the United States of major traffickers; and programs intended to strengthen local justice and law enforcement systems. However, it was the preponderant role designed for both U.S. and local military forces that led critics to denounce the "militarization" of U.S. drug policy. This militarization includes the role carved out for military forces in domestic law enforcement operations, the training of civilian police forces in paramilitary operations and strategies, and the provision of the vast majority of drug war resources to military and police forces, to the detriment of economic development and democratic institution-building programs.

As the Cold War was coming to a close, U.S. military forces in the region— primarily the U.S. Southern Command (SouthCom)—were seeking a new mission.[3] Though many within the Defense Department were skeptical of military involvement in combating illicit drugs, SouthCom enthusiastically embraced the War on Drugs as a means of not only maintaining but expanding its role, influence, and presence in the region. Its hefty budget and 3,000 permanent military and civilian personnel make it a formidable force within the hemisphere,[4] and the head of SouthCom can be found visiting Latin American countries far more than high-level State Department officials. Journalist Dana Priest reports: "More people work there dealing with Latin American matters than at the Departments of State, Commerce, Treasury, and Agriculture, the Pentagon's Joint Staff, and the office of the secretary of defense combined."[5] As a result, SouthCom has taken on a "growing and disproportionate role in U.S.–Latin American relations."[6]

From its first involvement in counter-drug efforts, the U.S. military has seen that mission as well suited to the low-intensity conflict strategies honed in Central America in the 1980s. As with the Cold War, the drug war strategy relied on military forces to combat an "internal enemy" via jungle warfare or paramilitary-style operations. Similarly, military training and assistance is provided despite the human rights records of recipient forces and few, if any, incentives are provided for long-term institutional reforms.

However, in the wake of the September 11, 2001, terrorist attacks in New

York and Washington, the nexus between U.S. counter-drug and counter-terrorism strategy has become much stronger. Not long after September 11, the U.S. attorney general, John Ashcroft, declared, "Terrorism and drugs go together like rats and the bubonic plague. They thrive in the same conditions, support each other and feed off each other."[7] Though the narco-guerilla theory has been articulated by U.S. policy makers for over two decades, terminology referring to guerrillas or insurgents has been replaced by the "narcoterrorist" rhetoric that predominates today.

The national security strategies adopted by the Bush administration in the wake of September 11 are leading to the militarization of a range of non-traditional security issues, in addition to drug trafficking. In his annual statement to the U.S. Congress, SouthCom commander in chief General Bantz J. Craddock lists the following threats to "the stability and prosperity" in the region and hence to be addressed by SouthCom: "transnational terrorism, narco-terrorism, illicit trafficking, forgery and money laundering, kidnapping, urban gangs, radical movements, natural disasters, and mass migration."[8] This approach implies that military solutions are applicable to problems that often have socioeconomic roots, such as urban gang activity. While they may present challenges to law enforcement agencies, these issues necessitate multifaceted solutions. In fact, experience to date in confronting illicit drug trafficking calls this approach into question: the militarized U.S. War on Drugs has failed to make any dent in the supply or availability of illicit drugs.

The U.S. government now views the Latin American region almost exclusively through the counterterrorist lens, though the region poses no serious national security threat to the United States. U.S. policy makers have long pointed to the tri-border area of Argentina, Brazil, and Paraguay as a center for Arab radicalism. However, little evidence has been put forward to substantiate such claims, and whatever activity is taking place there appears to be minimal. Those Latin American groups on the U.S. State Department's list of designated foreign terrorist organizations include three in Colombia: the Revolutionary Armed Forces of Colombia (FARC), the National Liberation Army (ELN) and the United Self-Defense Forces (AUC). All of these groups derive substantial funding from the drug trade and other illicit activities, pose a significant threat to Colombian society, and are responsible for horrific atrocities. Their actions, however, are targeted inward, not outward; at most, they can be considered domestic, not international, terrorists. Moreover, applying the terrorism concept to these groups negates their political projects: both left- and right-wing insurgents are seeking territorial control and political power in Colombia.

Colombia, however, is the primary country in which U.S. counter-drug, counterinsurgency and counterterrorism agendas converge. Former South-Com commander General James Hill claims that "narco-terrorists in Colombia remain the largest and most well known threat in our region . . . by and large these groups consist of terrorists and criminals who operate outside of the rule of law in pursuit of illicit profits rather than political revolution."[9] Even before September 11, Colombia had become the primary recipient of U.S. military aid, training, and support in the hemisphere. Counternarcotics assistance to that country began to increase over the second half of the 1990s but took a big leap forward in mid-2000, when the U.S. Congress approved funding for Plan Colombia, a massive five-year aid initiative. Between fiscal years 2000 and 2005, Colombia received approximately four billion U.S. dollars, of which 80 percent was destined for military and police forces.[10] Smaller amounts of funding were provided to neighboring countries in an effort to prevent the Colombian conflict and drug trade from "spilling over" its poorly protected borders.

From the beginning, the line between counter-drug and counterinsurgency assistance and programs has been murky at best, though when Plan Colombia was approved as a counter-drug initiative, some restrictions were put in place to attempt to limit possible U.S. involvement in counterinsurgency efforts. That murky line was erased entirely after September 11. The Bush administration requested and received congressional support for eliminating restrictions on providing U.S. assistance and intelligence for counterinsurgency purposes. According to Adam Isacson, "This allowed U.S. aid to pay for a host of new non-drug military and police initiatives in Colombia."[11] For example, in 2003, the U.S. government provided millions of dollars to equip and train army battalions tasked with protecting oil pipelines in the northeastern part of the country. The number of U.S. troops and contract employees in Colombia escalated, reaching the 800-person limit mandated by the U.S. Congress. The U.S. counterinsurgency role was warmly embraced by Colombian president Álvaro Uribe, who was elected in 2002. He quickly became the primary hemispheric ally of Washington in its war on terror.

ANATOMY OF A POLICY FAILURE

Colombia is illustrative of the failure of U.S. international drug control policy to date. Both the U.S. and Colombian governments claim that the overall security situation in the country has improved but can point to no meaningful evidence to show a significant disruption to the illicit drug trade. This is evident with regard to both the fumigation policy and the availability and price of illicit drugs in the United States.

By the mid-1990s, Colombia had replaced Peru and Bolivia as the primary producer of the coca leaf used in making cocaine. Although U.S. officials credited their "Air Bridge Denial" strategy—intended to reduce the transportation by air of Peruvian coca paste to Colombian cocaine laboratories—more important was the spread of a fungus afflicting coca crops in Peru and the "verticalization" of the Colombian cocaine industry. After the successful dismantling of the Medellín and Cali cartels, they were replaced by smaller cartels that depend on locally grown coca rather than coca transported from Peru, with the costs that entailed. Violence and poverty fed the coca boom in Colombia, as internal displacement caused by the civil conflict, the growing concentration of land, and lack of employment opportunities all fed migration to coca-growing regions. Coca production in southern Colombia flourished, and poppy production followed as the country's heroin industry boomed as well.

The United States had supported aerial fumigation efforts in Colombia—the only country in the Andes to allow aerial eradication—since the 1980s, when marijuana was the target. By the mid-1990s, the United States pushed for and funded a large-scale fumigation campaign, this time primarily targeting coca plants. Under Plan Colombia, fumigation was carried out on a massive scale. From 2000 through 2003 alone, "the U.S.-backed fumigation

program sprayed herbicide on more than 380,000 hectares of coca, equivalent to more than eight percent of Colombia's arable land."[12] Overall coca
production was reduced but was still significantly higher than just a few years
before. In 2004, a record 130,000 hectares of coca crops were sprayed, but
according to the U.S. government's own figures, released in March 2005, the
total amount of coca under cultivation remained "statistically unchanged," at
114,000 hectares. In short, massive aerial fumigation has failed to make any
significant dent in coca production in Colombia.

In fact, aerial eradication has led to the proliferation of coca production
in other areas of the country. Similarly, suppressing coca production in one
area leads it to emerge somewhere else, either within the country or across
national borders. This is often referred to as the "balloon effect": squeezing
it in one place causes its contents to be displaced to another. In Colombia,
coca production was initially prevalent in three departments. By 1999, it had
spread to twelve and by 2002 could be found in twenty-two departments.[13]
Now it is often grown under shade and in smaller parcels, making it harder to
detect and fumigate. Higher-yield crops make the challenge even greater. In
the Andes as a whole, coca cultivation has remained remarkably constant
over two decades (see Figure 4.1).

Similar patterns can be found throughout the illicit drug trafficking industry. A study by the Washington Office on Latin America (WOLA) points
out: "Arrested drug lords are quickly replaced by others who move up the
ranks; dismantled cartels are replaced by smaller, leaner operations that are
harder to detect and deter. When drug-trafficking routes are disrupted by intensive interdiction campaigns, they are simply shifted elsewhere."[14] Even
larger and more frequent drug seizures may reflect increased drug production and trafficking, as traffickers seek to compensate for their anticipated
losses.

Like statistics on seizures, most indicators of success put forward by
drug policy officials may point to short-term tactical victories but do not
show progress in reducing the overall supply of illicit drugs. These include
the numbers of hectares of coca and poppy eradicated, illicit drugs seized,
and arrests of alleged drug traffickers. This scorecard approach to evaluat-
ing drug policy impact is also the basis for the annual certification process,

FIGURE 4.1

Coca Cultivation in the Andes

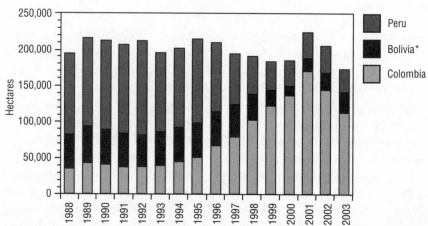

* Note: Beginning in 2001. USG surveys of Bolivian coca take place over the period June to June.
Source: U.S. State Department, *INCSR,* various years. Compiled by the Washington Office on
Latin America.

by which the U.S. government grades the performance of major illicit-
drug-production and transit countries in effectively combating the illicit
drug trade. A country that is "decertified" faces a range of sanctions, including cut-offs in U.S. assistance (with the exception of counter-drug or human-
itarian aid).[15]

Basing such decisions on these short-term indicators can be deeply problematic. For example, using arrest statistics as an indicator of success can lead
to the imprisonment of either innocent or low-level offenders swept up in
drug raids in order to meet arrest quotas. The most recent antidrug accord
signed between the United States and Ecuador actually mandates a 12 percent increase in arrests on drug charges. Such an agreement does not guarantee that major drug traffickers will be apprehended; it only ensures that
Ecuador's prisons will remain overcrowded. A study by the Latin American
Faculty of Social Sciences (FLACSO), based in Quito, found that most of
those imprisoned on drug charges in that country are "mules," or small-time

offenders who carry drugs from one point to another, and that they do so in order to cover the basic living costs of their families.[16] These "mules" are subject to a twelve-year mandatory minimum sentence.

The ultimate U.S. policy objective is to reduce the availability and use of illicit drugs. The supply-side strategy is based on the premise that international drug control efforts can drive up price and thereby drive down demand. In theory, supply shortages should lead to higher prices and lower purity. The higher cost of illicit drugs would discourage demand by new or infrequent users and encourage chronic users to seek treatment. By this measure, drug control efforts to date have had no meaningful impact.

According to U.S. government figures, the retail price of cocaine dropped steadily over the 1980s and early 1990s; thereafter, it more or less stabilized with periodic fluctuations. Heroin prices followed a similar route. Purity of both drugs rose and then stabilized. According to John Walsh, "As of midyear 2003, the estimated retail prices per gram of both powder cocaine and heroin were less than a fifth of their 1981 prices. Crack cocaine cost 44 percent less at mid-year 2003 than it did in 1986." He also points out that decreased prices are not related to slackening demand for illicit drugs.[17] In short, both the price and purity of illicit drugs are substantially lower than they were twenty years ago, indicating that the supply continues to be plentiful. At the same time that prices are going down, rather than up, U.S. spending on international drug control efforts has increased significantly (see Fig. 4.2). In other words, the more the U.S. government has spent, the farther it has gotten from reaching its stated goals.

That is because the policy is fundamentally flawed; it flies in the face of basic economic theory at every link in the chain of the illicit drug business. If coca eradication is successful, the price of coca rises, encouraging new production. The ability to impact prices in the United States via interdiction overseas is equally problematic. The vast majority of the profit margin from illicit drugs is gained once the drugs are in the United States; impacting price before then has an extremely marginal impact on U.S. street prices. Moreover, as noted by Francisco Thoumi, "the challenges to interdiction are overwhelming. In a globalized economy, searching for illegal drugs is frequently like searching for a needle in a haystack."[18]

With regard to domestic law enforcement efforts, Boyum and Reuter con-

82

FIGURE 4.2

U.S. Spending on International Drug Control vs.
U.S. Retail Cocaine and Heroin Prices

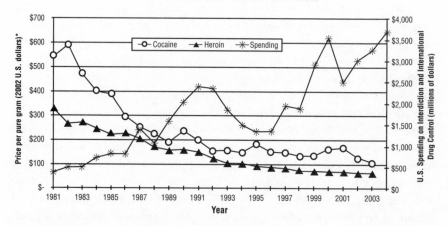

* Note: Prices shown are for purchases of ≤2g of cocaine, and for ≤1g of heroin. Heroin prices
have been divided by six to fit scale.
Source: Price data prepared by the RAND Corporation for the Office of National Drug Control
Policy (ONDCP): spending date from ONDCP. *National Drug Control Strategy.* Compiled by the
Washington Office on Latin America.

clude that "it is hard to find evidence that the sharp ratcheting-up of dealer
risks since the late 1980s has done much to reduce availability or increase
price."[19] They also found that, from a cost-benefit point of view, drug treatment is "far more effective than enforcement in reducing drug consumption."[20] These conclusions point to the need to refocus U.S. drug control
efforts on programs that target the demand for illicit substances, including
treatment and education programs that have proven to be effective.

THE DRUG WAR'S COLLATERAL DAMAGE

Not only is the drug war ineffective, it also has dangerous consequences. A
three-year investigation carried out by WOLA evaluated the impact of U.S.

international drug control efforts on democratization and human rights trends in Latin America and the Caribbean.[21] While recognizing the harm caused by the drug trade itself across the hemisphere, the study focused on whether or not current policy mitigates or exacerbates the myriad problems caused by illicit drug production and abuse. The conclusions reached illustrate the extent of the drug war's collateral damage.

One of WOLA's findings is that the drug war has enhanced the role of the region's militaries. As discussed above, the role of the military and the confusion of military and law enforcement functions are of particular concern for Latin America. The drug war was launched just as a period of military rule across the region was coming to a close. That period was characterized by military coups and other forms of political intervention as well as domestic counterinsurgency campaigns that resulted in massive human rights violations. Precisely as civilian elected governments were seeking to limit the military's role in domestic politics and policing, the U.S. government was advocating, via the drug war, a military role in domestic law enforcement, including intelligence gathering.

In addition to empowering military forces, the drug war created a confusion of roles and conflicts between military and police forces. In Mexico, military officials were put in command positions and now operate alongside police forces. In Bolivia, the military has been brought in to maintain public order when protests against U.S.-backed coca eradication erupt. A related issue is the militarization of local police forces, which are often trained in paramilitary or low-intensity conflict operations that are remarkably similar to that provided at the height of the Cold War. Often, local police forces receive training directly from the U.S. military, including U.S. Special Forces. This works against efforts across the region to professionalize and bring police forces under civilian control.

The lack of accountability and secretiveness that characterize most militaries in Latin America and the Caribbean present serious obstacles to limiting or preventing corruption when those forces are put into more direct contact with the drug trade. These problems are exacerbated by the "confidential" nature of counter-drug programs. For example, when Peruvian president Alberto Fujimori carved out a direct role for the armed forces in counter-drug efforts, the result was rampant personal and institutionalized corruption. Dozens of generals and other high-ranking military and police officials are now awaiting trial on corruption, drug trafficking, and other charges.

Another dangerous consequence of this approach is that the U.S. government has forged alliances with security forces with questionable and even deplorable human rights records. For example, as noted, Colombia is the primary recipient of U.S. security assistance in the hemisphere; yet it is also the country with one of the worst human rights situations and a record of impunity for those responsible. Collusion between right-wing paramilitary groups—many of which are implicated in drug trafficking—and members of the Colombian security forces occurs with disturbing frequency, even as the government forges ahead in its efforts to demobilize the paramilitaries. In fact, in recent years Colombia has witnessed a significant increase in threats against and the detention of human rights and labor activists. Attacks against them continue at alarming rates, even as the United States and Bush administration laud the country's improved security situation.[22]

In the case of Colombia, U.S. policy is contributing to a preexisting human rights crisis. In the case of Bolivia, on the other hand, U.S. counterdrug policy has directly resulted in human rights violations perpetrated by local security forces against coca farmers, including killings, illegal detentions, and mistreatment and even torture of detainees. As in Colombia, those responsible for such atrocities operate with complete impunity. Often, killings take place in the context of the social protests opposing coca eradication. Between 1997 and 2004, thirty-five coca growers and twenty-seven police and military personnel were killed and hundreds more injured.[23]

In both Bolivia and Peru, efforts to meet coca eradication targets set by the U.S. government have led to significant social conflict and violence. Peru's president Alejandro Toledo inherited a difficult situation in coca growing regions and within a year of taking office had to deal with "increasingly explosive protests stemming from unattended social demands that had accumulated during the ten-year government of former president Alberto Fujimori."[24] Pressure by the U.S. government to achieve "zero coca"—a reference to the policy adopted by the Banzer government in Bolivia—within five years exacerbated the situation. This demand far exceeded what Washington had asked of the authoritarian government of former president Fujimori, despite the fact that Peru was embarking upon a difficult democratic transition after the collapse of his authoritarian and corrupt government. Although President Toledo first adopted a policy of negotiation and voluntary eradication in exchange for alternative development assistance, the government ultimately had to resort to forced eradication in order to meet U.S. coca-reduction targets, resulting in a cyclical pattern of protests and violence in response to eradication efforts that continues today.

The case of Peru also showcases U.S. engagement in unholy alliances to further short-term antidrug objectives, all to the detriment of broader U.S. foreign policy goals. The U.S. government's primary interlocutor on drug policy during the Fujimori administration was Vladimiro Montesinos, the de facto national security advisor. The U.S. provided important political backing to Montesinos, even as evidence accumulated of his own involvement in the drug trade. Washington also provided counter-narcotics assistance to the Peruvian intelligence service, SIN, despite its involvement in death squad activity and as its role evolved to that of a Peruvian KGB. After the fall of the Fujimori government in 2000, the extent of Montesinos's corruption was laid bare. One of the U.S. government's key drug war allies was not only amassing a million-dollar fortune through drug related and other forms of corruption, he was also charged with selling guns to the Colombian FARC. Montesinos is now standing trial on over sixty charges; in Washington, calls by independent analysts for U.S. policy makers to evaluate what went wrong with U.S. policy toward Peru fell on deaf ears.

In countries such as Peru, the U.S. government has shown a tolerance for dictatorial regimes that are viewed as cooperative in the drug war. In a similar vein, U.S. policy makers have sacrificed civil liberties to show "zero tolerance" for drug trafficking. As in the United States, the U.S. government has promoted the adoption of harsh antidrug laws across the region that are often at odds with international norms and standards of due process, including the presumption of innocence and punishments that are commensurate with the gravity of the crime committed. Mandatory minimums that provide no leeway for judges in dictating sentences are also problematic.

Ecuador's Congress, for example, adopted U.S.-backed legislation in which the burden for conviction of defendants is so low that lawyers complained that they have to prove their innocence. Often, judges base convictions solely on police reports. Mandatory minimums have led to serious disparities in sentencing practices. The minimum sentence for drug trafficking is twelve years, and the maximum sentence is twenty-five years. However, the maximum sentence for murder is sixteen years. As a result, a small-time trafficker can end up with a higher sentence than a mass murderer.

Justice and prison systems across the region are further skewed by corruption. Adequate legal defense is rarely provided to poor defendants. Yet major drug traffickers can use their ill-gotten gains to bribe judicial officials for either reduced sentences or outright acquittals. If they are incarcerated, they can buy prison conditions that are more acceptable than the norm, along with a range of amenities. While the case of Pablo Escobar's golden prison was the most blatant, it was not an anomaly. It is also not uncommon for criminal chiefs to run their businesses from jail, as has been widely reported in Peru and Mexico.

Finally, forced coca eradication generates a range of negative consequences, generating the social unrest and violence referred to above. Aerial fumigation in Colombia is particularly problematic. In a country that already has millions of internal refugees as a result of the civil conflict, the destruction of peasant livelihoods leads to the further displacement of rural communities. It also fuels left-wing and right-wing insurgencies alike, as farmers seek other means of economic survival, thereby fostering political violence, and weakens "whatever loyalty peasants have to the state."[25] The environmental and health impacts of fumigation remain a subject of debate, though spray, drift and lack of effective targeting clearly damage licit food crops. And, as noted earlier, fumigation leads to the geographic dispersal of coca production.

Forced manual eradication also undermines the legitimacy of central governments and pushes people deeper into poverty. Illicit crops tend to be grown in areas with poor conditions for sustainable agricultural production, lack of infrastructure, and poor accessibility, hence limited market access. Farmers generally do not have opportunities to obtain credit or technical assistance. Most grow food crops for subsistence, along with coca or poppy as a source of cash income. Eliminating that cash income before viable economic alternatives are in place can devastate rural families, yet U.S. policy is based on the premise that coca must be eradicated first—or at least simultaneously—with the provision of alternative development assistance. To date, most of these development programs have yielded little success due to poor design, lack of resources, and the absence of effective participation and "buy in" by local communities.

Despite Washington's insistence to the contrary, forced eradication and alternative development efforts are incompatible. The repressive nature of eradication hinders the cooperation needed for effective, participatory development. The German government's foreign aid agency, GTZ, emphasizes that when poverty is the root cause of coca or poppy production, then repressive eradication measures are inappropriate and counterproductive:

> Alternative development initiatives should be free of deadlines and the precondition of total eradication of drug crops prior to the availability of viable alternatives. A more flexible and gradual reduction of drug crop production must be allowed to avoid problems related to economic and social suffering. Today many communities are forced to hasten the eradication process without viable alternatives, which has resulted in aggravated poverty and migration.[26]

Based on its extensive experience working in coca-growing regions of the Andes, GTZ concludes that when dealing with small-scale coca production, participatory and agreed-upon eradication targets can be set and met only when other sources of income are put in place.

U.S. policy makers view coca farmers as part of the criminal chain of illicit drug trafficking, or even "narco-cultivators." Martin Jelsma of the Transnational Institute takes a radically different view, arguing that small growers should be defined as "economic victims that have become 'addicted' to illicit crops for survival."[27] Jelsma and others argue for the development of a "pro-poor drug control policy"[28] that takes as its starting point the principle that all individuals have a right to a life with dignity[29] and hence should not be deprived of their only income source. A first step toward implementing these ideas in practice would be the decriminalization of small-scale coca production in all Andean countries. While more study is needed on how this approach could be implemented in practice, it is a step in the direction of creating a more humane, and ultimately effective, drug policy.

Adopting a "pro-poor" drug-control policy would promote greater political stability in Andean countries in particular. To date, opposition to U.S.-backed drug policies has contributed to the fall of governments in both Bolivia and Ecuador. In Bolivia, opposition to the violence and conflict generated by U.S. pressure to meet coca eradication targets was one factor leading to the protests that resulted in the collapse of the Gonzalo Sánchez de Lozada government in October 2003. The perception that drug policy was also contributing to Bolivia's economic crisis was a related factor. In fact, prior to the eruption of protests, President Sánchez de Lozada pleaded for more U.S. economic assistance, to no avail.

In Ecuador, ousted president Lucio Gutiérrez had campaigned on a platform of advocating a negotiated settlement to the Colombian conflict and developing a more autonomous national security strategy independent of U.S. policy. After his election in 2002, Gutiérrez reversed course in the face of U.S. economic and diplomatic pressure. He embraced Plan Colombia and the U.S. "cooperative security location," or military base, in Manta, Ecuador. Opposition to the Ecuadorian government's support for Plan Colombia and the U.S. presence at Manta were among the factors that brought his government down in early 2005.

INDEPENDENT VOICES

In both Bolivia and Ecuador, subsequent governments have taken more independent approaches to drug policy. Upon taking office in Bolivia, Carlos Mesa adopted a more lenient strategy with the well-organized coca growers. Given the range of controversial issues facing the country, including the production and sale of natural gas, the new government sought to mitigate conflict wherever possible. That trend has continued with his successor, Eduardo

Rodríguez Veltze. The mere fact that the country has had three presidents in less than two years is in part attributable to the U.S. government's' relentless pursuit of coca eradication. It has also proven to be a boon for the coca growers' leader Evo Morales. In historic elections on December 18, 2005, Morales won the presidency with over 50 percent of the popular vote. As the first candidate to win in the first round since Bolivia returned to formal democratic rule over two decades ago, he has an unprecedented mandate for change. His stated approach to drug policy—"coca, yes; cocaine, no"—has already provoked the wrath of U.S. officials. In addition to calling for the complete legalization of coca production, he advocates marketing coca for traditional uses, and industrializing the leaf for products such as toothpaste, soft drinks and chewing gum.[30]

In Ecuador, the Alfredo Palacios government, which took office after Gutiérrez fled, has returned to the previous platform of developing a more autonomous national security policy. While the government has said that it will honor the Manta agreement—itself questionable as it was negotiated behind closed doors and without congressional approval as mandated by the Ecuadorian constitution—it has adopted a more critical approach to Plan Colombia. Most concretely, calls have been renewed for Colombia to avoid fumigation along the Ecuadorian border due to the potential environmental and health consequences. Establishing a ten-kilometer fumigation-free zone along the border was a proposal that first emerged at the beginning of the Gutiérrez government but was quickly abandoned. As the Transnational Institute points out: "What concerns Ecuador . . . is the harm caused by Colombia because of the proximity of the armed conflict, illegal drug trafficking, and the existence and aerial spraying of crops."[31] After President Palacios elevated the case to the level of the OAS and United Nations, Colombian officials agreed to a temporary suspension of fumigation along the border.

In Peru, opposition to U.S.-backed drug policies has gone a very different route. In June 2005, the regional president, Carlos Cuardesma, in Cusco—which includes areas where coca has traditionally been grown for local use—signed legislation essentially legalizing coca production in three of the department's valleys by declaring the leaf a "cultural patrimony." In July, the regional president in Huanuco—a major coca producing region—followed suit. A similar norm was also adopted by the Puno region but did not go into effect due to infighting among the members of the Regional Council. In September, Peru's constitutional tribunal ruled on the matter, unanimously deciding that the regional governments did not have the authority to take such action. However, it also called on President Toledo to reevaluate the policy because of its lack of success to date. In particular, the tribunal members questioned the focus on coca eradication as opposed to interdiction efforts such as controlling the sale of chemicals used in manufacturing cocaine.[32] They also questioned the lack of an adequate agricultural policy, which pushes poor farmers into coca production.

Where U.S. drug policy has run into the most opposition, however, is Venezuela. When he first took office, President Chávez suspended U.S. antidrug surveillance overflights over Venezuelan territory. As bilateral relations between the two countries continued to sour, Chávez curtailed military-to-military counternarcotics cooperation. Finally, in August 2005, Chávez accused the Drug Enforcement Administration (DEA) of using its agents for espionage and suspended cooperation. Although efforts began almost immediately to reach a new accord to allow the DEA to operate in the country, accusations continued to fly back and forth. "The DEA was using the fight against drug trafficking as a mask," declared Chávez, "to support drug trafficking, to carry out intelligence in Venezuela against the government. Under those circumstances we decided to make a clean break with those accords, and we are reviewing them."[33]

After weeks of political jostling between the two countries, the September 2005 date for the annual U.S. certification report arrived. Not surprisingly, the U.S. government refused to grant a full certification to Venezuela and instead issued a "vital national interests certification." After the determination was issued, there was confusion in the Venezuelan press as to whether or not Venezuela was decertified or certified with a waiver. Technically, the country was certified with a waiver. But for all practical purposes, that is considered a decertification and hence that term is often used to describe such status.

The U.S. State Department determined that "Venezuela failed demonstrably to make sufficient efforts during the last 12 months to meet its obligations under international counter-narcotics agreements and U.S. domestic counter-narcotics requirements. . . ."[34] The litany of complaints cited includes harsh criticism of the Venezuelan government's law enforcement efforts, including a "negative publicity campaign" against the DEA, the removal of key high-level officials responsible for drug policy implementation and allegations of corruption.[35] In response, Venezuelan vice president José Vicente Rangel declared that his government "doesn't recognize" Washington's "moral, judicial, ethical, or political authority" to pass such judgments, noting that the United States is the world's largest consumer of illicit drugs.[36]

The Bush administration's decision not to grant a full certification to Venezuela cannot be fully understood outside of the context of its intense hostility toward Chávez and his Bolivarian revolution. Though Latin American leaders have refused to take up the U.S. call to treat Chávez as an international pariah, the Bush administration has forged ahead with its confrontational approach. It has also sought to portray left-wing or popular uprisings in neighboring countries as fomented by Chávez. For example, Bush administration officials have claimed that recent citizen uprisings in Bolivia were the result of efforts by Cuba's Fidel Castro and Venezuela's Hugo Chávez "to steer this revolution toward a Marxist-socialist populist state."[37] In an August 2005 tour of five South American countries, U.S. secretary of defense Donald Rumsfeld echoed these allegations.[38] To date, no evidence has been presented to back these claims, though they do offer the administration a convenient excuse for ignoring the root causes of the "radical populism" they fear.[39]

Issuing the national security waiver—as opposed to an outright decertification—allows the Bush administration to continue an important form of economic assistance for its policy toward the country: "democracy" assistance that is channeled to Venezuelan opposition groups. Issuing a national interests certification carries the stigma of decertification, and hence represents a slap in the face of the government while allowing the U.S. administration to continue funding "programs to aid Venezuela's democratic institutions, establish selected community development projects, and strengthen Venezuela's political party system."[40]

Ironically, this action was taken against Venezuela while Haiti was fully certified, even though it is the one country in the region that appears to be moving in the direction of a narco-state. U.S. officials repeatedly refer to Haiti as "the black hole" for transiting illicit drugs. Yet the State Department determination blandly states: "While Haiti made efforts this year to improve its performance, we reiterate our concerns . . . about the Interim Government of Haiti's inability to effectively organize law enforcement resources to permit sustained counter-narcotics efforts. Further, the national criminal justice system must be significantly strengthened in order to be effective and gain public confidence."[41] These charges could be lodged, from the perspective of U.S. policy makers, against most other Latin American and Caribbean countries and fail to reflect the reality of a country now routinely referred to in Washington circles as a failed state. Yet again, in terms of domestic politics, a stronger rebuke of Haiti could bolster criticisms of the Bush administration's decision to support the ouster of President Jean-Bertrand Aristide.

THE CUBA CONTRADICTION

Cuba provides another example of the ideological underpinnings of the present administration playing a significant role in the implementation of antidrug policy. The State Department's annual International Narcotics Control Strategy Report puts the drug issue in the broader context of its opposition to the Cuban regime. The 2004 report alleges that "the primary focus of the regime's aggressive posture with respect to all activities deemed 'illegal,' including narcotics trafficking, has been the repression of political and economic activities permissible in most normal societies." As Peter Kornbluh points out: "Opponents of any U.S.-Cuban initiative on drug trafficking argue that Havana is insincere in its commitment to waging a war on drugs and seeks only the international legitimacy that a counter-narcotics accord with the United States would bring."[42]

In reality however, at the operational level, counternarcotics cooperation between the United States and Cuba has improved considerably since the posting of a U.S. Coast Guard liaison officer in the U.S. Interests Section in Havana in 2001. Cooperation between the Coast Guard and the Cuban Ministry of the Interior is fluid and the Ministry is in close contact with the liaison officer whenever an interdiction operation in Cuban waters is taking place. If the United States is serious about interdiction efforts, such coordination is in fact essential, given Cuba's geographic location and the U.S. government's concerns about the flow of illicit drugs through the Caribbean, and in particular the Windward Passage.

The U.S. State Department often complains of the lack of resources that the Cuban government dedicates to interdiction efforts and lack of effective coordination of antidrug efforts with neighboring countries. Yet, the U.S. government is the lone voice criticizing Cuban drug policy within the international community. Other governments, such as Canada and Great Britain, claim to have excellent cooperation with the Cuban government, pointing out that the country is trying to show the hemisphere that it is serious about collaborating with counterdrug efforts. The British Ambassador to Cuba asserts that his government enjoys "a lot of cooperation" and that the Cuban government is putting "sufficient resources" into the effort, given its overall budget constraints and infrastructure deterioration.[43] Cuba has signed regional, multilateral, and bilateral accords with European and Caribbean countries and works closely with the UN Office on Drugs and Crime. Indeed, Cuba has been largely successful in keeping illicit drugs out of its own territory and has an exceptionally low incidence of drug use and addiction.

Ironically, the U.S. government's biggest complaint is that Cuba has failed to implement an "effective use of force policy." Concretely, this means that the Cuban government has been unwilling to shoot with the intent to sink boats that refuse to obey warning shots. When asked about this reluctance to use force, Cuban officials point out that if they were to kill even alleged drug traffickers on the open seas, they fear the incident would be used against them by the anti-Castro forces within the U.S. government.[44] In a June 2005 gathering of Caribbean counter-drug officials in Havana, Cuban officials repeatedly called for the United States to sign an antinarcotics accord to allow for increased collaboration. Such calls are routinely rebuffed by Washington, despite the ongoing operational cooperation just described.

94 COLETTA A. YOUNGERS

AN ALTERNATIVE APPROACH

U.S. international drug control policy is full of contradictions, has failed to disrupt the illicit drug trade, and has dangerous consequences for countries across the hemisphere and particularly in the Andean coca-growing regions. To date, successive U.S. administrations have dismissed discussion of policy alternatives. In the Washington policy-making environment, those advocating alternative approaches are often portrayed as morally wrong for being lax on drugs or stigmatized as promoting the legalization of drugs. It is time to open up an honest debate on how to confront more effectively the very real problems associated with the production and consumption of illicit drugs.

That debate should start from the premise that completely eliminating either illicit drug consumption or production is unrealistic. Economic incentives ensure that the production of illicit drugs, including synthetic drugs, will continue to meet demand, even if the costs are high for those drug traffickers and their employees who are apprehended. The challenge, therefore, is to mitigate the harm caused by drugs to individuals, societies and countries.

Moreover, the greatest impact on drug production and trafficking in Latin America and the Caribbean would be a significant reduction of the demand for illicit drugs in the United States, as it is still the U.S. market that is the driving force behind the illicit drug trade. Within the United States, this would require a fundamental reorientation of antidrug policy to put it in a public health framework. Strategies should be reoriented to focus on effective treatment and education programs, including treatment upon demand, HIV/AIDS programs, realistic prevention strategies, and community development.

The harm-reduction model can also be applied to international drug control efforts: policy makers should seek to reduce the harm caused by international counternarcotics policies themselves. This means abandoning both the one-size-fits-all model and Washington's heavy-handed approach. Latin American governments need the flexibility to develop their own antidrug strategies, appropriate for the on-the-ground realities that vary tremendously from country to country. Along these lines, many of the worst elements of U.S. international drug control policy discussed here should simply be eliminated, including most of the military components of U.S. counterdrug aid and training programs, the certification process and other mechanisms that link the provision of U.S. economic assistance to counter-drug aid, and forced and aerial eradication.

This new approach should be accompanied by a fundamental shift in U.S. resource allocation overseas—from military-oriented programs to economic assistance for equitable economic development, including support for the rural sector, which is so often neglected in today's development models. In addition, far more resources need to be allocated to programs to promote democratic institution building. This includes long-term efforts to reform police forces and the justice sector. Ultimately, it is in the long-term strategic interests of the United States to promote economic development and participatory democracy in Latin America and the Caribbean, as well as to build more equitable partnerships with its hemispheric neighbors. Such an approach would be more humane—and ultimately more effective—than the current national security and narcoterrorist framework for U.S. foreign policy toward the region.

5

Promoting Polyarchy in Latin America:
The Oxymoron of "Market Democracy"

William I. Robinson

"**I** don't see why we need to stand by and watch a country go Communist because of the irresponsibility of its own people," famously declared National Security Advisor Henry Kissinger in June 1970, referring to the democratic election that year of Salvador Allende as president of Chile.[1] In the preceding decade, Washington had spent millions of dollars in covert intervention to "marginalize" Allende and the left and bolster its favored parties, particularly the Christian Democrats. When Allende won anyway, Washington turned to a massive destabilization campaign against his government, with the collusion of the Christian Democrats—then headed by Patricio Aylwin—and other groups from the center and the right. The result was the bloody 1973 military coup.

The Chilean coup was part of a pattern in Latin America of military takeovers in the 1960s and 1970s with U.S. approval and often active assistance, in the face of mass struggles that broke out everywhere against the prevailing social and economic inequalities and highly restricted political systems. But Washington abruptly switched tracks in the mid-1980s and began to "promote democracy" in Latin America and around the world. In Chile, Aylwin and his party once again received U.S. assistance, this time as part of a "democracy promotion" program channeled through the National Endowment for Democracy (NED) and the U.S. Agency for International Development (AID), which would help Aylwin become president. Ironically, the return to power in 1990 of Aylwin and the party that openly participated in the 1973 military coup was projected around the world as the culmination of a "democratic revolution" sweeping Latin America. In different ways, this scenario—suppressing democracy and placing dictatorships in power, only to later organize a return to civilian rule under the banner of "democracy promotion"—repeated itself throughout Latin America and the world in the 1980s and 1990s.

GLOBALIZATION AND THE TRANSNATIONAL AGENDA

What is most striking about this shift from promoting dictatorships to promoting "democracy" is that it coincides with the rise of the neoliberal economic project. I suggest here that not only are these two linked, but that what Washington refers to as "democracy" has become a functional imperative of economic globalization. "Market democracy" may be an oxymoron for those who see the concentration of social and economic power brought about by capitalist "free" markets as fundamentally incompatible with the democratic exercise of political power. Yet the phrase cynically captures the ideological sales pitch that a new transnational elite has used to sell the project of global capitalism in recent decades. This new elite—the product of recent changes in transnational development—constructed and imposed a paradigm of "free markets and democracy" that was so hegemonic in the 1980s and 1990s that it came to be seen as common sense and those who challenged it as crazed heretics.

Over the past thirty years the world economy has experienced dramatic crises and restructuring as globalization has unfolded. Structural changes have profoundly transformed the social and political fabric of each nation, international relations, and the global system as a whole, giving rise to a new global capitalist bloc under the leadership of the transnational elite. The increasing global mobility of capital has allowed for the decentralization and functional integration around the world of vast chains of production and distribution and the unprecedented concentration of worldwide economic management, control, and decision-making power in transnational capital. As national economies are dismantled and replaced by an integrated global production and financial system, new corporate and bureaucratic groups have emerged. Their interests lie in advancing the global economy over any national economic projects. In recent decades, these groups gradually coalesced into a new global capitalist bloc led by a transnational elite comprised of the owners and managers of the leading transnational corporations and banks, as well as bureaucrats and technicians who administer the international financial institutions (IFIs), the upper echelons of state bureaucracies in the "North" and the "South"—developed and underdeveloped countries alike—and transnational forums including the Group of Seven, the Trilateral Commission, and the World Economic Forum.[2]

The promotion of "free markets and democracy" is intended to make the world both available and safe for global capitalism by creating the most propitious conditions for the unfettered operation of the new global production and financial system. One part of global restructuring was the so-called "Washington Consensus," or what came to be known as neoliberalism, a doctrine of laissez-faire capitalism legitimated by the assumptions of neoclassical economics and modernization theory, by the doctrine of comparative advantage, and by the globalist rhetoric of free trade, growth, efficiency, and prosperity.[3] But this transnational agenda has an explicitly political component, involving a shift in the policies of the United States and other capitalist powers from bolstering authoritarianism and dictatorship in much of the South to promoting "democracy." If the economic component is to make the world available to capital, the political component is to make it safe for capital. This endeavor involves the development of new methods of domination, new political institutions, and forms of transnational social control intended to achieve a more stable and predictable world environment.

Behind the policy of "democracy promotion" is the eternal problem that dominant groups face: how to maintain order and exercise effective social control in the face of popular pressures for change. By the 1980s it had become clear to dominant groups, and especially to emergent transnational elites, that the old methods of political domination would no longer work. Elite rule required renovation as people were becoming integrated globally, and many engaged in mass mobilization as they saw their ways of life profoundly altered by capitalist development. Sweeping changes in social control were necessary if the emergent global order was to hold together.

When transnational elites talk about "democracy promotion," what they really mean is the promotion of polyarchy. I use the term to refer to a system in which a small group actually rules, and mass participation in decision making is confined to choosing leaders in elections that are carefully managed by competing elites. This, of course, is the system in place in the United States. The concept of polyarchy is an outgrowth of elitism theories that developed early in the twentieth century to counter the classic definition of democracy as power or rule (*cratos*) by the people (*demos*). This classic definition was quite at odds with the rapid increase in the concentration of wealth and political power among dominant elites, and their ever-greater control of social life, that accompanied the rise of corporate capitalism. To bring the term "democracy" in line with reality, redefinition was necessary.

Early twentieth-century elitism theory argued, in the words of one of its leading exponents, Italian social scientist (and Mussolini admirer) Gaetano Mosca, that "in all societies, two classes of people appear—a class that rules and a class that is ruled. The first class, always the less numerous, performs all political functions, monopolizes power and enjoys the advantages that power brings, whereas the second, the more numerous class, is directed and controlled by the first, in a manner that is now more or less legal, now more or less arbitrary and violent."[4]

What Mosca meant by "now more or less legal, now more or less arbitrary and violent," was that elite domination could be maintained, and the social order preserved, through either democratic or dictatorial methods, depending on circumstances. Building on this elitism theory, a new polyarchic or institutional redefinition of democracy developed within U.S. academic circles closely tied to the U.S. policy-making community in the post–World War II years of U.S. world power. This redefinition began with Joseph Schumpeter's 1942 classic study, *Capitalism, Socialism and Democracy*, in which he rejected the "classic theory of democracy" defined in terms of the "will of the people" and the "common good." Instead, Schumpeter advanced "another theory" of democracy as "institutional arrangements" for elites to acquire power "by means of a competitive struggle for the people's vote." Explained Schumpeter, "Democracy means only that the people have the opportunity of accepting or refusing the men who are to rule them."[5] This redefinition culminated in 1971 with the publication of Robert Dahl's study, *Polyarchy*. By the time the United States assumed global leadership after World War II, the polyarchic definition of democracy had come to dominate social science, political, and mass public discourse. It is this conception that has informed the "transitions to democracy" and the veritable cottage industry of academic literature on the subject.

Polyarchy is not dictatorship, and the distinction between the two should not be derided. But the trappings of democratic procedure in a polyarchic political system do not mean that the lives of ordinary people become filled with authentic or meaningful democratic content, much less that social justice or greater economic equality is achieved. This type of "low-intensity democracy" does not involve power (cratos) of the people (demos), much less an end to class domination or to substantive inequality that is growing exponentially under the global economy. Mass movements for democratization around the world are movements seeking fundamental social change, including but encompassing much more than reforms leading to contested elections and other institutional structures of polyarchy. In contrast to more popular conceptions of democracy, which see political power as a means for transforming unjust socioeconomic structures and democratizing social and cultural life, the polyarchic definition explicitly isolates the political from the socioeconomic sphere and restricts democracy to the political sphere. And even then, it limits democratic participation to voting in elections.

Polyarchy is promoted in order to co-opt, neutralize, and redirect these mass popular democratic movements—to relieve pressure from subordinate classes for more fundamental political, social, and economic change in emergent global society. The crisis of elite rule that developed throughout the underdeveloped world in the 1970s and 1980s was resolved, momentarily, through transitions to polyarchies—the so-called "democratic revolution." During these contested transitions, transnational dominant groups tried to reconstitute hegemony by changing the mode of political domination—from coercive control exercised by authoritarian and dictatorial regimes to more consensually based (or at least consensus-seeking) new polyarchies.

At stake was the type of social order—nascent global capitalism or some popular alternative—that would emerge. While masses pushed for a deeper popular democratization, emergent transnationalized fractions of local elites, backed by the political and ideological power of the global economy, often counted on the direct political and military intervention of the United States and other transnational forces. They were thus able to gain a controlling influence over democratization movements and to steer the breakup of authoritarianism into polyarchic outcomes. These transitions constitute real political reform—"preemptive reform," in the words of former secretaries of state Henry Kissinger and Cyrus Vance—in an effort to contain mass popular movements.[6]

Promotion of polyarchy is a policy initiative that has become transnationalized under U.S. leadership. The United States and other core powers have conducted programs worldwide through diverse "democracy promotion" instruments as part of their foreign policy and military/security apparatuses. Various international organizations have also established "democracy units," and the IFIs have made aid and access to global financial markets conditional upon the recipient country having a polyarchic system.[7] I stress the collective nature of this new policy because I disagree with the prevalent notion that the emergent global capitalist order is based on U.S. hegemony. Analysis based on the nation-state is outdated and obscures our understanding of transnational dynamics in the new era. We are witnessing the decline of U.S. supremacy and the early stages of an emerging transnational hegemony as expressed in a new historic bloc that is global in scope and based on the hegemony of transnational capital.[8] In Latin America, the United States has sponsored the region's restructuring and integration into global capitalism, *not* as a project of U.S. hegemony in rivalry with other powers for influence but *on behalf of* a transnational project. In this age of globalization the U.S. state promotes polyarchy not to stabilize the old interstate system but to attempt to stabilize a new transnational capitalist historic bloc.

POLYARCHY AND NEOLIBERALISM

In Latin America, as elsewhere, the "transitions to democracy" became a mechanism to facilitate the rise to power of transnationally oriented elites.

During the 1980s and 1990s, alliances of local and global elites were able to hijack and redirect mass democratization movements to undercut popular demands for more fundamental change in the social order. In this way, the outcome of mass movements against the brutal regimes that ruled that continent involved a change in the political system while leaving intact fundamentally unjust socioeconomic structures.

Alongside the promotion of "democratic transitions," transnational elites and their local counterparts in the state and the economy (new "modernizing" or "technocratic" elites) used the structural power of the global economy to reorganize state institutions and to create a more favorable set of institutions for deepening adjustment. The new polyarchic civilian elites emerging from controlled transitions set about integrating (or reintegrating) their countries into the new global capitalism through a massive neoliberal restructuring—the well-known story of deregulation, liberalization, privatization, social austerity, labor flexibilization, and the like. The result in Latin America has been an unmitigated disaster for the popular classes. Throughout the 1980s and 1990s, as the global economy arrived in Latin America, the poor got poorer and the rich got richer; social conditions deteriorated for majorities as insecurity and marginality escalated.

Seen in historical perspective, the shift to polyarchy corresponds to the emergence of the global economy in recent decades. New modes of social control became a political counterpart to economic restructuring on a world scale, in the context of the transnationalization of the economy and of politics itself. Transnational capital emerged as the agent of globalization as the world capitalist system entered into a political and economic crisis in the 1970s. Symptoms of this crisis included economic stagnation, declining corporate profits, the growing strength of the nonaligned movement and its calls for a "new international economic order," and rising popular protests around the world. In the face of this crisis, transnational elites became convinced that both the economic and the political pillars of the system needed to be transformed. The economic goal was to restore growth and profitability through a new global production and financial system. The political goal was to reestablish authority—read "capitalist hegemony"—through new ideologies and by overhauling political systems around the world. On the economic

front, transnational elites began this project by reorganizing and dismantling national economies and redistributive projects and constructing a new
global production and market system.[9]

Polyarchy has been promoted by the transnational elite as the political
counterpart to neoliberalism, structural adjustment, and unfettered transnational corporate accumulation. The neoliberal program involved worldwide
market liberalization and the construction of a new legal and regulatory
framework for the global economy, along with internal restructuring and
global integration of each national economic system. The program called for
eliminating state intervention in the economy and sharply curtailing state
regulation over capital flows in all nations. The combination of the two was
aimed at creating a "liberal world order," an open global economy, and a
global policy regime that breaks down all national barriers to the free movement of transnational capital *between* borders and the free operation of capital *within* borders. The neoliberal model attempts to harmonize a wide range
of fiscal, monetary, industrial, labor, and commercial policies among multiple nations, as a requirement for fully mobile transnational capital to function simultaneously, and often instantaneously, among numerous national
borders. These programs became the major mechanism of adjusting local
economies to the global economy. What took place through these programs
was a massive restructuring of the productive apparatus in each adjusted
country—and the reintegration into global capitalism of vast zones of the
former Third and Second Worlds—under the tutelage of emergent transnational state apparatuses.[10]

But why does polyarchy become the political counterpart to this economic restructuring? Interaction and economic integration on a world scale
are obstructed by authoritarian or dictatorial political systems, which cannot
manage the expanded social intercourse associated with the global economy.
The turn to promoting polyarchy is an effort to modernize political systems
in each country incorporated into global structures so that they operate
through consensual, rather than direct, coercive domination. The demands,
grievances, and hopes of the popular classes tend to be neutralized less
through direct repression than through ideological mechanisms, political
co-optation and disorganization, and the limits imposed by the global econ-

omy. The universal imposition of economic or "market" discipline as the principal worldwide means of social control has tended to replace extra-economic or political discipline exercised by states as sites of direct social control.

In addition to mediating interclass relations, polyarchy is also a better institutional arrangement for resolving conflicts among dominant groups. Because of its mechanisms for intraelite compromise and accommodation, and with its hegemonic incorporation of popular majorities through elections and other mechanisms, polyarchy is better equipped in the new global environment to legitimize the political authority of dominant groups and to achieve a stable enough environment—even under the conflict-ridden and fluid conditions of emergent global society—for global capitalism to operate in the new world order. U.S. "democracy promotion" intervention, in this regard, generally facilitates a shift in power from locally and regionally oriented elites to new groups more favorable to the transnational agenda. Under the guidance of transnational fractions of local elites, neoliberal states promote the interests of global accumulation over national accumulation.

Polyarchy represents a more efficient, viable, and durable form for the political management of socioeconomic dictatorship in the age of global capitalism. Nonetheless, neoliberal states have been wracked by internal conflicts brought about by the contradictions of the global system. The "democratic consensus" is consensus among an increasingly cohesive global elite on the best type of political system for reproducing social order. Promoting polyarchy is thus a political counterpart to the project of promoting capitalist globalization. And "democracy promotion"—free markets through neoliberal restructuring—has become a singular process in U.S. foreign policy. As the U.S. AID explains, "Democracy is complementary to and supportive of the transition to market-oriented economies."[11]

Throughout the 1980s and 1990s Washington developed novel mechanisms of political intervention as it launched "democracy promotion" programs around the world and set about to transnationalize the policy. Political intervention programs have increasingly brought together an array of governmental and nongovernmental organizations, think tanks, financial institutions, multilateral agencies, and private corporations from the United States, Europe, and elsewhere. In 1980 the United States and the European Union each spent $20 million on "democracy"-related foreign aid. By 2001 this had risen to $571 million and $392 million, respectively. In 2003 the EU spent $3.5 billion while the United States was expected to spend a total of $2 billion for the 2006 fiscal year for polyarchy promotion.

U.S.-organized political intervention programs conducted under the rubric of "democracy promotion" involve several tiers of policy design, funding, operational activity, and influence. The first involves the highest levels of the U.S. state apparatus: the White House, the State Department, the Pentagon, the Central Intelligence Agency (CIA), and certain other state branches. It is at this level that the overall need to undertake political intervention through "democracy promotion" in particular countries and regions is identified as one component of overall policy toward the country or region in question, to be synchronized with military, economic, diplomatic, and other dimensions.

In the second tier, the U.S. Agency for International Development (AID) and several other branches of the State Department are allocated hundreds of millions of dollars, which they dole out, either directly or via the National Endowment for Democracy (NED) and other agencies such as the U.S. Institute for Peace (USIP), to a series of ostensibly "private" U.S. organizations that are in reality closely tied to the policy-making establishment and aligned with U.S. foreign policy. The NED was created in 1983 as a central organ, or clearinghouse, for new forms of "democratic" political intervention abroad. Prior to the creation of the NED, the CIA had routinely provided funding and guidance for political parties, business councils, trade unions, student groups, and civic organizations in the countries in which the United States intervened. In the 1980s a significant portion of these programs were shifted from the CIA to the AID and the NED and made many times more sophisticated than the often-crude operations of the CIA.

The organizations that receive AID and NED funds include, among others (the list is extensive): the National Republican Institute for International Affairs (NRI, also known as the International Republican Institute, or IRI) and the National Democratic Institute for International Affairs (NDI), which are officially the "foreign policy arms" of the U.S. Republican and Democratic parties, respectively, as well as the International Federation for Electoral Systems (IFES), the Center for Democracy (CFD), the Center for International Private Enterprise (CIPE), the Free Trade Union Institute (FTUI), and International Labor Solidarity. The boards of directors of these organizations include representatives from the highest levels of the U.S. foreign policy and political establishment and representatives from the transnational corporate world. U.S. universities, private contractors, independent intellectuals, and other "democracy" experts may also be tapped. All these organizations and actors coalesce into a complex and multileveled U.S. political intervention network.

In the third tier, these U.S. organizations provide "grants"—that is, funding, guidance, and political sponsorship—to a host of organizations in the intervened country itself. These organizations may have previously existed and are penetrated through "democracy promotion" programs and incorporated in new ways into U.S. foreign policy designs. Or they may be created entirely from scratch. These organizations include local political parties and coalitions, trade unions, business councils, media outlets, professional and civic associations, student and women's groups, peasant leagues, human rights groups, and so on. In the division of labor with the political intervention network, each U.S. agency works with a specific sector of the intervened society. For example, the IRI and the NDI specialize in political parties and they make "grants" to parties in intervened countries. For their part, the FTUI and the ILS target the working class and typically handle grants to trade unions in the intervened country. Local groups brought into U.S. "democracy promotion" programs are held up as "independent" and "nonpartisan," but in reality they become internal agents of the transnational agenda.

The interventionist network seeks to penetrate and capture civil society in the intervened country through local groups that have been brought into the fold. A veritable army of U.S. and international nongovernmental organizations (NGOs) and technical advisors, consultants, and "experts" conduct programs to "strengthen political parties and civil society," for example. They also lead workshops on "civil education," "leadership development," "media training," and so on. These "democracy promotion" activities seek to cultivate local political and civic leaders with a political and civic-action capacity. Under U.S. sponsorship, these groups typically come together into a "civic front" with interlocking boards of directors. They support one another and synchronize their political activities and discourse.

In the overall strategy, Washington hopes to create through its "democracy promotion" programs "agents of influence"—local political and civic leaders who are expected to generate ideological conformity with the elite social order under construction, to promote the neoliberal outlook, and to advocate for policies that integrate the intervened country into global capitalism. These agents are further expected to compete with, and eclipse, more popular-oriented, independent, progressive, or radical groups and individuals who may have a distinct agenda for their country.

PROMOTING POLYARCHY IN LATIN AMERICA

These processes are clearly illustrated in Latin America, which in many respects has been a laboratory for polyarchy promotion. By the late 1970s, authoritarian regimes there faced an intractable crisis. Mass popular movements for democracy and human rights threatened to bring down the whole elite-based social order along with the dictatorships—as happened in Nicaragua in 1979, and looked likely to occur in Haiti, El Salvador, Guatemala, and elsewhere. This threat from below, combined with the inability of the authoritarian regimes to manage the dislocations and adjustments of globalization, generated intraelite conflicts that unraveled the ruling power coalitions. This crisis of elite rule was defused, at least momentarily, through transitions to polyarchy that took place in almost every country in the region during the 1980s and early 1990s.

U.S. polyarchy promotion in Latin America has involved two phases. In the first, begun in the 1980s, the United States launched "democracy promotion" along with other interventions during mass struggles against authoritarian regimes and for popular democratization. The challenge of "preemptive reform" was to remove dictatorships to prevent deeper change. U.S. intervention synchronized political aid programs with covert and direct military operations, economic aid or sanctions, formal diplomacy, government-to-government programs, and so on. These programs linked with and helped place in power local sections of the transnational elite that swept to power in country after country, and who have integrated their respective nation-states into the new global order. The same elite groups that benefit from capitalist globalization also came in this way to control key political institutions.

In the second phase, launched in the 1990s, U.S. policy has aimed to "consolidate" democracy through broad "democratic aid" and other government-to-government and multilateral programs.[12] These programs sought to train the new transnationally oriented elites in the procedures of polyarchy, to inculcate a polyarchic political culture, and to strengthen a polyarchic institutional environment, as a complement to economic restructuring under the superintendence of the IFIs. These elites are helped in opposition to popular sectors and also against the far-right, authoritarian-oriented elites, "crony" capitalists, and other dominant strata opposed to the transnational project.

Transitions to polyarchy provided transnational elites the opportunity to reorganize the state and build a better institutional framework to deepen neoliberal adjustment. In undertaking this adjustment, the new elites have set out to modernize the state and society without any fundamental deconcentration of property and wealth, or any class redistribution of political and economic power.[13] Instead, the elites have implemented a transnational model of development based on a rearticulation with world markets, new economic activities linked to global accumulation, the contraction of domestic markets, and the easy availability to transnational capital of cheap labor and abundant natural resources as the region's "comparative advantage" in the global economy.[14]

The cases of Chile, Nicaragua, Panama, Mexico, Haiti, Venezuela, and Bolivia demonstrate these patterns.[15] In Chile, the United States, after orchestrating the 1973 overthrow of the Allende government, provided consistent backing for the military dictatorship of Augusto Pinochet until 1985, when, in response to a growing protest movement, it abruptly shifted support to the elite opposition and began to promote a transition. That year, the United

States began applying myriad carrot-and-stick pressures on the regime to open up and to transfer power to civilian elites. Simultaneously, it implemented political aid programs, through the AID and the NED, to help organize and guide the coalition that ran against Pinochet in the 1988 plebiscite and against the dictatorship's candidates in the 1990 general elections. U.S. political intervention was key to achieving unity among a splintered elite opposition, in eclipsing popular opposition, and in assuring elite hegemony over the antidictatorial movement between 1985 and 1987 when this hegemony was in dispute. From 1987 to 1990, U.S. intervention also was important in consolidating a reconstituted elite and in securing the commitment of much of that elite to the process—begun under Pinochet—of far-reaching neoliberal restructuring and integration into the global economy.

In Nicaragua, the United States supported the Somoza family dictatorship for nearly five decades. Foreign capital poured into Central America in the 1960s and 1970s, integrating the region into the global economy and laying the structural basis for the social upheavals of the 1980s. The Sandinista government that came to power in the 1979 revolution became the target of a massive U.S. destabilization campaign. Then, in 1987, the objective of this campaign changed dramatically, from a military overthrow of the Sandinistas by a foreign-based counterrevolutionary movement to new forms of polyarchy promotion that supported an internal, moderate opposition. This opposition, organized and trained through large-scale U.S. political aid programs, operated through peaceful, noncoercive means in civil society to undermine Sandinista hegemony. The shift from hard-line destabilization to polyarchy promotion culminated in the 1990 electoral defeat of the Sandinistas, a conservative restoration and installation of a polyarchic political system, reinsertion of Nicaragua into the global economy and far-reaching neoliberal restructuring.

In Panama, as in Nicaragua, military aggression was combined with political intervention to achieve a polyarchic outcome. In 1903 the United States orchestrated the country's independence from Colombia and brought to power a tiny white oligarchic elite (in an overwhelmingly black country) that would support its plans to build the canal. This elite was kept in power by U.S. support and numerous direct interventions until it was displaced, but only partially, by the populist 1968 coup led by General Omar Torrijos. Manuel Noriega, an unpopular CIA asset and close U.S. ally, came to power following Torrijos's death in 1981, opening a period of crisis and instability. Washington continued its support for the Noriega regime, despite its practice of electoral fraud and mass repression, until a combination of conjunctural geopolitical concerns and the broader shift to its new, worldwide strategy led to a decision to overthrow it. The destabilization campaign included economic sanctions, coercive diplomacy, psychological operations, and, finally, a direct military invasion. The campaign also involved a multimillion-dollar political intervention program to create a "democratic opposition" by bringing together "modernizing" groups from within the oligarchy tied to international banking and trade. Through the invasion, this "modernized" sector was placed in power—literally. Despite ongoing social conflict and an internally divided elite, neoliberal reform proceeded apace in the 1990s.

In Mexico, the ruling Institutional Revolutionary Party (PRI) was wracked by a power struggle in the 1980s. The "dinosaurs" (the old bourgeoisie and state bureaucrats tied to Mexico's corporatist import-substitution model of national capitalism) could not prevent the rise of the "technocrats," the transnational fraction of the Mexican elite that captured the party and the state with the election of Carlos Salinas de Gortari in 1988. This group implemented a sweeping neoliberal structural adjustment, thoroughly transforming the Mexican economy and integrating the country into global capitalism. The struggle between national and transnational fractions, however, was not fully resolved, and things turned violent in the early 1990s. Intraelite conflict combined with the widespread mobilization of popular classes and armed insurrections by the Zapatistas in Chiapas and other guerrilla groups in the states of Guerrero and Oaxaca made stability elusive and threatened the whole transnational project for the country.

There was a disjuncture between the economic dimension of the transnational project and the political dimension: An incomplete transition to polyarchy lagged far behind neoliberalism. U.S. policy makers wanted to see a functioning bipartisan system based on competition between the PRI and the rightist and neoliberal National Action Party (PAN). But too much pressure on the PRI could have opened up space for the popular classes. U.S.

strategy was therefore to provide strong and consistent support for an authoritarian state even while prodding it to complete a transition to fully functioning polyarchy. This included support for the Mexican state's brutal counterinsurgency program in Chiapas against the Zapatistas and their supporters. The electoral triumph of PAN's Vicente Fox in July 2000, however, may have completed a transition to polyarchy, bringing the political system in synch with economic changes. The Mexican case also underscores that the U.S. objective is to promote polyarchy and oppose authoritarianism only when doing so does not jeopardize elite rule itself. Indeed, the United States provided support in the 1980s and 1990s for mass repression in each of the cases discussed and in other countries as well, such as in El Salvador, Guatemala, Bolivia, and Colombia. A policy of conditional promotion of polyarchy is perfectly compatible with, and in fact regularly includes, the promotion of repression.

In Haiti, the United States sustained the Duvalier dictatorship at the same time it promoted a development model in the 1960s and 1970s which inserted the country into the emergent global economy as an export-assembly platform. This model helped uproot the rural peasantry—a class that had constituted the backbone of the social order for nearly two centuries—and hastened a mass movement against the dictatorship. In early 1986 a popular uprising brought down the Duvalier regime.

In Chile elites had gained enough hegemony over the antidictatorial movement to secure a polyarchic outcome, and in Nicaragua the Sandinistas led popular sectors in a revolutionary outcome. In Haiti, however, neither elite nor popular forces could gain any decisive hegemony. The elite was fragmentary and wedded to authoritarianism, and what's more, the small, transnationally oriented elite was poorly organized. Popular forces had no unifying political organization, program, or leadership which could facilitate a bid for power. Haiti became submerged in a national power vacuum and a cauldron of turmoil between 1986 and 1990. During this period, the United States introduced a massive "democracy promotion" program to cultivate a polyarchic elite and place it in power through U.S.-organized elections. The liberation theologist Jean-Bertrand Aristide and his Lavalas Party defeated Marc Bazin, who had been carefully groomed in U.S. political aid programs, in the 1990 elections. This was an upset for the U.S. program, but Aristide was overthrown in a 1991 military coup d'état, which was tacitly supported by the United States.

Aristide returned to office as a lame-duck president through a U.S. invasion in September 1994, having agreed as a condition for his return to office that he implement a neoliberal program and open space for the elite. Throughout the 1990s and into the new century, the NED and the AID provided support for a coterie of elite civic and political organizations that mounted opposition to Aristide's Lavalas Party. The Lavalas Party remained in power from 1994 to 2004 and managed to resist implementing the full packet of neoliberal reform, but it was unable to govern effectively and saw its program of basic change in the social order stifled by the local elite, the United States, and the IFIs. Aristide was again ousted in February 2004, this time directly by U.S. Marines on the heels of an uprising led by former Duvalierist paramilitaries and conservative political groups. He was replaced by the same collection of elites that had been cultivated by U.S. political aid programs since the 1980s. The ongoing conflict in Haiti underscores a complex scenario whereby the conditions for a stable polyarchic system continued to elude the United States yet neither elite nor popular forces could achieve any hegemonic order.

Venezuela had a polyarchic political system in place since the 1958 pact of Punto Fijo, but the exhaustion of the political and economic model that emerged from that pact led to a crisis of the system during the 1980s and 1990s. This was an era of transition from the preglobalization world capitalist system to the emerging globalist stage of capitalism. In Venezuela, the elite were thrown into confusion over how to face the crisis unleashed by the decline of the old model and the rise of neoliberalism. Among the various elite cliques and factions were some stubbornly rooted in the national circuits of accumulation developed in the post–World War II period of oil-driven expansion and import-substitution industrialization—circuits that were increasingly less viable. (We have, for example, the very modest nationalist project put forth by the government of Rafael Caldera between 1994 and 1999.) Others, meanwhile, sought a reinsertion of the country into new transnational circuits. The oligarchy became wracked by internal splits and disputes. No one faction could achieve its hegemony over the elite as a whole. The crisis of oligarchic power could not be contained as the popular classes began to make their own political protagonism felt from the 1989 *Caracazo* and on. This political protagonism, for a number of circumstantial and conjunctural reasons, eventually coalesced around the rise of Hugo Chávez and the Bolivarian government. The oligarchy, for the first time since polyarchy had been instituted, began to lose its grip on power.

The objective of the transnational project in Venezuela, hence, was not to facilitate a transition to polyarchy, since the country had a polyarchy since 1959. Rather, it was aimed at salvaging oligarchic power, at modernizing it, and at trying to identify and groom new groups among the elite who could reincorporate the popular classes into an elite hegemony and implement the new model of neoliberalism and insertion into global capitalism. But this project could not be implemented. What took place instead was the rise of a popular project contrary to the interests of the transnational elite and their local counterparts. The Bolivarian project had broken with elitist hegemony in Venezuela and the basic U.S. objective became to restore it. This is the context in which U.S. strategists turned to "democracy promotion" in Venezuela.

As is well known, the NED has dramatically expanded its programs in Venezuela since Hugo Chávez was elected to power in 1998. NED and re-lated AID programs for the anti-Chavista forces have been broadly documented, and include, among others: assistance for these forces to develop media strategies; regular trips to Washington for opposition politicians, business people, and trade unionists; new disbursements for the opposition Confederation of Venezuelan Workers (CTV); a series of workshops for opposition groups; and financing for numerous anti-Chavista groups. The NED doled out almost $1 million in the period preceding the 2002 coup d'état to the groups that were involved in the abortive putsch, while the Bush administration gave tacit support to the coup.

With the collapse of the coup and the subsequent failure of the anti-Chavista forces to win the August 2005 referendum, Washington has turned to a strategy of ongoing attrition involving a strategic shift from a "war of maneuver" that sought the quick removal of the Chávez government (coup d'état, business strikes, referendum) to an extended "war of position." The effort now is to regroup the opposition forces and to develop plans for the 2006 elections and beyond, without passing up any opportunity to weaken and destabilize the government on an ongoing basis. For these purposes "democracy promotion" programs have been vastly expanded.

In Bolivia, polyarchy promotion programs were relatively small-scale until the indigenous uprising that drove President Gonzalo Sánchez de Lozada from power in October 2003. Since then, millions of dollars have poured in to fund and organize discredited traditional political parties, support compliant ("moderate") indigenous leaders that could counter more radical ones, and to develop civic organizations under elite control to compete with militant social movements. One objective of these programs was to depoliticize the issue of natural gas and defuse popular demands for nationalization of natural resources. AID's Office of Transition Initiatives (OTI) spent no less than $11.8 million for these purposes during 2004 and 2005. One U.S. Embassy cable from La Paz quite candidly stated that one of the objectives was to "help build moderate, pro-democratic political parties that can serve as a counterweight to the radical MAS or its successors."[16] MAS, or the Movement Toward Socialism, is one of two militant indigenous organizations that organized mass uprisings that forced two neoliberal presidents to resign— Sánchez de Lozada in 2003 and Carlos Mesa in 2005—and have demanded the nationalization of gas and the empowerment of indigenous communities.

POWER, THE GLOBAL SYSTEM,
AND THE ANTIMONY OF CAPITALIST POLYARCHY

When we speak of democracy, we should recall that at issue is *power*, or the ability to meet objective interests, to shape social structure in function of these interests. What is most striking about the new polyarchies is the extent to which globalizing elites have been insulated from popular pressures and mass opposition to the neoliberal project. In Latin America, the transnational elite has demonstrated a remarkable ability to utilize the structural power of transnational capital over individual countries as a sledgehammer against popular grassroots movements. In Haiti, Nicaragua, and elsewhere, these movements were powerless to change the social structure, even when they gained access to the state, because of the ability of the global economy and the transnational elite to dictate internal conditions. In several countries, antineoliberal blocs elected their own candidates in recent years. But these candidates soon found it impossible to resist the pressures of transnational forces.

In Honduras, for example, Carlos Roberto Reina headed an insurgent progressive, social democratic–oriented faction within the Liberal Party and won the 1993 elections on a populist platform of opposition to the neoliberal program. He was backed by national groups among the elite who were threatened by the opening to the global economy, and by broad popular sectors whose resistance to neoliberal austerity mounted in the early 1990s. In his first year in office Reina met with International Monetary Fund (IMF) and AID officials and tried to negotiate greater flexibility in implementing adjustment programs that his predecessors had agreed to. But when threatened with suspension of new bilateral and multilateral credits, and with the denial of much-needed debt relief, the government caved in, and by 1995 had recommitted Honduras to the neoliberal program. Reina's own social base rapidly deteriorated, and his government faced a spiral of popular protest and loss of legitimacy in the mid-1990s. Similar stories can be told for Rafael Caldera's government in Venezuela, elected in 1993, and for governments elected in the 1990s and in the new century in Ecuador, Argentina, and elsewhere.

Voting against the dominant project by electing candidates who oppose it has not given electorates the ability to change that project. It is evident that the global system limits the ability of popular majorities to use polyarchy to have their will prevail. The power of global capitalism to impose discipline through the market usually makes the all-pervasive coercion of authoritarian regimes unnecessary. The concept of coercion here is not limited to physical coercion such as military and police force. Economic coercion as the threat of deprivation and loss, the threat of poverty and hunger, and so on forces people to make certain decisions and take certain actions, such that apparently "free" choices are made by groups that have in fact been coerced by structures, and by other groups that control those structures, into making particular choices.

Socioeconomic power, therefore, translates into political power: the political and the socioeconomic spheres cannot be separated. "Transitions to democracy" literature, drawing on theories of elitism, claim that democracy rests exclusively on process and that the political sphere can and should be separated from the economic sphere, so that there is no contradiction between a "democratic" process and an antidemocratic social order characterized by sharp social inequalities and minority monopolization of society's material and cultural resources. However, a central argument in this literature, and one that directly mirrors U.S. policy, is that polyarchy requires free-market capitalism and that promoting polyarchy is complementary to and supportive of promoting free-market capitalism.[17] The polyarchic definition of "democracy" thus claims to separate the political from the economic and yet it simultaneously connects the two in its actual construct, just as U.S. policy connects the two in the actual practice.

Hence when global capitalism is the concern, the political is expected to be linked to the social and the economic and "normal society" is capitalist society. But when economic inequalities and social justice are the concern, the political is expected to be separated from the social and the economic. By making this separation, such issues as socioeconomic exclusion, the exercise of power, the controls of material and cultural resources of society, and so forth become irrelevant to the discussion of democracy. What *is* relevant is simply political contestation among elite factions through procedurally free elections. This separation of the socioeconomic from the political sphere by policy makers and by mainstream social scientists is an ideological construct that does not correspond to reality but does help legitimate the political practice of promoting polyarchy and the interests it serves.[18]

Transitions to polyarchy have been accompanied by a dramatic sharpening of inequalities and social polarization, as well as growth in poverty, a consequence of polarizing processes inherent in capital accumulation liberated through globalization from the constraints of developmental and interventionist states and the countervailing powers of popular classes. Added to income polarization in the 1980s and 1990s was the dramatic deterioration in social conditions as a result of neoliberal policies that drastically reduced and privatized health, education, and other social programs.[19] Popular classes whose social reproduction is dependent on a social wage (the public sector) have faced a social crisis, while privileged middle and upper classes have become exclusive consumers of social services channeled through private networks. Global, neoliberal capitalism generates downward mobility for most people while it opens new opportunities for some middle-class and professional groups by separating global market forces from mediation by redistributive state structures as they mold the prospects for downward and upward mobility.

In fact, the United Nations Development Program's Human Development Index (HDI), an aggregate measure of well-being based on life expectancy at birth, educational attainment, and standard of living (GDP per capita in purchasing-power parity), actually *decreased* for many Latin American countries in the 1990s, including Argentina, Chile, Uruguay, Costa Rica, Mexico, Panama, Venezuela, Colombia, Brazil, Peru, Ecuador, Bolivia, and Guatemala. Between 1980 and 1995, some 94 million Latin Americans joined the ranks of the poor as the number of people living in poverty went from 136 to 230 million—an increase from 41 to 48 percent of the total population.[20] An explosion of the informal sector, mass unemployment and underemployment, the spread of hunger and malnutrition, and the epidemic reappearance of such diseases as malaria, tuberculosis, and cholera have accompanied the transitions to polyarchy and the integration of Latin America into the global economy. These trends are not particular to Latin America; they are part of a broader pattern under global capitalism.

Latin America's polyarchic regimes face growing crises of legitimacy and governability. Almost every Latin American country has experienced waves of spontaneous uprisings triggered by austerity measures, indigenous uprisings, the formation in the shantytowns of urban poor movements of political protest, and a resurgence of mass peasant movements and land invasions, all outside of the formal institutions of the political system, and almost always involving violent clashes between protestors and the states and paramilitary forces. But there has also been growing and increasingly coherent organized opposition from below. State repression organized by polyarchic regimes has been used throughout Latin America to repress protest against neoliberalism and has claimed thousands of lives.[21]

Popular uprisings and their forcible suppression highlight the relationship between the violation of socioeconomic rights and the violation of traditional human rights. In the end, the imperative of social order makes itself felt in coercive domination. Worldwide inequality in the distribution of wealth and power is a form of permanent structural violence against the world's majority. This structural violence generates collective protest, which calls forth state repression. On an ongoing basis, this repression turns structural violence into direct violence. Hegemony, Gramsci reminds us, is consensus protected by the "armor of coercion."[22] Polyarchy does not mean an end to direct coercion. It means that coercion is applied more selectively than under a dictatorship, and that repression becomes legalized—legitimated—by civilian authorities, elections, and a constitution.

In the long run, the transnational elite cannot promote polyarchy and also promote global capital accumulation and the class interests embedded therein. This has already become clear in Colombia and Mexico. Even though Washington has attempted to promote polyarchy in these countries, the need to save the state from popular and insurrectionary sectors has led it into an ever deeper alignment with local authoritarian political forces and paramilitary groups who have been strengthened by U.S. support. The social and economic crisis has given way to expanding institutional quandaries, the breakdown of social control mechanisms, and transnational political-military conflict. The revolt in Argentina, a string of leftist electoral victories in South America, the struggle of the landless in Brazil, peasant and indigenous insurrections in Bolivia and Ecuador, ongoing civil war in Colombia, coups d'état in Haiti, the Bolivarian revolution in Venezuela, and so forth: this was the order of the day in the first few years of the twenty-first century.[23]

This panorama suggests that the state structures that have been set up (and continuously modified) to protect dominant interests are now decomposing, possibly beyond repair, as the neoliberal elite that came to power in recent decades through "transitions to democracy" has lost legitimacy and the Washington Consensus has cracked. It is not at all clear in the early twenty-first century whether these fragile polyarchic political systems will be able to absorb the tensions of economic and social crisis without themselves collapsing. A long period of political decay and institutional instability is likely.

But we should not lose sight of the structural underpinning of expanding institutional crises and recall the fundamental incompatibility of democracy with global capitalism. The transnational model of accumulation being implemented since the 1980s does not require an inclusionary social base and is inherently polarizing. This is a fundamental structural contradiction between global capitalism and the effort to maintain polyarchic political systems that require the hegemonic incorporation of a sufficiently broad social base. Global capitalism generates social conditions and political tensions—inequality, polarization, impoverishment, marginality—conducive to a breakdown of polyarchy. This is the fundamental contradiction between the class function of the neoliberal states and their legitimation function. The same market that generates an affinity between capitalism and polyarchy, largely because the market replaces coercive systems of social control, also creates and re-creates the socioeconomic conditions that make genuine democracy impossible.

6

Latin America: Persistent Inequality and Recent Transformations

Luis Reygadas

Latin America has long been the world region with the highest levels of income inequality. Will it remain so after all of the sociopolitical and economic changes of recent years? The past decade and a half has witnessed democratic transitions, structural adjustment, globalization, powerful indigenous movements, and a leftward shift in the political landscape of many Latin American countries. This chapter explores whether these transformations will help to reduce inequality in the region.

WHAT IS UNIQUE ABOUT INEQUALITY IN LATIN AMERICA?

Latin America is not the poorest region on the planet—parts of Africa and Asia suffer greater misery, marginality, and gender inequality—yet it is the region where income inequality is greatest. Moreover, this inequality is persistent rather than transitory. Measured in terms of Gini coefficients—a widely accepted measurement in which a score of zero depicts complete equality and one signals a situation in which all resources are held by one sector and no resources accrue to another—Latin America stands out for its exceptional concentration of income. The average Gini coefficient was 0.522 during the 1990s, compared to 0.342 in the developed economies of the OECD, 0.328 in Eastern Europe, 0.412 in Asia, and 0.450 in Africa.[1] The distance between the income of the richest 10 percent and that of the poorest 10 percent is enormous, reaching 68 to 1 in Brazil and 55 to 1 in Guatemala.[2]

FIGURE 6.1

Distribution of Income in Latin American and OECD Countries

Country	Year	Gini Coefficient
Latin America		
Paraguay	1995	0.621
Brazil	1996	0.591
Bolivia	1996	0.588
Panama	1997	0.576
Colombia	1997	0.567
Nicaragua	1993	0.567
Chile	1996	0.564
Ecuador	1995	0.560
Guatemala	1998	0.557
Peru	1997	0.555
Honduras	1996	0.528
Mexico	1996	0.528
El Salvador	1995	0.505
Venezuela	1997	0.496
Dominican Republic	1996	0.481
Argentina*	1996	0.470
Costa Rica	1997	0.459
Uruguay*	1997	0.426
Average		0.533
OECD Countries		
United Status	1994	0.440
United Kingdom	1995	0.397
Australia	1994	0.391

(continued)

* Includes only urban areas.

FIGURE 6.1 (*continued*)

Distribution of Income in Latin American and OECD Countries

Country	Year	Gini Coefficient
OECD Countries		
Italy	1995	0.362
Canada	1994	0.354
Germany	1994	0.346
Norway	1995	0.294
Finland	1995	0.292
Sweden	1995	0.288
Luxembourg	1994	0.269
Average		0.344

Source: Miguel Szekely and Marianne Hilgert, The 1990s in Latin America: Another Decade of Persistent Inequality, Luxembourg Income Study, Working Paper no. 235, Syracuse, NY, pp. 5–7.

Latin America has exhibited the highest Gini coefficients of all world regions over several decades, and Paraguay, Brazil, Bolivia, and Panama are among the most unequal countries on the planet. But what makes Latin America unique is that the richest sector of the population receives a far higher proportion of income than their counterparts elsewhere in the world. The top 10 percent receives nearly half (48 percent) of total income, whereas the richest 10 percent in developed countries receives "only" 29.1 percent.[3] Indeed, if we omit the top 10 percent from calculations of the Gini coefficient, it turns out that Latin America and the United States have similar levels of income inequality: 0.353 compared to 0.386. Three Latin American countries—Uruguay, Mexico, and Costa Rica—even turn out to be less unequal than the United States, while another six—the Dominican Republic, Argentina, El Salvador, Guatemala, Peru, and Venezuela—have only marginal differences vis-à-vis the United States. Thus, if we consider only the disparities between the middle and lower classes, Latin America is not unlike other regions of the world. It is only when we take into account the highest segments of the income distribution pyramid that the landscape looks so exceptional. Comparing gaps between the top 10 percent and the next 10 percent of income recipients, there is a clear regional pattern: the top decile earns between 2 and 3.5 times more than the next decile everywhere in Latin America. Even in the relatively unequal developed countries (the United States, the United Kingdom, and Canada), the differences are only 1.6, 1.5, and 1.4 times, respectively.[4] There is strong evidence, then, that in all Latin American countries the enormous inequality is tightly correlated with the extreme wealth of the top 10 percent of the population. Poverty is of course much more worrisome from a human perspective, and it is related to social inequality, but to understand inequality in Latin America one has to explain not only the resilience of poverty but, above all, the persistence of extreme wealth.

That inequality endures in Latin America across historical periods (from colonialism to the present), different economic development models (from primary export–based to import substitution and neoliberalism) and distinct regime types (populist, authoritarian, democratic) suggests that it is a structural characteristic that permeates social institutions and that requires specific attention. There is no single cause that explains this regional peculiarity: it is the result of a concatenation of forces and the accumulation of many intersecting processes—economic, political, ethnic, social, and cultural—that have been analyzed extensively over the years.[5]

GLOBALIZATION, STRUCTURAL ADJUSTMENT, AND INEQUALITY: LATIN AMERICA, 1990–2005

How has inequality evolved in recent times, in the context of globalization? Has the region become more equitable or, to the contrary, have social asymmetries been exacerbated? Many people would respond immediately that the whole world has become more unequal, and that Latin America has as well. Others would put forth the opposite view, contending that globalization creates opportunities, that Latin America has democratized, and that given these welcome developments we will soon see more equitable societies so long as the "correct" economic policies continue to be implemented. Statistics are bandied about by both sides to support virtually opposite interpretations, yet the reality is that the relationship between inequality and globalization is far more complex than immediately meets the eye.

Several images can illustrate the tensions that accompany the construction of equality in Latin America at the dawn of the new century. In 2002, as a culmination to the Zapatista march toward Mexico City, indigenous people from Chiapas stood up in the Mexican Congress and projected their voices into the parliament and through the mass media across the world. A few years earlier, Benedita da Silva, a woman of African descent and of impoverished origins, had been elected mayor of Rio de Janeiro and subsequently was named Minister of Social Development in the Lula government. The Ecuadorean indigenous leader Luis Macas was appointed the minister of agriculture in 2003. Alongside these promising developments we find grounds for pessimism, as well. In Buenos Aires, which once was among Latin America's least unequal cities, poverty rates rose from 4.7 percent of the population in 1974 to 57 percent a quarter century later. The ranks of Latin America's poor, which had diminished from 118 million people in 1970 to 82 million in 1982, swelled anew to reach 210 million people in 1994 and 222 million in 2005. If in 1970 the richest 1 percent of the population earned 363 times more than the poorest 1 percent, the proportion had increased to 417 times by 1995.[6] On the one hand, then, politically excluded sectors have achieved voice and recognition: women, indigenous peoples, and blacks are now key actors in Latin America. Alongside these welcome changes, there have been democratic transitions, powerful social movements, strengthened civil society organizations, and participatory social policies. Yet, on the other hand, we have seen processes that have maintained or even aggravated inequalities: structural adjustment has been associated with a deterioration of welfare policies, asymmetries of integration into world markets, increasingly precarious employment, new forms of social exclusion, the rise of organized crime and the increase in violence, and political, social, and economic polarization. The debate about inequality in the region once again has taken on force, after a period in which it seemed to have lost centrality.

TRADE OPENING

One important issue in current debates about inequality in Latin America concerns the outcome of structural adjustment processes, which have included the opening to international trade, privatization of public enterprises, financial deregulation, reforms of pension systems, the elimination of subsidies, and many other measures. The most widely held view is that structural adjustment entailed the dismantling of state intervention in the economy, giving way to the free play of market forces. Some observers favor this transformation, while others oppose it, but both camps tend to share the notion that there was a transition from state regulation to market regulation. Yet that premise is false: rather than a shift from total statism to pure market, what took place was a transition from one sort of market to another, and from one sort of state intervention to another. In the process, oligopolistic and clientelist mechanisms that existed before the transition were reconfigured. At the same time, adjustment processes were not identical everywhere: there have been variations across countries, and the outcomes of different policies have been heterogeneous.

Trade liberalization consisted of the reduction or elimination of import tariffs, the promotion of export strategies, and the signing of various free trade agreements (Mercosur, the Andean Pact, CAFTA, NAFTA, the agreement between Mercosur and the European Union, and those between Mexico and the EU and Japan). Countries that were once strongly protectionist shifted over a very brief period to become highly open to foreign trade. As noted in the introduction to this book, the export sector of many Latin American countries has grown as a result: clothing in Mexico, Central America, and the Caribbean; nontraditional agricultural products in Central America and Brazil; electric products, electronics, and autos in Mexico; fruits and wine in Chile; soybeans in Argentina; and so on. This has had an important impact on employment levels and on hard currency earnings for some export regions, particularly some of the more dynamic zones of Chile and Northern Mexico, and in nontraditional agriculture in Central America and Brazil. In terms of inequality, some studies report diminished indices in export zones. For example, in some areas of Guatemala small and medium-sized landholders have gained a foothold in export sectors, producing greater employment, less land concentration, and higher female participation in the labor force.[7] The data for Mexico are striking: in the five regions of the country where the most jobs were created in export-oriented maquila industries (the Northern Gulf, Peninsular, North, North Central, and Pacific North), income inequality as measured by Gini coefficients declined. Conversely, those regions less connected to the export boom saw inequality increase.[8] The data are insufficient to reach firm conclusions, and more studies would need to be carried out to determine the causes of shifts in inequality in each region. Nonetheless, it seems plausible to argue that in those areas of Mexico where significant sectors of the population managed to become incorporated into export activities, inequality declined, and that those which remained at the margin of the shift toward export-oriented production experienced a worsening of inequality. This is hardly cause for celebration, for the improved Gini coefficients in export zones are small, and overall inequality in Mexico increased, from .534 to .564.[9] Moreover, the greatest benefits from exports have been concentrated in transnational companies and large domestic enterprises. Most of the jobs created in the export sector are of poor quality in terms of wages, working conditions, and stability. Meanwhile, the increase in inequality in those regions that have remained outside the export boom calls into question many of the arguments of those in favor of economic opening.

Similar patterns are evident elsewhere in Latin America. The opening of the economy has enabled Chile to maintain high levels of economic growth and to reduce poverty considerably, but it has not reversed the enormous increase in inequality that took place during the Pinochet dictatorship of 1973–89. During the 1990s, average incomes increased, but these improvements were unequally distributed: the income of employers rose from 25 times the poverty rate to 34 times that figure, whereas that of workers rose only from 3.5 to 4.3 times the poverty rate. As a result, the gap between the two groups, which at the outset of the decade stood at 7 to 1, reached 8 to 1 by the close of the 1990s.[10] Similarly, Brazilian export agriculture—particularly soybeans—has grown considerably, but this accounts for only 8 percent of total agricultural production in the country, and its benefits are concentrated in a very limited segment of the population. Today Brazil remains one of the most unequal countries on earth. Meanwhile, in Central America hundreds of thousands of people have secured jobs in clothing maquilas and in export agriculture, but an even greater number of people have been thrust into the informal economy, international migration, or the ranks of the unemployed or underemployed.

The flip side of trade liberalization in Latin America is the closing down of countless domestic industries and the deterioration of traditional agriculture, which have not been able to survive the arrival of low-cost imports. Consumers enjoy greater access to cheaper and better goods, but most of the population cannot take advantage of this advance given the decline in their disposable incomes. Trade agreements have not included compensatory measures that might have permitted the majority of agricultural and industrial producers to adjust to the new patterns of accumulation. The problem is not so much that Latin American economies began a process of trade opening, but rather that this was done in a manner that led inevitably to a highly asymmetric distribution of its costs and benefits. In societies with extreme structural inequalities, only the most dynamic firms and the most skilled segments of the workforce were able to successfully confront the sudden opening up of markets. Existing disparities conditioned the course of trade opening, which reproduced or magnified economic polarization. Thus, on top of the old inequalities was added a new layer, which separates those who managed to catch a first-class seat on the train of liberalization from those who had to ride in the second-class compartment. Transnational companies, captains of industry, and highly skilled workers prospered, whereas small and medium-sized entrepreneurs barely survived, maquila workers and those employed in export industries faced unstable and low-paying jobs, and the rest of the population found itself left in the cold, disconnected from the export boom propelled by globalization.

THE PLUNDERING OF THE FINANCIAL SECTOR

During the 1980s, Latin America experienced in traumatic fashion the consequences of its financial fragility. High levels of external debt, together with economic crises, inflation, and the voraciousness of international creditors—

encouraged by the IMF—triggered the debt crisis, leaving the region on the verge of bankrupcy. To deal with the situation, governments assigned vast resources to servicing their debts. In 1990 Brazil devoted 77 percent of its annual budget to this purpose, and as late as 1998, the corresponding figure in Mexico was 59 percent. The interest payments that Latin American countries have made in recent decades far exceed the total amount that was loaned to them in the first place. This financial dynamic has brought about a massive hemorrhaging of resources from the region to international creditors, to the extent that entire Latin American economies have been looted in the process. The internal distribution of this sacrifice has been highly asymmetrical. Inflation, hyperinflation, economic stagnation, and austerity policies provoked an enormous concentration of income. There was a brutal decline in the percentage of gross domestic product (GDP) accruing to wage earners: in Mexico it fell from 35.7 percent in 1970 to 29.1 percent in 1996; in Argentina from 40.9 percent in 1970 to 29.6 percent in 1987; in Chile from 42.7 percent in 1970 to 29.1 percent in 1983; in Peru from 35.6 percent in 1970 to 20.8 percent in 1996; and in Venezuela from 40.4 percent in 1970 to 21.3 percent in 1993.[11] Over a very brief period of time, decades of progress toward poverty reduction and equity enhancement was squandered and indeed reversed.

Subsequently, during the 1990s, Latin America experienced a modest economic recovery, inflation was controlled, and public finances were stabilized. Nonetheless, the tendency toward concentration of wealth was not reversed, although inequality did not increase as much as it had during the previous decade. Gini coefficients grew slightly in the majority of countries, and where there was a reduction it was only marginal. The classic Latin American pattern seems to be repeating itself: inequality increases rapidly in moments of crisis and remains constant or grows moderately during expansionary phases. Its modest growth since 1990 is due to various factors, including the so-called process of financial deregulation.

It is generally believed that Latin American governments adopted policies of financial and exchange-rate flexibilization, drastically reducing their involvement in both domains. But a more careful look shows that many governments intervened forcefully in the markets, to protect the banking and financial sectors. This is especially clear in Brazil, Mexico, and Argentina, the three largest economies in the region.

In Mexico, during the government of Carlos Salinas de Gortari (1988–1994), enormous latitude was given for the entry and exit of capital. This opening coincided with the overvaluation of the peso vis-à-vis the dollar and the issuing of public debt instruments paying high interest rates. Fueled by the enormous expectations created by the NAFTA negotiations, this encouraged the entry of speculative capital which sought to take advantages of opportunities for investment. This was no mere game of supply and demand but rather a systematic intervention of the government and the Banco de Mexico on interest and exchange rates in an effort to attract investments. This caused individuals and firms to take on high levels of debt. Banks accepted high levels of risk in extending loans, and a financial bubble was created amid an environment of extreme liquidity and high volatility. The bubble burst in 1994: interest rates soared, debtors experienced great difficulty meeting their commitments, and there emerged the specter of cessation of payments and a financial sector debacle. In December 2004 the peso was devalued, the stock market declined, and the effects reverberated throughout the international financial system.

The response of the Mexican government, backed by the United States and the IMF, was to inject resources into the system to save the Mexican financial sector. Far from respecting the free operation of the market, which would have led to the collapse of many banks due to their misguided lending policies, this was an intervention from the highest levels of the state, which distributed costs and benefits in a highly asymmetrical manner. Speculators took advantage of the moment when the market was at its high point and got out in time thanks to assistance from the government. By contrast, many small and medium-sized enterprises collapsed, and much of the middle class lost their savings and the goods they had acquired on credit. Above and beyond instances of outright corruption, the overall process represented an immense expropriation through which financial capital absorbed a large part of the profits while losses were distributed across the population at large.

A similar pattern occurred in Brazil, which for a number of years artificially propped up an overvalued currency. In 1998 the IMF and the Brazilian government spent $50 billion to maintain an exchange rate that did not correspond to economic reality. Where did the money go? According to Nobel Laureate Joseph Stiglitz, it did not disappear into thin air. Rather, much of it went into the pockets of speculators: some lost and others came out ahead, but overall they gained an amount roughly equivalent to what the government lost.[12]

The most dramatic case was in Argentina, where predatory practices exacerbated financial irresponsibility. Against all logic, the Menem and de la Rúa governments maintained a policy of peso-to-dollar convertibility, causing a serious decline in the economy's competitiveness and a sharp spike in unemployment. Once again speculators were able to pull out their money buying cheap dollars while the middle classes saw their consumerist dreams turn to nightmares when their savings were sequestered through the mechanism known as the "corralito." The crisis broke out in December 2001 amid impressive popular mobilizations that forced the resignation of several presidents over a span of a few weeks. The process of converting dollar savings into pesos was clearly assymetrical: small and medium-sized savers saw their buying power decline at a vertiginous rate.

In other Latin American countries similar patterns were repeated, with financial openings taking place without the presence of regulatory institutions adequate to prevent speculation and amid widespread corrupt practices. It is no coincidence that many of the great fortunes that have arisen in Latin America in recent years are tied to the financial sector. Many others who joined the ranks of the super-rich did so thanks to the privatization of public enterprises.

PRIVATIZATIONS WITH OVERTONES OF EXPROPRIATION

The sale of public enterprises has been one of the most hotly debated topics in Latin America over the past two decades. Intense polemics began with the first privatization programs of the 1980s and 1990s, and even today there are bitter disputes over whether new privatizations should take place or whether previous ones should be reversed. In Argentina one still hears criticism of

Menem for having sold the majority of state enterprises during the 1990s, while Bolivia has experienced strong protests against the privatization of water and gas. In Mexico, debate rages over whether the electricity and petroleum sectors should be privatized. There seems to be little space for middle ground in this debate, with most observers falling on one side or another: privatization is good, or it is terrible. There is ammunition for both sides of the argument. Critics of state enterprises are right that many of them operated in Latin America with limited attention to efficiency, and that they have been a focus of corrupt dealings by politicians, managers, and union leaders. Important restructuring is certainly needed, and in this task there may be an important role to be played by private capital and some degree of market pressure. In turn, critics of privatization are justified in contending that the majority of privatization processes have been plagued by corruption or have benefited a handful of private groups rather than society as a whole.

Since the 1980s many state enterprises in Latin America have suffered enormous problems: inadequate investment, technological backwardness, stagnant productivity, low quality and innovative capability, lack of profitability, and so on. Some of these problems are linked to corruption, patronage, and the inflexibility of government management. But these problems are also due to the fact that many of these companies have been decapitalized during years of bleeding resources to finance the state, whose operating budget relied excessively on such income. Public enterprises were also called upon to absorb huge subsidies to consumers, and their situation became all the more untenable with the profound financial crises of the 1980s. Clearly, a deep restructuring was essential. The problem arose with the ways in which that restructuring was pursued. There prevailed a simplistic interpretation according to which all of the problems facing state enterprises were due to corruption and rent seeking associated with public property, and that privatization would be sufficient to overcome these practices. From the perspective of inequality, privatizations ran the risk of throwing out the baby with the bathwater: they could eliminate the rent seeking and corruption that was rife in many state enterprises, but they also eliminated many of the processes of equalization that those enterprises generated by financing development and subsidizing disadvantaged sectors of the population. In practice, most priva-

tizations were done in such a way as to generate new inequalities, for they especially favored privileged groups that acquired public enterprises through
insider deals that were not transparent, and that turned many privatizations
into veritable expropriations of public property.

In Chile, privatizations began under the military regime of Augusto
Pinochet, which, during the 1970s, returned firms that had been expropri-
ated under the Allende government to their previous owners. In turn, during
the 1980s, private enterprises were created to administer pension funds
which increasingly replaced the publicly supported social security system. At
the same time, large public enterprises were dismantled and market criteria
were introduced into educational financing. These measures contributed to
making various segments of the Chilean economy more dynamic, but they
caused a greater concentration of wealth. Just eight economic conglomerates accounted for 65 percent of the capital invested in acquiring privatized
firms between 1974–78, and a handful of companies linked to the major
banks dominated administration of the privatized pension funds. The large
industrial and financial conglomerates allied with government officials to
control the privatization processes. Thus, public officials who had designed
the dictatorship's economic policies took on leading positions in both the
principal banks and the electricity and long-distance telephone companies.[13]
The other big problem was that energy and telecommunications enterprises
were privatized as monopolies, enjoying extraordinary concessions regarding property rights over water and satellite access. Far from eliminating rent
seeking, a new form of profiteering was created, bringing about an enormous concentration of wealth. If on top of this we consider the drastic decrease in wages during the first years of the military regime, it comes as no
surprise that Chile, having been one of the least unequal countries of Latin
America, became one of the region's most unequal: today, the richest 10 percent of the population controls 47 percent of national income.[14]

Another country where inequality rose significantly is Argentina. Prior to
the 1970s it was featured alongside Costa Rica and Uruguay as a noteworthy
exception to the general Latin American pattern of inequality; that achievement is now a thing of the past. The military dictatorship of 1976–1983
played an important role in diminishing the income of workers and the mid-

dle classes, as did hyperinflation and the profound economic crises of the
1980s.

The Peronist government of Carlos Menem, in power during most of the
1990s, oversaw one of the region's most aggressive privatization programs,
encompassing gas, electricity, water and sewage, steel, petroleum, and social
security. Argentina's privatizations did not unfold under a competitive or
transparent framework. Most of them generated monopolies or duopolies
that enjoyed immediate profits thanks to rate increases, the maintenance of
protected markets, and the absence of regulatory mechanisms. Large private
conglomerates that traditionally had controlled the Argentine economy
were strengthened in the process, as were a handful of U.S. and European
multinational corporations. The sale of public enterprises was undertaken
through pacts involving business and labor leaders with close ties to the government, whose senior officials gained high-level positions in some of the
newly privatized firms.[15] Ironically, the Menem government, which had been
labeled by its supporters and detractors as the champion of economic liberalization, in reality did not follow a neoliberal policy. Quite the contrary: it
governed the economy through the negotiation of rent seeking and clientelist agreements.

In Mexico, with the process of economic opening and privatization, a new
governing coalition emerged. Industrialists oriented toward the internal
market were replaced by participants in a coalition united behind economic
liberalization, who included large industrial and commercial enterprises, financial conglomerates, and a new generation of politicians united in favor of
market-oriented policies. This new elite steered the privatization process,
which between 1983 and 1993 shed several thousand firms. The most important of these was Teléfonos de México (TELMEX), which was acquired in
1990 by the Grupo Carso, owned by Carlos Slim, in alliance with France Tele-
com and Southwestern Bell. The competition for TELMEX was a shady af-
fair, and the new firm enjoyed a series of privileges, including preferential
treatment within the NAFTA framework, allowing it to function as a monopoly for several years and then to collect extremely high connection fees from
other firms.[16] More than a competitive deregulation of the telecommunications sector, what took place was a new regulation organized to benefit a new

private monopoly, which came to dominate a sector controlled by just a few firms. To this day TELMEX controls the majority of the local, long distance, and cellular telephone markets in Mexico, and the firm has also acquired shares of telephone companies in various Latin American countries. The privatization of TELMEX was the platform that enabled Carlos Slim to become the richest man in Latin America in just a few years' time. In Peru, Venezuela, and other countries in the region, a similar pattern of privatizations was evident. Led by distributive coalitions that tied government officials to leading businessmen, these processes of privatization fostered greater concentration of wealth and generated new bases of inequality on top of those that already prevailed across the region.

The problem was not only one of corruption—of which there was plenty—but rather that the lack of adequate regulations and oversight institutions reduced the positive effects of privatization and increased its adverse consequences. On the whole, it can be said that privatizations contributed more to exacerbate inequalities than to reduce them. Privatizations were carried out in a manner that strengthened the consolidation of privileged sectors, and necessary measures were not taken to promote competitive markets and distribute the benefits of change to the general public. In most cases institutions were not reformed, informal and formal rules governing relations between actors were untouched, and thus were reproduced the conditions that have enabled inequality to persist.

EMPLOYMENT INSTABILITY AND NEW FORMS OF EXCLUSION

Whereas financial plunder and privatizations affected the rich by creating enormous fortunes, the transformation of labor markets is an element of structural adjustment that left Latin Americans mired in poverty. The key feature of changes in labor markets has been the increasing instability of employment. One of every ten workers in the region is unemployed, and one in five is underemployed.[17] The majority of people classified as underemployed have extremely precarious jobs with low wages, poor working conditions, minimal job security, and the almost complete absence of benefits. One of the new forms of inequality, then, is that which distinguishes those who have a stable job from those who lack work or who labor in highly unstable conditions.

Since the 1980s, public employment has lost its relative importance in the region's labor markets. This is a product of privatization and of the decline of state expenditures accompanying efforts to maintain budget surpluses needed to pay off debt. Over the past decade, public sector employment has declined as a percentage of total employment from 41.7 percent in 1990 to 40.6 percent.[18] Meanwhile, private firms are creating few new jobs, and most of those they do create are either part time or consist of subcontracted work and other forms of highly precarious employment. The prevailing conditions in world markets oblige firms and governments to increase their efficiency and productivity, but achieving these objectives almost always entails wage reductions, particularly for the less skilled segments of the workforce.

In Latin America, the adoption of this path to competitiveness has had to do with specific historical circumstances: an adverse correlation of forces for unions, the advance of an antistatist ideology during the 1980s and 1990s, and the persistence of an enormous polarization in the world of work. This is all the more evident when one observes that, at precisely that moment, incomes of high-level government officials and business officials often rose. Because the burden of cutbacks was allocated in keeping with political and social structures, the costs of adjustment were highly unequal. In some cases, as in Mexico and some countries of Central America and the Caribbean, maquila export industries were promoted, generating many jobs but almost all of them of low quality and with wages well below the average for manufacturing sector. In other cases, as in Uruguay and Argentina, the low-wage, export-driven path was not followed, but jobs were sacrificed nonetheless. Thus, in some countries public and private employment declined while in others they disappeared to a lesser degree but in more unfavorable conditions. The fact is that over the past two decades the formal sector, both public and private, has exhibited diminished capacity to generate new and high-quality jobs.

This is the context that explains the enormous expansion of the informal sector, which has increased its presence throughout the region: whereas it accounted for 28.9 percent of jobs in 1980, that number had increased to 42.8 percent by 1990 and 46.4 percent at the beginning of the new century. In less than a quarter century, the informal sector went from being less than a third of all jobs to nearly half of urban employment. It is said that of the 29 million new jobs generated in Latin America between 1990 and 1999, 20 million corresponded to the informal sector.[19]

In recent decades, open unemployment reached worrisome levels: average urban unemployment rates reached 8.3 percent in 2000, matching the level of 1985, when the region was at the most extreme moment of the debt crisis. By the end of the 1990s, eight countries were suffering double-digit levels of unemployment.[20] In Mexico, the crisis of 1994–1995 provoked a sharp increase in joblessness, and Argentina, Uruguay, and Chile have since had high levels of unemployment for extended periods of time. In Argentina the concept of "new poverty" has arisen to designate the situation experienced by those who suffer extended periods of unemployment, many of whom once had good jobs as workers or employees. The notorious movement of the "piqueteros" had its origins in working-class neighborhoods among laborers experiencing long-term unemployment and demanding jobs or government subsidies.

If one includes the entire pool of the unemployed, those who emigrated abroad due to the absence of work, those who end up in the informal sector, and those who are in the formal sector but lack adequate protection, the universe of labor precariousness is greater still, encompassing nearly three-fourths of the labor force.

A paradox of globalization is the persistence of low wages for unskilled workers in Latin America. Many labor-intensive industries have shifted from wealthy countries to Latin America, whose receiving countries should in theory have increased wages. But this has not happened. Export industries grew rapidly, but workers' wages did not, even though there was a scarcity of manpower in areas of intensive industrialization. The limits on legal migration of workers, the greater mobility of capital, and the growing power of transnational corporations, together with the weakening of unions, have made possible a decrease in wages even in those regions in which the massive arrival of maquilas produced a shortage of available manpower. New industries have been influenced by wage polarization that characterized these zones. This explains why managers in many maquilas enjoy high incomes, while unskilled workers have low wages.[21] This is especially troubling in that it indicates that, as in other periods of its history, Latin America can shift its model of accumulation without modifying the structures of inequality that have long characterized the region.

The contemporary labor market in Latin America exhibits growing gaps between wages accruing to skilled and nonskilled labor. A study carried out in four countries (Argentina, Chile, Mexico, and Uruguay) found that between 1990 and 2000 disparities grew between skilled and unskilled workers. Incomes, social protection, and employment levels all became more unequal.[22] This is especially odd given that educational levels have become increasingly unequal and the demand for nonskilled workers in export sectors has increased, a trend that presumably would have served to diminish the wage gap between skilled and unskilled workers. Firms have used educational and skill levels to select personnel, not so much because they need workers of higher schooling as because the overabundance of workers allows them to be more selective in hiring.

THE DIGITAL DIVIDE AND DISCONNECTEDNESS

Another aspect of the new inequalities sweeping Latin America is the digital divide separating those with access to new technologies from those who are disconnected from them. The result is greater disparities in knowledge. For centuries the concentration of land and natural resources in the hands of the elite was the determining factor generating inequalities in Latin America. Then, during the nineteenth and part of the twentieth centuries, property and the control over industrial and service enterprises was crucial. During the last third of the past century and the beginning of the new millennium, what has become crucial is the relevance of scientific knowledge and access to modern technology. It is not that some sources of inequality substitute for others, but rather that they overlap and combine. The so-called digital divide almost always forms around old social and economic fractures: rich countries and privileged social groups find themselves in better condition to appropriate new resources, since they possess the economic, social, political, and cultural capital needed to do so.

Latin America lags behind the rich countries in access to computers and the Internet. In recent years, use of the Internet has grown rapidly across the region, but this has not been sufficient to eliminate the digital divide. In Latin America and the Caribbean there were just over 55 million Internet users by 2004–2005, representing 10 percent of the population, well behind the 66.8 percent with such access in the United States. While in the rich countries nearly two-thirds of the population uses the Internet, the figure is much lower in Latin America, and this is related to poverty and inequality: access to the Internet in the region is greater in countries that have reduced poverty rates, such as Chile (23.1 percent), in countries that have been less unequal, such as Costa Rica (18.7 percent) and Uruguay (11.7 percent), or in the larger economies such as Brazil (11.2 percent), Mexico (9.8 percent), and Argentina (10.9 percent). In the poorest and most unequal countries, inequalities in the penetration of the Internet are minimal: only 1.5 percent of Nicaraguans have Internet access, not unlike rates of 2.6 percent in Honduras, 3.0 percent in Bolivia, and 3.4 percent in Guatemala.[23]

High-income sectors and those with higher education were the first to gain access to the Internet, whereas the rest of the population still does not have it or accessed it late, slowly, and with greater difficulty. In Mexico in 2002, half of the richest 8 percent of the population had computers at home. By contrast, the two groups with lowest incomes, including nearly three-fourths of all households, had practically no access to computers (1.06 percent and 7.82 percent). The divide between levels of education is striking: of those who achieved only primary school education, only 1.3 percent used the Internet and 4.2 percent the computer, compared to 41.5 percent and 66.6 percent of those with higher education.[24] If knowledge has become a determining factor for appropriating wealth, in Latin America the new inequalities are being superimposed on old ones: statistics on wealth, education, and access to new information and communication technologies tend to coincide.

INEQUALITY BY EXPROPRIATION AND INEQUALITY
BY DISCONNECTEDNESS

What conclusions can we reach with regard to new inequalities in Latin America? What has been the result of structural adjustment and the transformations of recent decades? The optimistic view, which holds that Latin America is breaking with its history of inequalities, seems unjustified. Yet neither can we confirm the notion that globalization and structural reforms have been the primary cause of the expansion of inequalities. The principal problem lies in the social processes that shape the distinct manners in which Latin Americans insert themselves into the globalized network. On the other hand, there is evidence that prior inequalities have played a crucial role: the strength of existing structures, institutions, relationships, cultures, and practices is such that it conditioned outcomes and characteristics acquired by trade opening, privatization, labor market flexibility, and the introduction of computers and the Internet. From the outset, different social groups had highly unequal resources to confront the opportunities and risks created by these transformations. It comes as no surprise, then, that sectors endowed with greater economic resources, stronger social networks, and higher educational capital gained a vastly disproportionate share of the benefits created by globalization, whereas the majority of the population, more limited in prior endowments of such resources, had enormous difficulties dealing with changed circumstances.

On the other hand, some transformations of recent years aggravated inequalities. Trade opening in and of itself can be positive, but it was carried out without preparation and without regulating the power of large corporations. As a result, benefits have been concentrated in a small sector at the same time that we see a growing gap between those regions and the people who could incorporate themselves into export activities, and those who have been left behind. Exchange rate and financial policies, in turn, far from following the neoliberal principles that supposedly were being advanced, were in practice often characterized by plundering: governments and international financial institutions gave extraordinary support to bankers and speculators, provoking even greater concentration of wealth. Many privatizations were done with little transparency, and on occasion led to the expropriation of public wealth to the benefit of groups allied with state officials. Finally, flexibilization of labor markets reflected a correlation of forces that was highly unfavorable to workers and unions, and this encouraged both an increase in unemployment and greater vulnerability for those who retained their jobs.

On top of old inequalities, rooted in centuries of exploitation of the poorest and long-standing patterns of discrimination against women, black, and indigenous peoples, were added new inequalities. Based on processes of exclusion and greater precariousness, these inequalities deprived the majority of the population of economic citizenship and left them at the margin of productive networks, quality education, the appropriation of useful knowledge and stable jobs. The contemporary landscape of Latin America suggests a displacement of the central axis of inequality: various long-standing patterns of exploitation, looting, and discrimination (inequality by expropriation) remain active, yet more and more we see other mechanisms factoring in, such as opportunities hoarding, exclusion, and gaps between different levels of insertion into global networks (inequality by disconnectedness).

In general, the same sectors that suffered the old inequalities also experience the new ones. Those who yesterday lacked good land today have less schooling and more precarious jobs. Similarly, there is a tendency for Latin American countries that were most equitable in the past, before globalization, to remain so today, as is the case with Costa Rica and Uruguay, while the majority of countries that were unequal before economic opening maintain that characteristic in our times. But there have also been important changes. During the 1970s, inequality grew in some countries, including Argentina and Chile, which suffered bloody military dictatorships. During the 1980s, before economic opening and the introduction of new technologies, there was a strong increase in inequalities in Latin America overall, especially in Brazil, Panama, Peru, and Venezuela.[25] Levels of inequality have been maintained in the region over the past fifteen years, in which there has been a bit more growth and during which several countries transited toward political democracy.[26] During the 1990s, inequality rose in El Salvador, Nicaragua, Peru, Venezuela, and, to a lesser degree, Brazil, Honduras, Panama, and

Uruguay. Another group of countries saw little variation in indices of inequality. Such was the case in Bolivia, Chile, Colombia, Costa Rica, and
Ecuador. In Mexico, inequality rose slightly during the 1990s, but was reduced a bit after 2000.[27]

POLITICAL SHIFTS AND PERSPECTIVES ON INEQUALITY

Latin America enters the twenty-first century without having resolved the
perennial issue of inequality. Many parts of the region, and many social
groups, have remained behind on the road toward globalization. But Latin
Americans do not watch these circumstances passively. Rather, they undertake all sorts of action to overcome them. Subaltern groups have sought to
become inserted into global flows through various paths—which range from
internal and international migration to self-employment and incorporation
into maquila export industries—and through participation in various social
and political movements. Some of these movements have witnessed indigenous peoples—those most disadvantaged by inequalities—playing a central
role. The CONAIE (Confederation of Indigenous Nationalities of Ecuador)
in Ecuador, the EZLN (Zapatista Army of National Liberation) in Chiapas,
and indigenous groups in Bolivia are the best known examples of a striking
ethnic emergence in the region. There have also been various peasant movements, with the most conspicuous being the landless movement in Brazil
(Sem Terra).

Latin American cities, meanwhile, have been the stage for numerous
protests against governments identified with neoliberalism. Discontent is
enormous with respect both to structural adjustment policies and to the way
in which Latin American governments have confronted globalization. In the
first years of the millennium there have been significant political shifts: leftist
or center-left presidents have come to power in many countries, including
Ricardo Lagos in Chile, Hugo Chávez in Venezuela, Luiz Inácio Lula da Silva
in Brazil, Néstor Kirchner in Argentina, and Tabaré Vázquez in Uruguay. In
Mexico, the PRI lost the presidency in 2000 after more than seventy years in
power. In some countries, governments associated with neoliberal policies

have fallen after intense popular protests. Such was the case with Argentina in 2001 and 2002, Ecuador in 2000 and 2005, and Bolivia in 2003 and 2005.

It remains too early to evaluate the medium- or long-term consequences of this political shift. Some countries, such as Bolivia and Ecuador, remain unsettled by the upheavals and changes of government. Although Hugo Chávez has broadened his base of support, Venezuela is polarized between supporters and opponents of the president. Argentina managed to get over the economic morass and crisis of governability of 2001–2002, but political alliances remain fragile in that country, and the short- and medium-term economic perspectives remain uncertain. In Brazil as of this writing, Lula's government seems to have lost a significant portion of its initial popularity as a result of various corruption scandals, while poverty and inequality have diminished only slightly. In Mexico extreme poverty has fallen slightly thanks to a fortunate combination of macroeconomic stability, migrant remittances, high oil prices, and the continuity of poverty-reduction policies launched by the Zedillo government. Yet political forces remain sharply divided and economic growth is both limited and vulnerable. Chile stands out alone in the region for having managed a significant institutional consolidation and sustained economic growth. It is the only country that seems to be in shape to achieve the millennium development goals objective of reducing poverty by half by 2015, but high inequality coefficients persist. Uruguay and Costa Rica remain exceptional in the region, in that they are more equal than the remainder of countries, but they have experienced serious problems of economic stagnation, and, in the case of Uruguay, this is aggravated by the persistence of severe unemployment.

Amid this somber panorama one thing is clear: the poorest sectors of Latin America, particularly those of indigenous and African origins but also many of the urban poor, have become political protagonists questioning prevailing inequalities and actively opposing policies of a neoliberal bent. They have demonstrated a capacity to block structural adjustment policies, and even to overthrow governments. This provides cause for hope, in that it indicates that forms of expropriation and discrimination that foster inequality will meet sharp resistance. But this does not solve the problem of inequality through disconnectedness, nor does it guarantee a more equitable and inclusive development strategy. For the latter to be attained requires long-term political accords, institutional consolidation, continuity, and broadening of social policies and poverty alleviation strategies, as well as financial stability and economic growth.

In the era of globalization, the majority of Latin American countries are betting on opening their economies and increasing exports. This is not sufficient to reduce persistent inequalities. In Chile and Mexico, the two Latin American countries that have experienced greatest success in boosting exports, inequality coefficients have not changed significantly, for better or worse. This fact refutes simplistic assertions of those who believe that economic opening increases inequality and those who believe that it reduces it. Some regions and sectors in Latin America have managed to integrate themselves into processes of globalization, while others have remained behind, forming pockets of persistent poverty, disconnected from the more dynamic activities or connected to them in only a precarious manner.

Nor have things gone well for countries that have resisted opening their economies and carrying out structural adjustment. If in these times inequality was reproduced, it was not because Latin America opened itself to globalization, but rather because participation in economic opening was highly asymmetrical, with important segments of the population remaining excluded or disconnected. In contrast, in those Latin American countries with less inequality one finds more solid institutions, more equitable educational and health systems, and more enduring social programs and inclusionary cultures that offer opportunities to all citizens. The contemporary dilemma for Latin America is not only how to consolidate economic opening and structural adjustment demanded by globalization, but rather to do so in a manner that reverses long-standing patterns of inequality that have characterized the region throughout its history.

7

A Table to Eat On: The Meaning and Measurement of Poverty in Latin America

Araceli Damián and Julio Boltvinik

This chapter traces the evolution of poverty in Latin America over the last twenty-five years within the context of the main shifts in social and economic policy in the region. The opening section is based on poverty calculations by the UN's Economic Commission for Latin America and the Caribbean (ECLAC, or CEPAL by its Spanish acronym) since, despite the fact that ECLAC refers only to income poverty (which we later show to be a partial and skewed method), these are the only data available and they allow for a certain degree of comparison. The chapter goes on to discuss the limitations of the income poverty (or poverty line) method of measuring poverty, which is used widely by international organizations and governments. We contrast it with the Integrated Poverty Measurement Method (IPMM), which is an alternative approach that seeks to broaden our look when measuring poverty.[1] We then present data on poverty in Mexico using the IPMM and compare those data with the results obtained with three different applications of the poverty line method. The last section analyzes the evolution of poverty in Latin America from the gender perspective and shows that there is some evidence that poverty is becoming masculinized.

THE GROWTH OF POVERTY

Over the last twenty-five years, following the prescriptions of international organizations, the governments of Latin American countries have implemented economic and social policies based in "free market" principles, amounting to a "race to the bottom" strategy. As a result, poverty has grown and labor and social policy standards have been gradually reduced to the minimum.[2]

This race-to-the-bottom strategy assumed that by reducing the cost of labor, the economies of the region would more effectively compete in the international marketplace. Those organizations and governments, however, did not foresee the larger participation in the world market of India and China, whose labor costs are much lower than those prevailing in Latin America. Neither did they foresee that as a consequence of this policy of lower labor costs, internal effective demand would fall, slowing economic growth, despite the growth in exports.

Following the recommendations of the international organizations or perhaps out of their own conviction, governments in Latin America abandoned their active role in the economy, leaving their economies to drift, and at the mercy of unfair international competition. The liberalization of capital markets destabilized national economies by subjecting them to the whims of speculative capital. The obsessive pursuit of low rates of inflation meant the abandonment of the goals of full employment and economic growth. The drive to privatize favored the creation of monopolies, transferring the profits previously appropriated by the public sector to private hands.

Likewise, governments have followed the neoliberal principle that the redistribution of income, a long-accepted state responsibility, should be carried out through public spending targeted to benefit only the extremely poor—to enable them to compete in the marketplace—ignoring the rest of the poor, and rejecting the redistributive role of progressive taxation. Public income, according to neoliberal principles, should depend, instead, on indirect taxation.[3]

Poverty in Latin America has shown a tendency to rise since the early 1980s. The percentage of the population that is poor increased from 40.5 percent to 44 percent between 1980 and 2002 (see Figure 7.1). The number of poor people increased by 84 million, from 136 million in 1980 to 220 million in 2002, which amounts to an increase of 61.8 percent. These figures show us the inadequacy and the paltry results that structural adjustment policies have had in Latin America.

FIGURE 7.1

Incidence of Poverty and Extreme Poverty in Latin America: 1980–2002*

Year	Below the Poverty Line			Below the Extreme Poverty Line		
	Total	Urban	Rural	Total	Urban	Rural
1980	40.5	29.8	59.9	18.6	10.6	32.7
1990	48.3	41.4	65.4	22.5	15.3	40.4
2000	42.5	35.9	62.5	18.1	11.7	37.8
2002	44.0	37.8	61.8	19.4	13.5	37.9

*All figures are percentages of the total population.
Source: CEPAL, 2001, Panorama Social de América Latina, Table 1, p. 14, and CEPAL, 2003, Panorama Social de América Latina, Table 1.2, p. 50. Percentages are of individuals living in poor or extremely poor households.

On the other hand, the diversity in the levels of poverty among Latin American countries is very wide as can be seen in Figure 7.2, in which poverty incidence has been classified in seven categories, from very high, where the only country with available data is Honduras (with an incidence of 77.3 percent), to very low, where again there is only one country, Uruguay, with 15.4 percent of its population living in poverty.

FIGURE 7.2

Latin American Countries Ranked by Levels of Poverty: 2002*

Country	Level of Poverty
Extremely High	
Honduras	77.3
Very High	
Nicaragua	69.4
Bolivia	62.5
Paraguay	61.0
Guatemala	59.9

* All figures in percentages of the total population living below the poverty line.

High

Peru	54.8
Colombia	50.6
Ecuador (urban)	49.0
El Salvador	48.9
Venezuela	48.6
Dominican Republic	44.9
Argentina (urban)	41.5

Moderate

Mexico	39.4
Brazil	37.5
Panama	25.3

Low

Chile	20.6
Costa Rica	20.3

Very Low

Uruguay	15.4

Source: Authors' calculations based on data from CEPAL, 2004, *Panorama Social de América Latina*, Table 15, pp. 324–325.

It is important to note that the economic crises experienced in the late 1990s in various Latin American countries had very serious consequences. For example, the percentage of poor people in urban Argentina rose from 16 percent in 1994 to 41.5 percent by 2002, turning Argentina from a country with low levels of poverty in its urban areas into one with a high degree of urban poverty. For its part, Uruguay saw its level of poverty go from less than 10 percent to more than 15 percent over the same period, despite the fact that it continues to be the country with the least poverty in the region.

The overall evolution of poverty in Latin America in the 1980–2002 period and its levels in 2002 might be even gloomier than what these figures reveal, since the official data showing a reduction of poverty in Mexico between 2000 and 2002, a period of economic recession, have been seriously challenged. ECLAC maintains that there is a lack of comparability between the

2000 and the 2002 Household Income and Expenditure Surveys (ENIGH).[4] The organization notes that the changes in the survey sampling design affected mostly poverty in rural areas (settlements with fewer than 2,500 inhabitants), where extreme poverty is concentrated and where the reduction of poverty was observed.[5]

MEASURING POVERTY

The measurement of poverty entails two elements: (1) the observed condition of households and individuals; and (2) the norms according to which we judge who is poor and who isn't, norms that express our view of the minimum floor below which human life loses dignity and becomes degraded.

The dominant approach to poverty compares household income with the poverty threshold or poverty line, both of which are expressed in per capita income terms. In the works of the World Bank, the level of the poverty line is arbitrarily set. The method used by ECLAC to measure poverty by income is that of a normative food basket (NFB).[6] The basket is made up of a list of goods, each with its quantity and price, and is formulated to reflect the nutritional requirements and the observed diet of each country. Given that diets and prices vary from country to country, both the basket of goods and its cost will also vary.

ECLAC defines the extreme poverty line (EPL) as identical with the cost of the normative food basket (CNFB); it also defines a poverty line (PL) that is a multiple of the EPL, to allow for the purchase of goods other than food. To purchase the NFB, households with incomes equal to the EPL (or the CNFB) would have to spend 100 percent of their earnings on raw food, but they would find it impossible to consume it since the NFB does not include the requirements for its preparation and consumption (gas, pans, utensils, plates, a table, detergents, etc.). This definition of extreme poverty reduces human beings to an animal state, eating raw food on the floor with their hands.

While this method establishes minimum norms in terms of food consumption, no norm is defined for what households require to satisfy the rest of their needs. To estimate the poverty line (PL), the cost of the normative food basket (CNFB) is multiplied by the inverse of the proportion of income or total expenditures dedicated to the purchase of food as observed in a reference group of households. This proportion is called the Engel Coefficient. The NFB methodology has been criticized because of the instability of the Engel Coefficient.[7] Different criteria exist for selecting the reference group as well. The poorer the reference group is, the higher the proportion of income spent on food will be and hence the lower the poverty line. Therefore, the establishment of the poverty line becomes an arbitrary political exercise.

According to Óscar Altimir, the author of ECLAC's measurement method, the reference group should be so defined that its expenditure on food is equal to the CNFB (or EPL).[8] This author assumes that households that fulfill their food requirements also satisfy the rest of their needs. Empirically, this assumption does not hold true; there are households that satisfy their food requirements and nevertheless are poor according to the Unsatisfied Basic Needs (UBN) method. Conceptually, the assumption is not solid either since it supposes that households arrive at the satisfaction of all their needs simultaneously, which is denied by all theories of human needs. Therefore, the additional income requirement that is added to the EPL to obtain PL is a black box that makes it impossible to know what standard of living it allows.

The poverty line method also has serious limitations with regard to capturing the complexity of the problem of poverty. For example, ECLAC itself has affirmed that even when poverty (by income) decreases as a result of an increase in households' monetary resources, this doesn't necessarily and automatically result in a decline in malnutrition, since there would also have to be a reduction in the negative impact of other risk factors, including sanitary living conditions, access to drinking water, adequate sewerage and access to health services.[9]

One of the principal limitations of the poverty line method is that it assumes that the satisfaction of basic needs depends exclusively on current household income or on private household consumption. Thus, it does not take into consideration other sources of well-being such as household's accumulated wealth (including dwelling ownership); non-basic assets; access to free education, health care, and other free services; free time and time available for domestic work and study; and knowledge and skills.[10] A household without access to free health services and social security does not have the same standard of living as a household that does, even when the per-person income is the same in both of them.

Julio Boltvinik developed an alternative approach for measuring poverty that takes into account all the sources of well-being enumerated in the previous paragraph: the Integrated Poverty Measurement Method (IPMM), which combines the poverty line (PL) method, the UBN method, and the index of excess working time, which serves to identify time poverty.[11]

The PL method, which calculates poverty taking into consideration only one of the sources of well-being—current household income—corresponds to what Amartya Sen called the indirect approach to the measurement of poverty. By contrast, the UBN method is a direct method since it observes the satisfaction—or lack—of certain basic needs, such as housing or education, taking into account some of those previously noted sources of well-being, but without taking into account income or time. The IPMM, in addition to taking into account all the sources of well-being, overcomes the following serious limitations, noted by Boltvinik, of the conventional applications of the UBN method:[12] (a) the intensity of deprivation cannot be calculated, and hence no aggregated poverty index beyond the proportion of poor people or poverty incidence can be calculated; (b) poverty incidence depends on the number of indicators used; the more indicators that are used, the greater poverty incidence will be. In the IPMM, all UBN indicators are converted into a well-being metric scale and are combined through weighted averages, thus overcoming both limitations of conventional UBN applications.[13]

In the IPMM, the satisfaction—or lack—of some basic needs is verified in an indirect manner through income. These needs are generally: food, fuel, personal and household care, clothing and shoes, public transportation, basic communications, recreation and culture, payment of housing services, and expenditures associated with school attendance and health care. On the other hand, the satisfaction of housing characteristics, access to housing services (water, electricity, and drainage), household facilities, education level, and access to health services and to social security are verified in a direct manner through the UBN method. Finally, the index of excess outside-the-home work expresses indirectly the availability of free time and time for rest, education, and domestic work.

In the IPMM, a comprehensive poverty index is worked out, in two stages, for each household. In the first stage, household income is adjusted by dividing it by the index of excess outside-the-home work before comparing it to the poverty line in order to obtain income-time poverty. In the second, the combined index of UBN (that is obtained as a weighted average of its partial indices) is combined with that of income-time through a weighted average. All households that have a positive value in the resulting integrated poverty index (or IPMM index) are classified as poor.[14] Likewise, the IPMM allows for the evaluation of each household from a partial point of view, taking into account only one dimension or one component (income poverty, unsatisfied basic needs poverty, time poverty, or poverty as depicted by any of the components of UBN). This method offers a measurement of poverty that is not only comprehensive but is also more precise and dynamic than measurements based exclusively on income.

THE CASE OF MEXICO

There are two principal explanations for the findings that the poverty incidence in the IPMM is much higher than the ECLAC results. First, the IPMM is broader as it takes into account all sources of well-being. Second, the norms utilized in the income dimension, the only one shared by both methods, are more generous and explicit in IPMM not only for food but for all goods and services.

Figure 7.3 shows the evolution of poverty in Mexico with the IPMM and with three variants of the poverty line method: (1) that of ECLAC, which covers the period from 1968 until 2000 and is adjusted to national accounts;[15] (2) that of the World Bank, which covers the period from 1968–1996, in which the methodology is not explicit;[16] and (3) that formulated by Enrique Hernández Laos and Julio Boltvinik (HLB), which covers the period from 1968–2000 and is based on the poverty line calculated on the basis of the standard basket of essential goods defined by the government unit Coplamar, which is adjusted to national accounts until 1984 only.[17] The calculation of the IPMM covers the period 1984–2000 and is adjusted to national accounts up to 1992. The graph does not present data on poverty for 2002 and 2004 since the surveys used to calculate poverty in those years are not comparable with the earlier ones.

Mexico's National Household Income and Expenditure Surveys (ENIGH) of 2002 and 2004 show a decline in extreme poverty compared with 2000 (whether measured by the PL or IPMM) but a rise in nonextreme poverty as we (though not ECLAC or the World Bank) conceive it, defined with generous thresholds that take into account all human needs, satisfied at a basic but dignified level. The decline in extreme poverty, however, is not consistent with the evolution of economic indicators. For example, the per capita gross domestic product (GDP) grew barely 0.3 percent; unemployment grew during this period, and the number of formal employees registered at the Mexican Institute of Social Security (IMSS) declined by more than 200,000. ENIGH's data for 2002 and 2004 are, therefore, broadly contested.[18]

The three longest series, based on the PL method, show a period of decline in poverty between 1968 and 1981.[19] This trend reverts to a rise that persists in an almost continuous fashion until 1996. The IPMM, whose series begins in 1984, also identifies an upward trend in poverty since then and until 1996. The two versions of the poverty line method that continue until 2000 (ECLAC and HLB) show an accelerated decrease in poverty between 1996 and 2000, while with the calculations of the IPMM the reduction is very slight.

The two versions of the poverty line method that cover the entire period show that the percentage of the population living in poverty is slightly less in 2000 than in 1968 but much greater than the level in 1981. So, according to ECLAC, poverty in 2000 affected 41.1 percent of the population, only 1.4 percentage points less than in 1968, but almost 5 percentage points higher than that of 1981, almost 20 years before. According to the HLB series, the level of poverty in 2000 was slightly less than that of 1968 (4 percentage points) but 20 percentage points above the level at 1981. Last, in the series of

FIGURE 7.3

Four Versions of Poverty in Mexico, 1968–2000

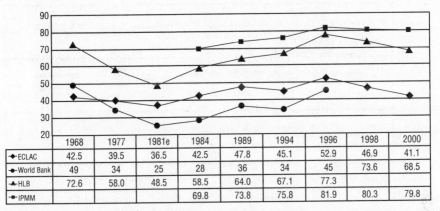

	1968	1977	1981e	1984	1989	1994	1996	1998	2000
◆ ECLAC	42.5	39.5	36.5	42.5	47.8	45.1	52.9	46.9	41.1
● World Bank	49	34	25	28	36	34	45	73.6	68.5
▲ HLB	72.6	58.0	48.5	58.5	64.0	67.1	77.3		
■ IPMM				69.8	73.8	75.8	81.9	80.3	79.8

All measurements are of the percentage of the Mexican population considered to be poor.
Sources: ECLAC: 1968, 1977, and 1984 are estimates of the percentage of individuals living in poor households as identified by the United Nations Development Program (UNDP), "Magnitud y evolución de la pobreza en América Latina," *Comercio Exterior* 42 (4), Abril 1992, Table 2, p. 384). Estimates for 1989–2000 are from CEPAL, *Boletín demográfico. América Latina y el Caribe: indicadores seleccionados con perspectiva de género,* 2002, statistical annex, Table 14, p. 221; World Bank: *Global economic prospects and the developing countries,* Washington, D.C., 2000, pp. 52–53; HLB: 1968–1984 are from Enrique Hernández-Laos, *Crecimiento económico y pobreza en México. Una agenda para la investigación,* Centro de Investigaciones Interdisciplinarias en Humanidades, Universidad Nacional Autónoma de México, 1992, Table 3.2, pp. 108–109. Estimates for 1989–2000 are authors' calculations based on the National Survey of Household Income and Spending (ENIGH).

the World Bank, poverty in 1996 (the final year of the series), though it is 4 percentage points lower than in 1968, is substantially greater than in 1977 and 20 percentage points higher than in 1981. Finally, the IPMM shows that poverty was higher in 2000 than in 1984.[20]

Figure 7.4 shows the evolution of poverty according to IPMM and its three dimensions (unsatisfied basic needs, income, and time) during the 1990s. It can be observed that while the incidence of integrated poverty rose between 1992 and 2000 (from 75.4 percent to 79.8 percent), the components of

FIGURE 7.4

Evolution of the Components of the IPMM in Mexico, 1992–2000

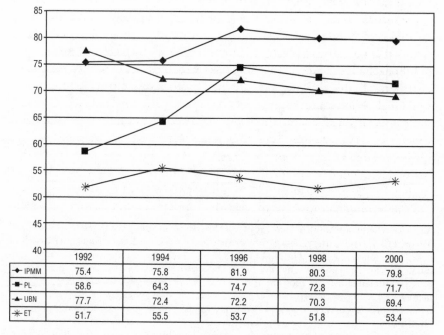

	1992	1994	1996	1998	2000
IPMM	75.4	75.8	81.9	80.3	79.8
PL	58.6	64.3	74.7	72.8	71.7
UBN	77.7	72.4	72.2	70.3	69.4
ET	51.7	55.5	53.7	51.8	53.4

IPMM is the integrated poverty measurement method; PL is the poverty line method; UBN is a measure of unsatisfied basic needs; ET is a measure of excess time at work.
Source: Authors' calculations based on the National Survey of Household Income and Growth (ENIGH), 1992, 1994, 1996, 1998, and 2000: National Institute of Statistical and Geographic Information (INEGI).

IPMM show different behaviors. Poverty measured by income increased greatly, rising 13.1 percentage points between 1992 and 2000 (from 58.5 percent to 71.7 percent); while poverty measured by time grew slightly and that of UBN declined (from 51.7 percent to 53.4 percent, and from 77.7 percent to 69.4 percent, respectively).

The income dimension is very sensitive to changes in economic growth, while the unsatisfied basic needs dimension tends to diminish with time.

This paradox is explained, above all, by two factors—first by the stock character of the majority of the variables of the UBN method (i.e., they exist and are measured at a given moment in time) vis-à-vis the flow character of the income variable (i.e., it is received per week, per month, etc., and is always calculated per period of time). While the flow variables can easily change their values, that is not the case with the stock variables, which can only experience marginal changes (except, for some stock variables, as a consequence of a catastrophe). In this way, the levels attained by stock variables at the present period are determined mostly by their level in the earlier period. Second, many indicators of the UBN method are determined by sources of well-being which can vary in the opposite direction with respect to household income during periods of recession. This is explained by the noncommodity character of many goods and services (e.g., education, health care, water, and drainage).[21] Even indicators such as housing (space and quality) that are partially determined by income are also determined by other factors, such as access to legal possession of land for housing; in the case of the poor population, the state of housing is widely determined by effective prevailing policies in the cities and by families building their own homes.

THE MASCULINIZATION OF POVERTY IN LATIN AMERICA

We now turn our attention to the question of gender. In recent decades, there has been growing consciousness of the unfavorable conditions of women who live in poverty, and it has been argued that the disadvantages these women face have grown more acute in the wake of the recurring economic crises. In the 1970s, a series of factors were said to have led to greater poverty in female-headed households: the fact that this type of household, most present in the poor strata, was increasing in number; that the women in these households had to assume more responsibilities, both domestic and extra-domestic; that they faced more joblessness, worked fewer hours, and received lower wages. Likewise, it was maintained that these were the households with the greatest number of dependents.[22]

In the 1980s, it was argued that in the wake of the innumerable economic crises that affected developing countries, women's living conditions, especially those with the least resources, were deteriorating. According to some authors, during these crises, women's duties of maintenance, reproduction, and replacement of the labor force became more intense.[23]

In the 1990s, it was argued that the feminization of poverty was a global phenomenon. According to Noeleen Heyzer, former director of the United Nations Development Fund for Women (UNIFEM), the number of women living in poverty had doubled over the previous two decades, and by the mid-1990s, women made up at least 60 percent of the 1 billion poor people in the world.[24] Likewise, in its *Panorama Social de América Latina 1995*, ECLAC included a chapter dedicated to the relationship between poverty and the female headship of households in which it is stated that "the notable growth of poverty registered in the region in the 1980s was reflected in a larger increase in indigent households headed by women. . . . Comparisons between both sexes allow the conclusion that in 7 of 11 countries, poverty is more frequent in households headed by women than those headed by men. The difference is most notable still in extremely poor or indigent households. . . . Extreme poverty, particularly in urban areas, affects above all households in which there is no husband."[25]

In the second half of the 1990s, some studies questioned the existence of an association between poverty and female-headed households.[26] Nevertheless, although these authors recognized the existence of other factors that influence the incidence of poverty (such as the type of household, the stage in the life cycle, access to property, etc.), they didn't deny that households headed by women were generally poorer than those headed by men. Thus, Arriagada, using data from Latin America in 1993, argued that "except for Argentina, Mexico, and Uruguay, in all households headed by women, whether they are extended, composite or nuclear families, there is a greater probability of poverty, as confirmed by different studies from the region.[27] The same occurs when examining the probabilities of indigence. . . ."

In the late 1990s, Lloyd commented that a recent review of the literature found that "households headed by women are poorer in general in most but not in all cases.

Income measurements by equivalent adult showed an even stronger relationship between poverty and female-headed households, where households with female heads were poorer."[28] Nonetheless, analyzing the data from different developing countries, she argued that no relationship exists between the percentage of people living in absolute poverty (defined according to the World Bank) and the percentage of female-headed households.[29] Further on, she says that "while female-headed households are frequently among the poorest, there does not appear to be an automatic relationship between female-headed households and poverty."

In the *Panorama Social, 2000–2001,* ECLAC notes that in Latin America, "the probability of being poor for the almost 91 million people belonging to female-headed households is similar to the average probability, which shows that this attribute does not connote by itself alone a condition of poverty."[30] This declaration rejects the opinion about the feminization of poverty expressed by the same organization in 1995.

The alleged existence of a feminization of poverty is not easy to elucidate. When poverty is calculated, the unit of observation and identification of poverty is not the person but the household. Poverty does not depend only on someone earning little, but also on the number of people who depend on that income. As the same literature on gender has pointed out, this form of approaching poverty has many limitations, since it doesn't expose the inequality within members of the household. Nevertheless, because of the difficulties of actually observing differences by gender or by generations within households, those of us who study poverty see ourselves always obliged to suppose total egalitarianism within the household, in such a way that everyone in the household is regarded as poor or as not poor. Thus, the feminization of poverty can neither be proved nor disproved. The only recourse left to us is either to compare some indicators of well-being between women and men or to analyze poverty according to the sex of the head of the household.

Despite our identification of the major limitations of the poverty line measuring method, and calling attention to the inequalities inside the household that all available poverty measurement methods can conceal (regardless of the sex of the head), this section seeks to contribute to the debate about whether or not a feminization of poverty exists in Latin America. Toward that end, we use the poverty calculations and some other sociodemographic indicators published by ECLAC for the countries of Latin America.

ECLAC's *Boletín Demográfico 2002* was produced with a focus on gender. Table 6b of the document refers to the "femininity ratio" of the poor population in 1999, calculated by dividing the number of poor women by the number of poor men and expressing the result as a percentage.[31] Based on this table, we would have to conclude that poverty affects women more than men, as the femininity ratio is greater than 100 percent in both urban and rural areas in eleven of the seventeen countries with available information. Another four countries have a femininity ratio greater than 100 percent in either their urban or rural areas and only two countries have a femininity ratio of less than 100 percent.[32]

Nevertheless, ECLAC makes a very obvious methodological error: it ignores the fact that in the majority of Latin American countries, women represent a larger percentage of total population than men. Therefore, to construct a femininity index of poverty that takes this fact into account, the data must be adjusted according to the relative proportion of women in each country. Figure 7.5 contains a femininity index of poverty corrected to reflect the relative weight that women have in the total population; the index is calculated for urban and rural areas, and, in contrast to ECLAC's original table, it also presents an index for the national total in each country and for Latin America as a whole. This index is expressed in relation to the unit. If its value is 1.00, it means that the probability of being poor if you are a woman is equal to the probability of being poor if you are a man.[33]

FIGURE 7.5

Gender and Poverty, 1999–2002

Country	Feminine Poverty Index
Latin America	1.01
Urban	1.05
Rural	0.95
Argentina	nd
Urban	1.05
Rural	nd

Bolivia	1.01
Urban	1.04
Rural	0.97
Brazil	1.00
Urban	1.05
Rural	0.91
Chile (1998)	1.03
Urban	1.05
Rural	0.92
Colombia	1.03
Urban	1.07
Rural	0.92
Costa Rica	1.10
Urban	1.17
Rural	1.05
Dominican Republic (1997)	1.07
Urban	1.10
Rural	1.04
Ecuador	nd
Urban	1.03
Rural	nd
El Salvador	1.04
Urban	1.12
Rural	0.98
Guatemala	0.97
Urban	1.04
Rural	0.95
Honduras	0.97
Urban	1.06
Rural	0.91
Mexico	1.02
Urban	1.03
Rural	1.01

(*continued*)

FIGURE 7.5 (*continued*)

Gender and Poverty, 1999–2002

Country	Feminine Poverty Index
Nicaragua	1.01
Urban	1.08
Rural	0.94
Panama	1.02
Urban	1.09
Rural	0.96
Paraguay	0.95
Urban	1.02
Rural	0.90
Uruguay	nd
Urban	1.06
Rural	nd
Venezuela (1997)	1.02
Urban	nd
Rural	nd

All figures represent the ratio of women to men living below the poverty line divided by the ratio of women to men in the country. A ratio higher than 1 indicates a "feminization" of poverty.
Source: Author's calculations based on CEPAL, 2001, 2002, *Panorama Social de América Latina.*

Based on this index, we can state that in the late 1990s in Latin America, a slight masculinization of poverty was present. Poverty affected women and men almost in the same proportions, since the standardized index shows 0.99 poor women for each poor man in the region. The value of this index is the same for urban areas as for the total population; only in rural areas is there feminization of poverty since the index is slightly greater than one (1.02 poor women for each poor man).[34] The countries that register masculinization of poverty are Paraguay, Uruguay, Brazil (whose value turns out to be decisive for Latin America as a whole), Argentina, Guatemala, and Honduras. In another six countries (Bolivia, Colombia, Ecuador, El Salvador, Mexico, and Nicaragua), the relationship is 1.00. Finally, Chile, Venezuela, Panama, the

Dominican Republic, and Costa Rica are the only countries that show feminization of poverty, which is most acute in the latter two.

With this data it is possible to argue that there is no evidence that at the end of the twentieth century there were a greater standardized number of poor women than poor men in Latin America. To complement this conclusion we have to verify whether there exists a feminization of poverty when one uses as an indicator the comparative incidence of poverty according to the sex of the head of household.

The data show that in 1999, in terms of income poverty, households headed by women were as likely to be poor as total households (43.1 percent).[35] But if we consider extreme poverty or indigence, households headed by women were less affected, with 17.5 percent in this condition, while for total households this percentage was 18.4 percent.[36] Therefore, indigence by household was slightly masculinized in 1999.

The *Panorama Social de América Latina* shows that in 2000–2002 poverty incidence in households headed by women in urban areas (no information is available for rural households) is lower than poverty incidence for all urban households. Therefore, we can say that total poverty (not only indigence) in urban households in Latin America was slightly masculinized in 2000–2002. The country-by-country data are shown in Figure 7.6.

FIGURE 7.6

Poverty by Gender of Head of Household
in Urban Areas in Latin America, 1990–2002

Percentage of Households Below the Poverty Line

Country/Year	Total	With Female Head
Argentina (Greater Buenos Aires)		
1990	16.2	11.3
2002	31.6	27.4
Bolivia		
1989	49.4	55.7
2002	44.9	39.7

(*continued*)

FIGURE 7.6 (*continued*)

Poverty by Gender of Head of Household
in Urban Areas in Latin America, 1990–2002

Percentage of Households Below the Poverty Line

Country/Year	Total	With Female Head
Brazil		
1990	35.6	41.4
2002	27.4	26.5
Chile		
1990	33.3	33.0
2003	15.2	11.3
Colombia		
1991	47.1	47.4
2002	44.6	45.9
Costa Rica		
1990	22.2	27.4
2002	15.9	27.1
Dominican Republic		
1997	31.6	38.0
2002	38.4	50.8
Ecuador		
1990	55.8	60.1
2002	42.6	46.1
El Salvador		
1995	40.0	43.5
2001	34.7	38.5
Guatemala		
1989	48.2	48.5
2002	39.0	42.5
Honduras		
1990	64.5	71.5
2002	60.5	60.7

Mexico		
1989	34.2	30.1
2002	26.0	26.9
Nicaragua		
1993	60.3	64.0
2001	57.7	61.0
Panama		
1991	33.6	40.0
2002	21.4	26.9
Paraguay (Asunción metro area)		
1990	36.8	41.7
2000	35.0	34.3
Uruguay		
1990	11.8	10.6
2002	9.3	8.0
Venezuela		
1990	33.4	45.0
2002	43.3	48.1

Source: CEPAL, 2004, *Panorama Social de América Latina,* Tables 17 and 22.

If we accept the statement by ECLAC in 1995 that the feminization of poverty was present in Latin America in the beginning of the 1990s, one of the conclusions that derives from the previous analysis is that the region went through a masculinization of poverty in the 1990s. Only some cases of a clear feminization of poverty by type of household are evident. This is the case in Costa Rica, El Salvador, and Nicaragua, countries where both at the beginning and at the end of the 1990s the incidence of poverty of female-headed households was greater than in male-headed households; moreover, the gap between them widened in the period.

The inequality of work-related earnings by men and women is another of the indicators usually linked to the question of poverty and gender. According to available data, the gap between the income of men and women narrowed in the 1990s (see Figure 7.7). In 1990, Uruguay had the biggest income gap, since income of women represented 45 percent of that of men. At the other extreme is the more egalitarian situation found in Panama, where the average income of women represented 80 percent of that of men.[37]

FIGURE 7.7

Women's Average Income as a Percentage of Men's
Average Income in Urban Areas: 1990–2002

Country/Year	Total Labor Income	Wage Income Only
Argentina (Greater Buenos Aires)		
1990	65	76
2002	59	71
Bolivia		
1989	59	60
2002	61	71
Brazil		
1990	56	65
2002	66	86
Chile		
1990	61	66
2003	64	84
Colombia		
1991	68	77
2002	77	99
Costa Rica		
1990	72	74
2002	75	85
Dominican Republic		
1997	75	90
2002	68	89
Ecuador		
1990	66	77
2002	67	87

El Salvador		
1995	63	79
2001	80	100
Guatemala		
1989	65	82
2002	58	81
Honduras		
1990	59	78
2002	76	95
Mexico		
1989	55	73
2002	63	76
Nicaragua		
1993	77	77
2002	69	82
Panama		
1991	80	80
2002	76	85
Paraguay (Asunción metro area)		
1990	55	63
2000	70	95
Uruguay		
1990	45	64
2002	72	71
Venezuela		
1990	66	79
2002	76	99

Source: CEPAL, 2004, *Panorama Social de América Latina.*

At the beginning of the current century, the income gap narrowed in most countries in the region, with Argentina and Guatemala having the greatest inequality (women's income representing 59 percent and 58 percent of that of men, respectively). The income gap between women and men narrowed by means of very different processes of change among groups of countries:[38]

1. In Bolivia, Honduras, and Venezuela, the average income of men and women fell. Nevertheless, the income of women fell to a lesser degree than that of men. Consequently, the reduction in the gap was not associated with an improvement in the situation of women, but rather was a product of a general impoverishment that affected most the income of men.

2. In Brazil, Mexico, Paraguay, and Uruguay, the income of women rose while that of men fell. Therefore, in these countries, women improved their economic situation vis-à-vis men.

3. In Colombia, Costa Rica, Ecuador, El Salvador, Panama, Paraguay, and Uruguay, the reduction in the gap is explained by a more rapid rise in the income of women than that of men. On the other hand, both in Panama and the Dominican Republic, work-related income rose for both genders, but that of women grew to a lesser degree than that of men, which resulted in a widening of the gap.

Another relevant aspect of female achievement relates to improvement in the education levels of women. From the perspective of gender, we find notable results as the average education levels of women have improved more than those of men. While in the early 1990s in only three countries (Argentina, Panama, and Uruguay) did young women (ages twenty-five to twenty-nine) have a greater number of years of study on average than men, by the end of the decade five countries were in this situation.[39] In addition, this achievement is observed in the rural areas of the Dominican Republic and, surprisingly, in rural Colombia and Honduras.

Among people ages fifteen to twenty-four, we also find significant advances. While in the early 1990s in eleven of the seventeen countries with available data, women had levels of education equal or higher than those of men, by 2000 this situation could be observed in almost all the Latin American countries (both in rural and urban areas). Mexico, Guatemala, and Bolivia are the exceptions, although the differences exist basically in their rural areas, since in the cities the average for men and women is almost the same.[40]

The overall income deterioration in most Latin American countries has resulted in many women having improved their situation relative to that of men due to the fact that men's wages have been more negatively affected than those of women. Despite that, some indicators of well-being have improved, and women have managed to advance more in areas such as education.

FINAL REFLECTIONS

The economic discontent of the Latin American population is widespread. The policies of structural adjustment carried out during the 1980s and 1990s did not succeed in achieving the economic growth and reduction of poverty that was promised by neoliberal elites and governments. Popular sectors with limited employment opportunities continue to swell the ranks of informality. Workers and independent unions, despite their resistance to labor reforms that seek to destroy their historically won rights, continue being battered by low wages and by strategies to weaken and/or dismantle their organizations. The middle class has ever-decreasing hopes of maintaining its standard of living, and middle-class youth face a dramatic level of unemployment despite their increasing levels of education.

Civil society, weary of suffering the attacks of the right in the name of a better future that has never arrived, has succeeded in bringing leftist and center-left parties to power. Although many of these governments have not substantially modified neoliberal economic and social policies (at times for a lack of consensus, and at times due to agreements with financial powers), in many countries of Latin America, society has not given up and continues propelling governments with a progressive vision of economic development to power.

Given the challenge faced by leftist and center-left Latin American governments to convert themselves into real, long-term political forces, it is essential that their economic policies focus on the raising of their people's living standards and do not restrict themselves to programs of macroeconomic stability. We now have more than two decades of experience with the neoliberal model, and any way you look at it, it has not produced results.

The following are some conclusions that flow from this essay, which any leftist or center-left government should take into account when putting its public policies into practice.

Measurements of poverty based only on income, being one-dimensional measurements that omit fundamental factors that affect living standards, are insufficient for an evaluation of how a country is progressing toward social development. Their vision is very limited in supposing that income is the only source of well-being. Furthermore, it is necessary to abandon minimalist definitions of poverty, like those of the World Bank or ECLAC, which establish subhuman poverty lines, defining, for example, the threshold of extreme poverty as the income required to purchase raw food, as though human beings were animals and could chew and digest their food in that form. The Integrated Poverty Measurement Method (IPMM), the multidimensional method discussed earlier in this chapter, incorporates indicators of all the sources of well-being and thus offers a more complete vision of human deprivation. The IPMM allows us to combine the different components of poverty and evaluate the situation of each household within that household's integrated index, showing simultaneously the partial dimensions: poverty as measured by the poverty line, unsatisfied basic needs, and free time. With this method, we can obtain a more exact and dynamic measurement of poverty, and thereby have a more adequate basis for the implementation of social policies designed to overcome many kinds of social deprivation.

At the same time, it is important that the definition of the poverty thresholds is based on norms that fully recognize the socioeconomic human rights expressed in a variety of international declarations; and in the definition of the requirements to satisfy basic needs, all the goods and services that allow for their genuine satisfaction should be included. For example, in estimating the costs of a minimally adequate diet, all the goods necessary for its preparation and consumption (utensils to eat with, gas to cook with, a table to eat on, etc.) should be included.

As for gender-oriented policies, it is necessary for progressive governments of the region to design public policies having as a background the gender poverty really observed in their countries rather than the assumed feminization of poverty, which has not been empirically verified. In this chapter we have found that poverty affects the sexes in approximately the same proportions. Nonetheless, at the level of the household, we have found that poverty in Latin America has gone through a process of "defeminization" or "masculinization" during the 1990s. In addition, we have identified ways in which women, in general, have improved their situation with respect to men; even in households in which living conditions have worsened, households headed by women have been less affected than those headed by men.

The reduction in income inequality by gender has taken place, above all, because of the greater decline of the income of men than that of women. Furthermore, in countries in which average income has risen, that of women has risen more rapidly. This is certainly contributing to the changes in gender relations and to women's quality of life.

On the other hand, many women who are working today, some of whom could find better-paying jobs, will continue facing serious difficulties in fully carrying out the dual tasks of providing for their family's income and taking charge of its reproduction. Some women will continue leaving their children alone during working hours due to the nonexistence of public child-care services.[41] Others will continue being witnesses to the frustration in which male members of their households live, as victims of layoffs, or whose wages, day after day, purchase less and less. These situations will continue generating family conflicts leading to violence and the disintegration of the home. Therefore, we have to be careful in overestimating what has been achieved, and instead point out areas which, given the changes in gender relations, require closer attention on the part of the state and society in general. Among these areas, public day-care service for children stands out. Noncommodified child day care must be seen as a basic human right, and should be available to all adults, men as well as women, who have young children and have to attend to activities outside the home—not only work, but studies as well. This is a right that every progressive government should vigorously support.

On the other hand, the data presented here lead us to question the usefulness of conditioned transfer programs targeted to the extremely poor, programs that are now spread throughout the region, like *Oportunidades* in Mexico, which provides educational support for children and young people, and which pays higher scholarships to women than to men who are studying at secondary and preparatory levels. The information shows that in most Latin American countries, women are achieving, without these differential supports, levels of education that are the same as or higher than those achieved by men. In any case, if we were to opt for these type of programs, scholarships in urban areas should be directed to higher levels of education since young people are already achieving secondary education in the majority of countries. As a result of austerity policies, however, public investment in postsecondary education has been abandoned, and therefore, there is insufficient room for the growing demand for this service. A large part of the youth-education problem is derived from supply restrictions, a problem that will not be resolved by subsidizing the demand for education, as is done by the *Oportunidades* program.

To overcome poverty, it is important not only to increase the population's levels of education but to generate conditions for the development of economic activity and thereby increase the opportunities for well-paid employment.[42] In the same way, the data presented in this chapter make clear the need to redesign these targeted programs which currently ignore the need to improve the education of adults who, in fact, are the ones suffering greater educational deprivation. This combination—employment opportunities and promotion of adult educational levels—would contribute to the improvement of living conditions of all members of the household.

8

Crime and Citizen Security in Latin America

Mark Ungar

A REGION UNDER SIEGE

Latin America is under siege by crime. Violent crimes—those involving physical harm, assault, and threat, from homicide to armed robbery—have risen at alarming rates. A 41 percent increase in homicides alone during the 1990s, to a rate three times the global average, has made Latin America the world's most crime-ridden region.[1] According to the World Health Organization, in 2004 there were 27.5 homicides for every 100,000 people in Latin America, compared to 22 in Africa and 15 in Eastern Europe. Since 1995, nearly a third of the population has reported being assaulted or robbed, well above the global average of 19 percent.[2] In the annual Latinobarómetro poll, the number of respondents who said they know someone victimized by crime jumped from 33 percent to 41 percent between 2004 and 2005. The murder rate nearly tripled in most of Central America, the Andes, and many states in Brazil between 1990 and 2004.[3] In Venezuela, crimes against persons nearly doubled and violent property crimes rose nearly threefold between 1990 and 2003. By one credible estimate, the lives and productivity lost to crime has cost the region over 12 percent of its gross domestic product—about $145 billion—each year.[4]

Even amid economic and political breakdowns across much of Latin America, nearly every national poll carried out in the region since the mid-1990s concludes that the crisis of citizen security represents the first or second most urgent concern for public opinion. Demands for more security have spurred some of the biggest public demonstrations since the transition to democracy—attracting over 200,000 people each in Buenos Aires and Mexico City in 2004. Killings by security forces and their inability to maintain order have even contributed to the collapse of five constitutional governments since 2000.

The poor performance of police and criminal justice systems serves only to exacerbate the prevailing climate of fear, abuse, and violence. One response to this crisis is the increasing adoption of iron fist policies that do not address the causes of crime. Another response is the continuation of abusive and increasingly ineffective policing. The police are part of a larger criminal justice system that is in disarray and that operates in societies where fear, stoked by sensationalist media, has led to increasing levels of vigilante justice and other forms of violence. These acts of a desperate citizenry represent a third, especially troubling, response to the crisis of security.

Of course, Latin America's citizen security crisis is also an economic and social one. In nearly every country in the region, a lethal combination of inequality, poverty, urban migration, and unemployment has been fueling skyrocketing rates of crime. Since 1980, Latin America's population has grown by 30 percent and the percentage living in urban areas from 65.1 percent to 75.6 percent. In fact, urban violent crime outstrips national rates in nearly every country. Murder has quintupled in Caracas; San Salvador's homicide rate, one of the world's highest, is double the national rate; and the number of murders in São Paulo and Rio de Janeiro is nearly three times Brazil's national average. Aggravating the dislocation of urbanization is Latin America's severe inequality, discussed in greater detail in the contribution to this volume by Luis Reygadas. The region's average Gini Coefficient, which measures inequality on a scale in which 0 is perfect equality, was 51.7 in 2004—well above the world average of 40. The richest tenth of Latin Americans earn 48 percent of total income while the poorest tenth earn 1.6 percent; the equivalent figures for rich countries are 29.1 percent and 2.5 percent.[5] The increase in violent and property crimes both reflects and intensifies this economic dimension of citizen security.

In societies with long-standing patterns of discrimination, crime is blamed primarily on marginalized groups such as youth, immigrants, the poor, and people of indigenous or African descent.[6] Combined with the lack of economic opportunities and cutbacks in services such as education, such discrimination has led above all to more violence by and against youth, from killings of street children to narcotrafficking by heavily armed gangs. Nearly 30 percent of all homicides in Latin America are of people between the ages of fifteen and twenty-four.[7] The tendency of public opinion and policy interventions to focus on those identified with crime leads to neglect of crime's root causes and policies that might address them, such as better community-police relations.

Crime has also led to a widespread fear, which finds its outlet not only in public support for a *mano dura,* but also through increases in private arms and vigilantism. Firearms are responsible for about 63 percent of killings around the world, but in Latin America—where arms are readily available through trafficking by organized crime and security agencies—they are responsible for well over 80 percent and have given Latin America and the Caribbean the world's highest rate of deadly firearms violence.[8] Many of those weapons are employed in the region's alarming rise in vigilantism, carried out by perpetrators ranging from spontaneous mobs to "social work" groups and clandestine organizations with police ties. For Guatemala alone, the United Nations documented nearly five hundred lynchings between 1996 and 2002. Many organized vigilante squads grow out of judicial or community policing councils, as in urban Bolivia and Ecuador's highland *Justicieros.* Acceptance and support of vigilantism appears to be high throughout the region. Over a third of Venezuelans—and up to 70 percent in some cities—favors "social cleansing" by para-police squads,[9] which have been reported in at least seven states and the capital. While suspected criminals continue to be vigilantes' primary targets, victims now include mayors, policemen, and "undesirable" individuals. In May 2004, a mob in the Peruvian town of Ilave beat their mayor to death after accusing him of embezzlement. In Mexico, where over a hundred lynchings were documented in the 1990s, angry neighbors in Mexico City were caught on tape in 2004 pouring gasoline on two undercover policemen misidentified as kidnappers.

TENTATIVE AND OFTEN FRUSTRATED REFORMS

The undeniable failure of prevailing responses to criminality, and the tension between those responses and efforts to strengthen fledgling democracies across the region, has led to various strategies for reform, with uneven degrees of success. Under tremendous pressure, governments have put forth a wide range of reform policies that fall into three general areas. The first is structural reorganization of police forces to make them more effective and accountable through regional decentralization, flatter hierarchies, better technology, more professional security, higher wages, oversight agencies, and stronger discipline. Highly militarized and centralized police have been broken up into preventive, investigative, and special-crimes divisions, while countries such as Mexico have created Public Security Secretariats and federal police agencies as well.

The second area of change is judicial and legal, ranging from more transparent selection of judges to enactment of clearer civil rights statutes. Most significantly, fourteen countries have adopted new penal process codes to strengthen defendant and due process rights, replace slow and biased written procedures with oral trials, transfer investigative authorities from the police to prosecutors (*fiscales*) in the attorney general's office (*Ministerio Público*), and create courts at the investigative and sentencing phases. Finally, the third and most innovative new citizen security policy is community policing designed to empower citizens to respond directly to crime through street patrols, joint policy councils with state officials, more autonomy for neighborhood police commissioners, and programs targeting such problems as drug abuse and domestic violence.

Many of these reforms are part of broader political changes, as in new civilian security structures formed by the peace accords in Central America. New presidents, governors, and mayors in many other countries have used their electoral mandates to revamp flawed security systems inherited from the past. Many of these changes have led to significant improvements. Restructuring has made police more effective, new penal process codes have sped up the criminal justice process, and community policing has reduced crimes such as domestic violence. Progress is evident from Uruguay, where better training has turned the police from among the least respected to one of the most esteemed state bodies, to Costa Rica, where community policing, improved police education, and systematized information has cut citizens' sensation of insecurity in half. Similarly, Chile's national police, the Carabineros, have boosted security through the autonomous neighborhood units of the *Plan Cuadrante,* while in some areas of particularly high conflict, such as the Mexican state of Guerrero and the Honduran city of Danlí, citizens have formed their own security programs. Even amid an ongoing civil war, Colombian cities have implemented successful citizen security policies. In Cali, where homicide rates had shot up from 23 to 90 per 100,000 people between 1983 and 1993,[10] a plan was introduced to strengthen police-based institutions and augment citizen participation in antiviolence strategies. The result was a drop of six hundred murders per year.[11] In the capital city of Bogotá, community advisory committees, citizen security schools, and neighborhood crime prevention fronts also have decreased violent crime.[12]

Because of pressure for immediate results, however, most criminal policies continue to be short-term actions focused on arrest and incarceration. Although long-standing distrust of security forces does create support for civil rights and legal oversight, particularly after egregious acts of police violence or exposure of police corruption, the fear that is pervasive across the region usually trumps such demands: even citizens who fear the police do not want to hinder their ability to fight crime. Outrage over police involvement in the 1993 massacre of seven Rio street children, for example, did not lead to lasting change. Politicians, with short terms in office and often tenuous control over state institutions, are reluctant or unable to take on the much-needed improvements in investigation, finances, and management. So they combine or replace such reforms with *mano dura* (iron fist) and "zero tolerance" proposals, which are popular, easy to formulate, and sail through legislatures, but which rarely bring durable progress.

The *mano dura* is abusive and ineffective in Latin America because it selectively applies the "broken windows" theory,[13] which argues that since crime begins with physical deterioration and different forms of harassment that intimidate law-abiding citizens, it can only be prevented with detentions for misdemeanors and antisocial behavior. The unprecedented 70 percent drop in New York City's homicide rate in the 1990s is widely attributed to this approach, and has led to similar efforts throughout Latin America. But to be effective while not eroding civil rights, zero tolerance policies require solid professional training for officials, clear laws, strong oversight, greater coordination with social services to address the causes of crime, and more courts to process detainees. In Latin America, however, "zero tolerance" has been implemented without such supports or accountability mechanisms, turning it into a continuation of predemocratic practices. A typical case is that of El Salvador, where about a third of the 2,500 murders in 2004 were gang-related,[14] and where the government cracked down in July 2003 with the *Plan Mano Dura,* resulting in more than 8,000 arrests. But this emergency measure failed to stem the violence, and judges released many detainees for lack of evidence. So in 2004, a new president widened the police's arrest powers and launched *Plan Super Mano Dura.* This intensification of zero tolerance enjoys 70 percent public approval but has been harshly criticized by human rights groups for allowing arbitrary arrests and legalizing discrimination. Indeed, zero tolerance thickens the line being drawn between public order and police on the one hand, and human rights and delinquency on the other. Security officials frequently criticize human rights groups and public defense attorneys with the refrain of "Where were they when the crime was committed?" Such a false division has even reached the point where government policy makers criticize new penal process codes as too "guaranteeist" for Latin America's violent reality.

These failed experiments have increased the appeal of community policing, designed to empower citizens and skirt dysfunctional state institutions. Uruguay's citizen security program combines regular meetings with logistical support centers and empowered local commissioners; Guatemala established security schools for citizens; São Paulo has active citizen councils with grassroots participation, and the community policing programs in Paraguay's capital are pilot programs of a national plan. Many countries also have judges of the peace and mediation centers to resolve minor conflicts. Despite this variation, community policing has reduced crime and fear in neighborhoods throughout Latin America. Many programs do not get needed financial and institutional support, however, and are dismissed as "social work" by the police, who usually do not carry out supportive structural changes such as communications training for street officers or increased personnel to respond to increased demand. Many programs also falter on poor coordination between the police, which are usually national agencies, and the municipal government, which provides most of the services—such as street lighting and women's shelters—that address the sources of insecurity. In addition, the citizen forums that are a centerpiece of community policing are sometimes never convoked, making many programs vulnerable to co-optation by local commissioners or organized criminals. Most communities lack the experience and resources to make up for these shortfalls, much less break down the misunderstanding, fear, distrust, and violence that characterizes their relationships with the police.

If the temptation toward iron fist policies, and the weakness of efforts to implement community policing, represent two dimensions of the citizen security crisis in Latin America, a third dimension concerns the agency on its front lines—the police. One reason why police agencies throughout the region do not adapt and improve is the deeply entrenched nature of their practices and power. Throughout Latin America's history, the police have been responsible less for stopping crime than for suppressing political opposition and marginalized social sectors. In the colonial period, policing was carried out by irregular bodies with wide discretion and controlled by town councils and *caudillos,* or regional strongmen. Upon independence, this role continued for decades as the region was embroiled in internal and regional wars.

In the more stable second half of the nineteenth century, most countries adopted constitutions protecting due process, codified criminal and civil codes, and professionalized their police forces. With weak judiciaries and low levels of societal participation, however, these developments had little impact on practice. Most police continued to be controlled by *caudillos* or the warring conservative and liberal parties. Even in relatively small Ecuador, for example, efforts to nationalize the police did not come until 107 years after independence. With immigration and industrialization at the beginning of the twentieth century came the growth of unionism and socialism and other challenges to the status quo, and these were often met with state violence and criminalization. Labor strikes throughout the Southern Cone, for example, were brutally broken up by police and military forces. When the military began taking power in that part of the region during the 1920s and 1930s, the police and criminal justice systems were incorporated into the state's repressive apparatus and used to squelch all forms of political opposition. This was particularly pronounced during the Cold War. Courts, legislatures, and other oversight bodies were either complicit in this repression or silenced.

Much of this legacy survived Latin America's transitions to democracy. The police's link to powerful presidencies, coupled with fears that reform will dilute crime fighting, helps security agencies resist changes that clash with their interests and are regarded as meddling or punitive. One of the bases of current zero tolerance policy, for instance, is the large number of internal regulations and edicts that most Latin American police have been acquiring since the colonial era, which permit detention for a wide range of subjectively defined traits and behaviors, from "vagrancy" to "suspicion of criminal intent." The provision in Chile's 1901 penal code allowing police officers to make arrests based on physical appearance, for example, was not eliminated until 1998. Venezuela's 1939 Law of Vagabonds and Crooks, which allowed detention of anyone deemed "suspicious," was one of the main bases for police detentions until it was finally declared unconstitutional in 1997. Yet even when such regulations have been struck down, most governments try to replace them with new "social control" laws, include them in temporary operations that remain after the operation ends, or step up other powers such as detaining people to check their criminal records.

Poor training and criminology increases dependence on such tactics. Most police academies still emphasize physical preparation and formalistic knowledge of laws rather than analysis and discussion of criminal policy and social conditions. In Mexico, where forty-one academies had no minimal educational requirements for entry and 56 percent of active duty officers had no formal education, the government responded by strengthening and standardizing materials. But most countries continue providing only three to five months of training for police officers or, as in the case of Guatemala, have lowered standards to fill the ranks. Once on the force, most top officers lack both the time and incentives to incorporate criminology into their activities. Combined with unclear laws, such poor planning has serious consequences for citizen security, encouraging among other things the excessive use of force. Most police have only general UN guidelines on the use of force without training or discussion of how these norms apply in practice. Indeed, cadets in many countries complain of receiving only a few practice sessions before being issued their guns. The result is excessive violence and a culture of systematic cover-up by the police. In Venezuela, death results in over 40 percent of incidents of civilian resistance to police. The Rio de Janeiro police killed 1,195 people in 2003, compared to 300 in *all* of the United States the same year, and São Paulo's police killed 7,500 between 1990 and 2000—far more than those killed during the twenty-one years of military rule from 1964–85. Increasing military involvement in policing multiplies the likelihood of such violence. Not only is the military unsuited and unprepared for internal policing, but their involvement threatens both civil rights and civilian control. In nearly every country, however, military forces have been brought into street patrols, special operations, suppression of protests, takeovers of sensitive areas, drug trafficking activity, control of prisons, and saturation of high-crime neighborhoods.

When the police become politicized by disputes between governments or parties—much like in the nineteenth century—the possibility of change becomes even more remote. In Venezuela, for example, police forces and policy have been caught up in the rivalry between the president, who controls the national forces, and the agencies of municipal forces run by opposition mayors. International support can help break such deadlocks by overcoming internal politics and financial constraints, and many citizen security projects have depended entirely or in part on external funds. Important examples include security sector restructuring supported by the United Nations, antiviolence programs funded by the Inter-American Development Bank, police training promoted by the United States, and comprehensive packages like a 2005 loan extended by the Central American Bank of Economic Integration (BCIE) to Nicaragua for communications modernization and rural police units. But external support often leads only to temporary improvement because of the lack of domestic reforms. The judicial changes and citizen training of Guatemala's well-designed community policing programs, for instance, dropped off once the international stage was over. Similarly, in the

Dominican Republic, a community policing program sponsored by the Organization of American States was slowed down by a newly elected president's purge of many police officers tied to the opposition party.

Even when they are open to change, many police agencies are simply incapable of absorbing it. Poor coordination between preventative and investigative bodies, inadequate or nonexistent information sharing, institutional territoriality, inadequate budgets, poor training and salaries, little professional security, archaic hierarchies, and exhausting work schedules all make officials both resentful and reluctant to take on the extra work to implement new policies. These difficulties have been multiplied by proliferation of agencies. On nearly every issue, from health to education, Latin American governments are being decentralized to enhance performance and proximity to citizens. But in the security sector, decentralization has led to a record number of regional and municipal police forces that repeat the ineffective and abusive practices of their national counterparts. Amid increasing inequality, it has also led to an economic fragmentation of agencies with little incentive to cooperate. Among Lima's twenty-three municipalities, for example, some pay for top-rate private services and others barely scrape together a police force at all. Of the dozen overlapping police forces in Venezuela's Federal District, the wealthy ones have ten times more police officers than the poor ones.

Also hampering citizen security is the poor state of criminal investigation. Inadequately trained police and prosecutors throughout Latin America haphazardly carry out basic steps such as crime scene protection. Since such actions deprive them of the scientific ability and information to resolve the crime, police resort to intimidation, raids, and mass roundups—depriving them of reliable and cooperative witnesses, the other element needed for successful investigation. Raids in poor Lima neighborhoods net hundreds of people in a search for a single suspect—a practice that public support and weak judicial control has helped make an "engrained" part of policing, says one Peruvian official.[15] With continual bottlenecks in the criminal justice system, those caught up in such sweeps are usually held long past the legal maximum time for detention without charge, which is twenty-four hours in most countries. The usual response from officials, though, is to increase that time to two or more days.

Along with investigation, information is a pillar of citizen security policy. Crime statistics should shape and drive daily operations, internal management, and long-term planning. Some governments, such as Brazil's Minas Gerais state, have developed comprehensive new databases in collaboration with university specialists. In most of Latin America, though, statistics are uneven, incomplete, and unreliable. Typically, there are marked differences in the crime rates reported by the preventive police, the investigative police, the judiciary, and the *Fiscalía* (roughly equivalent to the attorney general). Most countries also lack computerized databases and professional statistics agencies, resulting in poor coordination compounded by police decentralization. The biggest cause of informational unreliability, though, is the fact that most crimes are simply not reported—accounting for an estimated 75 percent of crimes in some countries.

The weakness of police institutions and the absence of transparency are even more evident with regard to budgets, for governments exhibit little or no control over disbursement and spending of law enforcement funds. Police officers are among the worst paid state officials, taking home around $200 a month—barely enough to support a family in most countries. Budgetary problems have led countries such as Nicaragua to suspend promotions and salaries. Along with weak oversight and discipline, poor remuneration has allowed corruption to flourish in the security sector, from street bribes to organized crime. Many cadets at Peru's School of Superior Police Studies cited "informal financial opportunities" as a major incentive for joining the force.[16] Many countries have taken steps to stem corruption, from prosecution of commanders to assignment of women to bribery-prone traffic beats. But the power and resources of drug trafficking and other organized criminal networks limit the impact of such actions. To make ends meet, many officers also moonlight for the private security sector, which has grown so astronomically since the 1980s that private security agents outnumber public ones in most big cities. Many of these agents neglect their regular work, either through physical exhaustion or favoritism toward after-hours clients.

These conditions have made the police one of the least trusted among state agencies. In a typical poll, over 56 percent of Mexicans expressed "no confidence" in the police and over 75 percent believe that they are corrupt and criminal.[17] Poor performance by the police also comes from poor man-

agement. Lower ranking personnel are scapegoated for mistakes and dis-
couraged from innovation. Most street officers spend most of their time
monitoring a single corner without supervision or authority to interact with
the community, and, in many cases, without a radio.[18] Rather than rewarding
positive actions or specific skill development, promotion in most police
agencies depends almost entirely on the officer's seniority, academy exam
score, and relations with superiors. Most forms for individual promotion are
usually no more than a page, with few questions about specific achievements
or skills.

But the police's performance is limited by that of the larger criminal justice system in which it works. Inadequate training, skeletal budgets, corruption, bureaucracy, and political favoritism have trapped judges, prosecutors,
public defenders, and other criminal justice officials in a cycle of inefficiency,
myopia, and public scorn. Fewer than 2 percent of homicides are resolved by
Latin America's notoriously slow and biased criminal justice systems. In Mexico, just 3 percent of all crimes reach a trial and sentence.[19] In Colombia, 35
percent of homicides reached trial in the 1970s, but just 6 percent did in the
1990s.[20] In most of Latin America, not surprisingly, public confidence in the
legal system rarely surpasses a dismal 25 percent.[21]

New penal process codes have begun to speed up creaky criminal procedures, but at the same time have exposed these limits. Stricter rules on evidence collection, detention, questioning, and level of proof—as well as new
responsibilities for judges and *fiscales* (prosecutors)—have not been backed
up by needed training and funds. Antagonism between police and justice officials is rife throughout the region, with each side blaming the other for continuing bottlenecks and impunity. Trust and cooperation are particularly
scarce when the judicial police are under the executive branch and not the
Fiscalía, which now directs criminal investigations. In jurisdictions where
some judges use the new code and others use the old one, furthermore, the
resulting confusion feeds into the politically potent argument that the new
codes are soft on crime, with police complaints of having to release criminals
receiving wide and sympathetic media coverage.

In many countries, investigation of such abuses is now carried out by national ombudsmen or internal affairs units in the police. Units in Peru,

Ecuador, and Argentina have made significant headway in holding security forces accountable, but others have been stalled by financial and political restrictions. Limited capacity for independent investigations has forced Guatemala's Office of Professional Responsibility to forfeit many cases. In countries such as Mexico, inconsistent adherence to disciplinary procedures, politicized dismissals, and insufficient documentation have led courts to reinstate many police and judicial officials accused of abuses. And getting to the courts does not necessarily reduce impunity. In Venezuela, for example, the conviction rate of police officers is less than 20 percent that of civilians charged with similar crimes.

Penal reforms have also had limited impact on public defense and prisons. Despite guarantees of free legal defense and the need for it by the vast majority of detainees, the only Latin American country with a sufficient number of public defenders is Costa Rica. Elsewhere, public defenders take on far too many cases to be effective on most of them—with average caseloads of up to 300.[22] Along with the *mano dura,* poor public defense has led to a 50 percent increase in Latin America's prison population, crowded into facilities at rates of up to four times intended capacity. Peru's Lurigancho prison was built for 1,000 people but holds over 7,000,[23] and an estimated 60 to 70 percent of Rio de Janeiro's small-time drug convicts would not be in prison if they had better lawyers.[24] Vermin, disease, hunger strikes, and deadly riots have become part of daily life in the region's penitentiary systems. In most of them, well over half of all prisoners are awaiting trial, often long past the two years that regional law advises as a legal limit.

Governments are beginning to respond, though, such as by releasing those held for minor crimes or who have already served more than the time of the maximum sentence of the crime for which they were detained. Alternatives to sentencing through mediation and community service are also being promoted with positive results in many countries. There is just a 6 percent recidivism rate among the 4,000 beneficiaries of Costa Rica's community service, for example, far below the 80 percent for those who serve time. But even with such alternatives, most judges still opt for imprisonment—reflecting judicial support for a *mano dura* in most countries. Opinion polls show active public hostility toward measures to improve prisons, in addition, and candidates around the region say that expression of concern for prisoners can derail their campaigns.

THREE EMBLEMATIC CASES

To illustrate how the crisis of citizen security is unfolding in Latin America, we turn now to more detailed consideration of three countries: Honduras, Bolivia, and Argentina. The situation in these countries is representative of broad patterns emerging across the region. Honduras is resorting to an iron fist to crack down on crime, and in the process is weakening new democratic reforms in ways that are also evident in many other countries and in subnational regions. In Bolivia, as in much of the Andean region, a weak state and unstable government prevent successful implementation of coherent policies. For its part, Argentina, like many other countries in the Southern Cone and several Brazilian states, is attempting with some success to transform the traditional, repression-based model of law enforcement into one based on accountability and citizen participation. Located in different parts of Latin America and with diverse economic and political structures, these countries demonstrate the extent to which the citizen security crisis is affecting the entire region. Despite differences among them, each of these cases highlight the conditions—public fear, short-term policies, and state ineffectiveness—that combine to inflame the citizen security crisis across Latin America.

Honduras: the Mano Dura

In countries such as Honduras, the crisis is characterized by a *mano dura* overshadowing democratic reform. It might have been otherwise. A poor Central American country emerging out of Cold War conflict, Honduras transferred public security authority from the armed forces to a newly created civilian police force in 1996, followed by new police laws in 1997. A new penal process code created oral trials, enhanced the powers of the *Fiscalía*, included alternative dispute resolution mechanisms such as mediation, and established new courts at the investigation and sentencing stages. Also enacted were judicial reforms such as creation of a judicial council to select most judicial personnel.

But the aggressive "zero tolerance" policy of President Ricardo Maduro, elected in 2002 on an anticrime campaign platform, has undermined these changes. The focus of his government's policy is youth gangs *(maras)*, who even police acknowledge commit less than a third of all crimes but are blamed for almost all of them. Anti-*mara* rhetoric saturates the media and— with high levels of approval from the public, the Honduran Congress, and the judiciary—dominates criminal legislation and law. The centerpiece of this policy is Provision 322, a penal code amendment punishing gang membership with up to twelve years of imprisonment. The 2002 Law of Police and Social Co-Existence gives the police vague powers to "control" people in certain areas and to detain "vagabonds"—people who lack an honest means of living.

These conflicting trends reflect the fundamental divide between constitutional rights and the iron fist underlying Latin America's citizen security crisis. Many Honduran gangs now shun tattoos and other evidence of gang membership, for example, which often leads prosecutors and judges to declare a lack of the higher level of proof required for conviction under the code. This reluctance to prosecute angers security officials, increasing the use of mass raids, forced confessions, preventative detention, and extrajudicial killing.[25] Declaring that the new code is excessively "guaranteeist," the minister of security says that its protections for the accused hinder the fight against crime and so should be scrapped.[26]

Citizen security and rights are also impeded by the poor preparation and funding for the police. The six months of training for cadets focuses on use of arms, with little legal or sociological education. Many police are functionally illiterate, are paid an inadequate average monthly salary of $225, and work long shifts in patrols with one vehicle in neighborhoods of up to 70,000 residents. Further impairing citizen security is poor investigation. About 90 percent of the police's budget goes to the Preventative Police, whose officers, while receiving practically no investigative training, pass themselves off as investigative police, intimidate witnesses, and fail to protect crime scenes. But the solution proposed by those state officials who acknowledge the problem is to give the police more autonomy—such as more than twenty-four hours to investigate a detainee. The lack of a centralized information network also impedes the formulation of a larger criminal policy. With the preventative police, investigative police, the morgue, and the judiciary all reporting different statistics on crimes as serious as homicide, long-term planning is impossible.

The accountability measures accompanying Honduras's security restructuring have also been weakened. Two of the main accountability agencies are the National Council of Interior Security (CONASIN: *Consejo Nacional de Seguridad Interior*), which advises the government on criminal policy, and the Internal Affairs Unit (UAI: *Unidad de Asuntos Internos*), which investigates wrongdoing. But CONASIN is rarely convened,[27] and when the Secretariat of Security was established in 1997, its control over law enforcement agencies led to "counter-reform . . . characterized by halting the process of purging corrupt officers and those involved in rights violations and in death squads."[28] Distrust between the Security Ministry's investigative police and the *Fiscalía*—which officially directs the police in criminal investigation— further obstructs citizen security. The UAI, meanwhile, has been weakened since its formation by deficient resources, unclear regulations, and rivalry with the Security Secretariat's Office of Professional Responsibility, which the new police law was supposed to eliminate.

But what has led to the most controversy is the UAI's investigation of youth killings. Most officials agree off the record with the estimate of over 1,600 extrajudicial killings of people under the age of twenty-three between 1999 and 2003, with about 39 percent of cases having evidence of police responsibility.[29] But when UAI chief María Luisa Borjas[30] implicated Security officials in at least twenty of these killings in September 2002, she began receiving death threats, her staff was cut, and, two months later, she was fired. Parallel investigations by *fiscales,* meanwhile, have lacked the institutional, political and legal support to instigate real change.[31]

As in many other countries, the drug war has further militarized the police and brought the police into regular policing. Since 2002, soldiers have been used in police sweeps and inundations of gang-controlled urban areas and in taking control of prison riots. Many of the 200 inmates who died in prison violence between 2003 and 2005 were killed by soldiers who came to restore order. No official has been found responsible.[32]

It is important to point out, however, that new policing strategies have helped to reduce crime in some areas. The national community policing program has used preventative strategies, such as regular community meetings and fixing street lights, to reduce homicides, robberies, and domestic violence in many of the country's most crime-ridden areas. In one notoriously dangerous San Pedro Sula barrio, for example, the murder rate has been cut in half.[33] There has been resistance by other police toward the program,[34] but of more serious concern are instances in which the program has served as a channel for abuse. The police official heading one of the more successful community policing programs was arrested for killing youth as part of an extermination squad, and the head of the citizen policing group describes how it attacks local delinquents.[35] Prosecutors and human rights commissioners believe that there have been thousands of unreported vigilante attacks since 2002.[36]

Bolivia: Continuities Amid Frustrated Reforms

Like countries such as Honduras, those in the Andean region face citizen security crises characterized by societal polarization, drug trafficking, and a lack of support for police and legal reforms attempted during the 1990s. In Bolivia, persistently high crime rates—including a homicide rate as high as 60 per 100,000 people since the 1982 democratic transition—has led to demands for crackdowns.[37] But amid sharp economic inequality, secessionist pressures, a violent coca eradication campaign, and protests that have brought down two presidents since 2003, public and political order must first be stabilized. Doing so, however, requires use of a police force that is one of the main causes of the crisis. Police strikes, in fact, instigated the violence that led to the ouster of President Gonzalo Sánchez de Lozada in October 2003. Twelve security plans have failed since 1990, and the security budget has nearly quintupled since 1990 without tangible results.[38] The depth of Bolivia's citizen security emergency is hardly in doubt: public opinion polls rank the police as the country's most (or second most) corrupt and untrustworthy institution, strikes by police officers have spurred larger political protests, and the force has proven incapable of exerting peaceful control during paralyzing political unrest.

By its own admission, the police have been responding toward an "ungrateful" population with "brutality, authoritarianism, and violence."[39] Police laws do not discuss human rights in sufficient detail, actions such as forced entries without a warrant are common, and many anti–drug trafficking statutes entrench discrimination against indigenous communities.[40] Despite an overhaul of the police academy to change the focus from physical preparation to law enforcement, the curriculum remains centered on the use of arms and control of social groups. And a great deal of violence has been perpetrated by police agencies and military-police operations created to carry out the anticoca campaign begun in 1998.[41] The Special Antinarcotics Force, the Rural Area Police Patrol Unit, the Joint Task Force, the Expeditionary Task Force, and other anticoca forces have carried out extrajudicial killings, mass detentions, and states of siege. Although this violence has led many of them to be downsized or removed from the coca-growing regions, they helped open up a rift in society that has spilled over into ongoing antigovernment unrest.

Mechanisms to hold the police accountable for such actions are weak. When trying to stop unconstitutional police actions like the use of clandestine agents, the *Defensoría del Pueblo,* Bolivia's main accountability agency, complains of being blocked by court ineffectiveness and government attacks for being on the "wrong" side of the division between human rights and citizen security.[42] Most other accusations against police go to the Office of Professional Responsibility (DNRP: *Dirección Nacional de Responsibilidad Profesional*), which investigates cases, and to the Superior Disciplinary Tribunal (TDS), which tries and disciplines the accused. Modification of the Disciplinary Code, higher budgets, and new due process guarantees have increased the number of TDS prosecutions.[43] The *Fiscalía*, meanwhile, has also tried more cases, including its first conviction of police generals in 2004. But aside from the few high-profile prosecutions, the vast majority of cases handled by the disciplinary system are for abandonment of posts among the poorly paid lower ranks. Reflecting the country's sharp ethnic and class divisions, these ranks are filled by the indigenous groups that comprise the majority of Bolivians.

As is the case elsewhere across the region, the criminal justice system—from police investigation to sentencing—is in bad shape. Within the police, a lack of equipment and the constant rotation of officials prevent development of expertise and stable management. Within the judiciary, the new 1999 Criminal Procedure Code (COPP), which replaced written with oral trials and put the *Fiscalía* in charge of investigations, has been backed by international funding and projects to increase public access. Yet the reform is not being implemented coherently. Unprepared prosecutors still use much of the old code, with a confusing mix of inquisitive and oral procedures, and police chiefs say their officers are not trained to follow new procedures of gathering evidence, interviewing suspects, and protecting crime scenes. The *Fiscalía* says it has "no control" over the police and that its access to information in criminal cases is "precarious."[44] Meanwhile, there are far too few public defenders to serve the many defendants who need them. As a result of these problems, only about one of every five cases is resolved.[45] Frustration with the criminal justice system has also fanned vigilantism in Bolivia, with over seventy documented lynchings since the late 1990s.

Police corruption represents a far more entrenched obstacle to reform. Since its transition to democracy in 1982, no fewer than eighteen police commanders have been forced out of office under accusations of criminal activity, cover-ups, torture, and extortion. For the lower ranks, the most common targets of corruption are indigenous people, street merchants, poor women, youth, community activists, and prison detainees. A lack of budget transparency sustains such activity. The police overcharge in procurement contracts, the retirement fund processes illicit funds, many officers of the Customs Police continue receiving salaries after being fired,[46] and only a fraction of the millions of dollars taken in by the Identification Agency through its handling of drivers' licenses and identification cards is transferred to the government.[47] This financial free reign allows the police to ignore state directives, rebuff repeated attempts to make accounting transparent,[48] and avoid public management laws.[49] As in most other Latin

American countries, favoritism in promotions perpetuates such corruption by advancing those who cooperate in it.

Argentina: Incipient Reforms

An incipient yet more promising set of responses to Latin America's citizen security crisis entails a turn toward alternative models. Like countries such as Chile, Uruguay, and Costa Rica, as well as many states in Brazil and Mexico, most of Argentina is trying to reorient its security systems from repression to accountability and citizen participation. But it is a daunting challenge to turn around practices of a police force that has carried out repressive policies of both democratic and military regimes throughout Argentina's history. Despite personnel purges, new rights guarantees, stronger discipline, and other reforms after the 1983 democratic transition, the twenty-four provincial police forces and the federal police (PFA: *Policía Federal Argentina*) enjoyed continuity in both structure and authority. As crime doubled and violent crimes rose 65 percent between 1990 and 2000—while the poverty rate shot up from 22 to 43 percent in tandem with record levels of unemployment and inequality—so did public demands for a *mano dura*.[50] But rising crime also exposed police ineffectiveness and violence. In the city of Buenos Aires, where the PFA enforces the law, well over half of all police actions were misdemeanor detentions, allowed by pre-1983 edicts, while one out of every four killings were committed by a police officer.

In provinces where these and other futile *mano dura* tactics combined with exposure of police violence and corruption, the public began to support efforts to bring the police in line. In Buenos Aires Province, then-governor and presidential hopeful Eduardo Duhalde overhauled the province's notoriously violent and corrupt police in 1997. It was divided into functional divisions and decentralized into the province's judicial departments, each accountable to the province's civilian secretary of justice and security. Also established were a bicameral security commission, a new penal process code, and citizen forums at the community, municipal, and department levels. Regrettably, within a few years, the reform collapsed under the pressures of climbing crime rates, police resistance, and opposition to it by Duhalde's successor,[51] who promised "bullets for murderers" in his campaign and, after taking office, widened police powers and appointed a right-wing former military official as chief of security.

The failure of this approach to stem crime or police corruption, however, has brought a return to reform in Buenos Aires—under the same architect as the 1997 measures. This latest initiative, with support from the federal government's national security plan, focuses on community policing. It includes creating community police in ninety-five cities with chiefs elected by citizen forums and under the orders of the mayor. The mayors of several towns have used this power not only to alter police structure, but also to expand programs for troubled youth and other marginalized groups. Citizen forums will also be in charge of police promotions, based not on seniority but on efficiency. The new plan also includes creation of a special force for high-crime areas and another focusing on organized crime. Similar developments are taking place in other provinces, including many that embraced *mano dura* in the 1990s. In Mendoza, where comprehensive police reform in 1999 was modeled after that in Buenos Aires and faced a similar backlash, many community policing programs are once again being adopted. One high-crime municipality has a series of programs, designed by citizen committees, that target youth truancy, after-hours alcohol sales, and other specific causes of insecurity.[52] Santa Fe, Misiones, Córdoba, Chubut, and other provinces are forming or reforming citizen security councils and alternative dispute resolution mechanisms, while the province of La Rioja is restructuring its entire police force based on a community policing model.

Admittedly, this approach has not yet prevailed over the *mano dura* in Argentina. After a massive rally in April 2004, for example, the national congress approved a battery of measures to toughen penal law. In Mendoza province, where the accountability agencies and citizen forums created by recent reform are starved of resources, the provincial legislature passed seventeen *mano dura* laws in a single afternoon without any substantial debate. The prison system remains inhumane and overcrowded throughout the country, and politicians continue to tread carefully when discussing civil rights.

As Argentina and other countries show, efforts to address Latin America's citizen security crisis are often weaker than the obstacles in their way. The resulting lack of progress is undermining democracy throughout the region.

Free elections and constitutional rule are no longer sufficient for the survival of Latin America's democratic regimes; they must also demonstrate efficacy on fundamental responsibilities such as public safety. But citizens are becoming increasingly disillusioned with the empty promises and endless debates on crime that they are associating with democracy, drawing unfavorable comparisons with military regimes regarded, if nothing else, as able to maintain order. Crime is also weakening constitutionalism. With their control over the security apparatus and the political agenda, executives push policies through legislatures and the judiciary, throwing off the balance of power between the three branches of government. Constitutional guarantees are also being eroded, with most human rights abuses—from killings on the street to due process violations in the courts and inhumane conditions in the prisons—occurring within the criminal justice system. Perhaps more troubling still, as citizens arm themselves and turn against each other more often than they organize for reform, crime is debilitating the kind of civil society that supports due process and equality.

At the same time, however, democracy provides the most viable solutions. Citizen security cannot improve without popular participation, transparency in police operations, adherence to human rights standards, and social services for marginalized sectors—all of which are possible only under democratic government. So while many of Latin America's attempts to improve citizen security may not overcome obstacles in the short run, the advances under democracy—such as fairer and faster legal codes, more accountable police structures, and community-based projects—should prove to be more durable in the long run.

9

The Politics of Memory, the Languages of Human Rights

Katherine Hite

[H]uman rights must become a language not of compromise and a phony reconciliation, but instead the means to pursue a well-defined political will guided by a program of social justice.
—Richard Wilson, *The Politics of Truth and Reconciliation in South Africa: Legitimizing the Post-Apartheid State*

Today virtually no Latin American state or society escapes the challenges of having to "come to terms" with haunting memories of recent and not-so-recent pasts. While countries throughout the region have undergone major transitions from regimes that systematically and massively violated human rights, there is no such thing as closure on mass atrocities, no matter how distant the brutality. For many individuals, families, and communities, the violent and enormous loss of life renders reconciling such losses remote—as many as 30,000 dead and disappeared in Argentina, close to 70,000 in Peru, approximately 200,000 in Guatemala alone. What does it mean to be "reconciled" with the rape and disappearance of a daughter, the cold-blooded murder of a brother, the burning of a town hall with dozens of children forcibly trapped inside? Traumatic memories of human rights abuse do not simply fade away.

Calls to remember atrocious pasts and to bring perpetrators to justice raise other pressing concerns, including the very immediate problems of ongoing violence and social injustice—police brutality, high crime rates, political corruption, and social inequality. Impunity for past human rights violations may very well signal impunity for perpetrators of violence in the present. The overwhelming majority of human rights victims come from societies' poorest sectors. Demands to right past injustices invariably shade into demands for social justice in the here and now.

The politics of memory and coming to terms with human rights violations of the past pose a range of important analytical questions or problems. Drawing primarily from Argentina, Chile, Guatemala, and Peru, this chapter will explore what political purposes memory debates serve, including how processes and policies that address past human rights violations might contribute to facilitating democratic praxis. Ideally, democracies are those in which citizens confront and debate their painful pasts free from fear of reprisal. Memory politics can conceivably promote greater understandings of cultural and political difference as well as acknowledgment of injustices. Yet, as will be discussed here, explorations of painful memories have proved constrained. Fear often pervades discussion of the past in ways that champion the victors, privilege the powerful, silence voice, and discourage debate. Moreover, politicians have become increasingly adept at manipulating memory debates toward ends that serve their own agendas as well as repress cultural and political difference. To reconcile—or what anthropologist John Borneman has termed "to render [former enemies] no longer opposed"— proves exceedingly difficult and multi-layered.[1]

TRUTH TELLING

Policy proposals for coming to terms with human rights violations of the past, or so-called "retroactive justice" policies, have generally included investigative commissions (commonly known as "truth commissions"), trials for accused violators, compensation for victims and their families (like monthly stipends and educational scholarships), and symbolic reparations in such forms as public memorials or protection from obligatory military service for victims' family members. The reaches and limits of retroactive justice policies arguably mirror leaders' and societies' perceptions of the degree of actual authority that can be exercised over human rights–violating incumbents and their accomplices.

Government-sponsored truth-telling processes are largely symbolic exercises to produce official and societal acknowledgment of past atrocities and to drive home the message of *nunca más,* never again. In the wake of a brutal military regime (1976–82), Argentina's transitional government established a truth commission that would become an important model for the region. Argentine president Raúl Alfonsín (1983–89) appointed a blue-ribbon panel, the National Commission on the Disappearance of People (CONADEP), headed by well-known novelist Ernesto Sábato, to lead the investigatory process. Survivors of human rights abuse, families of human rights abuse victims, and human rights organizations provided testimony and documentation. In 1984, CONADEP rendered a major report, *Nunca Más,* that attempted to order, temporalize, organize, educate, and suggest an understanding of Argentina's painful national past. The commission also provided a series of institutional reform recommendations to attempt to ensure against future human rights abuses. *Nunca Más* became an immediate bestseller, and its perceived success as an official symbolic document influenced subsequent truth commission designs in the region and elsewhere.

Nevertheless, government-orchestrated (and in the cases of El Salvador and Guatemala, United Nations–orchestrated) processes of truth telling are fraught with debate over political intent: What truths should be privileged and what downplayed? Where should remembering begin? Should testimonies be private or public? Can witnesses be subpoenaed? How will findings be deployed? Truth-telling designs have significant political implications— some anticipated, but some, like the irruptions of memories themselves, unanticipated.[2]

Anthropologist Richard Wilson argues that government-sponsored truth commissions attempt to craft narratives of the past that render the present more governable, that "manufacture bureaucratic legitimacy" for the state.[3] At first glance, such would appear to be the case for the truth commissions of Chile (1991) and Peru (2003), both of which include the term "reconciliation" in their official titles, suggesting an intention to build consensus and foster national unity. The United Nations–sponsored Guatemalan truth commission, in contrast, defines itself as a body for "historical clarification," explicit in its intent to examine long histories of violence and injustice that make even the concept of reconciliation more distant.

Chilean president Patricio Aylwin (1990–94), the country's first elected leader in the wake of the seventeen-year military regime, set the democratic leadership agenda by placing the need "to clarify the truth and do justice to the subject of human rights, as a moral exigency unavoidable for reconciliation" at the top of his five-point program of governmental tasks. As in Argentina, the Aylwin government established a blue-ribbon truth commission charged with responsibility for investigating the details of deaths and disappearances (though not those who were tortured and survived) under the dictatorship. Denied the powers of subpoena, the commission worked behind closed doors and gathered documentation from families whose loved ones had been executed or disappeared. Commissioners and staff also drew amply from the previous work and documentation of several Chilean human rights organizations, as well as from political parties and labor unions that provided lists of their dead and disappeared members.

In 1991, after working for six months, Chile's Truth and Reconciliation Commission ultimately produced a succinct interpretation of the country's past as well as a series of recommendations for reparations to victims' families and for establishing a "human rights culture" in Chile. In an illustration of the political importance of how the past is temporalized, the report's telling of history begins with the Cold War, the Cuban Revolution, and Chile's political insertion in this world and regional context.[4] The first Chilean group upon whom the report focuses is the MIR (Revolutionary Left Movement), founded in 1965 as a Cuba-inspired group that advocated socialist transformation through violence if necessary. The report then describes the broader Chilean left and its many factions and the ways revolutionary discourse contributed to political polarization, intensifying toward its final consequences in the overthrow of the leftist Popular Unity administration of Salvador Allende (1970–73).

The choice to frame the violence in a Cold War context, in which a national radical left arose, is deliberate. Despite the fact that all state-sponsored repression, all systematic human rights abuse, including deaths and disappearances, occurred under the dictatorship and not before, commissioners determined it was in the interest of national reconciliation to begin with the radical left, to locate a context that appeased the powerful Chilean right. The commission did emphasize that political polarization between the left and right by no means justified the right-wing dictatorship's aim to eliminate the left.

The commission provided specific documentation of those who had been executed and disappeared, and it made a series of recommendations regarding compensation for victims' families. Citing the need to leave judgment of guilt or innocence to the courts, the commission did not publicly name known human rights violators. Rather, the commission viewed its role as providing meticulous documentation of the most heinous abuses, a sound methodological approach, a series of guidelines and recommendations to ensure against such violations in the future, and an account of the "deterioration" of a political consensus that had been a hallmark of Chilean democracy. Interestingly, while the commission was careful to provide definitions of human rights norms and the violations of those norms, the report did not provide a definition of "reconciliation" as a concept.

In a publicly televised speech, President Aylwin thanked the commissioners, who came from both the center-left and right of the political spectrum, for their work, and he issued an emotional public apology as head of the state to all the victims of human rights violations. Aylwin exhorted the military to cooperate voluntarily and the judiciary to assume a proactive human rights–minded agenda toward reconciliation, neither of which was forthcoming under his tenure. Three weeks after the public release of the report and Aylwin's appeals, leftist extremists assassinated the outspoken right-wing leader and Senator Jaime Guzmán, a political and legal architect of the Pinochet regime. The Chilean right successfully used Guzmán's assassination to stymie efforts to engage the public in a collective exploration of Chile's past.

In Guatemala, the 1999 UN-sponsored Historical Clarification Commission (CEH) report produced documentation and analysis that could very well lead to outcomes the military had expected to avoid. In 1994, the

Guatemalan military ostensibly settled for a truth commission that would be, in the words of Guatemalan defense minister Mario Enriquez, "Just like in Chile: truth, but no trials,"[5] which was certainly the case for Chile at that time. Moreover, the Guatemalan military insisted that the CEH agree to conduct an investigation into the past that would not name individuals responsible for the killings.

CEH staff members traversed the Guatemalan countryside and gathered over 8,000 testimonies from their own interviewing and from the work of well-known Guatemalan human rights and indigenous rights groups. In fact, the CEH built upon a truth-telling model and report developed as a project of the Guatemalan Catholic Church, known as "the Recovery of Historical Memory" (REMHI). The model was based on a sensitive, careful drawing-out of victims' testimonies, emphasizing the notion of a "restorative history" that recognized the agency and meaning of survival amid such long-standing violent conditions.[6] The risk of providing testimony and documentation itself took on new meaning when, in April 1998, two days after the release of the REMHI report, the director of the REMHI project, Bishop Juan Gerardi, was assassinated. His murder brought significant attention to the atrocities continuing to take place with impunity in Guatemala, and REMHI project members proved instrumental to the CEH process.

The CEH staff included diplomats, social workers, anthropologists, historians, and others, both Guatemalan and foreign. The result was a report that reached deep into the history of unequal and racist social, cultural, and political relations in the country. Entitled *Memory of Silence*, the report provided evidence of systematic patterns of military and security forces abuse, including dozens of massacres in indigenous communities throughout the rural highlands. The CEH estimated that, under the thirty-six years of Guatemalan military reign and armed conflict, the vast majority, over 93 percent, of the 200,000 killed were civilians murdered by the military and state security agencies, while the remaining were killed by guerrillas.[7] It concluded that the scorched earth tactics of General Efraín Rios Montt (1981–83) constituted genocide, a crime not covered by Guatemala's 1996 Amnesty Law. Guatemalan indigenous activist and Nobel Peace Prize winner Rigoberta Menchú used the CEH report in her launching of a case against Rios Montt in Spanish court.

In a certain sense, the task of the Peruvian Truth and Reconciliation Commission (CVR) proved far more complicated than that of the Chilean or Guatemalan one. In contrast to Chile, Peru experienced systematic human rights violations under three democratically elected presidents from distinct political parties and alliances (Fernando Belaúnde from 1980 to 1985, Alan García from 1985 to 1990, and Alberto Fujimori from 1990 to 2000), each confronted with a powerful and extremely violent guerrilla movement, the Shining Path. While the Guatemalan truth commission confronted a context of internal armed conflict in which human rights abuses were committed on both sides, the Guatemalan insurgency was far weaker than the Shining Path, and human rights abuses in the Guatemalan case were overwhelmingly committed by the state. In Peru, by contrast, both state security forces and guerrillas committed massive abuses, and, as in Guatemala, the vast majority of the atrocities took place in the highlands against the indigenous. In addition, local and regional indigenous communities organized self-defense committees—at times in collaboration with state security forces, but often not—who fought the Shining Path and killed suspected Shining Path militants and collaborators. Other indigenous groups joined the Shining Path. The CVR thus faced the formidable task of investigating a range of cases in which local and national elected politicians were implicated in repression and denial, and in which members of the indigenous communities collaborated in the killings. In addition, the commission was charged not only with investigating the abuses during the major internal armed conflict (1980–93), but also with documenting President Fujimori's increasing abuse of power after militarily defeating the guerrilla movement (1993–2000).

Influenced in part by the South African Truth and Reconciliation Commission, the CVR conceptualized its mission as one of (1) promoting reconciliation through extensive documentation and analysis of two decades of violent conflict; (2) close attention to communities that had been the most directly affected by the conflict; (3) nationally televised public hearings (though unlike the South African process, no one could be granted amnesty in exchange for truth telling); and (4) detailed recommendations of the institutional reforms deemed necessary to facilitate reconciliation and prevent future conflict. Peruvian and international anthropologists played key roles in communicating the CVR's mission to indigenous villages and in gathering testimonies. To demonstrate their commitment to investigating abuses in the highlands, truth commissioners bore witness to several mass exhumations.

The Peruvian commission produced a nine-volume report that addressed the range of perpetrators and facilitators of violence at the national, regional, and local levels, from state security forces to elected local and national officials, political parties, vigilante groups, and guerrillas—all implicated, according to the CVR, to one degree or another in the violence that had wrought the country. In its summary volume, the commission provided a discussion of the concept of reconciliation and its components. The CVR defined reconciliation as "a process of reestablishment and recasting of fundamental ties among Peruvians . . . [that] has three dimensions: (1) the political dimension, involving a reconciliation between the State and society, and between political parties, the State and society; (2) the social dimension, encompassing reconciliation of civil society institutions and public spaces with society as a whole, with special consideration for marginalized ethnic groups; and (3) the interpersonal dimension, involving members of communities or institutions who found themselves in conflict."[8] Underlying this concept of reconciliation was the recognition that the twenty-year conflict had violently weakened, and in many cases destroyed, communal trust, that responsibility for the violence had to be shared, and that reconciliation required multiethnic, multilingual, pluricultural, and ecumenical sensitivity.

From the outset, the CVR report sparked (and continues to spark) important debate. The report challenged Peru's largely urban middle class to address the structural marginalization of the countryside and, inherently, the racist general character toward indigenous populations. It criticized the failure of a range of political parties and leaders to stem the waves of human rights abuse by both the military and the Shining Path. In response, beginning in August 2005—on the second anniversary of the release of the report—criticism of the CVR escalated. Politicians scapegoated the commission for contributing to ongoing discord. Those on the right denounced the CVR for condemning the military, which the right claimed saved the country from the Shining Path. Politicians on the left questioned the framing of the report as one in which the security forces were only reacting to a growing guerrilla threat while established political party leaders across the spectrum failed the country.[9] In addition, commentators both left and right have raised questions about how the CVR calculated the number of dead, claiming the figure of 69,000 was too high.[10]

In spite of the intense criticism of the CVR, the Peruvian report has proved a catalyst for ongoing dialogue, fueled by educational institutions, an active press, and a range of nongovernmental organizations that include both vibrant human rights advocacy groups and think tanks. Many question left-wing political party failures to denounce guerrilla abuses, as well as both the left's and right's lukewarm defense of democracy during the 1980s and 1990s. Analysts have also signaled the ways in which the report demonstrated the lack of civilian expertise regarding questions of security, counterinsurgency, and the military as institution.[11]

There are thus unanticipated dimensions of truth commission reports that can hardly be considered symbolic. Spanish judge Baltasar Garzón used the Chilean truth commission report to build his path-breaking case against former Chilean dictator Augusto Pinochet. The Guatemalan truth commission charge of genocide opens up the possibility of prosecuting violators in national, regional, and international courts. The Peruvian Truth and Reconciliation Report proved a major catalyst for exhumations at the sites of reported massacres, and, like the Guatemalan report, it helped lay the groundwork for prosecutions of major human rights violators.

RETROACTIVE JUSTICE AND DEMOCRATIC-INSTITUTION BUILDING

Truth-telling processes are related to justice, or "accountability," issues: Are trials of persecutors feasible or advisable? Will the convicted be punished? Should amnesties be considered, and if so, under what conditions? In countries with weak or fragile political institutions, including countries in transition from military rule, political analysts disagree over the relationship between strengthening democratic institutions and implementing retroactive justice policies. On the one hand, it would seem self-evident that a country devoted to democracy and the rule of law would seek to investigate past wrongdoings and hold its citizens accountable for human rights crimes. Ar-

gentina, for example, became the first (and only) democratizing regime in
Latin America to put all nine of the country's former military junta leaders
on trial for the murders and disappearances of scores of the country's citizens during the 1976–83 dictatorship.

On the other hand, telling the whole truth and nothing but the truth and
holding former repressors accountable are easier said than done, particularly when former violators and their supporters remain powerful political
actors. Unlike the discredited Argentine military that, in addition to a record
of systematic human rights violations, left in its wake a disastrous economy
and a military defeat in the Falkland Islands by the British, the armed forces
in countries in transition like Chile and Guatemala continued to wield enormous power and autonomy, refusing to cooperate with truth commissions
and vetoing prosecutions of its members for human rights violations. For
countries in transition from authoritarian rule, in which military institutions
exercise major prerogatives, retroactive justice policies arguably place the
transition at risk.[12] In Peru, mass atrocities took place under popularly
elected administrations that granted the military and security forces carte
blanche in their war against the Shining Path. Elected politicians ignored
human rights groups' condemnations of the massive abuse, and many politicians were implicated in mass repression and denial. These realities discourage the domestic pursuit of aggressive retroactive justice policies.

Yet democratic political regimes bear a moral responsibility for conduct-
ing retroactive justice policies, and postponing or evading retroactive justice
projects further weakens the legitimacy of democratic institutions. For example, only days after the UN-sponsored truth commission in El Salvador released its report condemning dozens of military and civilian human rights
violators and urging they be held accountable, the Salvadoran government
passed a sweeping general amnesty law. Many argue that the continued high
level of violent crimes in El Salvador, from gang-related violence to kidnapping rings, is inextricably linked to consistent patterns of impunity for former violators.[13] In addition, systematic impunity for human rights violators
can cause significant sectors of society to de-link from the new regime, exac-
erbating public skepticism toward democratic legitimacy.

Retroactive justice policies can be politically efficacious. Purging the primary civilian and military institutions of close adherents to previous human rights–violating regimes can serve to remove institutional obstacles that block the effective functioning of new regimes. Moreover, new regimes can take advantage of the opportunity to demonstrate their strength and distance their autonomy from individuals and institutions of the past. By establishing a dramatic break with the violence of the previous regime through aggressive retroactive justice measures, reformist elites can earn political legitimacy and avoid a premature *desencanto,* or disenchantment, with democratic institutions.

Nevertheless, prosecution of former human rights violators has arguably become the most far-reaching in those countries that have achieved a comfortable degree of democratic political stability. Generational turnover within the military and the judiciary, international pressure and action against former repressors, and continuing demands from the grass roots facilitate the possibilities of due process. The Argentine and Chilean cases demonstrate that legislating closure on mass atrocity ultimately does little to deter demands for truth and accountability and can prove unviable as national and international political and legal contexts shift.

In Argentina both during and after the precedent-setting trials of the former military junta leaders in 1985, the Alfonsín government (1983–89) faced small-scale military rebellions by officers protesting military budget reductions, forced retirements of generals, and continued prosecutions of the many military officials implicated in the human rights violations. Argentines massively condemned the rebellions, urging the government to stay the course. Nevertheless, in 1986 and 1987, Alfonsín successfully proposed legislation that both put a deadline on court case filings by the families of the victims (known as the Full Stop Law) and protected officers who could claim they were following orders (known as the Due Obedience Law).

In addition to military rustlings, economic instability plagued Alfonsín's administration, and many analysts and advisers counseled the need to "turn the page" on the past to address inflation, unemployment, and fiscal crisis. In fact, much of the conventional wisdom of the 1980s asserted that the lesson of Argentina's ambitious retroactive justice policies—trials and convictions of the generals, continued investigations and prosecutions of other human rights violators, and compensation for the victims—were too costly for a redemocratizing regime facing a host of political, social, and economic challenges. In 1989, Alfonsín left the presidency amid continued military rebellion and economic crisis.

Shortly after assuming office, Argentine president Carlos Menem (1989–99) struck a deal with the military that decreed pardons for all those who had been convicted in return for an end to military uprisings. It was a severe blow to human rights victims. Yet the human rights movement, other important civil society groups, and key members of the judiciary refused to accept the constitutionality of closing the books on human rights criminality under the dictatorship. Through the 1990s, human rights groups, journalists, and judges focused on crimes excluded from the Due Obedience Law, particularly those involving abductions of children of the disappeared, to press for new convictions. By 2000, four of the formerly pardoned junta leaders and dozens of lower-ranking officers had been charged and imprisoned for child kidnapping and illegal adoption. In 2005, first the Argentine Congress and Senate and then the Argentine Supreme Court revoked the previous amnesty laws that had protected the military from prosecution for violations.

Carlos Nino, the late Argentine legal theorist and chief architect of Alfonsín's human rights policies, claimed that retroactive justice strengthened "the moral consciousness of society . . . [to] help overcome the corporatism, anomie, and concentration of power that all too long have been hallmarks of Argentine society."[14] While Nino recognized the Argentine process as imperfect, such imperfections, he argued, came from an administration that had attempted to conduct a truth and accountability process precisely within the letter of the law to reinforce the legitimacy of the historic Argentine constitution. Nino charged that those within the scholarly community who opposed retroactive justice based their arguments primarily on short-term political self-interest, failing to recognize the contribution of retroactive justice efforts to an epistemic democratic community.

From the outset of his term, Argentine president Néstor Kirchner (2003–present) embraced a platform of coming to terms with the atrocities of the past. Among several symbolic-discursive acts, Kirchner announced that a military training school, the Escuela Mecánica de la Armada (ESMA), once a notorious center of torture and forced disappearance, would be converted into a museum of memory. Himself a product of a generation of persecuted young leftists under the dictatorship, Kirchner has attempted to claim a moral high ground by championing measures to lay forth Argentina's painful past and hold its chief architects accountable.

In Chile, former dictator General Augusto Pinochet is now internationally discredited as a crook as well as a human rights violator, and after more than a decade of reticence to confront the many violent dimensions of the dictatorship, Chilean courts and politicians began to advocate an aggressive range of retroactive justice policies. Since Pinochet's London arrest in 1998—a full twenty years after the 1978 military-decreed amnesty law—Chilean courts have prosecuted more than 300 military officers for human rights violations. In 2004, based on more than 20,000 testimonies, the Chilean executive issued a lengthy report on systematic torture practices under the dictatorship, and the government established a set of compensation policies for former torture victims. In fact, current Chilean president Michelle Bachelet is herself a former political prisoner and the daughter of a constitutional general who died in a Pinochet cell.

Nevertheless, while memory politics have dramatically shifted in Chile over the past decade and a half, it is by no means a linear process. Chilean president Ricardo Lagos (2000–2006), a Socialist leader who served in the Justice Ministry during the Allende government, inexplicably issued a presidential pardon to the convicted murderer of Tucapel Jiménez, a prominent Christian Democratic labor leader assassinated in 1982 on his way to a planning meeting for a national strike against the dictatorship. Lagos also supported discussion of legislation to establish a full stop law similar to the one that was ultimately revoked in Argentina. The grassroots, nongoverning Chilean left linked these stances to what it claimed was a governing left quite distant from social justice concerns both past and present.

In contrast to the concerns and anxieties of the 1980s and 1990s transition periods, neither the Argentine nor the Chilean regime fears that retroactive justice policies will prove destabilizing today. Both cases attest to the fitful yet persistent process of memory politics. On the other hand, in

Peru, retroactive justice proceeds amid ongoing political volatility and intimidation. Luís Alberto Ramírez, a man who had given testimony against a general and three other high military officials, was shot and wounded twice in front of his home. He took temporary refuge in Chile, but he, his wife, and their children were followed and photographed in Santiago, and they returned to Lima to live under police protection.[15] Head of the Peruvian Truth and Reconciliation Commission Salomón Lerner also received several death threats, threats that seemed to coincide with the significant rise in prosecutions (378 as of October 2005) of human rights violators, both military and civilian.

Amnesty International titled one of its 2003 reports on Guatemala *Deep Cause for Concern*. The report noted that in spite of concerted efforts among local, national, and international human rights groups with extensive UN support, politically related violence had risen sharply in ways all too reminiscent of patterns in the armed conflict years.[16] After the 1996 Guatemalan government endorsement of the Peace Accords, indigenous and ladino human rights advocates and legal human rights defenders had been murdered, paramilitary groups were continuing to operate, and the many institutional reforms established by the Peace Accords appeared a distant dream. Prosecutions in two well-known cases—the murder of Bishop Gerardi and the murder of anthropologist Myrna Mack—have taken place, albeit amid tremendous uncertainty regarding possible appeals as well as the unknown whereabouts of Mack's convicted killer, Colonel Juan Valencia Osorio, Guatemala's only senior officer to be convicted for human rights violations. In the course of the investigation into Gerardi's assassination, seven witnesses were killed, while six witnesses, two prosecutors, and one judge fled the country.

MEMORY DISCOURSE

As collective memory pioneer Maurice Halbwachs emphasized, individual and collective memories of the past are subject to—are at the service of—the present. What gets publicly voiced is contingent upon both the political dynamics in a given time and place and the intersubjective dynamics of human relationships and exchange. Halbwachs underestimated the many competing narratives that challenge a notion of unitary nationally inscribed collective memories, or master narratives, but he did signal the fluidity of memory in relation to local and national identity imperatives. In addition, there are psychoanalytic and psychosocial cultural traditions that both privilege and downplay public expression of memory or that "out" memories in quite varied ways.

For example, scholars of Argentina claim that it is no coincidence that the country has its share of notorious human rights violators who have publicly laid bare memories of atrocities they themselves have committed. The most well-known case is that of retired navy captain Francisco Scilingo, who confessed to Argentine journalist Horacio Verbitsky his role in such acts as dumping naked bodies from airplanes over the south Atlantic. In a country with a strong psychoanalytic tradition, Scilingo claims his need to confess is a product of his posttraumatic stress disorder, and that he can no longer repress his unconscious.[17] Scilingo's confession served to resuscitate grassroots efforts to hold former human rights violators accountable for their actions. Argentina is also the site of HIJOS, a group of children of the disappeared whose chief action has been to out former violators.

HIJOS inspired a similar group in Chile, in a political and cultural milieu that was arguably more repressive, more self-censuring. In Chile, fear and anxiety marked much of the 1990s. After seventeen years of dictatorship and a largely military-directed transition, it was clear that the democratic political leadership was fearful of a still powerful military and its equally powerful authoritarian supporters. In a country with a highly institutionalized political party system, the fact that the leadership retreated from memory politics relegated memory debates to the margins. Public opinion polls often indicated that "human rights" was low on the list of daily concerns, yet memoirs and other written as well as documentary, feature film, and theatrical accounts of the repressive past were consumed avidly. It would take events largely outside the country as well as shifts within the Chilean judiciary and military to open political space for public explorations of the past. Symbolically embracing this new space, Chile's president Michelle Bachelet began her administration in March 2006 with a host of public actions to commemorate victims of

the Pinochet dictatorship, from her own father who died as a political prisoner of Pinochet to three human rights advocates and Chilean Communist
Party militants whose throats were slit by state security forces in 1985. In a
moving opening of a memorial to the *degollados* (the "slit throats"), Bachelet
broke from presidential protocol to deliver an account of her personal devas-
tation over the murders of the three men. Bachelet named Estela Ortiz, a
widow of one of the three men, to head a national preschool program.

While calls to remember atrocious pasts have been consistently embraced
by sectors of the grass roots, there is also a considerable desire to forget. This
desire is not limited to the political elite, for whom resurrecting painful pasts
can prove contentious and costly. The wish to forget can also be heard from
communities most directly affected by armed conflict, including formerly
displaced families who lost loved ones and who are uncertain they can return
either physically to their former communities or mentally and spiritually to
their memories of violence and loss.

In their studies of communities in Ayacucho, Peru, the region in which
most confrontations between the military and the Shining Path occurred,
scholars Ponciano del Pino and Kimberly Theidon reveal a pattern of narra-
tion in indigenous accountings of the recent past they have termed "toxic
memory." Toxic memory emerges from experiences of intense, direct violence within a community for which there is no recourse, no possibility of social justice nor remorse from the perpetrators. According to Theidon, "The
forms of violence suffered *and* practiced influence the reconstruction
process when the fighting subsides. The fratricidal nature of Peru's internal
armed conflict means that in any given community, ex-*Senderistas,* current
sympathizers, widows, orphans, and veterans live side-by-side. This is a
volatile social landscape. It is a mixture of victims and perpetrators . . ."[18]
Theidon argues that the military-led counterinsurgency strategy that allowed
Shining Path militants to return to their villages without the requirement
that they make reparations or apologize is tantamount to losing the political-
ideological and moral battle with the Shining Path.[19] Public memory debates
in such settings are explicitly constrained by the knowledge of what violence
particular agents are capable of exacting and by power dynamics that make
no guarantees that such violence will be prevented in the future.

In addition, the proliferation of truth commissions, memory debates, and the like can be interpreted as a sign of leaders striving for credibility in this new world of human rights–speak and truth talk. In contrast to an earlier period in which political leaders attempted to "move on," to "turn the page" on painful memories, politicians are increasingly resorting to political manipulations of memory, championing explorations of the past, instrumentalizing memory to serve their agendas or enhance their status. Politicians have found that talk can be cheap. In the 2000 elections in Mexico, for example, president-elect Vicente Fox made a commitment to reopen state files to investigate past human rights abuses by the state under former president Luis Echeverría. It was clear that Fox championed this commitment to symbolize that his leadership was a major break from the past. Fox also had a team of advisers that included former university student organizers for whom the 1968 and 1971 massacres were direct experiences.

In an attempt to defend and bolster himself and curry favor with the Peruvian military, former Peruvian president Alan García (1985–90) resurrected the all-too-recent memory of the militarily defeated Shining Path as a haunting presence and ongoing threat. During his term in office, García gave the military virtually unchecked authority to wage a counterinsurgency campaign against the Shining Path. In a rather miraculous comeback from his presidential record of gross economic and security mismanagement and corruption, García returned to the country after several years to reclaim his party's mantle. The former president asserted that to hold the armed forces accountable for their counterinsurgency tactics "plays into the hands" of the Shining Path.[20] García charged that the Shining Path might have been "militarily but not politically defeated and therefore looks for ruses to present itself as a victim."[21] This assertion exacerbates the anxieties that are clearly felt in many of the indigenous communities most hit by the violence of the 1980s.

Peruvian human rights groups continue to press for García himself to be held accountable for massive abuses under his stewardship, including the death of 118 inmates during a 1986 military action to reassume authority after a prison revolt at El Frontón prison. While the ex–commander in chief of the armed forces testified that he received orders from García to attack the

prison, the former president has yet to be prosecuted. Ayacucho special prosecutor Cristina Olazábal sought prosecution of García for the assassination
of sixty-nine peasants in Accomarca, but Olazábal was accused of political
motives for seeking the former president's prosecution.

Over many years in Guatemala, powerful state officials—both civilian and
military—have become experts at rhetorical commitment to human rights
while human rights abuses continue apace, and in some cases escalate.
Shortly after President Alfonso Portillo (2000–2004) appointed a commission in 2003 to investigate illegal armed groups and clandestine security organizations, attacks against human rights defenders rose sharply. Portillo's
successor, President Oscar Berger, issued the first public statement on behalf
of the Guatemalan state acknowledging both the state's responsibility and
denial of justice in the 1990 Myrna Mack murder case, while threats against
the Myrna Mack Foundation increased. In May 2004, while facing charges of
genocide as well as a range of other crimes, former president Efraín Rios
Montt was placed under house arrest, yet he managed to host an elaborate
wedding party for his daughter, attended by U.S. Ambassador John Hamilton. Rios Montt is today both a popular politician and an ordained minister
of the Gospel Outreach/Verbo evangelical church, based in California. The
same man who preaches the gospel and clean living authored scorched-earth
tactics responsible for thousands of deaths.

Some of the most hard hit and formerly displaced indigenous communities in both Peru and Guatemala have sought a re-foundational communal
identity through evangelism. According to one seminal study of the community of Uchuraccay, Peru, the site of the massacre of eight Peruvian journalists
in 1983, the village had one evangelical family before the violence. Little
more than a decade later, close to half the population of the area in which this
community is a part self-identifies as evangelical.[22] Moreover, the villagers of
Uchuraccay have developed narratives that constitute re-foundational identities for their community and that distinguish their understandings of the
massacre of the journalists from those of the families of the journalists themselves. While the families of the journalists remember and commemorate January 26 as the day their loved ones were killed, the villagers of Uchuraccay
remember July 16 and December 24, 1983, as days they were attacked by the

Shining Path, and they do not recognize January 26. For those of Uchuraccay, October 10 has become a celebratory date marking their return to the community after years of displacement.[23]

CONCLUSION

Throughout Latin America, from Uruguay to Brazil, Chile, and Argentina, government actors—both military and civilian—who assumed they had largely shut the books on human rights violations under the dictatorships they replaced now accept that they were shortsighted and naïve. As part of the "unfinished business" of peace in El Salvador and Guatemala, forensic teams' continuous unearthing of mass graves suggests that in spite of the fact that holding perpetrators accountable has thus far proved elusive, evidence for mass atrocities will not go away and neither, therefore, will calls for due process.

Declassified documents in Mexico resurrected officially unacknowledged state-perpetrated massacres in 1968 and 1971, as well as politically motivated assassinations throughout the 1970s—Mexico's "dirty war"—forcing a public revisiting of atrocious pasts all these years later. Declassified documents in the United States laid bare the reach and depth of U.S. government instigation and collusion in human rights abuses throughout the Americas over the decades, and U.S., Chilean, Salvadoran, and Guatemalan citizens press U.S. courts to hold past U.S. and Latin American government officials accountable. In spite of (and because of) dramatic regime changes and shifts in the global balance of power from the 1980s to the present, states and societies are peeling away layers of memories and amnesia to fulfill, at least in part, a need to interpret contemporary politics as both a break from and continuous with the past.[24]

Memory debates often appear as codes that over the years have undergone several iterations. In the 1980s in Argentina, Uruguay, and Brazil, and in the 1990s in Chile, El Salvador, Guatemala, and Peru, cries to remember centered primarily on demanding that governments and societies recognize heinous human rights abuse and victims' suffering. Underneath the cries, memory debates were also thickly wound up in left political-ideological positions and tensions of the left that date back to heady political victories and bitter political defeats, intense fractionalization, and even fratricidal conflict that facilitated state repression. Increasingly, memory discourse throughout the Americas is emphasizing agency over victimization—that is, reclaiming the pain of the fractionalization and internal discord within the left and between the left and center particularly, but also recounting the many forms of resistance in the face of brutality by the state (and in the Peruvian case, by the Shining Path as well). Memory discourse resurrects commitments to justice and questions past and current political agendas at the local, regional, and national levels.

Memories are associational, uncontrollable, triggered by the unexpected as well as the mundane, recalled individually and collectively, retrieved suddenly and fitfully as well as deliberatively and deliberately. Moreover, it is clear that memories of atrocious pasts continue visibly to haunt the present because they are constitutive of contemporary human rights violations, violence, injustice, and impunity. Throughout Latin America, left activists died for their beliefs, and many thousands more were murdered as suspected supporters. There is thus both a *literality* to traumatic memories and a sense of déjà vu when a human rights worker is shot in a restaurant in Guatemala City, or a political militant turns up dead in a ditch outside San Salvador. In the best of scenarios, states and societies attempt to facilitate environments in which painful memories of human rights atrocities can be explored and addressed with openness and understanding, vitally linked to an agenda of social justice.

10

Give or Take Ten Million: The Paradoxes of Migration to the United States

Judith Adler Hellman

Much that has been written about the recent decades of international migration in the Americas links this flow of humanity to the process of "globalization," as if the acceleration of migration were a direct consequence of the complex processes that increasingly come under this catch-all term. If, however, we think of globalization as having begun when regimes in the region began to abandon protectionist policies, drop their tariff barriers, and open their borders to imports from around the world, then we are looking at a relatively recent phenomenon that dates from the mid-1980s. The large-scale movements of migrants in the Americas, on the other hand, can be traced back to the nineteenth century and have continued throughout the twentieth century, intensifying over the last four decades.

To be sure, it has never been easy to track with precision the flow of migrants from one country to another in Latin America and the Caribbean or from the region into the United States, Canada, Europe, or, more recently, Japan. While some official statistics are available to indicate how many grandchildren of Italian and Spanish immigrants to the Southern Cone have claimed their right of return to Europe or how many Peruvians of Japanese descent have resettled in Japan, it is far more difficult even to estimate other migratory flows: How many Haitians work in the Dominican Republic? How many Grenadians or Anguillans have been drawn into the relatively robust labor market of Trinidad and Tobago? How many Nicaraguans have set out for the agricultural fields of Costa Rica? How many undocumented Mexicans pick fruit, trim lawns, wash dishes, bus tables, iron shirts, clean offices, roll sushi, clear construction sites, mind children, paint trim, sell tamales, deliver pizza, stitch apparel, or wash cars in the United States? Some authorities estimate five to six million undocumented Mexicans live and work in the United States. Others put the figure at somewhere between ten and fifteen million. Is it possible to agree on a figure—give or take ten million?[1]

What we can say is that long before anyone had ever uttered the word "globalization," harsh conditions in rural Latin America and the Caribbean— in particular, the declining prices of agricultural goods—led people to leave the rural areas for nearby towns and cities. Today the continued deterioration of conditions in the countryside have pushed increasing numbers of rural people to travel further afield to seek their fortunes—or at least to provide for their family's survival. Moreover, rural migrants have been joined in their international peregrinations by their urban compatriots, people from the cities who are often the daughters, sons, or grandchildren of peasants whose rural exodus in the 1950s and 1960s shifted the demographic profile of the Americas from largely rural to urban societies.

NEW PATTERNS

Thus, while we lack accurate, reliable figures on international migration in the Americas, what we do know is that today, as over the last three decades, millions of women, men, and sometimes children have found their way from their villages, towns, or city neighborhoods in Latin America and the Caribbean to destinations thousands of miles away where—one way or another—they manage to find work, housing, social networks, and social services. However, when we compare the current migration process with the patterns of past generations, some significant differences do emerge. The number of migrants is higher and growing. The migrants are coming from a wider range of communities and circumstances within their own countries. They continue to set forth from what are often referred to as traditional migrant sending regions, historically marked by severe poverty, but now they come as well from "nontraditional" zones where large-scale exodus was previously unknown. Even those who come from the traditional sending communities are less likely to work, as in the past, in agriculture and more likely to find construction, industrial manufacturing, and service sector jobs.[2]

The migratory flows include more women than in the past—except in the case of migrants from the Caribbean, where women, often seeking jobs in domestic service, have long outnumbered men. The migrant pool today is made up of people with higher levels of literacy, more urban experience, more skills, more extensive personal networks that connect them to other migrants already established abroad, and—yes, thanks to the globalization of the media—more knowledge of the societies into which they hope to move.

Ironically, for all the personal resources that these migrants bring with them in the form of higher levels of literacy, skills, and job training, the overwhelming majority remain in minimum-wage, low-skilled, nonunionized sectors of the economy. In the international division of labor, it falls to these people to take on the jobs that those with more secure status reject, and many different industries in North America that have faced and will face overwhelming competition from Asian producers have "rescued" themselves either by outsourcing their production—that is, sending part or all the production offshore to low-wage export zones around the world—or by employing migrants from those same countries in sweatshops and other nonprotected work environments in the United States and Canada. In short, a poor Jamaican might "choose" to work in a minimum-wage job either in the Jamaica Plains neighborhood of Boston or just across the East River from Manhattan in Jamaica, Queens, or in the low-wage export zone at home in Jamaica.

MEXICAN MIGRANTS

While the trickle of documented and the flood of undocumented migrants to the United States includes people from every country in the Americas, it is Mexicans who account for the overwhelming majority of undocumented migrants who live and work in the United States. Indeed, it is estimated that people of Mexican origin—both documented and undocumented—now represent two-thirds of all Hispanics in the United States. Mexican migration to the United States has had profound reciprocal effects on the two countries. The in-migration of Mexicans over the past two decades has influenced U.S. politics and culture in ways that go far beyond the impact of any other recent immigrant group. At the same time, the continuous outflow of young workers to the United States has affected Mexico's labor markets, popular culture, family structures, and national income in ways that are common among small Caribbean countries, where the number of citizens working abroad often outnumbers the economically active population at home. But among Latin American countries, Mexico is unsurpassed in the importance of migration as a social, economic, and political phenomenon. For all these reasons, this chapter will focus on Mexican migration.

This increased movement of Mexicans across the U.S. border is only the latest chapter in an ongoing tale of physical—if not always social—mobility. Through the 1960s, the massive migration to Mexico City quintupled the population of the capital in a decade. From the 1960s through the 1980s, as peasants poured into the Federal District at a rate of more than a thousand per day, secondary Mexican cities (such as Guadalajara, Monterrey, Puebla, and Veracruz) also drew rural migrants, and the border region with the United States began to attract first tens of thousands—and eventually millions—of poor, generally rural Mexicans who sought work in the *maquila* plants in the newly formed export zone.

The 1990s was the decade in which internal migration within Mexico gave way to an accelerated international migration to the United States. The implementation of NAFTA in 1994 involved changes to the agrarian reform legislation designed to "harmonize" Mexican peasant agriculture with the enterprises of private U.S. and Canadian farmers. These measures created greater poverty in rural Mexico, intensifying the "push" factors that had long stimulated the exodus of rural people from their villages. As successive economic downturns threw peasant production into crisis, rural Mexicans responded by moving to the cities, but also by setting out for the traditional immigrant receiving areas of the United States (California, Texas, and Chicago). In addition, however, they also moved to new destinations, particularly Georgia and the Carolinas, the Pacific Northwest, the New York metropolitan area and neighboring states, onward into New England, and even to Alaska! By now it would be difficult to find any corner of the United States, however remote, that has no population of Mexican migrants.

WHY MIGRATE?

In attempting to explain why Mexican migration has grown so rapidly, most analysts, as we have noted, focus on the intensification of poverty produced by neoliberal policies. However, in addition to grave economic problems like the shortage of arable land, the declining prices of agricultural commodities, and the lack of employment opportunities in both the countryside and the cities, some important—and not well understood—social changes have stimulated the impulse to leave home, friends and family behind to pursue individual and family migration projects.

One stimulus to rural exodus is that migration offers women an escape from the most oppressive village-based forms of patriarchy. The ideological commitment of many progressive people to denounce neoliberalism and its pernicious effects has led some analysts to ignore the very simple fact that many women who migrate, or who support the migratory projects of their husbands—with the hope of joining them at a later date—do so in order to raise the funds to build an independent housing unit, a "neolocal household," to escape the absolute tyranny exercised by the mother-in-law over the daughters-in-law in the patrilocal household. As Nancy Churchill explains: "In the countryside, peasant women are subject to patriarchal vigilance by both men, boys, and older women, all of whom are responsible for watching over their virtue, and by extension, the honor of the family. When women marry, the responsibility for vigilance passes from their fathers and brothers to their husband and his father and mother."[3]

When a young woman's husband migrates and leaves her behind in his parents' home, she comes under the authority of both her mother and father-in-law. However, in practice, it is the *suegra*, the mother-in-law, who rules inside the walls of the house, controlling the time and labor power of the young women of the household. To the extent that a young wife whose husband has gone off to the United States is physically confined to his parents' home, the *suegra*'s domination of her daughter-in-law is total and often oppressive. Nonetheless, because this aspect of women's subjugation does not fit the categories of those who focus on antiglobalism and runs counter to essentialist feminist concepts, it is often overlooked or ignored in discussions of migration.

Another motivation for migration that is also often absent from discussions of the phenomenon among progressive people are the changes among poor people in Latin America and the Caribbean in their conception of what are life's basic necessities. Any consideration of the migratory process that does not sentimentalize the migrants points to the astonishing lengths to which migrants go—leaving loved ones behind, running great personal risk crossing the desert, living without formal rights as an underclass in a racist society—to acquire material goods. To be sure, migrants are likely to direct their first remittances to improving their dwellings, acquiring land and better agricultural equipment, purchasing a car or truck, or underwriting a modest business venture. Moreover, an estimated 20 percent of Mexican families are absolutely dependent on remittances to meet their need for food, clothing, and shelter. However, any careful survey of sending communities also highlights the degree to which the desire for such products as televisions, computers, cordless phones, cell phones, DVD players, and a variety of consumer goods that, in very recent memory, would have been seen as luxuries—if they were known at all—plays a part in stimulating migration, as these possessions have come to be redefined as "meeting basic needs."

WHO GOES? WHO STAYS?

When we examine who migrates and who stays home, it becomes evident that those who leave are by no means the poorest in the village or neighborhood because financial and human capital are needed to finance the trip. Indeed, if we can find any predictor that would account for the decision to undertake the journey northward it is the presence of family, village, or neighborhood networks that facilitate and stimulate people to consider resolving their problems by joining friends and relations *al otro lado*, on the "other side."

Ironically, the strength of migrants' networks provides key advantages to employers in the United States as well as to the migrants themselves, as Wayne Cornelius has noted in his study of labor markets in San Diego County: "No costly advertising is required; no employment agency fees need be paid. Job vacancies can be filled almost immediately; in most cases, immigrants already working in the firm know that a vacancy is about to occur even before the employer does. High-quality workers are virtually guaranteed, even without screening of job applicants since the immigrant's social network vouches for his or her reliability, productivity and good character."[4]

In some sectors—notably restaurants, landscaping, building maintenance, and low-tech manufacturing—this survey discovered that 80 percent of those employed had found their jobs through their migratory networks.[5]

But how do would-be immigrants finance their trip? Depending on whether they wish to go only as far as Southern California or hope to reach destinations on the East Coast or the north of the United States, the cost of transportation and "coyotes" (smugglers) fees may reach four thousand dollars or even more. Often the trip is sponsored by a relative who is already established in the United States and can provide not only an advance on future wages to pay for the trip, but also housing upon arrival and help in finding a job. Alternatively, the migrant may be sponsored by relatives back home in the sending community, and indeed the acceleration of international migration has led to the revival of the traditional system of *acapadores*—that is, the money lenders who historically provided credit to peasants who mortgaged their future crop in order to have access to immediate cash to meet basic family needs or to buy the seed and other agricultural inputs to cultivate their land.

Nowadays, parents mortgage their land to finance their son's crossing. If the remittances don't begin to flow back to the village very soon after the migrant's arrival in the United States, the parents stand to lose all. In other cases, migratory journeys are underwritten by the local *cacique,* or political boss, who expects to be repaid with votes as well as cash. Still another source of funds may be the village priest. While some priests take a passionately strong stand against migration, especially of women and young people, others play an active role in facilitating the trip northward in part because remittances have become a key resource for an underfinanced Church, supporting both religious festivals and the repair and upkeep of the church buildings.

POLITICAL AND SOCIAL PROFILE OF THOSE WHO MIGRATE

While it is often remarked that the total numbers and social characteristics of the undocumented Mexican migrants to the United States cannot by definition be known, in fact a long-term study carried out in Tijuana by researchers from the Colegio de la Frontera Norte (COLEF) provides some interesting insights.[6] Before the COLEF team began its survey in the 1980s, the data on border crossings focused narrowly on those who had failed in their attempt to cross. The United States Immigration and Naturalization Service (INS, or *"migra"*) kept statistics gleaned from questionnaires applied at detention centers where would-be migrants who had been apprehended by the border police were interviewed before being deported to Mexico. However, the COLEF team interviewed would-be migrants as they waited at the border for nightfall to cover their attempts to leap the fence that divides Tijuana from San Ysidro, California.

Thus the COLEF findings, by definition, were based on a more complete sample, including those who would subsequently succeed in their effort to cross the border as well as those who would later be caught by the *migra*. Apart from finding larger numbers of women traveling unaccompanied by relatives, plus far more urban Mexicans with higher levels of education than had previously been supposed, the data assembled by the COLEF team show that the profile of would-be migrants from rural Mexico resembles that which typically belonged to the peasant leaders of the past. In particular, rural school teachers, traditionally the most influential figures in their villages (often exceeding the importance of the village priest), make up a disproportionate part of the transnational migratory flow. Indeed, these studies confirm that those who leave their rural villages to try their luck in the United States have higher levels of literacy, education, and technical training than those who stay behind, even if it becomes their destiny to work, as we have noted with respect to undocumented immigrants as a whole, in the lowest rungs of the service economy.

POLITICAL IMPLICATIONS

The question of who goes and who stays behind has some clear implications for political mobilization in Mexico. Given fairly widespread and uniform conditions of impoverishment in the subsistence agricultural sector of Mexico and the generalized availability of at least provisional or rudimentary migration networks in all areas of Mexico, we need to distinguish the people who stay put and organize collective action to transform their circumstances from those who pursue an individual exit strategy—that is, national or international migration. Any attempt to explain who chooses which alternative life strategy raises a number of key questions: Are those who leave the countryside the same people who, in the past, provided the leadership and membership of the peasant movements that previously mobilized significant areas of rural Mexico? Are the rural Mexicans with the greatest cultural resources the ones most likely to emigrate? If they are, what happens to those who are left behind? Under what circumstances are those who have chosen the exit strategy of migration to the United States able to reconstitute themselves as a collective force to pursue political action?

As migration to the United States has become vastly more difficult, costly, and perilous, how and why people make the social, economic, and political choice to migrate or to stay put is not simple to explain. In an ironic turnabout, participation in a peasant mobilization, until very recently an activity that a rural person might undertake at the peril of his or her life (risking injury or death at the hands of the army, the *guardias blancas* of the landlords, or paramilitary troops), may not be as dangerous today as crossing into the United States at the points along the border that are less intensively patrolled by the border patrol—that is, those crossings that require a two- or three-day hike through the Arizona-Sonora desert. Moreover, rural people's choice to remain in or to leave their village is a decision that is now made in a national context of an increasingly plural political system that features greater freedom of expression and association.

Thus, in weighing the decision to stay and to engage in political struggle at home or to emigrate, rural Mexicans are now acting within a structure of political opportunity that potentially offers more ample openings for collective action than would have been the case before the current process of transition to democracy began. At the same time, those Mexicans who decide to emigrate do so in a post–September 11 context in which control of the U.S.-Mexican border has been tightened and the rights of both documented and undocumented noncitizens residing in the United States have been curtailed. Under the circumstances, the fundamental questions of who stays, who goes, who returns, who engages in collective action, and where this activity unfolds have significant political consequences at both the local and national level in Mexico.

However, the political implications of migration are not limited to local and national Mexican politics. Although far from their place of origin and living as an underclass abroad, documented and undocumented Mexican migrants to the United States often come together as "transnational communities," forming hometown associations that engage in a variety of activities designed to reinforce ties to the home village. These clubs pool their members' remittances to finance the construction of health clinics, the renovation of the central plaza of the town or village, or the repair of the school or church. They also sponsor public events, fiestas for the patron saint, team sports, carnival rides, rodeos, and concerts. As Garcia Zamora notes, the clubs' trajectory generally begins with sponsorship of public events and public works, but once the basic infrastructural needs of the home communities have been met, they may, in a later phase of their development, turn to income-generating projects, recognizing, as they do, that the central problem of their communities is the lack of employment opportunities.[7]

Energetic as the collective activities of the hometown associations may be, they rarely focus on village politics in support of one party candidate or another. Nonetheless, although they are largely nonpartisan, the efforts of the hometown clubs have been recognized by the governors of those Mexican states that have the highest rates of out-migration, and these politicians have brought their political campaigns north to the United States, meeting frequently with the club members and leaders to press the migrants to invest in their home states.[8]

Thus, in addition to all the other projects they undertake with the fruits of hard labor in the United States, the migrants and their hometown associations are increasingly posed by politicians in Mexico as the answer to the problem of stimulating economic development. As it is, individual and collective remittances sent by migrants working abroad to their families in Mexico—$16.6 billion US in 2004 and an estimated $20 billion in 2005—have come to constitute the mainstay of the economy of countless villages, towns, and cities. Altogether, remittances exceed foreign exchange earnings from tourism, manufacturing, and agricultural exports and are surpassed only by oil earnings in importance as a proportion of foreign exchange.

But as if it were not enough that migrant workers self-exploit to make up the shortfall in social spending from the state that should and would make the lives of those left behind more bearable, today the Mexican state increasingly presumes that collective and individual remittances will be productively invested in the hometown—particularly in the development of infrastructure—and that this investment will make up for the shortfall in public spending. To stimulate this process, programs of matching public to private funds have been promoted. Since 1992, for example, every dollar contributed by Zacatecas hometown associations to the funding of projects back home has been matched by the Zacatecas state and the Mexican federal governments, each adding a dollar in a so-called Two-for-One program. In 1998 the addition of a dollar from the *municipio* turned the program into Three-for-One, and in 2000 the Vicente Fox government made it a nationwide policy under a Citizens' Initiative Program.[9]

In return for the migrants' self-exploitation in the interest of supporting their families, developing the infrastructure of their hometowns, and providing investment capital, the official Mexican position has changed from one that heaped scorn on migrants for "abandoning" their homeland, culture, and families to a new construction of migrants as national heroes and their remittances as expressions of their patriotism. This new appreciation of the migrant as patriotic hero is evident in the written material that the Mexican government has waiting at the airports for migrants who return from the United States:

> Welcome home, countryman [President Vicente Fox writes]. Please accept greetings and my recognition for your effort and your sacrifice of being far from your loved ones and your homeland for a long period.

The migrants constitute a great example. Their spirit of struggle and valor have earned them the admiration of one and all. . . . In your absence we have continued working to protect your rights and to make your visit to Mexico, your homeland, as pleasant as possible. To assure that your arrival and departure are safe we have put in place the Paisano Program which offers attention, information, and orientation and will record any complaints and accusations [you may have].

And yet, even as remittance-sending immigrants are now officially lionized, and the Three-for-One program has spread across Mexico, it is clear that the money earned by poor immigrants in the United States cannot replace investments by the state or the private sector. "Why ask migrants to invest their remittances productively and to use them 'efficiently' (creating multiplier effects in the local or regional economy), when the private sector does not do so?" asks a declaration issued by a group of thirty-two experts on Mexican migration issues who met in Cuernavaca, Morelos, in April 2005:

> Existing transnational migrant organizations have proliferated thanks to their own work, and to a lesser extent, to government support and incentives. As a result, these organizations currently enjoy a certain amount of prestige and political power. Recognizing the importance of migrants' collective contributions to local development is fundamental. But once again, these collective donations cannot solve deep and globally rooted structural asymmetries, much less address the absence of effective regional and national development policies.[10]

Increasingly, then, the Mexican state relies on collective remittances to replace public spending. This is a situation produced by the contraction of the state under neoliberalism and it is a turn of events that is actually foreseen and celebrated by neoliberal ideologues. The inappropriateness—indeed, the profound perversity—of this growing dependence of the state upon the downtrodden individual is all the more shocking when we consider that the funds collected by the hometown associations are largely contributed by people who are not merely poor but who have earned these dollars under conditions of extreme exploitation and at great personal risk to themselves.

THE RISKS THEY TAKE

In the course of the Clinton and Bush administrations, crossing the border has become an ever more dangerous and expensive undertaking for those undocumented Mexicans who are determined to pursue work in the United States as their family survival strategy. Successive U.S. administrations have responded to the complaint that the country has lost control of its borders by "beefing up" border security with the construction of higher fences, the purchase and deployment of more sophisticated and effective detection equipment like hidden electronic sensors, helicopter surveillance by day, night-vision cameras by night, and the assignment of more officers to patrol the most heavily utilized border crossing points, particularly at Tijuana, on the Pacific coast, and along the Texas border. With the institution in 1993 of Operation Blockade (hastily renamed "Operation Hold-the-Line") in El Paso, followed in 1994 with Operation Gatekeeper in the San Diego sector of the border, spending on border enforcement grew year by year until, by the new millennium, it had tripled.

The tragic outcome of the intensification of enforcement along the border, as Wayne Cornelius has graphically demonstrated, is to push would-be migrants away from the heavily patrolled traditional crossing points and into the Arizona-Sonora desert, a zone marked by extremes of heat and cold, a total lack of water, and rough terrain that requires those who would cross to spend days walking through one of the least habitable environments in the hemisphere, risking death by dehydration, the bites of poisonous snakes and insects, or at the hands of bandits or U.S.-based vigilantes. It has forced a higher percentage of migrants to engage the services of coyotes, or people smugglers, and it has quadrupled, and in some cases quintupled, the cost of crossing while increasing the number of deaths to an average of more than four hundred a year, counting only those cases where remains were actually recovered by the U.S. border patrol or the Mexican police.[11]

As it turns out, the huge expenditure of financial and human resources intended to close off the border with Mexico can be said to have had no effect whatsoever on the continued and expanded presence of undocumented Mexicans in the United States. Although INS statistics measure "apprehensions," these figures tell us little about the effectiveness of programs like Operation Gatekeeper because the same unfortunate would-be migrants may be caught several times in the same night and are likely to continue their efforts to cross until they are successful—at which point they disappear from the statistical records of the INS. In a remarkably contradictory assertion, both the Clinton and Bush administrations have argued that a rise in apprehensions indicates the efficacy of the border patrols and their detection equipment, while any drop in apprehensions is claimed as evidence that the border operations have worked successfully to deter Mexican migrants and that fewer Mexicans are attempting to cross.[12]

THE CONTRADICTIONS

In reality, the presence of Mexicans in the United States, as we have noted, is so ubiquitous and widespread that anyone in the United States who looks around intuitively understands that closing off the border to Mexicans (as well as the Central and South Americans who may cross with them) has not deterred the continued flow of undocumented migrants into U.S. society. Would-be migrants find their way across in any case, and the intensification of the effort to exclude migrants has only made the crossing more dangerous and a lot more expensive for those who would attempt it. The response of undocumented Mexicans to these measures has been—logically enough—to give up their annual trip to their homeland, to remain longer in the United States, and often to make the sacrifices necessary to pay for their families to join them in the United States. Thus, the policies intended to tighten up the border and keep migrants out have, instead, had the effect of containing more of them within the United States.

Recognition of this reality is now reflected in public opinion in the United States. For example, a *Washington Post* survey conducted in January 2005 found that 61 percent of U.S. citizens questioned thought that undocumented migrants should be allowed to keep their jobs and apply for legal status.[13] Clearly, if it is the political will of U.S. citizens *not* to have undocumented migrants living among them, their political representatives will need to find a formula through which undocumented people who are resident in the country can receive proper documents and the full range of rights and guarantees available to legal residents. The construction of higher fences and deployment of more manpower and machinery at the border will not accomplish this goal.

It is striking to see that while a great show has been made of closing the border, the alternative approach of going after those who illegally employ undocumented migrant workers has until recently been conspicuously neglected as the U.S. Congress has provided large loopholes that permit U.S. employers—both large and small—to escape any legal responsibility for hiring a workforce comprised of undocumented immigrants. There is no legal responsibility for employers to verify the authenticity of the green card or Social Security card presented by a worker and no serious penalty for filling a factory with hundreds of undocumented workers. Thus, notwithstanding all the heated rhetoric about porous borders, and the periodic anti-immigrant outbursts of members of Congress, legislators have not put in place the disincentives that would discourage U.S.-based employers from adopting as their standard business strategy the use of unprotected, undocumented migrant workers as cheap labor.

The clear contradictions of U.S. federal policy on immigration and documentation of workers in the U.S. economy bespeaks a profound ambivalence of a political elite that claims that it wants to promote free trade in goods while prohibiting a free market of labor. The official position that excludes the free movement of labor across borders produces policies that are at odds with the manifest need for these workers in the economy.

Indeed, these contradictions give rise to some of the strangest coalitions in U.S. politics. The Essential Worker Immigrant Coalition lobbies Congress and the White House on behalf of fast-food restaurant chains, the hotel industry, slaughterhouses and meatpacking firms, nursing homes, and agribusiness, and this kind of "proimmigrant" coalition faces off against populist anti-immigrant groups that fear that a decline in wages will be the inevitable consequence of the entry of more immigrant workers, both documented or undocumented. Social justice advocates who are concerned with immigrants' welfare find themselves linked to small-business people who are eager to employ immigrant workers even if only to exploit them as cheap labor. Business people who hope to meet the challenge of lower production costs abroad by employing undocumented workers in the United States find themselves in the same Republican Party with those who want to stem the flow of foreigners at all costs, including even racist vigilantes who have appointed themselves as "minutemen" to guard the border. And even as Congress moved in 2000 to pass a bill that would grant tens of thousands of visas to temporary high-skilled workers, mostly bound for high-tech jobs, coalitions of business and immigrant groups pushed to extend the visa program to include low-skilled temporary workers.

IMMIGRATION REFORM: PRE- AND POST-SEPTEMBER 11

Given the complexity and contradictory nature of the interests at stake, it is not surprising that every official unilateral or bilateral attempt to address the problems of labor market mobility, border security, and the rights of immigrant workers, has ended in an impasse. Whether we look only at the debates and the results under the most recent two administrations, or begin with the long, sad history of bilateral negotiations from the *bracero* program (1942–64) through the 1986 amnesty offered to three million undocumented immigrant workers who were already in the United States, we can only conclude that these are intractable problems that are unlikely to be resolved any time soon. Certainly from the time that the United States' superior bargaining position enabled its representatives to take labor mobility off the table in the negotiations leading up to NAFTA, the goal of guaranteeing rights and security and the chance for a dignified life in the United States for all who live and work there has come no closer to fulfillment.

Perhaps the greatest hopes were raised during George W. Bush's first presidential campaign in 2000. In an effort to attract Hispanic voters to the Republican Party, Bush met frequently in a series of folksy, cordial encounters with his "friend," "neighbor," and "fellow rancher," the governor of the State of Guanajuato, Vicente Fox, himself the leading candidate for the Mexican presidency and, by July 2000, president-elect of Mexico. Once in office, Bush appointed a Cabinet-level panel charged with formulating recommendations on how some of the estimated three million undocumented Mexican workers might apply for legal status if they could meet eligibility requirements based on their employment history and length of residence in the United States. Of course, this proposal, coupled with a program of recruitment of "temporary workers" who would hold short-term work visas, immediately set off protests from non-Mexican immigrant groups that demanded similar opportunities as well as counter protests from xenophobic groups in the United States that simply want the exclusion of foreigners in general and nonwhite foreigners in particular.

Nonetheless, the proposal won the backing of the AFL-CIO leadership, which had come to see the degree to which legalization of the undocumented workforce would enable organized labor to unionize low-wage workers and to fight the kind of exploitation that occurs when a huge pool of cheap labor is readily available to employers. As the *New York Times* editorialized on July 23, 2001,

> Granting temporary visa holders meaningful rights is also important to low-skilled American workers. This is one reason labor unions have reversed their past opposition to legalizing the status of undocumented workers. They no longer worry about illegal immigrants displacing American-born job seekers as much as they worry that Mexican workers here will drive down wages for all low-skilled workers. It is in no one's interest that undocumented workers, assuming most are here to stay, be relegated to an underground economy.

As promising as this initiative seemed when, on September 6, 2001, Bush and Fox announced their intention to pursue these changes, the terrorist attacks five days later brought the entire discussion to an end. To make matters worse, as Philip Martin wrote, "the combination of an economic downturn and the September 11, 2001, terrorist attack has altered the U.S. immigration debate."[14] Before the attacks, the pressing immigration issue was how to legalize the status of three to four million unauthorized Mexicans in the United States. Legalization would have shifted the focus from preventing the entry of unauthorized foreigners to regularizing their status in the United

States. Since the attacks, the big issue has been how to prevent foreigners from entering the United States and committing terrorist attacks. In the minds of many Americans, the image of "immigrant" changed after September 11 from hard-working foreigners seeking the American dream to potentially deadly threats.

In fact, following September 11, the INS simply stopped processing immigration and visa applications. This policy decision left roughly 20,000 people who were already slated to come to the United States sitting in limbo in refugee camps around the world. Legislation was designed to "prevent future acts of terrorism" by altering the procedures for granting visas, greatly reducing the number of visas issued and increasing inspection and control at the U.S. borders with Canada and Mexico by tripling the number of Customs Service inspectors working at ports of entry.

Bush's 2004 presidential campaign prompted a brief reprise of the immigration policy discussion. Once again, he hoped to attract Hispanic votes by offering a program that would allow undocumented workers to apply for temporary guest worker status for an initial period of three years, a permit that could then be renewed an indefinite number of times. Under the program, the "guest workers" would be granted most of the benefits enjoyed by U.S. workers, including the guarantee of minimum wage, the right to obtain a legal Social Security number and a driver's license, and a green card which would confer permanent resident status. Moreover, the proposal was "labor market sensitive" because it provided for more visas to be issued when employers showed a need. At the same time, to guarantee that the workers would leave the United States at the conclusion of their work contract, the plan provided for part of their pay to be withheld and turned over to them only on their return to their home country.

It is not surprising that this proposal found little favor either with immigrant advocates or with right-wing anti-immigrant groups. The sad reality is that there is little chance that any meaningful legislation could be put forward because of the contradictory nature of the demands on policy makers. Immigrant labor is crucial to the U.S. service economy. Moreover, the future competitiveness of the United States in a global economy depends absolutely on a continued supply of unprotected low-wage labor—that is, of people who will work *inside* the United States at wage rates and in conditions that approximate those of the export zones of the Third World. To be sure, U.S. manufacturers cannot match the rock-bottom wages and deplorable conditions of, say, Chinese factories. Yet, the logic of global capitalism demands that manufacturers reduce their costs of production to the lowest possible level, and this is—from the employer's perspective—best achieved by exploiting those whose legal status is insecure and labor rights unprotected.

Under the circumstances, only the countermeasure of reinforcing labor's capacity to organize workers is likely to bring any improvement in this situation. This is because in spite of the many changes in migration patterns detailed in this article, the plight of recent migrants to the United States is, in so many respects, the same as that faced by the "huddled masses" at the turn of the last century. Migrant workers' desperation to find and hold jobs makes them vulnerable to exploitation. Thus, the answer to the question of how best to counter this vulnerability is the one that Joe Hill himself would recognize and surely endorse.[15] If there is a "solution" to be found it is not a particularly novel one. It is a response that is called forth by the conditions that are widespread today but that were also characteristic of a period of immigration a full century before anyone ever thought to impose a model called neoliberalism. The "answer" consists of a call for recognition of the crucial role that immigrants play in the economy and society of the United States and other advanced industrialized countries. It requires those lucky enough to hold citizenship in the "host" country to think hard about the kind of society in which they wish to live and in which they wish their children to live. And it depends, as it always has, on the success of the struggle to strengthen labor rights and human rights in general.

Note: This chapter was written prior to the mid-2006 developments in the U.S. immigration debate.

11

The Left in South America and the Resurgence of National-Popular Regimes

Carlos M. Vilas

THE LEFT: IDEOLOGY AND POLITICS

Like any other political classification, the left-right dyad is historically determined. It varies with times and circumstances, and its relevance for an understanding of political processes, organizations, or governments is contingent on a number of factors. While in a very broad sense we can refer to "the left" as relating to "the unfolding of progress and change," some recent experiences suggest that "change" and "progress" do not always go together.[1] Many of the outcomes of the political and socioeconomic transformations that have occurred during the last fifteen years in the former Soviet republics do not easily fit with the ideas of progress that inspired many of their promoters. Neither is it easy to equate progress with some of the most notorious changes brought about over the past two decades by neoliberal macroeconomic adjustment—such as poverty and inequality growth, labor market disintegration, deepening social fragmentation, and increasing public insecurity.

Nor can we accept at face value Norberto Bobbio's assertion that the fundamental distinction between the left and right is "the contrast between a horizontal or egalitarian vision of society and a vertical or non-egalitarian one," which is to say "the different attitude assumed by men in regard to the ideal of equality."[2] As a matter of fact, economic and social policies implemented by the governments of the democratic *Concertación* in Chile—governments conventionally considered to be on the left—have stimulated a deepening of social inequalities, in spite of their efficacy in reducing poverty.[3] Moreover, during the last decade the question of social inequality has been incorporated into the agendas of the most relevant actors of financial globalization and neoliberal capitalist restructuring, such as the IMF, the IDB, and the World Bank.[4] Concern for inequality is associated with the need to strengthen the institutional stability of governments that have been facing increasing levels of social unrest because of the introduction of neoliberal reforms. This official concern is also associated with the need to put leverage on the pace of economic growth. Much more than the "ideal of equality" and of justice alluded to by Bobbio, such institutions are worried about the uneasy compatibility of social inequalities and political governance.

There are no criteria in Bobbio's argument that allow us to specify the kind of inequality against which a politics of the left would address itself. Every society encompasses a great many inequalities. The relevant inequality for both political analysis and policy making, however, is that which involves collective actors: *social* inequality that sweeps up individuals and their families because they belong to a particular social group—be it social class, ethnicity, nationality, sex, age, place of residence, religion, habits or life preferences, or any other. It is not enough that individuals are, or are considered to be, different from each other. Differences turn into inequality when the institutional structure of power relations allots specific effects to those differences—such as access to economic resources, entitlement to political participation, social prestige, or others. Without this reference to a society's power relations, as well as its subjective translation of those relations into ideologies, symbols, and values and its objectification of power as social practices and institutions, inequality ends up as an abstract matter of some individuals' personal characteristics being different than others.

Attempts to arrive at a general definition of the left frequently lose sight of its political dimension. What is at stake in such an attempt is the identification of a specific political position with regard to the structure of power in a society and to the effects generated by that structure. While this is a task that has a theoretical or ideological dimension, the identification of a *political* left must focus on how that dimension translates itself into collective actions relative to other actors, to the organization of society, and to its insertion into the international political arena.

The classification of a certain position on the political spectrum refers as much to the general ideas that inspire it as to the effects of the intervention of the actors who hold that position on relations of power, on the allocation of resources, and on the organization of society. These effects depend on a wide set of factors. Ideology is one of them insofar as it sets the greater objectives and the broad horizon to which political actions are addressed. We must keep in mind, however, that the advances along this trajectory are a result of the characteristics of the road to be traveled—the institutional and factual settings as well as the identity, objectives, and interests of other actors; of their actions and reactions; of the available resources; of the scope of alternatives it is possible to propose and the ability to enhance them; of historical trajectories, and so on. The biblical admonition, "By their fruits you shall know them," is not to be mechanically applied to politics, as the fruits of political action do not rely just on the will of this or that actor. However, it is an interesting warning with regard to the distance that frequently lies between intentions (ideologies) and outcomes.

The processes of progressive social change carried out in Latin America during most of the twentieth century emphasized the reform of the political system with the aim of extending participation to social groups until then excluded, together with a more progressive distribution of national income— i.e., attempts to expand the social and economic frontiers of democracy. Proposals of transformation included confronting the social organization of production and reforming systems of private property (from the elimination of the semifeudal *latifundio* and the configuration of variants of a mixed economy to the abolition of capitalist ownership of the means of production), enhancing the political and social participation of workers and other popular sectors, the secularization of culture, and an insertion with larger relative autonomy into the international system. Around this nucleus of basic ideas one can differentiate positions and strategies that were more or less radical and more or less "reformist," positions and strategies that articulated with international currents or organizations—such as the Communist or the Social Democratic Internationals—and those that were mainly framed by "third way" definitions. One can also identify a variety of methodological or operational differences—for example the debates over armed versus institutional struggle.

It has never been easy in Latin America to agree on what is meant by the left. Phenomena of wide popular appeal with long-lasting impact on the design of their societies and political institutions, such as the Mexican and Bolivian revolutions, and the many varieties of national-popular regimes—such as Peronismo in Argentina, Varguismo in Brazil, "national liberation" in Costa Rica, Velasquismo in Ecuador—connect with difficulty to a standard concept of the left.[5] If we put aside extreme cases—e.g., nobody doubts that the military dictatorships of Pinochet or that of Videla et al were on the right and that the Chilean Popular Unity was on the left—the political record of Latin America offers a marked predominance of situations in which the conventional left-right dichotomy is unsatisfactory or even forced.

Part of this problem stems from a certain tendency to reduce the brand "left" to the Socialist and Communist parties or ideologies. The political proposals and experiences of progressive transformation have never been their sole property, nor have they consistently played relevant roles in political regimes that have activated processes of progressive social change. Furthermore, in several moments of their existence, those progressive regimes, while impelling policies of political and social transformation—universal suffrage, progressive labor and social security legislation, furthering workers' unionization, implementing agrarian reform, enhancing the national stake in basic resources, progressive redistribution of income—not only confronted the opposition of traditional power holders or of foreign powers who felt their hegemony threatened, but also were enmeshed in power competitions with Socialist and Communist parties.

In uneven measures, in multiple, reciprocal combinations and with ingredients taken from the most diverse theoretical positions (liberalism, positivism, romanticism, Marxism, nationalism, social Catholicism, and others) proposals for change and social progress were embodied by a wide variety of social and political organizations. Together they expressed a dissatisfaction with the kind of capitalism prevalent in Latin America. This was a capitalism that was a combined outcome of colonial imposition, the subordinate articulation of preexisting social formations, a peripheral insertion into the structure of international power, the subsequent modifications of national and regional economic structures, and accelerated processes of urbanization. It was, in brief, a type of capitalism whose phenomenologies displayed sharp differences vis-à-vis the European models.

Many were the carriers of ideological formulations. However, the conversion of ideas into organized collective strategies for social and political change and, furthermore, for gaining access to political rule corresponded to few. It was possibly the Chilean political system of the 1960s that most closely approximated the European configuration of political coalitions and confrontations and the conventional correlation between social class and political ideology. There was a Socialist and Communist left with a solid stance in the working class; a conservative right voicing the interests of the economic elites and their foreign ties; and a liberal center appealing to the middle classes.

In the other countries of the hemisphere, however, the processes of transformation were prompted by the aforementioned national-popular regimes, rooted in the urban and rural popular masses as well as in segments of the middle and even upper classes, with an emphasis on national development, social and political democratization, and an open inclination toward economic nationalism.

This not always harmonious complex of ideas and social roots came to power by electoral means in some cases (Battlismo in Uruguay, Peronismo in Argentina, the Chilean Popular Front in 1936, Vargas in Brazil in 1951), in other cases as the product of armed revolutions (Mexico, 1910–1915; Bolivia, 1952; Cuba, 1959; Nicaragua, 1979), and in still other cases through civilian-military actions leading to institutional breaks (Brazil, 1937; Guatemala, 1944; Costa Rica, 1948; Peru, 1968). Reactions from the Communist and Socialist parties ranged from open opposition—including electoral coalitions with parties of the right and participation in military coups as in Argentina during the first Peronista government—to alliances and support. The Chilean experiences of the Popular Front (1936–1941) and the Popular Unity (1970–1973), in which the Socialist and Communist parties shared political power with the Radical Party, or the eventual incorporation of the Cuban PSP (People's Socialist Party) into the revolution led by the 26 of July Movement, stand out in stark contrast to what was the predominant stance of Communist and Socialist parties. What came to be known in some countries of the region—and in some political parties and unions—as the "national left" combined an adherence to non-Soviet versions of Marxism with the assertion that in semicolonial countries such as those of Latin America, the immediate task was not a socialist transformation but an antifeudal, anti-imperialist one.

ADAPTATION AND REFORMS

As is well known, over the past two decades these and other revolutionary or reformist experiences confronted a number of setbacks and unexpected turns that led not a few participants in Latin American politics to cast doubts on the feasibility, or even the desirability, of a systemic confrontation with capitalism and a subsequent fundamental transformation of society. By "systemic confrontation" I am not referring to the questioning of capitalism as a mode of production but to a questioning of the particular type of capitalism that has effectively emerged over the past two or three decades as a result of neoliberal reforms. The commitment to a structural redesign of society and the state has thus given way to a variety of sectoral initiatives and proposals of much more moderate change.[6]

The return to representative democracy after periods of military dictatorship coincided in a number of Latin American countries with the implementation of neoliberal reforms. The new democracies found themselves having to come to terms with the new social and institutional ground set forth by those reforms. Yet neoliberal adjustment involved much more than changes in social and economic organization, as it propelled substantial shifts in power relations among social classes and other social actors. Wage workers, campesinos and small farmers, small and medium entrepreneurs oriented to the domestic market, women and young people—the social bases of the programs for reform of the preceding decades—all lost ground within the new designs as governmental commitment to social well-being was subordinated to the accomplishment of the new macroeconomic concerns.

The rebuilding of representative democracy in the 1980s and 1990s took place in settings of accentuated social vulnerability. According to the UN's

Economic Commission for Latin America and the Caribbean (ECLAC), 136 million people in Latin America were living in poverty in 1980. Ten years later the figure had climbed to 200 million, while in 2003 ECLAC's estimate was 225 million.[7] The sustained growth of poverty took place in the framework of an accelerated growth of social inequality. Income inequality during the years of the neoliberal experiment grew significantly in the region as a whole and, with a few exceptions, in every country.[8] It is worth stressing that poverty growth and the deepening of social inequality took place as most Latin American economies were robustly growing. In addition to rebutting the neoliberal hypothesis of the "spillover" of the fruits of growth, the perception of the unequal distribution of gains and losses contributed to the erosion of the legitimacy of a political system tolerating, or even promoting, such a result.[9]

As several Latin American scholars have pointed out, the way in which wide sectors of the Latin American population conceive of democracy was not reflected by the actual performance of these reconstructed representative regimes. People's evaluations of political regimes, and not only democracies, tend to be heavily influenced not just by institutional or procedural questions but by the effective content of the decisions made within the framework of these procedures and institutions.[10] Yet the democratic transitions in most of the Latin American countries from the mid-1980s on resulted in political regimes that in one way or the other adapted the procedures and institutions of representative democracy to the goals and rationale of the so-called Washington Consensus—what former U.S. president Bill Clinton referred to as *market democracies:* representative political systems whose principal commitment is the advance of capitalism in its particular neoliberal recipe.[11] People's demands for social improvement were relegated to the back burner or directly discarded in the name of the preservation of so-called "macroeconomic fundamentals."

The tension between this restrictive conception of democracy and people's aspirations for a democracy of higher density, especially in settings of great social vulnerability, proved to have explosive effects in several countries. Mass popular protests led in recent years to unscheduled government changes and to the toppling of presidents in Ecuador, Argentina, Peru, and Bolivia. Within the framework of deep economic crises, persistent government corruption, or a combination of the two, huge mass mobilizations forced the resignation or removal from office of governments that had arisen not long before in clean and competitive conventional elections. Popular anger thus toppled Abdalá Bucaram, Jamil Mahuad, and Lucio Gutiérrez in Ecuador, Alberto Fujimori in Peru, Fernando de la Rúa in Argentina, and Gonzalo Sánchez de Losada and Carlos Mesa in Bolivia.

The fact that these popular explosions have not, in and of themselves, generated political and social transformations does not diminish their relevance. They alert us to the precarious stability of social settings characterized by the conflictive coexistence of the principles of citizen equality and popular sovereignty on the one hand and the inequalities and privileges for the very few typical of these social settings on the other. Yet the subsequent political changes that have taken place in countries such as Argentina in 2002–03, or more recently in Bolivia with the presidential election of MAS leader Evo Morales, are clear by-products of people's rage and persistent mass protest.

A NEW LEFT

All this sets the context for the emergence of a number of governments attempting to close the gap between people's expectations and demands, while trying to avoid an across-the-board open conflict with economic power holders. Either for reasons of linguistic inertia or because of previous, more radical performances of some political parties, such experiments have been placed on the "left" or "center-left" of the political spectrum. The Workers Party (PT) in Brazil, *Frente Amplio* (Broad Front) in Uruguay, democratic *Concertación* in Chile, and possibly Kirchnerism in Argentina—and their respective governments—qualify for such a classification. The Mexican Party of the Democratic Revolution (PRD) as well the Bolivian Movement Toward Socialism (MAS) may also fit into this category.

Beyond their many specific differences, the common denominator of these groups has been their attempt to grant policy stimuli to the growth of investment, production, and employment in order to allow for a progressive satisfaction of social demands in a framework of monetary stability, institutional governability, and democratic participation. In achieving this, the state is expected to take on a more active role than in the neoliberal strategy, monitoring the performance of markets and, in general, operating through conventional mechanisms of active fiscal and monetary policies: taxes, exchange and interest rates, economic regulation, and so on. At the same time, these governments do acknowledge that, in specific areas, markets are inefficient and the state must take on more direct responsibility and involvement in questions of environment protection, poverty alleviation, infrastructure development, and job creation, for example, as well a more balanced involvement in globalization. If the neoliberal recipes of the 1980s and 1990s found their inspiration in the Washington Consensus, proposals from this new left seem to be inspired by recommendations to resort to "broader tools and goals" to achieve development and stronger social cohesion as well "to move on towards a post-Washington Consensus."[12]

In a variety of ways, these and other approaches can be understood as fruits of a convergence of organizations, tendencies, theoretical perspectives, and political experiences toward the need to provide these reborn democracies with effective commitment for reform and social sensitivity. Many of the leaders and political organizations that are implementing them have reached the highest levels in national governments or have competed for them after successful performances in municipal, provincial, or state governments. Landing at the highest levels of national political decision making has not been the effect of a surprising leap from the lowlands but the culmination of a prolonged accumulation of forces—power building as well as governance know-how. It has not, by and large, involved the coming to power of political outsiders—as was the case of former neoliberal mavericks like Alberto Fujimori or radical reformist Hugo Chávez—but the work of well-known and experienced participants in electoral, parliamentary, and administrative struggles. It has been a *war of position,* to borrow from Gramsci's metaphor.

As usual, such arrivals have advantages together with shortcomings. The main advantage is the knowledge they have gained regarding the challenges to institutional political power, its procedures and tools, and the ability to build alliances together with collecting experience in mastering the political timing of complex issues. The risk is that after coexisting with traditional politics for so long, this new left ends up absorbing some of the worst habits of politics-as-usual, thus diluting its own proposals for transformation into a short-run pragmatism. After all, the new left is as much an attempted answer to people's demands as an outgrowth of the political regime it criticizes.

Hugo Chávez represents a particular case. The radical stance of his proposals and his transgressional style have much to do with his own political trajectory—solidly sustained in successive electoral victories—which is totally detached from the traditional political system.[13] In some ways, this is also the case of Argentine President Néstor Kirchner. In no way a newcomer to politics, Néstor Kirchner's career as a politician and government leader evolved mainly in his remote, underpopulated native province of Santa Cruz, which has very important mineral (especially oil and coal) and fishing resources but is relatively marginal to the national political system. Kirchner's political style—confrontational rhetoric vis-à-vis economic or corporatist vested interests, direct communication with the people, a tough negotiator with regard to foreign debt or multinational firms—contrasts with conventional political manners of preceding administrations, as do a number of governmental decisions and policy definitions on issues such as economic policy, regional integration, human rights, and civil-military relations, among others.

Propelled to government through the votes of the lower and middle classes, motivated by their hopes for well-being and progress, this new left must make this source of democratic legitimacy compatible with the political times and the many restrictions that appear in their particular arenas. This is not an easy task, due to both the magnitude of interests they confront and the diversity of perceptions, expectations, and identities that converge in the buildup of these new proposals. When we look inside these organizations or governments, what we usually find is a micro-universe of groups, political "lines" and tendencies, a variety of proposed actions as well as ways to implement them, and so on. Within each of these organizations "left" and "right" tendencies coexist. It is not infrequent that the accommodation of political currents, internal commitments, and external alliances—which, taken together, provide votes and make electoral victories possible—all give rise to tensions and eventual breakups when they move from the diagnostic stage to implementation, from political opposition to government, or from academic critique to implementation. There is also the stubborn logic of electoral arithmetic, which spurs the achievement of alliances and arrangements with other political forces either because of political common grounds or as a way to sum up as many votes as needed to gain access to government, or both.

In most of these governments, strong tensions exist between the urgency of popular demands on the one hand and the demands of economic powers and external pressures on the other. This attests to the conflict between sustaining the macroeconomic balances of preceding governments and the promotion of a type of development that brings together upward accumulation and downward distribution. The Chilean Democratic *Concertación* is a relatively successful case in which these tensions have been addressed. Through a progressive tax reform and the temporary regulation of international financial flows, economic policies achieved high growth rates, a successful articulation with the international economy, and improved social well-being. At the same time, the preservation of deeply rooted traits of the former macroeconomic scheme (especially a very high concentration of wealth) has contributed to a very unequal appropriation of the fruits of the new design, which places Chile as one of the Latin American countries with deepest social inequality.[14]

In more than one feature, the Chávez government looks like the left of this new governing left. Supported by the sustained increase in oil prices as an effect of U.S. policies in the Middle East, Chávez is financing a series of far-reaching social reforms—particularly in health care and education—encouraging the development of a regional political network of governments in order to keep pressures from Washington in check, and challenging positions of power traditionally held by large corporations, the technocratic elite, the mainstream press, and the Catholic Church hierarchy, all within the context of intense popular mobilization and subsequent electoral victories. The key to Chávez's political autonomy is state control of Venezuela's oil resources, which lends financial resources to fund social policies and Venezuela's increasing involvement in regional affairs.[15] It is not the first time that Venezuela has enjoyed the bonanza of high export prices. In the past, oil income funded dictatorships such as those of Juan Vicente Gómez and Marcos Pérez Jiménez, as well as corrupt fiscal mismanagement, as in the first government of Carlos Andrés Pérez. The current situation bears witness to the difference a government with alternative political goals can make.

On the other hand, Brazil's PT government made the option to keep, and in some ways reinforce, the neoliberal macroeconomic design, even at the expense of alienating the industrial elites as well as relevant segments of the working class that constituted traditional PT's supports. Some well-known social programs—"Zero Hunger," for example—have taken time before producing significant results, due to both the complexity of the problems they address as well as the broader institutional arena in which the government has to perform. Similarly, little progress has been made in access to land for poor farmers. Devoted to appeasing the fears and distrust of financial sectors and the U.S. administrations because of its previous performance as a radical left, even Marxist, party, the PT, once in government, resorted to drastic redefinitions of proposals, concepts, and political styles whose radicalism had paved, over the years, its electoral road to government. These redefinitions have poured gas over the fire of internal discussions, disagreements, and party splits, an uncomfortable situation that former president Fernando H. Cardoso has pointed to with badly disguised irony.[16] More recently, allegations of corruption and misappropriation of public funds by high-ranking PT leaders suggest that the new, pragmatic left is not immune to some of the worst temptations in traditional politics.

The most pathetic example of the relinquishing of ideals is the traumatic experience of FREPASO *(Frente por un País Solidario)* in Argentina from 1999 to 2001. A political party grown out of a consistent opposition to the neoliberal government of Carlos Menem during the 1990s, FREPASO was unable to manage the electoral alliance that enabled it to share power in the national government with the conservative Radical Party in the 1999 presidential elections, and it ended up handing over the most important political decisions to the most right-wing participants in the alliance—those most closely connected with the macroeconomic neoliberal design that had supposedly been rejected in the polls. Withdrawal from electoral commitments isolated the government, while serious allegations of corruption and bribery accelerated the rapid desertion of party leaders, legislators, and, especially, voters. All this removed legitimacy from the government, eventually leading to the December 2001 breakdown, President de la Rúa's resignation, and the virtual withering away of FREPASO as a relevant player in Argentine politics.[17]

A RESURGENCE OF POPULAR NATIONAL REGIMES?

The following statement by Tabaré Vásquez a few days after assuming the presidency of Uruguay illustrates the pragmatism and national anchoring—as opposed to the "internationalism" of the traditional Socialist and Communist left—used by this new left to carry out its proposals:

> [I]f you ask me whether, from an ideological perspective, our government's program is a socialist program, I will say it is not. It's a national program, a deeply democratizing one, a program that seeks solidarity, social justice, economic growth with justice, in other words, human development. . . . The changes we are going to make are Uruguayan-style changes or they won't happen. . . . [T]his is a peaceful change, gradual, thought-out, serious, profound, responsible, with the broad participation of all actors in the economic, political and social life of the country, that works towards the main objective of our government, which is to improve the quality of life for all Uruguayans, stemming from our historical mandate raised on the night of the formation of our country . . . when Artigas said that those most in need will be the most privileged; that the cause of the people does not allow for the slightest delay.[18]

Argentine president Néstor Kirchner made similar declarations when he assumed power in 2003:

> The idea of rebuilding a style of national capitalism that creates alternatives so that upward social mobility is reinstated is key to our project.

We don't want to close ourselves off to the world. It's not a matter of ultramontane nationalism, but of intelligence, observation and commitment with the nation. It's enough to see how the more developed countries protect their producers, their industries and their workers. It's a matter of . . . allowing a new Argentina to be born with social progress, where children can aspire to live better than their parents based on their own efforts, capabilities, and work. To achieve this, we must promote active policies that allow for development and economic growth in the country, new job creation and a better and more just distribution of income. It is understood that the state plays a main role in this. . . . It's not about putting pendulous movements in place that move us from an omnipresent state that crushes private activity to a deserting, absent state, and to continuously move from one extreme to another, in what appears to be an authentic national mania that prevents us from finding just, sensible and necessary balances. We want to have what is necessary for our development in a new design that allows for an intelligent State.[19]

At the risk of putting new wine in old bottles, it is important to stress some similarities between these statements and popular national Latin American regimes of the twentieth century. Like many of those regimes, present experiences are a result of broad political-social convergences that join popular mobilizations to the periodic involvement in electoral processes; resort to broad multiclass appeals in the name of national interests beyond sectoral interests, except when within a given political moment the prioritization of sectoral objectives is assumed to have beneficial repercussions for all.

Tabaré Vázquez's reference to the ideology of the national hero Jose Gervasio de Artigas brings to mind the close association of Hugo Chávez's Fifth Republic Movement with the thought and action of Simón Bolívar. In what can be seen as the rejuvenation of a long Latin American tradition, the nation has been raised here as the symbolic reference point for the calling together of a broad array of actors, regardless of their sector or class affiliation. The nation is conceptualized as the unifying expression of the people and thereby a collective subject, activated around a program of political action.

This appeal to the nation thus avoids the individualist atomization of the liberal concept of the citizen. The people of this nation are a people of citizens, yet citizens situated in specific socioeconomic settings. In a sense, this is a republican concept of the people and the nation that comes from the French Revolution and the writings of the Abbot Sieyes. But at the same time it is an approach that positions citizens in specific living conditions—Georges Burdeau's *l'homme situé*—that picks up the socialist critiques (both Marxist and non-Marxist) of the traditional, liberal concept of citizenship.

This new left also distinguishes itself from leftist movements of the past in that it has a more plural, differentiated vision of "the people" and "the nation," not subsuming those concepts within predetermined actors in the world of labor or the world of politics—be it the working class or the political leader.

The advances in recent decades of the political culture of the left have played an important role in the recognition of the plurality of the popular sectors and, therefore, the incorporation of their hopes and demands into its political action programs. No less decisive has been the decomposition of the worker's movement and its decline as a reference point in popular movements. In fact, the gradual disappearance of class references in the political discourse of the new left expresses this relative decline of the political weight of unions, and the self-assertive participation over the past decades achieved by a broad array of social movements.

The resurgence of the idea of the people-nation as an all-embracing synthesis of multiple social identities recovers a dimension of political struggle and conflict as seen "from below." With unequal levels of intensity—the Chilean *Concertación* being to the right and the Chávez government to the left—politics now revolves around social oppositions: the poor vs. the privileged, the excluded vs. the integrated, the people vs. the elites. The recourse to these oppositions becomes plausible because it inserts itself into the most notorious characteristics of the social map: the fragmentation of the labor market, unemployment, and social polarization. The political invocation of the antagonisms that cross the social map has great mobilizing potential. It is quite different from the discourse of the democratic transitions of the 1980s that centered around political-institutional oppositions like democracy vs.

dictatorship deprived of any socioeconomic consideration; it also contrasts, of course, with the rhetoric of a "consensus building" of the 1990s regimes under the aegis of the "Washington Consensus."

However, the recourse to a confrontational focus—just as typical of Socialist and Communist lefts as it was of national popular regimes—is not matched by a strategic design for systemic transformation. Rather, as we said earlier, it is accompanied by proposals for sectoral reforms together with a tougher dialogue with external actors like transnational corporations, the international financial institutions, and European and U.S. governments. The sectoral nature of the proposals for change translates ideological options (flowing from the governing experiences of the revolutionary left) as much as they obey the dilemmas faced by the moderate left when it wins elections, assumes power, and confronts stronger-than-expected obstacles to sovereign governance: the heavy burden of foreign debt, the internalization among domestic decision makers of the assumptions of financial globalization, the weakened capacities for state management, advanced processes of social anomie, and the changing agendas of hegemonic players in the international arena.

Pressed by the votes and hopes of the people for progress and well-being, the new left must make its democratic legitimacy compatible with the present political moment in international arenas that continue to be unfavorable to the adoption of profound changes. This is not an easy task given the variety of perceptions, expectations, and identities that converge in the organizational constitution of each of these new movements. In the governance of the new left it is not unusual to see the plurality of tendencies that voted the government into power turn into divisions when the phase changes from diagnosis to implementation, or from critique to implementation. The statements by Néstor Kirchner and Tabaré Vázquez, as quoted earlier, can also be interpreted as attempts to prevent desertions and divorces similar to those experienced within the PT during Lula da Silva's presidency.

The focus placed on the national character of policies and on the strengthening of state capacities implies, in operational terms, a correction of the globalizing bias that characterized the preceding decades. There is an improved balance between the processes of globalization and domestic politics, with the regional dimension acting as a hinge and mediator between them. This change in perspective, however, implies no swing toward economic nationalism or the state takeover of private companies. Nor does it imply the administrative control of prices, regulation of the job market, or governmental promotion of import substitution, all of which were pillars of the "classic" populism of national popular regimes.

For its part, the reactivation of debates around the strengthening and eventual broadening of Mercosur, the signing of complementary energy and production agreements, and the coordination of foreign policy actions all indicate a greater valuation of the regional arena as a launching platform to strengthen national strategies for development and broadened external autonomy. The construction of greater autonomy and decision-making ability in the definition of the objectives of international relations implies an assumption of different perspectives and focal points from those that govern the policies of globalization's dominant players toward Latin America and the Caribbean. These new left governments, which together rule over almost half the Latin American GDP, have been able to postpone the enactment of the FTAA to an uncertain future date, oppose the U.S. invasion of Iraq, and condemn the embargo of Cuba—three "hot button" issues in White House policies toward Latin America. The Chávez regime has actively supported the successful renegotiation of the Argentine foreign debt, purchasing part of it with fixed terms for Argentina. In addition, its oil sales to Cuba at preferential prices has made Venezuela the main trading partner of the island. An agreement between Venezuela, Argentina, Brazil, and Uruguay recently brought about the birth of TeleSur, a TV station owned by these four countries that will try to become a cultural as well as political alternative to the CNN network.

The moderation and pragmatism of the new left and its notable adhesion to the values of representative democracy do not, as yet, have an apparent equivalent on the right. Venezuela is a particularly illustrative example, given the anti-Chávez coup attempt of April 2002, the call from ex-president Carlos Andrés Pérez to resort to violence just before the referendum of 2004, and the current escalation in verbal aggressions from a number of high-ranking U.S. government officers.[20] With a bit more sophistication—and with less foreign involvement—the aborted maneuverings of the Mexican political establishment to block Mexico City's popular mayor, Andrés Manuel Lopez Obrador, from becoming the PRD's presidential candidate in the 2006 elections forms part of the same less-than-democratic opposition.

These aggressive maneuvers have coincided with the new rhetoric coming from some U.S. foreign policy makers, who have placed national popular proposals in the same space filled by the Communist threat during the Cold War.[21] In this rhetoric, "radical populism" is a name given to various regimes that are suspect in the world of global business and among the more ideological tendencies of the U.S. political system. According to this diagnosis, populism incites waves of economic nationalism, feeds social conflict, and puts hemispheric governability in danger, thus threatening to become a political-ideological precursor to international terrorism. The conclusion is obvious: populism easily qualifies for inclusion on the list of "rogue states."[22]

It is a sad irony that those who began to qualify the Chávez regime under the brand "radical populism" are U.S. academics with a cautious sympathy toward the experience.[23] The Chávez and other progressive governments are interpreted as populist for presenting social conflict as the central axis of politics. This is something, as already discussed, that is not exclusive to populism, nor is the experience of a political leader who relates directly to the people, without or beyond the mediation of parties or other organizations. In addition, they are considered to be radical experiences because they encourage policies of social and political change, as opposed to (1) the neoliberal imprint, and to (2) some aspects of U.S. government policies toward the region. They lay in sharp contrast with the strongly personalized, authoritarian governments of recent decades that implemented neoliberal reforms in Peru (under Fujimori) or Argentina (under Menem), for example, and that nurtured so-called "neoliberal neopopulisms" of the 1990s.[24] What began as an academic positive evaluation of these governments thus became transformed, in the hands of Washington policy makers, into a genuine threat.

If the warnings of the most recalcitrant right are correct, Latin America has entered a new wave of neopopulism that puts the governability of democracies and international security of the United States at risk. The fact that these warnings cannot be sustained objectively, neither in the reality of the present nor in the foreseeable future, in no way diminishes the danger they contain. It would not be the first time that the most disastrous political decisions have been based on incorrect information, shortsighted interests or prejudices, or simply because they can be made because of overwhelming material superiority in the unleashing of terror and violence.

FINAL CONSIDERATIONS

Left, right, and center are relational metaphors; the existence of each calls for the existence of the other two. Discussion of the relevance of locating a certain force on the political spectrum must include the configuration of the political circumstances, the available options, and the effective prospects for conserving or transforming the present state of affairs. These are more important aspects than generic ideological definitions or conventional political labels. This does not imply that we should get rid of theories and ideologies in the identification or understanding of political options, but it does mean that we must recognize that the ability of normative ideas to deliver actual changes always relies on relationships of power, the ability of human beings and organizations to operate upon them, on political agreements and confrontations, and on the coalitions and tensions that energize the life of society. One of the most visible political achievements of the new left is precisely the recognition of the complexity of the relationships in which great, general ideas are to be enforced. Nevertheless, together with the overemphasis on ideological issues, a not-minor danger is that principles will be left by the wayside. The distance between pragmatism and opportunism can be short as well as abbreviated by the urgencies of electoral arithmetic.

The term "new left" used to group together the varying Latin American political expressions we have discussed in the previous sections is quite arbitrary. Upon closer analysis, their differences are as numerous as their similarities. In this chapter, I have given priority to the similarities because it is the similarities rather than the differences that allow us to identify new aspects of the regional political scene. These similarities also highlight continuity with certain aspects of the national popular experiences of the twentieth century, which have returned to prominence in the landscapes of social deterioration caused by neoliberalism.

The identification of a kind of political kinship linking the progressive proposals and political styles of these contemporary experiments with aspects of the national popular regimes of the twentieth century makes sense to the degree that it proceeds with extreme caution. Ideas tend to survive the eras that gave birth to them, but political regimes always express the moment in which they function, and they derive their effective identity from those contemporary moments—something already observed by Aristotle some twenty-five centuries ago.

To call attention to this kinship does not imply that the new left is looking back. It means that, together with the challenges posed by new times and new settings, it is addressing the many issues raised during those previous experiences and that remain pertinent after decades of authoritarian governments, democratic frustrations, and neoliberal experiments: national integration, social security, popular participation, and the social efficacy of democracy.

12

De Protesta a Propuesta: The Contributions and Challenges of Latin American Feminism

Norma Chinchilla and Liesl Haas

INTRODUCTION: LATIN AMERICAN FEMINISM AT A CROSSROADS

Over the last three decades, Latin American feminists have introduced new vocabularies and new ways of "doing politics" into the lexicon of Latin American social movements and civil society. In many ways, Latin American feminists have heeded Chilean feminist Julieta Kirkwood's call to "transform the world,[1] introducing concepts such as "the personal is political," "democracy at home and in the nation," and the "social construction of masculinity and femininity." Feminists across the region have also heightened appreciation for the politics of daily life and the power of civil society at the same time that they have expanded commonly accepted notions of citizenship, democracy, and human rights. They have made their mark on Latin American history by helping to undermine patriarchal, exclusive, and authoritarian elements of traditional culture and envisioning an alternative society "beyond neoliberalism," based on solidarity, cooperation, pluralism, freedom, and respect for human rights. In the process, Latin American feminists have not only fought to make national governments accountable to women, but have taken advantage of changes triggered by globalization to build a regional and global women's movement that is unprecedented in its reach and potential for coordinated action.

Despite its undeniable successes, Latin American feminism today stands at a crossroads characterized by new possibilities as well as serious challenges. Its internal composition and dynamics as well as the context in which it operates are changing. Paradoxically, perhaps, Latin American feminism has continued to gain ground precisely when neoliberal economic reforms have made women's lives more difficult and threaten to undermine legal and other gains. In response to feminist gains, a strong right-wing movement with transnational ties has emerged to challenge feminism ideologically and politically.

Internally, Latin American feminism has become more diverse, which extends its reach and grounds it in multiple realities. Yet diversity presents challenges for coordinated action, all the more so since feminism has also become more dispersed through geographic space and into multiple layers of political institutions and civil society. Feminists enjoy access to new forms of power but at the same time must grapple with new inequalities in access to resources, voice, and political space. Diversity and dispersion create new challenges for the practice of democracy and pluralism within women's movements similar to those in society at large. Feminist nongovernmental organizations (NGOs) and feminist influences in cultural institutions, together with feminist participation in political parties and state agencies, have opened access to new tools with which to challenge obstacles to women's equality.

At the same time, however, these forms of incorporation create new inequalities and opportunities for co-optation. The creation of transnational alliances and international conferences on women's rights increases the visibility of feminism, provides resources for women's organizations, and gives women a new arena in which to practice citizenship and exercise rights. But once again positive changes carry with them potentially deleterious consequences: an emphasis on transnational mobilization can also distract feminists from the particular challenges to women and feminist movements in their home countries. A participant in the eighth Latin American and Caribbean Feminist Encuentro in the Dominican Republic encapsulated the views of many activists when she wondered, "How are we supposed to navigate in a world in which so much has changed?"[2]

LATIN AMERICAN WOMEN'S LIVES IN THE CONTEXT OF NEOLIBERALISM AND GLOBALIZATION

To appreciate the contributions and successes of Latin American feminism, one must recognize the depth of the challenges faced by Latin American women and the ways in which their historical exclusion has been exacerbated in recent decades by neoliberal economic policies and incomplete democratization. Underfunded and often fragile legal systems combined with weak enforcement of laws related to equality of opportunity mean that advances in public policy in such areas as access to education, salary equity, domestic violence, and reproductive health often fail to alter the reality of women's lives. And the current context of a growing opposition movement from the political right and the Catholic Church threatens to erode the gains feminists have made, including their access to political power through increasing representation in political parties and the state.

Overall, women's growing access to education in Latin America is something to celebrate. The most dramatic positive change in women's access to social resources in recent decades is that 87 percent are now enrolled in primary and secondary education, and more women than men are now enrolled in universities. Restrictions on women's education, such as a Chilean law allowing schools to expel pregnant students, have been struck down in many places. Nevertheless, women's access to education varies widely across the region. Aggregate statistics mask high (and sometimes growing) rates of illiteracy among rural women, especially indigenous women.

Another potentially positive change is the growing percentage of women who have access to paid labor outside the home. Overall, approximately one third of the official (paid) labor force (EAP) in Latin America is now female. Yet increased access to jobs for women has not gone along with a reduction in poverty. Nor, in the majority of cases, has it brought about notable increases in the economic well-being of women and their families. As a result of neoliberal policies of stabilization, liberalization, and privatization, poverty is being feminized at a rapid rate and women's burdens from a double or triple day of work are heavy. Even where feminists have succeeded in passing salary equity legislation, women's wages are 60 to 80 percent those of men, and the gender gap in male and female wages increases as educational levels increase. Women's growing participation in the labor force is concentrated in precarious, low-wage, low-productivity jobs and, to a high degree, in the informal sector. Furthermore, the proportion of families headed by a female alone (now a quarter to a third of all Latin American households) or where there is a male present who is unemployed is increasing throughout the hemisphere. Lack of publicly funded day care creates heavy burdens for poor women who work outside the home. Prostitution is on the rise, in part through migration to other countries, and increasing numbers of women are choosing to migrate to more developed countries in order to support their families by sending remittances.

The problem of violence against women has been a central mobilizing issue for Latin American women's movements since the 1980s. However, structural adjustment policies enacted in recent years have entailed reductions in state funding, both for social welfare and public security, and together with increasing inequality these have made violence an even more urgent issue for feminist activism over the past decade. The passage of domestic violence legislation throughout the region in the 1990s and the ratification of the Inter-American Convention on the Prevention, Punishment and Eradication of Violence Against Women (CEDAW) by Latin American governments has not translated into consistent enforcement on the ground, and public and private violence against women remains endemic in many places. The absence of domestic shelters in most Latin American countries renders domestic violence legislation largely symbolic since, in practical terms, women are unable to leave abusive partners. More dramatically, the ongoing killing of young maquila workers in Mexico has spread from Ciudad Juarez to other Mexican cities, and the even greater numbers of women who are victims of "feminicide" in Guatemala, most likely with police complicity, threatens to become a pattern elsewhere.

There have been large gains for women in terms of life expectancy overall but small gains in the area of reproductive rights and access to reproductive health services. Public opinion surveys in Latin America show consistent support for contraceptive use and the decriminalization of abortion, and some countries, notably Brazil, have made great strides addressing reproductive health, including HIV prevention. Throughout the region, feminists are demanding public debate on these issues. Yet in much of Latin America, the opposition of the Catholic Church and the political right to sex education, affordable contraceptives and safe, legal abortion hampers the ability of governments to respond to feminist demands for reproductive education and healthcare. In Chile, for example, AIDS is increasing but the Catholic Church has pressured the government into censuring public service campaigns aimed at preventing the spread of HIV.

Across the region, the absence of available contraception and access to safe abortion means that many women continue to resort to sterilization or clandestine abortions as their only means of controlling reproduction. An estimated one out of every three pregnancies in Peru, for example, ends in abortion. In Chile, the principal form of birth control is abortion, and botched abortions are the primary cause of maternal death. In Paraguay and Peru, complications from clandestine abortions are the second most important cause of maternal death, and the total percentage of maternal deaths caused by unsafe abortions is higher in Latin America and the Caribbean than in any other region of the world. In some countries, such as Chile and, more recently, El Salvador, abortion is not permitted even to save the life of the mother. In Mexico City, where abortions are now allowed under a broad range of conditions, the lack of response within the public health system still often leaves poor women without the option. And rural women who increasingly lack access to public health facilities cannot obtain abortions even when they are legal.

Such challenges in access to economic resources, reproductive health, and an environment free of violence temper but do not negate the real political gains feminists have made in other areas since the 1990s. With increasing numbers of feminists entering political parties, women's ministries, or feminist NGOs, women are better positioned than in the past to address these concerns. Yet the ability of Latin American feminists to mobilize around such issues is complicated by the diversity of feminist organizing in the region, deep divisions within feminist movements over political participation, and the continued marginalization of women and women's rights issues within the state.

THE EMERGENCE OF LATIN AMERICAN WOMEN'S MOVEMENTS

Current tensions within Latin American feminism have their roots in the origins of second-wave feminism in Latin America[3] and the nature of grassroots women's emergence as a mass political force in a number of countries in the 1980s, as well as in a rapidly changing regional and global context. The very factors that gave grassroots women power as a political force in opposition to dictatorships—their seemingly "nonpolitical" nature, their embrace of traditional gender roles, and their relatively narrow mobilizing concerns (economic survival and human rights)—magnified their influence. Once the dictatorships were overthrown, the eclectic ideological and class base of these movements, the wide range in the level of political experience of their members, and the tradition of an oppositional relationship of grassroots movements in relation to the state made unified collective action by women more difficult. In addition, as formal democracies replaced dictatorships in Southern Cone countries, peace accords were signed in countries such as El Salvador and Guatemala, and political reforms made pluralism more possible in countries such as Mexico, feminists experienced new sorts of divisions. On the one hand there were those who believed that the time was ripe for women to move from resolute political opposition ("protesta") to try to access power in democratic institutions and generate practical political alternatives ("propuesta"). On the other hand were those who believed that feminism should focus on consciousness raising and cultural transformation and aspire to be a radical and utopian force for change, uncontaminated by "cooptation" into inherently patriarchal institutions. Current strategic debates about the proper focus of feminist energies derive, in part, from these historical changes.

During the 1980s and early 1990s, women in many parts of Latin America organized at the grassroots level to respond to violations of basic human rights and the challenges of daily survival, made more precarious as a result of neoliberal reforms. Although these struggles typically originated out of women's attempts to fulfill rather than critique their roles as mothers and wives or focused on their identities as members of other social groups (the urban poor, peasants, mothers of the disappeared) without a gender specific focus, the experiences and sense of empowerment that women acquired often led them to an incipient critique of gender inequities and the beginnings of a feminist vision for political and social change.

Thousands of Latin American women first acquired a political vision as a result of organizing around the issue of human rights. In the midst of war and dictatorship, women in a number of countries came together as wives, mothers, and other relatives of the disappeared to challenge powerful and repressive governments to end their human rights violations and give a public accounting of what had happened to their relatives. Demonstrating remarkable courage and tenacity, women in Chile, Argentina, Uruguay, Brazil, Guatemala, and El Salvador developed novel political strategies to call attention to the human rights abuses of military governments. Although different women in grassroots human rights groups experienced changes in consciousness, ideology, and agendas for change to different degrees and in different ways, virtually all talk about being transformed by their experience of acting collectively in the public sphere to demand that governments end repression and protect human rights. The ability of women in human rights groups such as the Mothers of the Plaza de Mayo in Argentina, Family Members of the Detained and Disappeared in Chile, and GAM in Guatemala, to unite across class, age, and ideological lines to protest repression and military dictatorships served as an inspiration and model for the broader democratic opposition that followed.

Others, particularly poor urban women, acquired their political consciousness as a result of efforts to respond collectively to severe economic crisis resulting from neoliberal economic policies. They experimented with ways to ensure their families' survival by sharing the costs of these crises and by demanding housing, food, and water from the state. In Chile, Brazil, Argentina, Ecuador, and Bolivia, women organized community kitchens that often became the most reliable source of food in poor neighborhoods. In Peru, women went further and created the Community Kitchen Movement, which effectively lobbied for funding from Caritas, a Catholic social service agency, and other nongovernmental organizations.

As in the case of women in the human rights groups, women's experiences organizing around economic issues eventually broadened their political focus. In Mexico in 1981, for example, urban women formed the National Council of the Urban Popular Movement (CONAMUP in Spanish) in response to an economic crisis accentuated by structural adjustment policies, including devaluation of the peso in 1982, drastic cuts in state investments in education, health, social security, and social welfare, and elimination of subsidies for basic consumer items. CONAMUP pressured the government for increased resource allocation to the poor while it attempted to change oppressive social conditions that affect women such as domestic violence. In similar fashion, the Rural Women Workers' Movement (MMTR), formed in Brazil in 1989, eventually moved beyond its original focus on securing equal working conditions and benefits for rural women to a political agenda that included abortion, sexuality, and challenges to the gender hierarchy. By 1992, the MMTR boasted a membership of over 30,000, an active local leadership of about 500, and branches in 110 southern Brazilian counties.

In some Latin American countries this incipient feminist consciousness of women organizing around human rights and to assure their families' survival was strengthened as a result of their contacts with feminists from the political left, some of whom saw themselves as advocates of "popular feminism." Inadvertently, the support and protection that Latin American Catholic Churches provided for human rights groups, the poor, and persecuted members of the political left created a space in which feminist activists made contact with women organizing around human rights and economic issues. These connections were particularly influential in Brazil and Chile, where left-wing feminists brought an explicit discussion of gender and women's rights to their participation with human rights groups and other community organizations. Many of these connections took place through Christian Base Communities, although in Chile, the Vicariate of Solidarity, the Church's official human rights institution, provided a particularly serendipitous location for Socialist feminists seeking political protection from the military government to make contact with women from the Family Members of the Detained and Disappeared and other community organizations. So powerful was this connection that when Pope John Paul II visited Chile in 1987, he demanded that the Vicariate expel the feminists.[4]

The emergence of Latin American feminism in a context of political repression and dictatorship in Southern Cone countries (and critiques of the authoritarianism and limited democracy in other countries) profoundly shaped the framing of women's rights in the region. Taking a page from feminist struggles in North America and Europe, Latin American feminists in the 1980s decried the public-private divide that marginalized women's oppression from political debate. Arguing that "the personal is political," feminists called for public response to the problems of domestic violence, women's health, and lack of equal opportunities for women. But Latin American feminists went further, politicizing women's rights as inextricably linked to the larger struggle for democracy and arguing that democracy was incomplete without women's equality. Chilean feminist Julieta Kirkwood coined the slogan "Democracy in the nation and in the home," which became a rallying cry for women's movements across the region. The violence of military rule was connected to the violence women suffered in the home, and domestic violence became a central issue of women's rights that united feminist activists. Out of their experiences with corrupt and authoritarian governments, feminists throughout Latin America demanded the creation of democratic societies that would be inclusive of women and responsive to women's demands.

The unity women achieved in the 1980s in the struggle against authoritarianism, and later, in the fight against violence against women, temporarily obscured the divisions among women. Mobilizing around traditional gender roles proved an effective strategy to call attention to human rights abuses and increasing poverty, but the post-transition period of the 1990s revealed the extent to which many grass roots women activists remained ambivalent about feminism. Among committed feminists, divisions emerged over whether, and how, to engage with new democratic governments. In the shifting political terrain of the 1990s, feminists sought new ways to maintain the integrity of their organizations, continue to mobilize women around a multitude of pressing needs, resist cooptation by political parties and the state, and, where possible, create effective strategies to influence government policies on women's rights. The inherently contradictory nature of many of these goals—most notably the delicate balance between political independence and political engagement—constituted formidable challenges for Latin American feminism.

LATIN AMERICAN FEMINISM AND DEMOCRATIC TRANSITIONS

The political transitions of the 1990s presented Latin American feminists with a new set of opportunities as well as challenges. After decades of dictatorships and civil war, transitions to democracy created a proliferation of new channels for political participation. Guatemalan feminists, for example, succeeded in organizing a women's sector in the Civil Society Assembly and inserted gender specific demands into the 1996 Peace Accords in a historically unprecedented move. While little has been done since the accords to implement the demands, the effort is an important example of ways that feminists attempted to mobilize in the new political landscape. In Argentina, Brazil, Chile, and Uruguay, political parties reemerged after the transition and "New Left" parties like the PT (Workers Party) in Brazil and the PPD (Party for Democracy) in Chile made concerted efforts to attract women to the parties. Mexican women in the 1990s joined alternative political parties in growing numbers and gained leadership positions in the PRD (Party of the Democratic Revolution) and ran as candidates for state offices. Governments throughout the region created National Women's Ministries to focus on gender equality at the national level. Chile's Sernam (National Women's Service), Brazil's National Councils for Women's Rights, and Argentina's National Women's Council spearheaded legal reforms on such issues as domestic violence, marriage and property laws, and education reform.

Yet this same period saw the splintering of the broad-based women's movements that had emerged with such force in the 1980s. Feminist organizations, which had played a crucial role in the struggles for democracy under dictatorships, faced the daunting task of radically redefining their relationship to states that continued to resist women's full political incorporation. Women who were able to make common cause during the dictatorships around issues of human rights, violence against women, and economic privations now found themselves divided over fundamental questions of political strategy. Outside the state, women continued to organize around a multitude of issues, but their efforts were limited in a number of cases by decreases in funding from international donors once the transitions were deemed over.

In this complex political context, several issues dominated debates within feminist organizations: How could feminists influence state policies without allowing the state to co-opt their political agenda? How could feminists increase their representation in the political parties and in the legislatures? How could feminists keep the new women's ministries accountable to women? And finally, how could feminists continue to nurture the movement and keep mobilization alive in the face of chronic funding shortages and the reemergence and dominance of traditional political actors?

FEMINIST PARTICIPATION IN DEMOCRATIC POLITICS

Following the transitions to democracy, political parties as the official interlocutors between civil society and the state reemerged or were created anew. Left-wing parties, in particular, courted women's votes, but feminists were deeply divided over whether to participate in the parties, where they risked diluting the feminist agenda, or to remain autonomous from the state and risk political marginalization. This dilemma was perhaps starkest in the Southern Cone, where stable political parties had historical roots. In Mexico, the opening of the political system and the emergence of alternative political parties like the PRD expanded women's political opportunities, even before the defeat of the PRI at the presidential level in 2000 signaled a significant transformation of the Mexican political system. In Central America, feminists attempted to influence the male-dominated culture of political parties from within, but, with the exception of Costa Rica, many more remained outside of political parties, preferring instead to focus on mobilizing women to exercise citizenship, on negotiating with political parties and the state, and contributing to the creation of a new political culture.

Parties of the left of Latin America were generally the most open to women's participation during this period, including that of feminists. Feminists have had particular success in gaining leadership positions and being chosen as candidates in the newer, more eclectic left parties like the PRD in Mexico, the PPD in Chile and the PT in Brazil. Even within the most progressive parties of the left, however, feminists have had to fight for full inclusion. Much of the openness to women's rights that we see globally in the political left is the result of intense work by feminist party members to force incorporation of feminist issues into the party platforms. In the case of Brazil, for example, feminists made significant inroads in the PT but only after intense internal struggles with the traditional left wing of the party, which was based in the trade union movement.[5] In Mexico, the PRD was the first party to voluntarily institute quotas for women's representation in party organisms and state institutions such as the Congress, but internal debates over the issue kept women's representation lower than in the PRI.

Because the left has been the most open to women's participation, the advancement of women's rights in many Latin American countries is closely linked to the fate of the left. After 1989, as neoliberal reforms consolidated, leftist parties were forced to reconsider their economic platforms, and their political viability became linked to their willingness to "renovate" and accept the basic tenets of liberal capitalism. With radical economic reforms off the political agenda, even Socialist presidents, such as Chile's Ricardo Lagos and Brazil's Lula da Silva, have crafted new political identities that are more Social Democrat than Socialist. Where the left is a minority party, or governs as part of a cross-party coalition, as is the case in Chile, the ability of the left to shape national policy is limited, further diluting the policy impact of feminists within the parties.

Feminists' initial efforts to gain influence and candidate seats in the parties were frustrated because parties often placed them too low on candidate lists to win election and shut them out from internal leadership posts. Across parties of the center-left, and at times even in alliance with conservative women on the right, feminists began to campaign for the creation of gender quotas for women's representation. Mobilization by feminist organizations was critical in helping women overcome the opposition of male party members to this demand. In 1991, Argentina instituted mandatory minimum quotas for women of 30 percent of each party's candidate positions. In the late 1990s, in response to feminist pressure, a number of other Latin American countries followed suit. Costa Rica's quota law, instituted in 1997, mandates that 40 percent of candidate position be given to women. This is the highest quota percentage of any Latin American country. Mexico (2001), Ecuador (2000), Bolivia (2000), Brazil (2000), and Panama (2000) all passed quota laws with a minimum 30 percent threshold for women's representation. Peru (1997) and the Dominican Republic (1997) passed a 25 percent quota law, and even Paraguay, one of the most historically authoritarian countries in Latin America, passed a 20 percent quota law in 1996. Venezuelan feminists suffered a major defeat when the quota law passed in 1997 was later rescinded. Since the imposition of quota laws, women's legislative representation in many of these countries has increased dramatically.

This increase in women's representation, however, has called into question expectations about women's legislative behavior once elected. As women enter the parties of the right as well as the left, easy assumptions about women's "natural" political interests have given way to an acknowledgement of women's multiple allegiances and often conflicting ideologies. While many women elected from the right have resisted feminist efforts to address issues of women's rights, in some instances, women have made political alliances across parties in pursuit of common policy goals. In Chile, for example, women from the left and right cooperated on domestic violence, day-care, and sexual assault legislation. Mexican women from the PRI, PAN, and PRD have worked together on poverty legislation and domestic violence laws. In Argentina and Mexico, cross-party alliances among women proved critical in forcing the parties to agree to quota laws. While these occasional cross-party alliances offer hope that feminist arguments will find root among conservative women, to date these interactions remain the exception rather than the norm.

NATIONAL WOMEN'S MINISTRIES

The creation of National Women's Ministries throughout Latin America in the 1990s is testament to the political strength feminists gained in the course of political transitions, reinforced, in some countries, by pressures from international donors. As new democratic governments sought women's votes, feminists demanded the creation of permanent institutions within the state that would focus on women's rights and legitimize a feminist policy agenda to the rest of the government. Rather than depending on particular parties or political leaders to support feminist policies, feminists hoped that these ministries would provide a permanent space within the state for feminist demands and create new avenues of political participation for women.

Indeed, women's ministries across Latin America have successfully challenged legal discrimination against women in a number of areas. In Mexico, Chile, Brazil, Argentina, Uruguay, and Peru, women's ministries pushed for domestic violence legislation and more equitable marriage and family law. The property rights of married women were strengthened in Chile, Brazil, and Argentina, wage and employment discrimination were targeted throughout South America, and ministries in Brazil and Mexico confronted significant political opposition to reform rape and sexual assault laws and to promote reproductive rights. The Chilean Ministry expanded day-care options for working women and instituted employment protection and benefits for domestic workers. Throughout the region, women's ministries pressured their governments to ratify international agreements on women's rights, from CEDAW to the Platform of Action from the Beijing Conference.

Yet women's ministries have also posed a number of challenges for feminists seeking to influence government policy. Under conservative governments they are not staffed by feminists and can easily be used to block or undermine feminist efforts to change discriminatory laws. In Brazil, the National Council on Women's Rights was closed for several years before being revitalized in 1995, and in Uruguay and Peru, national women's ministries survived only a few years in the 1990s, before being disbanded following a change to more conservative government.

In Mexico, feminists have voiced concerns that, under President Vicente

Fox's administration, conservative opposition within the PAN blocks the work of the women's ministry. Under any political administration, the fact that the top positions in the ministries are politically appointed means ministry leaders must balance allegiance to their particular parties against the demands of feminists outside the state. In Chile, for example, Sernam was headed by Christian Democrats from its creation in 1990 until 2000, during which time it refused to support feminists' efforts to legalize divorce and therapeutic abortion.[6] With the appointment of a Socialist to head the ministry in 2000, Sernam became willing to support divorce legislation. The ministry continues to avoid the issue of reproductive rights, however, because of the strength of opposition to such reforms in the rest of the government.

The politicized nature of women's ministries complicates their relationship with feminists outside the state and serves to confirm feminist suspicions about the risks of engagement with the state. A common complaint from feminists in many countries is that the women's ministries choose their policy agendas and implement their own programs without much consultation with feminist organizations. A leading Chilean feminist complained, "When Sernam needs the women's movement, it makes it visible, and when it doesn't need the movement, it makes it invisible."[7] Many feminists complain that the women's ministries avoid conflict with the rest of the government by implementing projects focused on women's traditional roles, such as poverty alleviation programs for female-headed households, avoiding more politically contentious feminist issues. Women's ministries have also shown a clear preference for cooperation with the most politically traditional professionalized NGOs which tend to promote a narrow range of political proposals more closely connected with middle-class feminists than with poor and working-class women, lesbian women, or indigenous, black, or mulatto women.

The degree of political independence of women's ministries from the rest of the government plays a major role in the ministries' relationship with feminists outside the state and in the types of policies the ministries promote. Some agencies are independent ministries, such as Chile's Sernam, the National Councils for Women's Rights in Brazil, and Argentina and Venezuela's National Councils for Women. Independent ministries have a freer hand in deciding what issues to pursue and how to frame their proposals. In other countries, the agencies fall under the jurisdiction of other government ministries. This is the case, for example, with Bolivia's Sub-secretary for Gender (under the National Secretariat for Indigenous Issues, Gender, and Generations), Costa Rica's National Center for the Development of Women and the Family (under the Ministry of Culture, Youth and Sports)[8] and Colombia's Council for Youth, Women, and the Family (under the Office of the President).

Where women's agencies are subject to the direction of other agencies, their ability to promote women's rights within the government is limited. Yet independent agencies, like Sernam, are considered low status ministries within the government (with correspondingly low status budgets), and they struggle to legitimate the theme of women's rights to the rest of the government. As indicated by the titles of some agencies, in a number of cases women's rights agencies are combined with ministries or subministries focusing on children and the family. Where this is the case, it is logically more difficult for government officials to promote policies that expand women's equality outside their traditional roles within the family. In federal systems, agencies may exist at both the national and state levels, as is the case with Argentina, Mexico, and Brazil.

FEMINISM AND CULTURAL TRANSFORMATION

Outside of the state, Latin American feminists created an impressive web of civil society institutions during the decade of the 1990s. Women's studies programs in universities, feminist research centers inside and outside of universities, and a wide range of nongovernmental organizations helped feminists to develop expertise in research, formal and informal education, the arts, media and public relations, lobbying, and advocacy. Together these NGOs, research centers, and women's studies programs gave feminists important new tools for "doing politics" and cultural transformation.

As in the case of women's ministries, however, professionalization and "NGOization" presented feminists with new challenges and contradictions as well as new forms of power. On the one hand, access to salaried personnel, funding, and an institutional structure made it possible for some activists to develop the kind of networks and expertise necessary to operate at multiple levels—subnational, national, regional, and global. At the same time this process siphoned off experienced feminist leadership from grass roots organizations, weakening, in many cases, the very non-State, non-NGO movements that could hold states and NGOs accountable. The visibility and availability of NGO feminists, together with their access to technical expertise and funding, increasingly put them in a position of being the ones consulted by governments and national and international institutions.

In the absence of mechanisms of consultation and accountability to respond to the new organizational context, this growing inequality in access to resources and official sites of power and the "crisis" of representation that resulted led to conflicts about "who speaks for whom" and how democracy and citizenship can be guaranteed among feminists as well as in the society at large. National and regional mobilizations for the fourth World Conference on Women in Beijing only exacerbated these concerns. The large infusions of resources that accompanied national planning processes inevitably favored some groups and NGOs over others, even while it also made diversity in that process and in attendance at the Hairou Forum at the Beijing conference possible. While serious discussion of these issues was difficult once the Beijing planning process was in motion, they inevitably came to the forefront in post-Beijing reflections on future Latin American feminist strategies and processes.

LATIN AMERICAN FEMINISM IN THE NEW MILLENNIUM: TRANSNATIONAL AND DIVERSE

The diversity and transnationalism that characterize Latin American feminism today were accelerated by events that took place in the 1990s, particularly technological changes associated with globalization that facilitated networking, and regional and international conferences, culminating in the fourth World Conference on Women in Beijing in 1995. These factors, together with the favorable political climate created by transitions to democracy in South America and peace accords in Central America, and the presence of private and public international funding, strengthened the desire to make common cause with women across the region and the world that had been there since the first World Conference on Women in Mexico City in 1975.

By the late 1980s and early 1990s, cyberspace and in-person connections linking women's groups and individual activists to their counterparts across Latin America, North America, and Europe proliferated. Theme-oriented international alliances were organized around issues of violence, health, reproductive rights, sexuality, HIV/AIDS education, popular education pedagogies, and indigenous and Afro-Latin women's rights. Periodic Latin American and Caribbean feminist *encuentros*—Bogotá, Colombia (1981); Lima, Peru (1983); Bertioga, Brazil (1985); Taxco, Mexico (1987); San Bernardo, Argentina (1990); Costa del Sol, El Salvador (1993); Cartegena, Chile (1996); Juan Dolio, Dominican Republic (1999), Playa Tambor, Costa Rica (2002), and Serra Negra, Brazil (2005)—were an opportunity to negotiate regionwide policy agendas and mobilizing strategies. Latin American feminists' transnational ties also received important impetus from international conferences, such as the 1992 UN Conference on Environment and Development in Rio de Janeiro, the 1993 World Conference on Human Rights in Vienna, the 1994 International Conference on Population and Development in Cairo.[9]

Transnational activism is based on a belief that many of the problems that women face today cannot be solved on the national level alone and that a globalized world calls for a globalized approach to women's rights. Indeed, research suggests that the development of global norms on women's rights may be influential in setting national level policies on a variety of feminist issues.[10] And the tight web of networks that developed among feminists and other women activists within Latin America and the Caribbean in the 1990s did make cross-national and regional responses to economic and political changes increasingly viable.

But transnational activism presents risks as well as advantages for domestic feminist politics. The advantages include not only broadening the scope of a potential field of action but also gaining access to international resources and expertise, learning new organizing techniques and creating new venues where citizenship can be exercised and human rights claims made. The latter is especially important to women's organizations that face severe marginalization, repression, or isolation in their home countries. The risks include the diversion of energy and resources into establishing and maintaining international connections at the expense of focusing on urgent local and national problems.

In the case of UN-sponsored conferences, transnational feminist activism can also mean that feminists from less developed countries and regions enter into a particular "logic" where the predetermined rules of the game are not in their favor. For example, self-professed "autonomous" feminists participating in the sixth Latin American and Caribbean Feminist Encuentro in Costa del Sol, El Salvador, in 1993, argued that directing energy toward influencing institutions governed by a "profoundly patriarchal logic" would weaken the rebellious and potentially subversive role of feminism. Other Encuentro participants were skeptical of a regional planning project that depended heavily on U.S. government and nongovernmental financing and that would inherently favor feminist NGOS and individuals with professional feminist expertise.

While some of these concerns were borne out in the course of the Beijing experience, what could not be anticipated was the degree to which the Latin American feminists, together with the international NGO network of which many were a vital part, found ways to subvert and influence the rigid bureaucratic rules and practices that traditionally framed the process. The NGO regional preparatory meetings, for example, were scheduled to overlap directly with governmental preparatory meetings and, during the conference itself, single-issue and regional conferences coordinated their activities on a daily basis and lobbied government delegates to a degree not seen in previous conferences. In a strategy designed to make the conference "a conference of commitments," they pressured governments to state explicitly which elements of the final document they would implement by the year 2000.

No one could have imagined, as well, the degree of diversity that would emerge in the course of preparations for the Beijing conference and other regional activities of the 1990s. Spurred on by international funding that often made diversity a condition, regional encuentros, conferences, and thematic networks ("redes"), throughout the 1990s, black women from favelas, indigenous women, rural women, young working-class women, religiously identified women, women union members, lesbian women, older women ("la tercera edad"), disabled women, and young women were increasingly visible. At the 1994 NGO forum in Mar de Plata, Argentina, held in preparation for the Beijing conference, the more than a thousand participants present embodied a range of feminist practices and spaces of action never before seen, from prominent feminist scholars and the "founding mothers" of Latin American feminism to government officials, development agency staff and consultants, Catholic theologians and lay activists from Catholics for Choice, black feminists, eco-feminists, self-proclaimed "popular feminists" and "Peronist feminists," and political party activists. Participation in the Latin American and Caribbean tent at the NGO tent in Huairou (the nonofficial part of the Beijing conference) was equally diverse. Brazil alone had delegates at the conference from over a thousand women's and feminist organizations and the Mexican delegation included 250 feminist groups. The conditioning of outside funding for the process on guaranteeing diversity, what some called "globalization with difference," had paid off. In the two years of preparation leading up to the fourth World Conference on Women in Beijing in 1995, it became clear that second-wave feminism in Latin American had transcended its relatively isolated, homogenous, stigmatized urban middle-class origins and become a much more diverse and decentered movement.

While the greater diversity of groups and individuals claiming the right to be included in the category "feminist" presented new challenges and tensions, discussions about how to weave feminism into other identities and threads of social and civic life had never been more vibrant or rich. The new diversity as well as a new regional and global context was serving as a motor force for a broader feminist vision. With the importance of classical feminist issues such as domestic and sexual violence, the need for subsidized day care, and reproductive rights acknowledged, to different degrees, feminists used the Beijing planning process to call for a broad vision and agenda, one which, in the words of the Brazilian movement, would "see the world through the eyes of women" or "see social change through a gendered lens" rather than as a specific set of issues primarily of concern to women such as sexual violence and abortion. Others talked about "developing a feminist agenda for public policy" rather than just a "feminist policy agenda."

The unprecedented activation of diverse groups of women throughout the region in a multiplicity of spaces in preparation for Beijing also served to push the boundaries of traditional definitions of citizenship. Indigenous women, for example, a growing number of whom now felt comfortable claiming feminism as one of their identities, created their own autonomous space by convening the First Continental Encuentro of Indigenous Women of the First Nations of Abya Yala (continent of Life) in August 1995 in Quito, Ecuador. In Beijing, they occupied a global space where their identities and proposals were visible and from which they could be reflected back to their countries of origin, giving them legitimacy that they might not otherwise be able to achieve. By achieving recognition and legitimacy, exchanging experiences, and establishing networks of solidarity for future coordination, indigenous women modified and broadened their "subjective citizenship" (borrowing from Virginia Vargas).

At the same time, the Beijing conference further clarified the growing strength of the opposition to feminism. Vatican representatives as well as conservative Catholic and Muslim organizations protested the conference's focus on reproductive health and choice and challenged the concept of gender as a Trojan horse for lesbianism. These groups publicly challenged feminist claims to represent women's interests.

Despite these challenges, the Beijing conference concluded with an ambitious Platform for Action that included preserving most of the gains of previous conferences (including the three previous conferences on women and the ones focused on human rights and population) and agreed on twelve critical areas of concern that constitute the main obstacles to women's advancement: poverty, education, health, violence against women, armed conflict, economic structures, power sharing and decision making, mechanisms to promote the advancement of women, human rights, the media, the environment, and the girl child. Debate was heated, especially on issues related to women's health, but, in the end, the Platform was adopted by consensus although reservations were expressed, orally or in writing, by some forty countries on specific provisions.

THE LESSONS OF BEIJING

Feminists emerged from Beijing with a sharpened understanding of the need to move beyond the dichotomous divisions that had weakened the movement, a clear recognition of the growing challenge of internationally connected antifeminist opposition groups, and the need for a balance among local, national, and international activism. Since Beijing, some feminists on different sides of strategy debates—policy advocacy "versus" movement building, local organizing "versus" global citizenship, autonomy "versus" penetration of the state and dominant institutions—have attempted to reflect critically on feminist activism of the 1990s, including the preparation for Beijing, in order to illuminate possible future paths. While some advocates of feminist autonomy continue to counterpose it to other strategies, most realize that all autonomy is relative and any serious feminist movement needs a combination of forms. Those who have thrown themselves into policy advocacy, on the other hand, recognize the dangers of a strategy that focuses exclusively on negotiations with governments and international organizations without counter-balancing it with grass roots movement building outside of institutions.

In the wake of Beijing, feminist advocates of pursuing global citizenship have acknowledged that, although local levels benefited in many ways from the strategy, in other ways, local processes paid a price by having the focus on a process so far away. In fact, some researchers conclude that the very focus on international conferences and networking has distracted feminists from the more localized struggles within their own countries. Susan Franceschet argues that the net effect of transnational activism within a particular country is highly context specific. Where a well-organized and well-funded feminist movement exists, and where political institutions are responsive to pressure from outside groups, the creation of global agreements on women's rights can spur national governments to make needed reforms. However, small and resource-poor groups, and organizations in less democratic institutional settings, may find that their participation in transnational conferences leaves them sidelined from relevant domestic debates.

Latin American feminists are looking for ways to rebuild women's movements outside of NGOs and state and nonstate institutions so as to provide the balance, accountability, and nourishment that feminist participation in those institutions requires. There is a need, as well, many feminists believe, for frameworks and discourses that acknowledge changed contexts. Rather than adopting a narrow or more purist definition of what it means to be a feminist (the famous *feministómetro,* or feminist yardstick implicitly called for by radicals) or reproducing mechanically arguments and frameworks from the past, there is a need, they argue, for new ways of couching old issues. The growing diversity of Latin American feminism, together with the increasing challenge from conservative opposition groups, challenges feminists to seek new allies even as they resist the cooptation or dilution of the movement's goals. For example, is it possible for feminists to join forces with the Catholic Church to fight poverty while resisting Church pressure to alter their support of reproductive rights? Is it possible to incorporate a defense of reproductive rights within a broader framework of human rights, in a way that could diffuse rather than instigate opposition? How can Latin American feminism continue to broaden its cultural and political influence while maintaining the clarity of vision necessary for collective action?

CONCLUSION

In the post-Beijing period, Latin American feminism faces a number of challenges—a continuing right-wing religious backlash, deteriorating economic and social conditions resulting from neoliberal reforms, halfhearted or outright resistance to implementation of the goals of the Platform for Action by national governments, and the fragility and disappointing performances of even populist civilian democratic governments. In addition, Latin American women's movements appear much more fragmented and unable to act collectively than in the past. Where some see fragmentation, however, others see a new diversity and a wider feminist reach, within and across countries, including globally, that create a foundation for a potentially stronger movement in the future.

Ten years after the Beijing conference and five years into the new millennium, Latin American feminism finds itself at another of its historic strategic crossroads. Latin American feminists are calling for a combination of critical reflection about what can be achieved through different avenues of change (dominant institutions and the state versus movement building outside) and a broad view of feminism to respond to right-wing attacks, deteriorating economies, and the promotion of "fundamentalisms" such as neoliberalism and rigid religious views that promote exclusion rather than inclusion. Increasingly, key Latin American feminist leaders see their movement as not just a set of issues and agendas specific to women but as a worldview that looks at the world through a feminist lens and ask not only "what is good for women" but what is good for democracy and what will contribute to a more humane and just society for all. Latin American feminism increasingly is, as Jean Franco has argued it should be,

> a position (not exclusive to women) that destabilizes both fundamentalism and the new oppressive structures that are emerging with late capitalism. As a secular nonessentialist and counterhegemonic movement, it must confront other global institutions, not only the Vatican but also the World Bank, a confrontation that involves more urgently than ever the struggle for interpretive power.[11]

It is in this struggle for interpretive power and the creation of new cultural symbols and practices, in the strengthening of democracy and citizenship, and in the continuing daily effort to transform dominant institutions and political parties from inside and out, that feminism remains central to struggles for a "world beyond neoliberalism" in Latin America today.

13

Negotiating Multicultural Citizenship and Ethnic Politics in 21st Century Latin America

Shane Greene

PERU ELECTS A NEW "INCA"

Peruvian president Alejandro Toledo entered office in July 2001 only after successfully mobilizing the popular sectors against the corrupt and authoritarian regime of his predecessor. In November 2000 Alberto Fujimori had fled to Japan and renounced his third presidential "victory" amid large-scale protest rallies over apparent electoral fraud led by Toledo and following the public release of the so-called "Vladivideos." The discovery of the videos, secretly made and stored by Fujimori's right-hand man, Vladimiro Montesinos, revealed a massive conspiracy to bribe high-ranking officials in the legislative and judicial branches of the Peruvian government.

In becoming Peru's next president, Toledo explicitly brought ethnic politics to the fore of public debate. He proudly accepted his popular nomination as Peru's new Pachacútec—the Incan emperor widely credited with expanding and renovating the ancient empire—on the basis of a decision to strategically position his own indigenous Andean background against Fujimori's as a political "outsider," the product of Japanese immigration to Peru. Waving the rainbow-colored flag of Tawantinsuyu (the Quechua name of the Inca's "four-corners" empire) and occasionally donning the garb of Andean staff-bearers to lead his public protests, Toledo configured his place within a centuries-old mythology still lodged in the popular Peruvian consciousness: the return of the Inca.[1]

Although his humble Andean background makes him seemingly more "authentic," Toledo's constant gestures to the Inca past on the campaign trail are not new to mainstream Peruvian politics. Paying rhetorical homage to Peru's Incaic roots has long been prominent in the political discourses of even the most aristocratic and evidently nonindigenous Peruvian ideologues, nation makers and *indigenista* intellectuals. Historian Cecilia Méndez aptly describes how the Peruvian elite has constructed the country's nationalism with constant rhetorical appreciation for the Inca patrimony. Implicit in this, of course, is the everyday disparagement of "assimilated" present-day indigenous people of the Andes and their migrant counterparts in coastal cities. Peru's nationalist ideology, she says, is best captured in the phrase *"Incas si, indios no"* ("Incas yes, Indians no").[2]

Since assuming office, Toledo has lessened his use of neo-Incaic symbolism even while attempting to convert his indigenous image into a workable multicultural agenda for all of Peru's ethnic minorities. Following multicultural models found elsewhere in Latin America this includes not only native Andeans but also indigenous Amazonians and Afro-Peruvians. In effect, Toledo was forced to move beyond his political posturing as the returning Inca in the face of overtly political demands from social movements that have tired of facile, rhetorical flirtations with the pre-Colombian past. Indigenous representatives from Peru's Andean and Amazonian regions now explore the possibilities of uniting their social causes and putting an end to decades of organizing separately under different ideological banners: the Andeans as "peasants" and the Amazonians as "natives." While Afro-Peruvians have become increasingly active in negotiating their own ethnic claims with the Toledo administration, a workable alliance with indigenous leaders has not materialized.

The various political actors speaking on behalf of Peru's ethnic populations are participants in emerging social movements—patently global in scope—that seek legitimation from a regime of rights, responsibilities, and opportunities afforded by a transnational indigenous citizenship on the one hand and a transatlantic, Afro-diasporic citizenship on the other. In this sense Peru is only one example of a fast-growing and now prominent trend toward multicultural citizenship and ethnic politics across the entire Latin American region.

ETHNIC POLITICS IN REGIONAL AND GLOBAL CONTEXT

Scholars commonly explain the prominence of ethnic rights agendas in terms of much broader global trends that are clearly visible in the Latin American context. They cite multicultural legislation, environmental ideologies, globalization, democratization, neoliberalization, the expansion of international advocacy networks, and the correlated waning of class politics with expanding "identity" based movements.[3] In a recent book on this subject Donna Lee Van Cott demonstrates that at least eight Latin American countries have explicitly incorporated multicultural rhetoric into their constitutions.[4] New constitutions in Brazil (1988), Colombia (1991), Ecuador (1998), Venezuela (1999), and proposed reforms in Peru (2002) are good examples of the constitutional dimensions of Latin American multiculturalisms.

The recent trend toward multicultural legislation seeks to redress the long history of institutionalized racism and colonial legacies that evolved into state-led ideologies of *mestizaje*. During an earlier republican era, with a few exceptions, most Latin American states explicitly promoted the ideas of biological and social mixture as a means of nation building.[5] The *mestizo* figure thus emerged not as a simple social "fact" of historical, cultural, and reproductive exchanges between colonially constructed "races." Rather, the mestizo also ultimately came to symbolize the nation itself, a representation which served to obscure, and even ideologically eliminate, the cultural and ethnic differences within nations. Not coincidentally, this meant primarily those differences associated with the races that European colonialism constructed as "inferior": primarily postconquest Amerindians and descendants of the African slave trade.

For peoples of agrarian background with identifiable cultural "traits" (i.e., non-European languages, customs, collective claims to territory, etc.) the re-

cent trend toward state recognition of ethnic difference has meant an opportunity to rethink their classification as part of a rural peasantry. Processes of
reindigenization of the agrarian peasantry are found all over Latin America.
A good example is the world famous Zapatista rebellion which began in 1994
in the impoverished southern state of Chiapas, Mexico, as a militant form of
indigenous Mayan protest. The Zapatistas perfectly timed the start of the
movement to contest the implementation of the North American Free Trade
Agreement (NAFTA) and changes in Mexican legislation that left communal
land systems first granted during the postrevolutionary Cardenas era open to
the threat of expropriation. A more recent example is the revolutionary up-
heaval in the capital streets of La Paz, Bolivia, in 2003, which took on explicit
ethnic overtones and resulted in the ousting of the Bolivian president. No-
ticeably, this dynamic of re-ethnification is not present merely in *el campo* but
also in *la ciudad*, challenging common assumptions about the way indigeneity and class line up with rural and urban spaces.

Historically, native peoples from tropical hunting-gathering societies have
always been defined by the racial categories of European colonialism, never
to be temporarily "promoted" to a class status in Marxist modernization
terms. Highly decentralized forms of political organization, forested environments, an often greater detachment from the modernizing frontier, and
the occasional presence of visual signs of "Indianness" (e.g., nakedness, body
paint, adornments) made them the most obvious targets for the "civilized"
world's racial scorn.

The recent globalization of indigenous movements stems from some
identifiable antecedents in the latter half of the twentieth century. Agrarian
reforms throughout Latin America in the 1950s and 1960s play a significant
role. So too do certain catalyzing events that refocused attention on the
ethnic status of Indians in the Americas, in particular the 1971 Barbados
Conference and the 1980 Russell Tribunal.[6] More recently, international
agreements and activities associated with the International Labor Organization, the United Nations Work Group on Indigenous Peoples, and the Organization of American States have dramatically heightened the world's
awareness of indigenous issues.

While certain national contexts are dominated by discussion of indigenous/state politics (Bolivia and Guatemala are two clear examples), other states view the trend toward ethnic recognition as one addressed to both indigenous and Afro-descendent constituencies. There are some signs of convergence between Afro and indigenous movement actors in terms of how the state seeks to incorporate them. In some Afro communities, particularly those identified with histories of collective resistance to slavery and the establishment of semiautonomous maroon communities, entitlement to a collective ethnic identity evolves from broader historical claims to a collective territory, natural resources, and cultural traditions in a manner not dissimilar to that of indigenous communities. In fact, in some cases, like that of the Garifuna of Central America, collective claims are articulated in terms of a hybrid Afro-Indigenous ancestry.

Despite the long histories of exchange that exist between those identified as "black," "Indian," "mestizo," and so on, states now seek to construct an anti-mestizaje model. Multicultural legislation thus goes in the direction of de-mixing and requires that states and ethnic actors think in terms of a rationalized "map" of distinct and separately bounded ethnic identities. In this sense, the ongoing construction of Afro-descendant identities diverges from indigenous identity politics in many contexts, creating as many obstacles to like-minded or allied political action as there are possibilities for it. For example, Afro-Peruvians, mainly Lima urbanites and provincial agricultural laborers (almost exclusively located on the coast), find it difficult to align their civil rights oriented struggle with the agendas of Andean and Amazonian representatives. The latters' discussions tend to revolve around natural resource rights, collective land claims, and indigenous language recognition, none of which precisely address the agenda of racism, equal opportunity, poverty-level wages, and distinctive musical traditions that blacks have organized around. In this sense, Afro-Peruvians seem self-consciously aware of what several observers have already reported as the tendency for state concerns with the status of indigenous peoples to overshadow the plight of peoples of African descent.[7]

State recognition of Afro-descendants' collective ethnic status is probably most visible in Brazil and Colombia, where legislation has been passed to demarcate "maroon remainder" and "black" communities respectively. Article 68 of Brazil's 1988 constitution opened the door for recognition of *quilombos* (maroons or escaped slaves). The centuries-long history of slaves escaping from Brazilian plantation owners, taking refuge in the country's interior and constructing semi-autonomous maroon communities is now formally legitimated by the state's decision to give collective title to the ancestral "remainders" of these historic sites. In an attempt to occupy the multicultural opening, and in coordination with the country's urban black leaders, the quilombo movement began to intensify its pressure on the state following ratification of the 1988 constitution. In doing so they espouse a "liberation" narrative in which cultural heroes of slave resistance figure prominently, most often the legendary Zumbi of Palmares. As a result of talks and public demonstrations in the mid-1990s, President Fernando Henrique Cardoso signed a decree that sought to address their demands and create a land titling commission. In recent years as many as 700 quilombo communities have been identified, although the pace of granting formal title has been predictably slower and takes place amid conflicting claims on rural lands.[8]

Colombia's 1991 constitution served as a similar collective ethnic opening for that country's rural Afro population. While black organizers have a much longer history in the country their eyes were clearly awakened when the government announced plans to reform the constitution. The Constituent Assembly charged with deliberating over constitutional reforms in 1990 was subjected to multiple claims by both indigenous and Afro-Colombian actors as well as academics working with these populations. In keeping with the state's longer legislative history of conceptualizing "Indians" as distinct ethnic groups, the new constitution grants some immediate and tangible political benefits to indigenous populations (for example an ethnic quota of two indigenous representatives in the congress). While the ethnic language was substantially weaker, Transitory Article 55 required the formation of a special committee to study the situation of Afro-Colombians, specifically those in the Pacific coast region where a law was deemed necessary "for the protection of the cultural identity and rights of these communities."[9] Following up on the constitutional mandate, in 1993 the Colombian legislature passed a law defining blacks in the "Pacific basin" area as an "ethnic group" and the result has been a complicated process of attending to and formalizing their collective lands, now legally recognized under the category of *comunidades negras*.

The noticeable trend toward Latin American states creating multicultural opportunities for ethnic groups to take advantage of is in no way a "risk-free" step forward. Indeed, there are important limitations to policies that address injustices based on histories of colonial and national racism and state efforts to expand the scope of democratic citizenship. In this sense, Charles Hale offers a framework to understand the possible "menace" multicultural recognition entails for those ethnic movements and actors that question the political and economic limits of state multiculturalism and get labelled "too radical" in the process.[10] When ethnic claims are categorized as "radical," critics are quick to accuse the ethnic actors who articulate them of "reverse-racism." Yet, as Hale points out, accusations of ethnic radicalism often turn out to be terribly convenient from the point of view of international development institutions like the World Bank whose neoliberal policies in fact encourage the state trend toward ethnic recognition. The "radical" label tends to conceal the ways that states use multicultural rhetoric as a means to officially permit ethnic participation while also strategically limiting ethnic actors' capacity to enact significant political and economic change. In other words, the limitations are inherently part of the multicultural opening. They are evident in the constant refusal to acknowledge those "radical" claims that might point to underlying structures of political marginalization and economic inequality to which ethnic actors are continually subject.

Recent presidential politics in the Andean region are particularly illustrative here as a sign of just how public, contradictory, and potentially "menacing" ethnic politics have become. Since the 1990s the Confederation of Indigenous Nationalities of Ecuador (CONAIE) has emerged as the leader of one of the world's most powerful indigenous movements. The organization began in the mid-1980s as an effort to consolidate representation of both Amazonian and Andean groups. But it became globally famous for organizing massive demonstrations in the early 1990s, a mobilization tactic it has used periodically to apply direct pressure on the state. By the mid-1990s Ecuador's indigenous movement evolved into a dual-strategy political actor. CONAIE continues to operate as a social movement but it is now directly attached to a political party, known as the Movimiento de Unidad Plurinacional Pachakutik, which has been successful in occupying municipal and national electoral seats.[11] Indeed, in 1996 Luis Macas, a multiterm president of CONAIE, became the first indigenous person to be elected to Ecuador's National Congress.

Over the last several years the CONAIE-Pachakutik alliance has resulted in a new form of indigenous electoral power. But it has also been witness to considerable political setbacks. Despite the fact that indigenous peoples are estimated at as high as 40 percent of the population in Ecuador, electoral strategies typically force ethnic actors to seek out alliances with other political actors, particularly at the national level. The consequences are sometimes controversial and, as one might expect, often contradictory. In 2000 CONAIE leaders supported a coup led by a former military colonel, Lucío Gutiérrez, that ousted President Jamil Mahuad. The takeover was short-lived but the indigenous-military alliance ultimately led to Gutiérrez's successful bid for the presidential office in 2003 due in significant part to CONAIE support. In a seemingly stunning "victory" for multicultural causes everywhere, Gutiérrez appointed two indigenous leaders to his cabinet. Luis Macas became the minister of agriculture while Nina Pakari became the first indigenous woman to be appointed as head of Ecuador's Ministry of Foreign Relations.

Not long after Gutiérrez occupied the presidential office, CONAIE realized its mistake. Instead of delivering on his promises of social equity the president instead sought to implement an IMF-backed economic plan that resulted in higher taxes and higher daily living costs (particularly in the prices of fuel, cooking gas, and bus fares). Negotiations over these economic measures between Gutiérrez and his indigenous supporters turned tense and soon led to street demonstrations in protest of the president's economic plan. By August 2003 the indigenous-military alliance had dissolved completely. Gutiérrez fired Macas and Pakari from his cabinet and CONAIE formally renounced all former allegiances to the president. However, Gutiérrez's most unpopular move came in 2005. Using the pretext of an "anticorruption" campaign, he arbitrarily and illegally fired the country's Supreme Court judges. This was apparently also his last move since it resulted in massive public demonstrations in Quito and provoked a decision by the congress to remove him from the presidential office. In mid-April he fled to Brazil seeking refuge.

Forced to reflect on this chain of events in a 2005 interview, ex-CONAIE leader Macas expressed considerable regret over the alliance of 2000 that led to Gutiérrez's election. He further clarified that in the wake of the president's departure, Ecuador's indigenous movement leaders took a decision on April 28 to refrain from all participation in state institutions for the near future. He recounted the events with a tinge of nostalgia about the glorious "then" of the indigenous movement in the early 1990s as compared to the more embattled (and perhaps embarrassing) "now" of the last few years:

> To compare, it [the indigenous movement] is not the same as it was in the early 1990s, when it was very strong, had a real presence, and, above all, was accepted and seen as credible by the national society. Today, unfortunately—and perhaps because of the quick evolution the indigenous movement has had in Ecuador—it has suffered from a kind of stagnation and I think, for that matter, a series of external manipulations have been produced that come principally from the government.[12]

To the case of Ecuador's ex-indigenous-supported, ex-military ex-president, one must now add the remarkable victory of an indigenous leader to the Bolivian presidency in December 2005. Elected with a majority 54 percent of the vote, Evo Morales is a self-identifying Aymara Indian and leader of Bolivia's coca growers' movement. Comparing him to Hugo Chávez in Venezuela, U.S. news reports depict Morales as the latest leader of a leftist resurgence taking hold of the region due to his self-professed socialism and his "war" against the U.S. "War on Drugs" associated with the country's coca eradication programs.[13] Indigenous advocates see Morales's triumph as the latest indication that democracy creates significant political opportunities for indigenous spokespersons. Open elections not only allow them to influence the state's highest offices of political authority but, given the right conditions, to occupy those offices as well.

Morales's rise to the fore of public politics in Bolivia is the complex result of a state-sanctioned call for broader popular participation in governance, a series of deepening political crises, and continued unrest over neoliberal reforms and U.S. drug policy. Bolivia's experiment with neoliberal reforms began in 1985 with the passing of the so-called "New Economic Policy" (Supreme Decree 21060), which had an immediate and widespread negative impact on the state mining industry. By the 1990s the government sought to combine neoliberal economics with a form of multicultural decentralization. In 1994 the administration of President Gonzalo Sánchez de Lozada (popularly known as "Goni") promulgated a "Popular Participation Law." The intent was to promote both the decentralization of state resources and an expansion of democratic practices among those sectors historically marginalized from them. Unlike in most Latin American states (Guatemala representing the other exception), Bolivia's indigenous citizens in fact constitute the majority of the population and the law was in large part directed at them. Thus, the first article of the law states, "The Present Law recognizes, promotes, and consolidates the process of popular participation by articulating indigenous, peasant, and urban communities with the juridical, political, and economic life of the country." [14]

Bolivia's indigenous majority, however, is politically organized in complicated and fragmentary ways. The country's "popular sector" organizations consist of everything from native Aymara nationalists and peasant and labor syndicates to coca-growers' organizations and urban neighborhood associations (due to the significant numbers of indigenous peoples living in cities like Cochabamba and El Alto, outside of La Paz). Since the end of the 1990s the country has experienced repeated bouts of political unrest fueled by popular discontent with successive administrations and deep ethnic divisions. Under the elected government of Hugo Banzer, who also headed a dictatorship during the 1970s, massive protests erupted in the city of Cochabamba as a result of an effort to privatize the municipal water system in 2000. After the state sold the water rights to a subsidiary of the U.S.-based Bechtel Corporation, the overwhelmingly poor residents of Cochabamba witnessed their water bills skyrocket and took to the streets. Following a general strike and stalled negotiations thousands of protesters again blockaded the city streets in February 2000, an action to which Banzer responded with police repression that turned violent. The conflict came to a climax in April when renewed clashes between thousands of protesters and military officials

resulted in the death of a teenager. The state finally backed down and conceded to the Cochabambinos who demanded that the water rights be returned to the local community.

An even more dramatic confrontation with Bolivia's neoliberal state came
to a head in 2003 surrounding the exploitation of a natural gas reserve that
lies in the eastern lowlands of Bolivia and which the state had conceded to a
consortium of foreign hydrocarbons corporations. The so-called "Bolivian
Gas War" stemmed from initial uproar in 2002 when President Jorge
Quiroga (who took over the presidential office for an ailing Hugo Banzer)
proposed a pipeline that would export the gas through Chile instead of
through Peru. The culture of protest that has developed in the highlands
over foreign corporate influence in the state's economic plans was tinged
with a strong nationalistic sentiment peculiar to the relations between Bolivia and Chile. Proposing to export gas through Chile also rekindled the
long-standing popular resentment of Bolivians toward their southern neighbor (due to Bolivia's having lost access to the Pacific coast during the War of
the Pacific in the late 1800s).

Quiroga postponed making a final decision about the pipeline, choosing
instead to leave the gas controversy to his successor, Gonzalo Sánchez de
Lozada, who was elected to a second presidential term to begin in late 2002.
When President "Goni" made his preference for the Chile option known,
popular unrest escalated into a violent confrontation with the military during the months of September and October 2003. Thousands from the pre-
dominantly indigenous and highland cities of El Alto and Cochabamba
organized protest rallies and street blockades. The military responded with
actions that led to the death of at least seventy persons. When the excessive
use of force became apparent Goni not only lost virtually all popular support
but also the support of top civilian and military officials, including that of his
own vice president, Carlos Mesa. On October 18 Sánchez de Lozada resigned from office and, like so many other troubled political elites from
Latin America have done before him, sought refuge in the United States.
Mesa, who inherited the office from Goni, fared little better. After an unsuccessful national referendum on the gas issue Mesa voluntarily resigned in
mid 2005, claiming that the nation had become ungovernable. The conflict

continues to deepen as peasant, labor, and indigenous movements based in the Bolivian highlands call for the nationalization of the gas reserves and probusiness interests in the lowland city of Santa Cruz demand privatization backed by a regional movement that threatens secession if necessary.[15]

During these successive years of political turmoil, Evo Morales emerged as Bolivia's indigenous "promise." He has been actively involved in Bolivia's *cocalero* movement, which seeks to defend the coca growers' livelihood and cultivation of the plant from the threat posed by U.S. backed coca eradication programs. Many of the coca growers he speaks for are also directly affiliated with a political party, the Movement Toward Socialism (MAS), that Morales leads. His national political career began in 1997 when he was elected to serve as a deputy in Bolivia's lower house, but he became increasingly visible when he placed as the runner-up candidate in the elections that returned Sánchez de Lozada to office for a second term in 2002. In public statements on the 2005 campaign trail Morales repeatedly made it clear that his presidential priorities would emphasize a reversal of the 1985 neoliberal economic policy and of coca eradication programs, as well as the nationalization of Bolivia's gas reserves and the creation of an all-inclusive Bolivia for all Bolivians. How far exactly he is willing to go to deliver on such promises is hardly clear at the moment as he faces the difficult task of balancing Bolivia's internal chaos and his own internal competitors with the demands of negotiating with international institutions at the beck and call of the U.S. superpower.

Thus, however tempting it might be to suggest that Morales's election in 2005 represents an automatic "victory" for ethnic causes, indigenous or otherwise, this would clearly be an oversimplification. The 2001 election of Alejandro Toledo in Peru began with very similar public celebrations of an "indigenous" victory.[16] Once Toledo faced the realities of an office that demands a balance of competing civil society interests with global market politics, his indigenous triumph evolved into a confrontation with social movement actors that expect more from a "multicultural" state than simply more of the same old indigenista-style rhetoric disguising underlying political-economic interests. By 2004 Toledo's ostensible "indigenous" victory had landed him in a slump of single-digit approval ratings and repeated public denunciations by the very ethnic representatives to whom his multicultural initiatives were addressed. This may be a lesson of caution that Morales should learn before attempting to create a "new" inclusive Bolivia in the name of the ethnic majority.

A CLOSER LOOK AT PERU'S MULTICULTURAL MOMENT

Unlike Bolivia's indigenous socialist president, Peru's President Toledo proved to be something closer to an indigenous neoliberal, which was not a terribly surprising outcome given his Stanford training as an economist and prior stint as a World Bank official. To recall Hale's concept of the multicultural menace, we might say that the Peruvian state's recent attempt to "promote" recognition of the ethnic status of indigenous and Afro-descendant actors seeks simultaneously to "nudge back" their more "radical" demands. Despite the indigenous image of the president, the Toledo administration has skilled itself in refusing to acknowledge as legitimate, or as often as not to simply ignore, those ethnic claims on the state that seek to alter the structure of power and economic influence that maintain Peru's inequalities.

The famed foreign first lady, an anthropologist and student of Quechua, emerged as a key player in this respect. Eliane Karp founded the Comisión Nacional de Pueblos Andinos, Amazónicos, y Afro-Peruanos (CONAPA) in late 2001, a state-led initiative that intended to represent the interests of Peru's Andean and Amazonian peoples and later extended its efforts to black Peruvians. CONAPA got off to an ambitious start by working on a constitutional reform agenda with multiple ethnic spokespersons. By 2003 CONAPA had spiraled downward into a series of troubles that led to a yearlong standoff, primarily between the administration and various Andean and Amazonian actors who repeatedly denounced the commission for its lack of transparency, its financial mismanagement, and the behind-the-scenes cronyism that seemed to account for most of the decision making. One Afro-Peruvian actor, an urban representative from a Lima-based NGO, steadfastly pledged his allegiance to Karp's cause throughout the entire ordeal. Another, from another Lima-based NGO, withdrew entirely from the commission. The latter bowed out because it appeared to be little more than a publicity stunt organized by the First Lady. To use his words from an interview, "era puro foto" ("It was nothing but photo opportunities"). In July 2004 Toledo finally acknowledged the criticisms, disbanded CONAPA, and called for a new and improved Instituto Nacional de Desarrollo de los Pueblos Andinos, Amazónicos y Afro-Peruano (INDEPA), the creation of which was approved by Congress in December of that year.

In what may come as a surprise to observers of indigenous politics in Peru, the various social-movement actors involved in these confrontational negotiations with the state represent a nascent—and still rapidly evolving—alliance between Andean and Amazonian community representatives under an explicitly "indigenous" banner. This may take some by surprise since contemporary scholarship insists that there is no significant indigenous movement in the country.[17] In fact, unlike neighboring Ecuador and Bolivia, Peru is often cited as a notable exception in the Latin American context, an aberration from general trends of ethnic-based claims trumping class-based politics.

Explanations for the ostensible absence of indigenous movements vary but they inevitably assume that the Peruvian national context is somehow peculiarly insulated from today's global indigenism and Latin America's growing grassroots indigenous mobilization. For some analysts, an explicitly "indigenous" identity remains a highly devalued political currency in Peru, specifically for the Andeans who have historically organized under the banner of agrarian unions and "peasant" syndicates.[18] Instead of appropriating their indigenousness as a political tool, they argue, Andean peoples articulate political projects for progress by utilizing other ideologies based on their peasant status or ethnic hybridity. According to anthropologist Marisol de la Cadena, rather than opposing indigenous identities to mestizo ones Andeans adopt a strategy of ethnic hybridity, infusing indigenousness with the signs of social mobility implied in the logic of mestizaje. Considering the explosion of an explicitly *indigenous* politics during Toledo's presidency, it might be time to rethink some of these assumptions. It is true that use of the term "indigenous" remains uncommon in many local Andean communities, compared to "peasant" or other provincial forms of self-identification. But in

the last few years the term increasingly circulates in peasant and ethnic movement organizational rhetoric, suggesting something about the impact of
global multicultural politics in Peru and the possibility of a rediscovery of indigenousness in the Peruvian Andes.

The emergence of joint Andean and Amazonian claims of an explicitly
"indigenous" sort during the Toledo presidency is due to processes that pre-
date the administration and that extend beyond the country's internal regional dynamics. Peru's emerging indigenous movement draws significantly
from several international arenas of rights claims and social advocacy decades in the making and central to indigenous projects everywhere. These
include conventions that recognize indigenous peoples' rights—for instance, the International Labor Organization's Convention 169, which gives
indigenous peoples the "right of consultation" in projects that affect their
territories.

Since the early 1980s, the UN has also been a primary international legal
context in which indigenous leaders infuse local causes with a more universal
notion of ethnic citizenship. Through the Working Group on Indigenous
Peoples, the UN helped promote and release the "Draft Declaration on the
Rights of Indigenous Peoples" in the early 1990s. The Draft proposes to recognize a series of collective rights that would redress the wrongs indigenous
populations suffered under European colonialism and the assimilationist
campaigns of postcolonial nation-states. All such international legal proposals, debated extensively by indigenous representatives, are careful to define
collective rights in concert with the West's historically dominant notions of
human and individual rights. Attempting to tie indigenous peoples to the
rule of law within liberal state democracies avoids the thorny issue of ethnic
separatism, which most indigenous groups do not advocate and is first on the
list in the "radical" ethnic agenda category Hale identifies. However, international indigenous-rights law legitimates the contemporary discourse about
distinct indigenous "peoples" possessing a fundamental right to collective
"self-determination." Ideologically, this guarantees them a sense of semi-
autonomous existence within their respective nation-states and allows them
to perceive themselves as part of an emerging indigenous citizenry on an international scale.

The dramatic worldwide impact of indigenous-environmental advocacy alliances is also of great importance here. Indigenous rights are now commonly promoted as part of a package with environmental justice issues, in significant part due to the privileged moral position indigenous peoples have come to occupy with respect to nature. Although promoting indigenous peoples as inherently conservationist is a matter of great contention, sometimes leading to great disappointment on environmentalists' part, one thing is clear: since the end of the 1980s, many indigenous groups have emerged as the most visible global representatives of environmental conservation. The various symbolic and practical victories won by Amazonian people opposing World Bank dam projects that threatened their rainforest territories are exemplary in this regard.[19]

Many indigenous spokespersons now display their cultural traditions, material practices and spiritual values as symbols of sustainable societies in opposition to the rampantly destructive tendencies of corporate capitalism. Or, for that matter, they look for their own market opportunities within the bounds of current "sustainable" development initiatives and ecologically oriented enterprises.[20] Thus, images of the indigenous as spokespersons for sustainability do not merely circulate as symbolic currency. They also serve as political and occasionally financial capital convertible into real-world possibilities for mobilization, international support, and thus leverage with the state.

In Peru, the international advocacy networks and conservationist alliances of Amazonian movements that were developed in the 1980s and 1990s helped create the ideological space necessary for Andeans to reevaluate their "peasant" status and consider exchanging it for, or at least combining it with, that of the ecologically inclined "indigenous" peoples. The agrarian identity of Peru's Andean peoples was made official by the state's reclassification of Andean "indigenous communities" as "peasant communities" during General Juan Velasco's reformist military revolution of the late 1960s and early 1970s. Yet born from that same revolutionary era was a different popular political consciousness that did define itself in ethnic and cultural terms. The Velasco state recognized Amazonian peoples' titled settlements as "native communities" during the same period it was redefining

Andeans as peasants. Velasco enacted the Native Communities Law in 1974, resulting in the rapid growth of local ethnic organizations among all the major indigenous groups in the Amazon and the birth of the national Interethnic Association of Development in the Peruvian Jungle (AIDESEP), which has sought to represent Amazonian peoples nationally and internationally since 1980.

The Amazonian natives' organizational efforts initially sought to protect their newly won communal land holdings by federating individually titled "native communities." During the 1980s the Amazonian movement diversified with the emergence of dozens of new local federations and a rival national-level organization. AIDESEP and its founding president, Evaristo Nugkuag, played an absolutely critical role in expanding the global reach of the Amazonian cause internationally. In 1984 he received help from the nongovernmental organization Oxfam to host a meeting in Lima.[21] AIDESEP invited indigenous organizational representatives from five Amazonian countries (Peru, Ecuador, Bolivia, Brazil, and Colombia). The result was the creation of the now globally recognized Coordinator of Indigenous Organizations from the Amazon Basin (COICA), the only continental Amazonian organization of its kind. Nugkuag, who served as president of both AIDESEP and COICA, became a key promoter of a strategic global alliance between Amazonian and environmentalist organizations. During his tenure, COICA invited every major international environmental NGO to Peru in 1990 to sign the Iquitos Declaration. The document formalized a strategic eco-indigenous alliance with global conservationists for which the Amazonians have since become famous.

Only since 1997 or so have the political projects of Andean "peasants" and Amazonian "natives" started to converge around ideas of an "indigenous" citizenship in Peru. A joint Andean-Amazonian organizational effort initially emerged that year as a result of a human rights meeting in Cuzco. The original architects of this biregional agenda sought to realign the Andean "peasants" with the Amazonian "natives" with an explicitly indigenous political message. Amazonian leaders from the organization AIDESEP initially played a strong role in establishing the effort. But Andean representatives became increasingly involved since 2001 due to the leading role played by a recent organization that represents Andean communities known as CONACAMI.

Born amid Fujimori's neoliberal dismantling of state industries and a massive expansion of foreign mining claims in Andean provinces in the late 1990s, the Coordinadora Nacional de Comunidades Afectadas por la Minería seeks to call attention to the social and environmental impact of these extractive activities. Realizing the global potential of combining their ecological concerns with ethnic concerns in today's ideological climate, CONACAMI has "rediscovered" Andean indigeneity and seeks to politicize it. In negotiating with the state they now make constant references to the UN Draft Declaration on the Rights of Indigenous Peoples and the International Labor Organization's Convention 169. They have also publicly declared that the term "peasant" should be considered synonomous with "indigenous" in Peru. In short, they seek to practice an eco-indigenous politics similar to that the Amazonians have been pursuing for decades. In the context of an explicit turn toward an ethnic identity model under Toledo's multicultural government, and in light of at least one sector of Andeans who have come to embrace an eco-indigenous political identity, even Peru's oldest and most historic "peasant" unions are not immune. While decidedly ambivalent about the ethnic trends they too portray themselves as "indigenous" on occasion as a means to build alliances with other social actors and to negotiate the state's multicultural opening.[22]

The role of Afro-Peruvians in this process is equally complex. As one might expect from an administration (and indeed a nation) obsessed with its Inca patrimony, Toledo's multicultural model was and is conceived primarily in terms of indigenous populations. Afro-Peruvians serve as a kind of ethnic afterthought. This is quite literally the case since the First Lady's original efforts did not include Afros and indeed they were not even invited during the preliminary rounds of discussion. According to multiple first-hand Afro-Peruvian accounts, Afro actors were eventually asked to join in the multicultural initiative on the basis of a precedent set by a 1999 World Bank development project that the Fujimori government had neglected and CONAPA took charge of. The program was specifically targeted for "indigenous and Afro-Peruvian peoples" and thus CONAPA was established to include them as part of its otherwise essentially indigenous mission. While alliances have formed between Amazonians and Andeans in the process of CONAPA's gradual transformation into INDEPA Afro-Peruvian actors have maintained a relative distance. They appear unsure of what, if any, possibilities exist for alliances with indigenous actors given the differences in their objectives and an often lukewarm reception of the other's ethnic cause on both sides.

As a result, Afro-Peruvians have organized a more or less independent response to the state's call for a multicultural model, albeit with substantial difficulties and with considerably more direct intervention by state actors. The main social movement that represents Afro communities at the grassroots level in Peru is the Movimiento Negro Francisco Congo (MNFC). Afro-Peruvian intellectuals founded MNFC in the mid 1980s, partly as a civil rights campaign inspired by the success of black movements in the United States but also, more locally, as an act of symbolic recuperation of a figure from Peru's history of slave resistance. Francisco Congo was an eighteenth-century *cimarrón* (escaped slave) and leader of the *palenque de Huachipa* outside of Lima. Essentially an urban Limeño phenomenon in its original instantiation, the MNFC has since remade itself to try to include representatives from various agricultural towns and rural communities on Peru's coastline, where there are significant historical concentrations of Afro-Peruvians. Since the early 1990s the Afro-Peruvian presence has slowly emerged as a more visible one nationally and internationally. This is due in part to the creation of several nongovernmental organizations that serve as the "professional arm" of the MNFC and multiple cultural associations that promote Afro-Peruvian performances which are now witnessing the success of international musical icons like Susana Baca and Eva Ayllon.

To the evident gap between indigenous and Afro in Peru one must add the gap between urban and rural. It is particularly evident in terms of how the divide between Afro-Limeños and provincial Afro-Peruvians on the coast has been deepened rather than resolved through the state's multiculturalism. Once Afros were included the First Lady's multicultural commission sought out Afro-descendent representation exclusively from Lima-based NGOs that work with Afro-Peruvian populations. In the last couple of years Afro actors have attempted to make the ethnic representation more inclusive by establishing *Mesas Técnicas* in multiple coastal communities as a means to consult with the base specifically about the multicultural commission's efforts. However, most of the negotiation and decision-making takes place in Lima through the "Mesa Afro-Peruana" in the Peruvian Congress, which is attended by some (but not all) Afro-Peruvian NGOs, cultural associations, and interested individuals and run by Congresswoman Martha Moyano. A Fujimori supporter in the 1990s without much of a history of attention to ethnic politics, Moyano has essentially remade herself under the Toledo administration into a leader of the Afro-Peruvian cause (although without surrendering her faith in "El Chino"; she is also one of the ring leaders of the "Sí Cumple" party that seeks to bring Fujimori back to Peru).

As this chapter goes to press, Peru's multicultural experiment continues to evolve amid complicated and contested politics. A full year after the creation of INDEPA Toledo finally presented the public with four Andean, three Amazonian, and two Afro-Peruvian representatives who were elected to serve their respective "pueblos" in December 2005. Despite repeated demands for voting parity, the nine ethnic representatives are conveniently outnumbered by the ten governmental appointees that also sit on the Executive Council, a mix of ministry representatives and Toledo's hand-picked Director. In the month leading up to the elections Afro-Peruvian and indigenous organizations once again registered protest and several publicly withdrew from participation. Amazonian leaders from one organization cited the continual "lack of transparency" in INDEPA's administration and decision-making. Multiple Afro-Peruvian NGOs denounced Martha Moyano for continuing to speak on their behalf after having refused to participate in her congressional commission and requesting that she remove their logos from the letterhead she uses for communications about developments in the Mesa Afro-Peruana. The Movimiento Negro Francisco Congo publicly withdrew its support entirely from the electoral process. Popular discontent was palpable despite the fact that the INDEPA law stipulates that the elections are to be carried out "al interior de sus respectivos pueblos" ("from within their respective communities"), which most observers understood as a mandate for strict coordination with the social movement actors and organizations that directly represent Peru's ethnic communities.[23]

The lesson here seems clear. On his way out of office and with no romantic Inca imagery left to deploy, Alejandro Toledo leaves as his legacy an institution that intended to speak with and for Peru's ethnic minorities. Instead, it appears to primarily be speaking at them, as multiple actors push to realize the possible promises of a multicultural Peru all the while discovering its abundant limitations.

CONCLUSION

One clear message emerges from examining the specifics of the Peruvian case in the context of the recent and wider regional wave of state-supported multiculturalism in Latin America. Any definition of ethnic movements as social and political actors operating "outside" of, or as necessarily opposed to, state institutions and state power is simply misguided. Democractic mobilization against the state is also a means toward democratic participation in the state, and vice versa. Increasingly, we are witness to the multiple strategies that ethnic and affiliated social movement actors use to move fluidly back and forth between, within, and outside of the institutional apparatus of governance and legislative systems that we call "the state." Movements morph into political parties that adopt an ethnic discourse to mobilize ethnic electoral constituencies. If and when the party politics go bad, "reflections" from outside the party and electoral system are once again in order. Thus, movement leaders split their time and efforts between offices of civil society organizations, street mobilizations, international funding requests, and bids for governmental offices.

Furthermore, Latin America's ethnic actors engage in these negotiations with the state all the while discovering that they have both support from and substantial limitations imposed on them by what we sometimes refer to as the "international community." Their struggles are of course bound not simply to their nation-states and the influences of regional trends but also, ultimately, by the dual dynamic (and often dueling dynamics) of a globalized world: the ongoing demand for a greater democratization of institutions of governance and the continuing expansion of a market economy. The dimension of global democratization assures that ethnic claims in the region will continue to receive support from international civil society and social justice advocates eager for change. The dimension of global marketization assures that such claims will continually run up against the structural realities of a world in which ethnic difference is also an important marker of political marginalization and economic inequality.

This does not mean that, unlike the largely class and labor-based "revolutionary" movements of decades prior, ethnic movement actors are necessarily "nonrevolutionary" (nor obviously can they divorce themselves from the recurring question of class divisions). But it does mean that in the midst of imagining revolutionary scenarios based on ideologies of multicultural citizenship rather than the proletarian utopias of classical Marxism, new risks also, inevitably, emerge. In other words, we can expect that alongside any revolutionary "radicalism" there will also continue to be a very real degree of compromise, contradiction, and co-optation that takes place in negotiating the competing interests of ethnic struggle, neoliberal economic power, and democratic governance.

14

Labor and the Challenge of Cross-Border, Cross-Sector Alliance

Mark Anner

There has been a marked increase in the level of struggle throughout the Americas, as well as increased awareness by our peoples that genuine democracy, sovereignty, and social equality can only be achieved through an integrated process of popular solidarity.

—Hemispheric Social Alliance, April 2005[1]

Many observers concur that labor's only plausible response to corporate globalization is cross-border union solidarity. At the same time, there is also a growing realization that labor will have to build more effective alliances with non-labor-based social movements and nongovernmental organizations (NGOs). Cross-border and cross-sector alliances are plagued with potential sources of conflict and inherent power imbalances, but these tensions are surmountable. Indeed, labor's future relevance may be linked to its capacity to form broad social alliances.

This chapter analyzes two very different efforts to bridge the labor-NGO, North-South divide. The first is a combination of unions and NGOs in the United States and Central America that focus on violations of fundamental workers' rights in apparel export processing zones. A second effort, in which South American unions play an important role, is the Hemispheric Social Alliance (HSA). This transnational NGO-labor coalition has raised broad macro issues of governance focusing particularly on the antidemocratic character of current proposals for a Free Trade Area of the Americas (FTAA).

OVERCOMING HISTORIES OF DISTRUST

The relationship between labor centers in the United States and Latin America has always been politically charged and at times contentious. During the Cold War, Latin American labor unionists accused the U.S. union movement of being protectionist and an instrument of reactionary U.S. foreign policies. At the same time, large segments of the Latin American labor movement were susceptible to nationalist appeals that led them to support local elites at the expense of solidarity with their fellow workers in other countries of the region. Labor unions and activist groups have faced numerous differences within both the United States and Latin America. In the United States during the Vietnam War, a dramatic divide existed between the prowar union leadership and anti-war activists. In Latin America, some labor unions were unwilling to give space on the workers' movement agenda to the interests of women, informal-sector workers, and marginalized minority groups.

The perversions of Cold War union practices have been well documented, with writers quick to point out the contradictions between the rhetoric of solidarity and union practices. Åke Wedin, in describing the pattern of U.S. and German union policies in Latin America, provocatively titled his book *International Trade Union "Solidarity" and its Victims,* while Beth Sims detailed the AFL-CIO's collaboration with U.S. foreign policy objectives in Latin America in her book *Workers of the World Undermined.*[2] Nor did Southern unionists always set their priorities along strong international ties with their Northern counterparts. During import substitution industrialization, many unions in South America and Mexico developed a corporatist ideology that prioritized a harmonious relationship with the state rather than class confrontation.[3]

Economic and political shifts from the 1970s to the 1990s have modified many old patterns. During the 1970s and 1980s, Latin American unions fought dictatorships and developed close ties to popular organizations, many of which persist today. In the United States, union decline in some sectors has created the opportunity for social movement unionism to replace status quo business unionism.[4] Albeit somewhat tenuously, U.S. unions are also building links to other social movements as seen in the 1999 protests in Seattle against the World Trade Organization (WTO). Internationally, regional trade pacts such as the North American Free Trade Agreement (NAFTA) and international trade institutions such as the WTO have created an incentive for labor to organize across borders. And in many cases, activists have joined forces across countries to protest labor rights violations in developing countries by attacking corporate brand-name images in developed countries. Combined, these trends create conditions for what Peter Evans refers to as "counter-hegemonic globalization."[5]

Yet regressive responses to globalization have far from dissipated. Despite increased economic integration, domestic labor strategies often take priority over international solidarity—in the North, for instance, union protectionism remains a concern. And in cases where labor internationalism is prevalent, weaker Southern actors find that their Northern counterparts tend to dominate campaign strategies and agendas. Even in highly internationalized sectors, business unionism, which shuns class solidarity in favor of narrow workplace issues, may prevail.

A progressive response to global neoliberalism will have to overcome these trends and embrace cross-sector, cross-border alliances. Eroding union densities, deteriorating working conditions, and the growth of the informal economy cannot be reversed by formal-sector workers acting alone. If it is to succeed, "social movement unionism"—in the practical as well as the ideological sense—must include women's organizations, human rights groups, landless movements, peasant communities, and faith-based organizations. At the same time, since corporate headquarters lie outside Latin America, Latin American activists need Northern allies to assist them in targeting multinational corporations (MNCs) and international institutions.

The Western Hemisphere has become the site of a series of innovative efforts. One such effort consists of a collection of diverse and differentiated organizations that work in concert to improve the balance of power that workers confront as they struggle to gain basic rights in oppressive, labor-intensive industries in Latin America. This "anti-sweatshop movement" is more than a transnational network. It encompasses a matrix of organizations in which the distinctively different capacities of the organizations involved are integrated in a way that gives this assemblage of groups much more effectiveness than the sum of its individual parts.

The second effort similarly entails a dense set of organizational alliances, but its goals are more political and substantially removed from the shop floor. This is the coalition of labor organizations and NGOs that is trying to defend democratic governance in the hemisphere against the anti-democratic threat posed by the neoliberal governance model embedded in the Free Trade Area of the Americas (FTAA). The most obvious organizational embodiment of this coalition is the alliance of alliances called the Hemispheric Social Alliance (HSA).

Analyzing these two very different cases together conveys a sense of the range of actions that new North-South and labor-NGO alliances are undertaking. It illustrates the strengths and accomplishments of the new initiatives bridging the double divide. It also illustrates the challenges that these new constructions continue to confront; the greatest of which involves power imbalances within these complexes, and shifting priorities of coalition members. The ability to overcome declining living standards and influence economic, social, and political decisions that affect their lives, will depend in part on the capacity of participants in these emerging alliances to administer their differences.

EPZS AND WORKPLACE-CENTERED CAMPAIGNS

One of the greatest challenges facing labor in the Caribbean basin is presented by Export Processing Zones.[6] These zones have been notoriously hard to unionize, yet they are too important to ignore. They are often the principal source of employment in the manufacturing sector. And their net export earnings have surpassed the export value of commodities such as coffee and bananas that had dominated these economies for over a century.

In Central America, when EPZ production boomed in the early 1990s, unions tried organizing using traditional organizing strategies. They were not very successful. In El Salvador, while the unionization rate of the traditional manufacturing sector was 10 percent, in the new EPZ jobs, unionization was less than 1 percent. In Honduras, only 6 percent of EPZ workers were unionized compared to 27 percent in the non-EPZ manufacturing sector. Inefficient labor courts, corrupt workplace inspectors, and open anti-unionism on the part of top-level government representatives were partly to blame. But the larger problem was the international system of outsourcing through which multinational apparel firms contracted out the labor intensive component of this low-end sector to highly mobile firms. In such a context, local and national strategies would always meet with limited success, so Central American unionists needed a northern ally.

In the United States, the textile and apparel workers' unions were in a crisis of their own for a different but related reason: rising imports from low-wage regions like Central America. From 1960 to 1993, employment in the U.S. textile and apparel industries dropped by 23 percent and unionization fell by 54 percent. From its peak in 1959, when 852,000 workers were members of textile and apparel unions, by 2000, the number had dropped to 225,000. The sector had lost 74 percent of its members, and less than 18 percent of workers were organized. This decline in union power affected wages, as average real wages for apparel industry production workers declined by 19 percent from 1968 to 1993. Indeed, in real terms a worker in 1957 earned more than a worker in 1995.

In the past, U.S. textile unionists relied on political allies to push through protectionist measures when the industry was in trouble. But by the 1990s, as the Clinton administration adopted a free trade agenda, protectionist political strategies were no longer feasible. This allowed a progressive segment of unionists within the newly formed textile workers' union, UNITE, to propose an alternative strategy: to form alliances with the very people some believed were "taking their jobs."[7] The goal of these alliances was to organize unions in the Export Processing Zones and improve working conditions to stop the "race-to-the-bottom" dynamics that allow apparel jobs to continually move to the countries with lowest wages and weakest unions.

In coordination with the International Textile and Garment Workers'

Union (ITG), UNITE developed contacts throughout the region and held local and regional workshops to diffuse its organizing strategy known as the "fishbowl" model. This model encouraged slow, clandestine ("underwater") organizing to build a broad base of support before going public (breaking the "water's" surface) in order to be best prepared to respond to the anticipated management backlash. The model includes: (1) identification of factories to target based on the perceived vulnerability of the brand-name corporation for which they produced, (2) slowly recruiting and training of workers in the factory who would become the main organizers, (3) rapid recruitment of the largest number of workers possible through extensive home visits, and (4) presentation of documentation for the legalization of the union accompanied by in-plant demonstration of support and transnational protests directed at the brand-name company producing in the plant.

The main criticism that the U.S. unionists had of the Central American model of organizing was that it did not carefully identify targets before beginning campaigns, and that the documentation to legalize unions was often presented when the organizers had the legal minimum to form a union (often between thirty and thirty-five workers). While this fulfilled the requirements of the law, it did not give the workers much associational power to confront the anticipated backlash from management. There was general agreement that unions should organize as many workers as possible before presenting the documentation, but whether they should wait until reaching the 50 percent threshold (especially in factories with 800 or more workers) was the subject of discussion.

Target selection for the campaigns was hotly debated between the U.S. and Central American unionists. The U.S. unionists said that they would be the ones to decide which companies to target since these were U.S. companies and they knew more about their vulnerabilities. The Central American unionists were uncomfortable with this loss of control over the strategy. Moreover, some argued that the most important element in choosing campaigns was the disposition of the workers to join a union, not the vulnerability of the MNC. A few local unions refused to work with their U.S. counterparts. But others accepted, and during the late 1990s and early 2000s, dozens of organizing drives were initiated in the region using the fishbowl model. Three of the companies targeted by these drives were Kimi and Yoo Yang in Honduras, and Tainan in El Salvador.

Kimi was a Korean-owned factory that produced for Gap and Macy's. The organizing drive was led by a U.S. unionist assigned to Honduras by UNITE and the ITG. With the guidance of this unionist, Honduran activists classified workers according to their perceived level of support (prounion, undecided or antiunion) and then aggressively targeted the undecided segment of the workforce through house visits where organizers would inform workers of the benefits and importance of joining a union. The union managed to recruit and train about 10 percent of the 700 workers, thus falling far short of the goal of 50 percent established in the model. It then moved toward short work stoppages to pressure the company into accepting the union.[8] Management eventually agreed to recognize the union. By March 1999, it negotiated a collective contract that raised wages and provided new benefits. The success was short-lived though; in May 2000, the owners closed the plant, destroying the union in the process. This same group of organizers using the same model began an organizing drive at Yoo Yang, which produced for Phillips–Van Heusen. Combined with international pressure on the parent company, in December 2000, the Yoo Yang workers succeeded in gaining legal recognition for the union, STEYY. After a year of continued local and international campaigning, the union and company signed their first collective bargaining agreement.[9]

In 2001, U.S. unionists and the ITG pursued a campaign in El Salvador. They did so by focusing on a Taiwanese-owned factory, Tainan, which produced for Gap, a company that was considered vulnerable to international campaigns. While the ITG was not as active in El Salvador as elsewhere (it had no paid staff in the country), its coordinator visited El Salvador frequently and convinced local organizers of the merits of the fishbowl model. The unionists conducted massive home visits that resulted in the recruitment of a significant percentage of the workforce, and the unionization of the plant in July 2001. By 2002 the union had 56 percent of the workers organized in one of two plants owned by Tainan, and they presented their demand to the company to negotiate a collective contract. However, the company—citing lack of orders caused by the unionization of the plant—

began dismissing workers instead, which greatly weakened the union. Then, in April 2002, the company announced it was closing the factory. The unionists fought back by placing pressure on Gap and Tainan's parent company in Taiwan. It was eventually agreed that Gap would contribute to the establishment of a partially worker-run factory for the unemployed workers of Tainan. The new factory, Just Garments, has been functioning ever since. At this writing, it has seventy-five production workers and an active union.

Given its limited success and following a change in its leadership, UNITE began to shift strategies. It focused less on cross-border organizing in the Americas of production workers and began to seek cross-border alliances with European labor unions to organize retail stores like H&M.[10] The AFL-CIO's American Center for International Labor Solidarity (ACILS) continued to pursue its own cross-border organizing efforts when possible.[11] Often, it found it had to modify the "fishbowl" strategy by petitioning to legalize unions before achieving support from 50 percent the workers, because while waiting to get more workers to join, the workers who already joined were being fired. The choice was either to legalize the union and protect the ones who had joined, or risk losing everyone.

Labor groups like the CUTH in Honduras, which chose not to work with the U.S. unionists, used militant activism at the base level combined with political pressure on state institutions. They demanded workplace inspections from the state and lobbied the Ministry of Labor for legal recognition of its unions. And they contacted non-labor solidarity groups to apply limited pressure to the MNCs. That is, while shunning the fishbowl model, they saw the benefits of including transnational pressure on MNCs as a component of their campaigns. The CUTH faced many difficulties in organizing unions and many workers were fired in the process. But by 1999, it had nineteen unions in the EPZ sector.

NGOS AND ANTI-SWEATSHOP ACTIVISM

The highly competitive, low-value-added nature of EPZs makes them conducive to violations of fundamental human and labor rights, and most workers in the sector are female. This has lead to a unique correlation of advocacy groups concerned with the EPZs: human and labor rights groups, religious organizations, and women's movement groups. Even prior to U.S. union activity in Central America, northern NGOs campaigned to address the sweatshop issue in the region. One of the more prominent of these groups was the National Labor Committee (NLC). The NLC was formed in 1980 by a group of New York unionists who were concerned about the AFL-CIO's support for U.S. policy in El Salvador. The NLC organized fact-finding delegations to El Salvador and wrote several reports that highlighted the dramatic level of labor rights violations in the country, including the systematic imprisonment and death-squad assassinations of union leaders. In 1992, when the war ended and more extreme forms of labor suppression subsided, the NLC began pursuing campaigns on behalf of workers in the country's mushrooming EPZs. These campaigns combined speaking tours with letter writing campaigns and protest activities outside retail stores. The goal was to shame carefully selected U.S. clothing retailers who had production contracts with targeted factories.

Other U.S. NGOs pursued similar campaigns. For example, the U.S. Guatemala Labor Education Project, with a full-time staff person in Guatemala City, documented labor rights violations committed by Phillips–Van Heusen in Guatemala, and more recently, after re-organizing itself as the U.S. Labor Education and Action Project (USLEAP), pursued campaigns throughout Latin America. Then, in the late 1990s, students began linking the global sweatshop issue to conditions under which campus products were made. In July 1998, student representatives from thirty universities came together in New York City and launched United Students Against Sweatshops (USAS), a coordinating body of student anti-sweatshop groups. By January 2000, USAS had 200 campus affiliates in the United States and Canada. For their first major campaign, students demanded that universities develop a stronger code of conduct for companies producing their apparel. Finally, Canadian NGOs like the Maquila Solidarity Network provided support to Central American NGOs, campaigned against companies within Canada, and provided useful analysis in both English and Spanish.[12]

Central American NGOs also had a strong motivation to become involved in addressing rights violations in EPZs. Several faith-based human rights groups were formed during the period of heightened violence in the 1980s to denounce the killings, torture, and terror, and to demand punishment of the culprits. By the 1990s, as the violence subsided, these groups were able to focus on other issues. In the case of the Jesuit University and the Catholic Archdiocese in El Salvador, their human rights departments began documenting violations in EPZs and provided legal assistance to workers who were illegally fired or otherwise victims of abusive treatment by management. And given the massive number of cases they received, these institutions began making public declarations in which they criticized the inability or lack of will on the part of the government to resolve these problems. In 1992, women linked to the opposition movement of the 1980s formed the Mélida Anaya Montes Women's Movement (MAM). The group sought to promote women's rights in the aftermath of the conflict. By 1996, it became involved in the EPZ issue by providing legal assistance to women whose labor rights were violated.[13]

The story is much the same in Honduras. Human rights and women's groups that were formed to focus on other issues found that the unfolding events in the EPZs required a shift in their priorities. For example, the Centro de Derechos de Mujeres (CDM) was founded to promote legislation to address the rising problem of domestic violence. But by the mid-1990s, as news of rights violations escalated in the EPZ sector, CDM decided to join forces with local labor unions. While the unions focused on organizing, CDM provided training to women in their legal rights as workers. To do this, CDM received funding from Oxfam, Norwegian People's Aid, and other groups. The Consultorio Jurídico Popular (CJP), a legal services organization, followed a similar trajectory. Formed to address family law for low-income people, by 1997 it became involved in the EPZ issue by providing legal counsel to workers whose rights had been violated.

NORTH/SOUTH, LABOR/NGOS ALLIANCES IN EPZS

Historically in the United States, much of the upper echelons of the labor movement shunned ties with what it considered more radical elements of society. This division was especially noticeable during the Vietnam War. In

Latin America, while the relationship between the old corporatist labor centers and NGOs was often strained, the relationship between progressive labor unions and NGO groups has been strong. If divisions existed, they were more often among political factions, not among social sectors. Thus, in the initial phase of the anti-sweatshop movement, while U.S. unions expressed skepticism of the role of NGOs in what was perceived as labor's domain, Central American unions and NGOs formed alliances. For example, in El Salvador in 1995, nineteen labor unions and NGOs came together to form the Coordinating Body for Jobs with Dignity in the Maquila (COSDEMA). The group was a remarkable show of cross sector unity. It successfully lobbied for a labor rights clause in the EPZ laws and assisted union organizing efforts.[14]

With time, the U.S. union movement began to see the benefits of alliances with carefully selected NGOs. U.S./LEAP and USAS were considered particularly trustworthy allies, while tensions with women's groups and NGOs like the National Labor Committee remained. Yet all these groups were active in the sector, and Northern-based organizations in the United States and Canada (and Europe) supported a large array of Central American unions and NGOs working on the EPZ issue. One survey showed that there were at least seven trade union and sixteen nonlabor (mostly NGO) EPZ projects in the region. Most often, unions worked with unions and NGOs worked with NGOs. But there were a significant number of Northern NGOs that worked with Central American unions and a few Northern unions that worked with Central American NGOs.[15]

In Mexico, the Kukdong case offers a strong illustration of the potential of these union/NGO alliances. On September 21, 2001, the first collective bargaining agreement between an independent union and a Mexican EPZ plant was signed by SITEMEX on behalf of the 400 workers at the Kukdong (renamed Mexmode) in Atlixco, Mexico. This led to an agreement in April 2002 to increase wages and benefits significantly. A wide array of labor organizations and NGOs were involved in this victory, including the Workers' Support Centre (CAT) in Mexico, the AFL-CIO Solidarity Center, and the Canadian Labor Congress (CLC). Solidarity groups included US/LEAP, the Campaign for Labor Rights, Global Exchange, Sweatshop Watch, the European Clean Clothes Campaign (CCC), the Korean House for International

Solidarity, and the Maquila Solidarity Network (MSN). This list of groups gives a hint of the organizational complexities involved in winning the basic right to organize. Students organized in USAS played a particularly strategic role since university sweatshirts were produced at the factory.

This whole organizational matrix was knit together by a set of internationally oriented labor activists, some of them inside the labor movement, some in the NGO world, many shifting back and forth between the two. The importance of network connections among these activists makes these groupings appear similar to the transnational advocacy networks (TANs) described by Margaret E. Keck and Kathryn Sikkink, but the fact that they are rooted in the labor movement gives the structure a different flavor.[16] Unlike the TANs, which are, in theory at least, made up of organizations whose reason for being is to defend "principled ideas or values," the organizational matrix of the "basic rights complex" also includes organizations that are directly accountable to (that is, elected by) a constituency with immediate interests grounded in the everyday struggles of hard political realities for livelihood and dignity, as well as long-term and ideological interests.

The challenge of these coalitions is to integrate principled ideas and values with everyday interests. Ideally, the logic of organizational relations would force groups and leaders to adopt a broad vision, even those whose natural tendencies might be to pursue their own interests in a more pedestrian, immediate way. Yet, while the basic ideological logic is robust, the organizational ties necessary to make it work require constant creative renovation. Viewed as a whole, the ideological and organizational matrix of these coalitions provides an important model of how alliances with NGOs can facilitate North-South labor alliances and how the combination can help give labor (and ordinary citizens) leverage against the naturally nonegalitarian thrust of global neoliberalism. Of course, even with the best of alliances, the high mobility of the apparel industry can lead to failure. This has led many activists to pursue a much broader campaign, one attacking the very structures of global governance.

DEFENDING DEMOCRATIC GOVERNANCE:
THE FIGHT AGAINST THE FTAA

In 1994, the United States hosted the first Summit of the Americas in Miami, which established plans to create a Free Trade Areas of the Americas (FTAA). The goal was to bring together thirty-four countries of the Americas (excluding only Cuba) and create the largest free trade zone in the world by 2005. Yet an emerging global social justice movement challenged the proposal and waged increasingly contentious protest events. In 1998, labor and NGOs from Canada, the United States and Latin America came together at the first "People's Summit" to discuss an alternative vision for regional integration. The People's Summit led to the formation of the Hemispheric Social Alliance (HSA) a year later.[17]

While in an earlier era, labor joined national social alliances to oppose the common enemy of dictatorship, now neoliberal globalization—with its adverse effects on labor, human rights, gender equity, the environment, and ethnic and racial minorities—created conditions for a cross-sector, North-South coalition. For labor-NGO alliances to have a broader impact on politics and policy, they must be able to cohere around shared goals that go beyond labor's immediate interests. Without a strategy for building more democratic forms of economic governance, nationally and globally, workplace struggles can only meet with limited success. The current labor-NGO coalition that has coalesced around opposition to the FTAA demonstrates the possibility of broader alliances built around the larger issue of democratizing economic governance.

Amid much debate and discussion, members of the HSA managed to draft an "Alternative for the Americas," which encapsulated a common vision based on deeply held beliefs and principles. The document notes, "No country can nor should remain isolated from the global economy." It adds, "We propose a world economy regulated at the national and supra-national levels in the interest of peace, democracy, sustainable development and economic stability. . . . As citizens of the Americas, we refuse to be ruled by the law of supply and demand, and claim our role as individuals rather than simple commodities governed by the laws of the market."[18]

The degree of political change represented by the movement against the FTAA is especially striking when compared with the character of hemispheric trade politics a decade ago at the time the fight over NAFTA began. In the NAFTA campaign, transnational alliances were much easier to form among environmental, human rights, faith-based, and women's groups, than among labor unions. This was due to "a history of mistrust, misunderstanding, and ignorance."[19] The labor politics of NAFTA also initially fell into a traditional mold of job competition. U.S. labor unionists decried the likelihood of job loss in the United States and the official Mexican Trade Union Confederation (CTM) supported the treaty on the belief that it would create jobs in Mexico. In the end, the cross-border coalition was unable to stop NAFTA, but the NAFTA experience had a profound impact on the successful campaigns that would follow. NAFTA allowed organizations to build trust and accumulate experiences. And the failure of NAFTA to deliver on jobs and sustainable development strengthened the conviction of movement activists that the expansion of the NAFTA model of free trade had to be stopped.

Alliance formation in the fight against the FTAA promised to be different. Here major labor centers from South America, such as the CUT/Brazil, were firmly opposed to the free trade agreement as was the Inter-American Regional Organization of Workers (ORIT).[20] ORIT emphasized the FTAA's undemocratic character and underlined the central importance of preserving the basic rights of all workers, regardless of what country they were working in or what their legal status was. It was not an "antiglobalization" position. ORIT advocated "a progressive version of economic globalization" that entailed the "globalization of human, economic, social, labor, cultural, and political rights." This represents a shift in both strategy and thinking. ORIT at first preferred a "free trade with a labor rights clause" approach, while NGOs were quick to take the "anti-globalization/No to the FTAA" stance.[21] And it was the first time that ORIT agreed to establish a structure to coordinate strategies and actions with NGOs. These shifts were influenced by the realization that the current model of economic integration was not improving the conditions of workers in the region. They also reflect changes in ORIT's membership. Following the end to the Cold War, progressive labor centers opted to join the organization, which helped to push ORIT's agenda more to the left. Finally, labor came to the realization that it did not have the power to defeat the FTAA alone. Broad social alliances became a political necessity.

HSA is a coalition of coalitions. Most of its members are umbrella organizations, each of which represents a coalition of NGOs or labor organizations. For example, the U.S. member is the Alliance for Responsible Trade (ART), itself a coalition of NGOs and labor groups, including the AFL-CIO. The Brazilian Network for People's Integration (*Rede Brasileira pela Integração dos Povos*, REBRIP) is likewise an alliance of labor and NGO groups. While HSA has not been able to find local labor-NGO alliances of the ART/REBRIP sort to work with in every country, it always tries to involve the labor movement in its activities, even when local labor-NGO alliances are not well developed. Thus in Ecuador, where labor-NGO alliances remain weak and CONAIE (the indigenous people's organization) played a leading role in organizing HSA actions around the November 2002 FTAA ministerial meeting in Quito, labor was still involved.

Southern organizations have played a central organizational role in the HSA. The Alliance's secretariat was first lodged with the Mexican Action Network on Free Trade (RMALC) and was then moved to REBRIP in Brazil, where Kjeld Jakobsen, the international affairs director of the CUT (Brazil's Central Trade Union Confederation), served as the executive secretary. Five of the eight organizational members of the coordinating body are based in Latin America. Spanish is the organization's de facto working language, and steering committee meetings move up and down the hemisphere along with FTAA ministerial meetings.

Forming a coalition of coalitions is not always a harmonious process. While ORIT is participating actively in the Alliance, several of ORIT's largest members—such as CTM/Mexico, CGT/Argentina, CTV/Venezuela, and Força Sindical/Brazil—are not. Often, these decisions are based on histories of distrust. One Argentine unionist explained why he supported the FTAA: "If the American unions are against it, it is because it must bring us some benefits at their expense. So we should be for it."[22] The HSA has managed to articulate labor-NGO alliances fully and effectively in only four or five of the thirty-four countries participating in the FTAA negotiations. The most active HSA chapters are in Brazil, Canada, Peru, and the United States.

HSA activities tend to focus on organizing parallel people's summits and protests at presidential summits and ministerial meetings. Ensuring that an alternative voice is heard at these events is one of HSA's greatest contributions, but this event-focused strategy has its limitations. Gathering activists from throughout the Americas is costly, and more energy could be spent by members actively working to influence their governments in between the big summit events.

Despite HSA's limitations, unions and NGOs have made important progress since the first Presidential Summit for Free Trade was held in Miami in 1994. HSA not only bridges the North-South, labor-NGO divide, but is exactly the kind of broad-based conglomeration of civil society groups that one would hope would be involved in any process of creating an economic constitution for the Americas. Equally important, HSA has been trying to involve ordinary citizens in the debate over its alternative vision through a process of "hemispheric consultation," which has involved public meetings and a series of referenda. In Canada, El Salvador, Mexico, and Peru activists worked to organize ballot or petition campaigns. Brazilian organizers completed an impressive referendum on the FTAA in which ten million people participated.

HSA is a solid demonstration that a North-South, labor-NGO alliance can generate a positive political agenda with respect to governance issues. Moreover, the alliance appears to have had an impact. In 2005, the Bush administration was unable to realize its goal of launching the FTAA as planned, and the HSA could claim some responsibility for that outcome. Of course, other factors also influenced this outcome, such as changes in governments in Brazil, Argentina, Uruguay, and Venezuela and the subsequent impasse between these governments and the government of the United States on issues such as subsidies to agro-businesses. But the shifts in Latin American governments can also be attributed to waves of organized popular discontent over market-oriented policies of the previous governments. The real challenge for the alliance is to move from blocking the FTAA to implementing its alternative vision of economic, political, and social integration. This will depend on the movement's capacity not only to extend labor-NGO alliances throughout the region, but also to generate sufficient mobilization among rank-and-file union members and ordinary citizens at the community level to make a political difference.

CONCLUSIONS

Effectively challenging the present model of corporate-dominated globalization in the Americas is an enormous task. In the apparel sector, the sales of firms like Liz Claiborne, Gap, and Nike surpass the GNP of most countries in Central America and the Caribbean. Company profits exceed the value of government budgets, and the salary of one C.E.O. can surpass the entire budget of a ministry of labor. At the same time, the U.S. economy accounts for over 80 percent of the combined GDP of the region. Latin American trade dependency on the United States is also high. Many countries send over half of their exports to the United States, while U.S. exports to the region only account for a fraction of total U.S. exports.

Activists in the region attempting to take on such powerful opponents realized that they needed to join forces based on common principles and tactics. The challenge was building cross-border and cross-sectoral alliances among groups with different visions and strategies. This was especially problematic for labor. Not only did labor unions have a different set of priorities, often focused more narrowly on workplace issues like job protection, they also had very different organizational structures. Labor unions tend to be large, centralized and bureaucratic organizations that shift strategies very slowly. Yet a combination of factors led the union movement to adjust priorities, shift tactics, and join forces across sectors. At the same time, labor's North-South divide had to be bridged. The history of U.S. labor union intervention in the region was not easily forgotten, despite the election of a more progressive leadership in 1995. And some Latin American unionists have raised questions about the recent activities of the AFL-CIO in places like Venezuela.

In the anti-sweatshop movement, labor and NGO groups often pursued separate paths, with labor focusing on organizing drives and NGOs on women's rights groups and media exposés. Despite the mutual statements of distrust and disapproval, the two strategies often complemented each other; NGO media exposés could make companies avoid the most blatant acts of labor rights abuses, and union organizing could ensure that media exposés translated into worker empowerment on the factory floor. At times, labor-

NGO/North-South alliances coalesced around concrete factory-based campaigns. When they did, labor was more successful in achieving deeper and more sustained improvements for workers.

The dynamics of cross-border, cross-sector alliances took on a different form in the Hemispheric Social Alliance. Here, while initial tension between the unions and NGOs was at times strong, the North-South divide was less pronounced. First, progressive southern labor centers joined the alliances with a discourse that moved beyond job protectionism to a broader vision of social equity and sustainable development. Second, the size and representativity of southern organizations prevented northern domination. Unlike alliances with small, under-funded, and under-staffed unions in Central America, union participation in the HSA comes from Brazil, Peru, Chile, Mexico, and Argentina. The CUT/Brazil alone represents over 7 million members, 2 million less than the AFL-CIO following its 2005 split. For the AFL-CIO this was perhaps the first time that it joined a coalition that it could not completely control.

In its call to participate in the third People's Summit in Mar del Plata, Argentina, of October 2005, the Hemispheric Social Alliance referred to "the common struggle to make another America possible: the America of popular creativity, and of the many faces of resistance; the America of alternatives to neo-liberalism and war; the America of our original people, of women in struggle, of farmers, of workers, of young people; the America of sexual, cultural and religious diversity—a people's America."[23] The North-South, labor-NGO alliances have a long way to go to achieve this goal. What they have shown is that to make another America possible, new forms of popular struggle are necessary.

Notes

1. Turning the Tide?

Eric Hershberg and Fred Rosen

1. A useful overview of the problem of inequality in Latin America is Kelly Hoffman and Miguel Angel Centeno, "The Lopsided Continent: Inequality in Latin America," *Annual Review of Sociology* 29 (August 2003): 363–90.
2. The term was first used by John Williamson and specified in his article "Democracy and the Washington Consensus," *World Development* 21, no. 8 (August 1993): 1329–36.
3. Fernando Fajnzylber, *Unavoidable Industrial Restructuring in Latin America* (Durham, NC: Duke University Press, 1990).
4. Rolando Franco, "Grandes temas del desarrollo social en America Latina y el Caribe," in *Desarrollo social en América Latina: Temas y desafíos para las políticas públicas,* ed. Carlos Sojo (San José: FLACSO Costa Rica/The World Bank, 2002), p. 67. Similarly, from 1950–1965 and 1965–1980, per capita growth rates for all of Latin America and the Caribbean averaged 2.0 percent and 3.5 percent, respectively, whereas they hovered around zero throughout the period between 1980 and 2000. See John Sheahan, *Patterns of Development in Latin America* (Princeton, NJ: Princeton University Press, 1987), p. 95, for per capita growth data between 1950–1980.
5. "Beyond the Washington Consensus," *NACLA Report on the Americas* 37, no. 3 (November/December 2003).
6. See the 2003 UNDP Human Development Report, pp. 266–68.
7. Judith Tendler, *Good Government in the Tropics* (Baltimore: Johns Hopkins University Press, 1998).
8. Nancy Birdsall and Augusto de la Torre, *Washington Contentious: Economic Policies for Social Equity in Latin America* (Washington, DC: Carnegie Endowment for International Peace and Inter-American Dialogue, 2001).

2. The Hegemony of U.S. Economic Doctrines in Latin America

Paul W. Drake

1. P.W. Drake, "The International Causes of Democratization, 1974–1990," in *The Origins of Liberty: Political and Economic Liberalization in the Modern World*, ed. P.W. Drake and M. D. McCubbins (Princeton: Princeton University Press, 1998); C. Lipson, *Standing Guard: Protecting Foreign Capital in the Nineteenth and Twentieth Centuries* (Berkeley: University of California Press, 1985).

2. J. Tulchin, *The Aftermath of War: World War I and U.S. Policy toward Latin America* (New York: New York University Press, 1971).

3. E.S. Rosenberg, *Financial Missionaries to the World: The Politics and Culture of Dollar Diplomacy, 1900–1930* (Cambridge, MA: Harvard University Press, 1999).

4. P.A. Gourevitch, *Politics in Hard Times: Comparative Responses to International Economic Crises* (Ithaca, NY: Cornell University Press, 1986).

5. J.L. Love, "Economic Ideas and Ideologies in Latin America since 1930," in *Cambridge History of Latin America*, vol. VI, ed. L. Bethell (Cambridge: Cambridge University Press, 1994).

6. E.V.K. Fitzgerald, "ECLA and Formation of Latin American Economic Doctrine," in *Latin America in the 1940s: War and Postwar Transitions*, ed. D. Rock (Berkeley: University of California Press, 1994).

7. A.O. Hirschman, "How the Keynesian Revolution Was Exported from the United States, and Other Comments," in *The Political Power of Economic Ideas: Keynesianism across Nations*, ed. P.A. Hall (Princeton, NJ: Princeton University Press, 1989).

8. T.J. Biersteker, "The 'Triumph' of Liberal Economic Ideas in the Developing World," in *Global Change, Regional Response: The New International Context of Development*, ed. B. Stallings (Cambridge: Cambridge University Press, 1995).

9. J.S. Odell, *U.S. International Monetary Policy: Markets, Power, and Ideas as Sources of Change* (Princeton, NJ: Princeton University Press, 1982).

10. For elaboration on these points, see J.M. Nelson, ed., *Economic Crisis and Policy Choice: The Politics of Adjustment in Developing Countries* (Princeton, NJ: Princeton University Press, 1990); J. Goldstein and R.O. Keohane, "Ideas and Foreign Policy: An Analytical Framework," in *Ideas and Foreign Policy: Beliefs, Institutions and Political Change*, ed. J. Goldstein and R.O. Keohane (Ithaca, NY: Cornell University Press, 1993); E.V. Iglesias, "Economic Reform: A View from Latin America," in *The Political Economy of Policy Reform*, ed. J. Williamson (Washington, DC: Institute for International Economics, 1994); J.I. Domínguez, ed., *Technopols: Freeing Politics and Markets in Latin America in the 1990s* (University Park: Pennsylvania State University Press, 1997); P. Van Dijck, "The World Bank and the Transformation of Latin American Society," in *The Politics of Expertise in Latin America*, ed. M.A. Centeno and P. Silva (New York: St. Martin's Press, 1998).

11. J. Williamson, ed., *Latin American Adjustment: How Much Has Happened?* (Washington, DC: Institute for International Economics, 1990).

12. T. Carothers, *In the Name of Democracy: U.S. Policy toward Latin America in the Reagan Years* (Berkeley: University of California Press, 1991).

13. S.P. Huntington, *The Third Wave: Democratization in the Late Twentieth Century* (Norman: University of Oklahoma Press, 1991); F. Fukuyama, *The End of History and the Last Man* (New York: Maxwell Macmillan International, 1992); Drake, "The International Causes of Democratization."

14. A.O. Hirschman, *Journeys Toward Progress: Studies of Economic Policy-Making in Latin America* (Westport, CT: Greenwood Publishing Group, 1965).

15. C.M. Conaghan, "Las Estrellas de la Crisis: El Ascenso de los Economistas en la Vida Pública Peruana," *Pensamiento Iberoamericano* 30 (1997): 177–206.

16. G.J. Ikenberry, "The International Spread of Privatization Policies: Inducements, Learning, and 'Policy Bandwagoning,' " in *The Political Economy of Public Sector Reform and Privatization,* ed. E.N. Suleiman and J. Waterbury (Boulder, CO: Westview Press, 1990); Biersteker, "The 'Triumph' of Liberal Economic Ideas."

17. M. Pastor, *The International Monetary Fund and Latin America: Economic Stabilization and Class Conflict* (Boulder, CO: Westview Press, 1987).

18. J.M. Nelson, ed., *A Precarious Balance: Democracy and Economic Reforms in Latin America* (Washington, DC: Overseas Development Council, 1994).

19. P.M. Haas, "Introduction: Epistemic Communities and International Policy Coordination," *International Organization* 46 (Winter 1992): 1–35.

20. Centeno and Silva, *The Politics of Expertise;* B. Galjart and P. Silva, eds., *Designers of Development: Intellectuals and Technocrats in the Third World* (Leiden: Leiden University, 1995); J. Markoff and V. Montecinos, "The Ubiquitous Rise of Economists," *Journal of Public Policy* 13, no. 1 (1993): 37–68.

21. C.M. Conaghan and J.M. Malloy, *Unsettling Statecraft: Democracy and Neo-liberalism in the Central Andes* (Pittsburgh: University of Pittsburgh Press, 1994).

22. J. Pinera, "Chile," in Williamson, *The Political Economy of Policy Reform.*

23. B.R. Schneider, "Las bases materiales de la tecnocracía: La confianza de los inversores y el neo-liberalismo en América Latina," *Pensamiento Iberoamericano* 30 (1997): 109–32.

24. A. Harberger, "Secrets of Success: A Handful of Heroes," *American Economic Review* 83, no. 2 (May 1993): 343–50.

25. M.A. Centeno, *Democracy Within Reason: Technocratic Revolution in Mexico* (University Park: Pennsylvania State University Press, 1994); Domínguez, *Technopols.*

26. J. Puryear, *Thinking Politics: Intellectuals and Politics in Chile, 1973–1988* (Baltimore: Johns Hopkins University Press, 1994).

27. H. de Soto, *The Other Path: The Invisible Revolution in the Third World* (New York: Harper and Row, 1989); N. Aslanbeigui and V. Montecinos, "Foreign Students in

U.S. Doctoral Programs," *Journal of Economic Perspectives* 12, no. 3 (Summer 1998): 171–82.

28. P. O'Brien and J. Roddick, *Chile, the Pinochet Decade: The Rise and Fall of the Chicago Boys* (London: Latin American Bureau, 1983); J.G. Valdes, *Pinochet's Economists: The Chicago School in Chile* (New York: Cambridge University Press, 1995); V. Montecinos, *Economists, Politics, and the State: Chile 1958–1994* (Amsterdam: CEDLA, 1998).

29. M. Urrutia, "Colombia," in Williamson, *The Political Economy of Policy Reform.*

30. B. Stallings and R. Kaufman, eds., *Debt and Democracy in Latin America* (Boulder, CO: Westview Press, 1989); J.A. Frieden, *Debt, Development and Democracy* (Princeton, NJ: Princeton University Press, 1991); E. Silva, *The State and Capital in Chile: Business Elites, Technocrats, and Market Economics* (Boulder, CO: Westview Press, 1996).

31. P.W. Drake, *Labor Movements and Dictatorships: The Southern Cone in Comparative Perspective* (Baltimore: Johns Hopkins University Press, 1996).

3. Latin America and the United States

Lars Schoultz

1. *Journals of the Continental Congress* 20 (June 1781): 705.

2. Roque Sáenz Peña, *Escritos y discursos,* 3 vols. (Buenos Aires: Jacobo Peuser, 1914–35), vol. 1, pp. 163–64. For the motivation behind the conference, see the official report of the excursion: U.S. Congress, Senate, *International American Conferences,* Sen. Exec. Doc. No. 232, pt. 3, 51st Cong., 1st Sess., 1890.

3. *The Memoirs of Herbert Hoover,* 2 vols. (New York: Macmillan, 1951–52), vol. 2, p. 69.

4. Harley A. Notter to Laurence Duggan, 12 September 1939, 710.11/2417 2, Record Group 59, National Archives.

5. 2 Stat. 666. For the congressional discussion, see *Annals of Congress,* vol. 22, pp. 269–80, 486, 1117–48.

6. Beaufort T. Watts to Henry Clay, 10 March 1828, Despatches from Colombia, Record Group 59, National Archives.

7. Monroe to John Quincy Adams, 10 December 1815, Instructions to U.S. Ministers, National Archives.

8. "Cuban Missile Crisis Meetings, October 16, 1962," presidential recordings transcripts, John F. Kennedy Library, Boston.

9. Robert E. Olds, "Confidential Memorandum on the Nicaraguan Situation," undated but noted "approximate date January, 1927," 817.00/5854, Record Group 59, National Archives. Emphasis added.

10. "Central America," address delivered before a Joint Session of the Congress, 27 April 1983, *Public Papers of the Presidents of the United States*, 1983, pp. 601–7.

11. General James T. Hill, commander, United States Southern Command, testimony before the Committee on Armed Services, U.S. House of Representatives, 24 March 2004.

12. Baruch to Franklin D. Roosevelt, 11 October 1938, Bernard Baruch Papers, Seeley Mudd Manuscript Library, Princeton University, Princeton, NJ.

13. Berle Diary, 6 and 10 January 1944 and 12 February 1945, Adolph Berle Papers, FDR Library, Hyde Park, NY.

14. John Cabot to Secretary of State Byrnes, 19 October 1945, *Foreign Relations of the United States* (hereafter FRUS), 1945, vol. 9, pp. 422–23. Germany had surrendered in May and Japan in August.

15. U.S. Department of State, *Consultation Among the American Republics with Respect to the Argentine Situation: Memorandum of the United States Government* (Washington, DC: GPO, 1946), pp. 65–66.

16. Braden to Messersmith, 8 March 1946, FRUS 1946, vol. 11, p. 233.

17. General James T. Hill, commander, United States Southern Command, testimony before the Committee on Armed Services, U.S. House of Representatives, 24 March 2004.

18. Southcom commanding general James Hill may tell Congress, as he did in 2004, that there is no useful distinction between a narcotrafficker and his terrorist activity, hence the term "narcoterrorist," but that, of course, is simply not true: terrorists seek political goals they perceive to be blocked by the United States; narcotraffickers seek to market their wares. The solution to terrorism is not obvious, but the solution to drug trafficking is clear: narcotrafficking will disappear if we either reduce the U.S. demand for drugs through education and treatment or (as some suggest, citing the experiment with Prohibition) legalize their use.

19. General Bantz J. Craddock, commander, United States Southern Command, testimony before the Committee on Armed Services, U.S. House of Representatives, 9 March 2005.

20. James A. Miner to Elihu Root, 19 November 1901, Elihu Root File, Philip Jessup Papers, Manuscripts Division, Library of Congress.

21. Hull to Sumner Welles, 1 May 1933, 711.37/178A, Record Group 59, National Archives. For an analysis of Cubans' historical tendency to seek refuge in the United States, see Guillermo J. Grenier and Lisandro Pérez, *The Legacy of Exile: Cubans in the United States* (Boston: Allyn and Bacon, 2003).

22. Philip Brenner, "The Thirty-Year War," *NACLA Report on the Americas* 24 (November 1990): 18.

23. "Remarks at a Campaign Fund-raising Luncheon, Miami, Florida," 16 August 1989, in *Public Papers of the Presidents of the United States*, 1989, p. 1093.

24. U.S. Congress, House of Representatives, Committee on Foreign Affairs, *Consideration of the Cuban Democracy Act of 1992,* 102nd Cong., 2nd Sess., 1992, pp. 167–68.

25. Clinton speech, 23 April 1992, reported in *Miami Herald,* 24 April 1992, pp. 1, 15. President Bush's concession is reprinted in *Consideration of the Cuban Democracy Act of 1992,* pp. 446, 464.

26. Interview with James Cason, chief, U.S. Interests Section, Havana, 8 March 2005.

27. Theodore Roosevelt, *Thomas Hart Benton* (Boston: Houghton, Mifflin, 1886), p. 175.

28. Samuel P. Huntington, "The Hispanic Challenge," *Foreign Policy,* March/April 2004, p. 32.

29. *Congressional Record,* 27 May 1993, P. H2938.

30. *Congressional Record,* 14 July 1993, P. H4677.

31. Diary entries for 19 September 1820 and 9 March 1821, *Memoirs of John Quincy Adams, Comprising Portions of His Diary from 1795 to 1838,* ed. Charles Francis Adams, 12 vols. (Philadelphia: J.B. Lippincott, 1874–77), vol. 5, pp. 176, 325.

32. "I cannot watch this brand of baseball any longer. A truly awful, pathetic, old team that only promises to be worse two years from now. It's just awful and bad to watch. Brain-dead Caribbean hitters hacking at slop nightly." Larry Krueger, KNBR's commentator quoted in *San Francisco Chronicle,* 6 August 2005.

33. "Ask Dame Edna," *Vanity Fair,* February 2003, p. 116.

34. Woodrow Wilson to Edith Bolling Galt, 19 August 1915, *The Papers of Woodrow Wilson,* ed. Arthur S. Link, 57 vols. (Princeton, NJ: Princeton University Press, 1966–87), vol. 34, p. 254.

4. Dangerous Consequences: The U.S. "War on Drugs" in Latin America

Coletta A. Youngers

1. Tom Barry, *Mission Creep in Latin America—U.S. Southern Command's New Security Strategy* (Silver City, NM: International Relations Center, 11 July 2005), p. 15.

2. U.S. Department of State, *2005 International Narcotics Control Strategy Report,* www.state.gov/p/inl/rls/nrcrpt/2005/.

3. The Pentagon has five geographical commands coordinating military activities and operations around the world. The U.S. Southern Command, or SouthCom, has responsibility for all of Latin America and the Caribbean, with the exception of Mexico.

4. Dana Priest, *The Mission: Waging War and Keeping Peace with America's Military* (New York: W. W. Norton, 2003), p. 74. Approximately 1,100 SouthCom staff are based in the region.

5. Ibid.

6. *Blurring the Lines: Trends in U.S. Military Programs with Latin America* (Washington, DC: The Latin America Working Group, Center for International Policy and the Washington Office on Latin America, September 2004), p. 3.

7. Quoted in Nancy Dunne and James Wilson, "Colombian Rebels Indicted," *Financial Times,* 19 March 2002.

8. Posture statement by General Bantz J. Craddock, United States Army Commander, United States Southern Command, before the 109th Congress House Armed Services Committee, 9 March 2005, p. 4.

9. Posture statement by General James Hill, United States Army Commander, United States Southern Command, before the House Armed Services Committee, U.S. House of Representatives, 24 March 2004, pp. 1–2.

10. For detailed analysis of U.S. assistance to Colombia, see the Center for International Policy Web site: www.ciponline.org/colombia/index.htm.

11. Adam Isacson, "The U.S. Military and the War on Drugs," in *Drugs and Democracy in Latin America: The Impact of U.S. Policy,* ed. Coletta A. Youngers and Eileen Rosin (Boulder, CO: Lynne Rienner Publishers, 2005), p. 48.

12. Maria Clemencia Ramirez Lemus, Kimberly Stanton, and John Walsh, "Colombia: A Vicious Cycle of Drugs and War," in Youngers and Rosin, *Drugs and Democracy in Latin America,* p. 113.

13. Ibid., p. 114.

14. Coletta A. Youngers and Eileen Rosin, "The U.S. 'War on Drugs': Its Impact in Latin America and the Caribbean," in Youngers and Rosin, *Drugs and Democracy in Latin America,* p. 6.

15. First legislated in 1986, the certification process was modified in 2002, such that countries are automatically certified unless the president announces a decertification. This and other reforms have lessened the bilateral tensions caused by the process, but it remains a blunt instrument, to be used at the administration's discretion.

16. "Blanco y Negro: La mayoría de detenidos es por narcotráfico," *Hoy,* 30 July 2005.

17. John Walsh, *Are We There Yet? Measuring Progress in the U.S. War on Drugs in Latin America* (Washington, DC: The Washington Office on Latin America, December 2004), p. 4.

18. Francisco E. Thoumi, *Illegal Drugs, Economy and Society in the Andes* (Washington, DC and Baltimore: The Woodrow Wilson Center Press and the Johns Hopkins University Press, 2003), p. 359.

19. David Boyum and Peter Reuter, *An Analytic Assessment of U.S. Drug Policy* (Washington, DC: The American Enterprise Institute, 2005), p. 95.

20. Ibid., p. 94.

21. See Youngers and Rosin, "The U.S. 'War on Drugs.' "

22. *Blueprint for a New Colombia Policy* (Washington, DC: Latin America Working Group, Center for International Policy, Washington Office on Latin America, and U.S. Office on Colombia, March 2005), p. 4.

23. Communication from Kathyrn Ledebur, Andean Information Network, 11 August 2005.

24. Isaias Rojas, *The Push for Zero Coca: Democratic Transition and Counternarcotics Policy in Peru* (Washington, DC: Washington Office on Latin America, February 2003), p. 1.

25. Thoumi, *Illegal Drugs, Economy and Society in the Andes*, p. 368.

26. GTZ, "Drugs and Conflict," discussion paper by the GTZ Drugs and Development Programme, September 2003, p. 23.

27. Martin Jelsma, "Revising and Integrating Drug Policies at the National and International Level: How Can Drug Reform Be Achieved?" paper presented at the Wilton Park Conference on Drug Policies and Their Impact, 27 March 2002, available on the Transnational Institute (TNI) Web site: www.tni.org/archives/jelsma/wilton.htm.

28. GTZ, *Drugs and Poverty: The Contribution of Development-Oriented Drug Control to Poverty Reduction,* a cooperative study of the Drugs and Development Programme (ADE) and the Poverty Reduction Project of GTZ, June 2003, p. 26.

29. Established in Article 11 of the International Covenant on Economic, Social and Cultural Rights.

30. "Bolivian presidential candidates take different stands on coca issue," *BBC Monitoring via COMTEX,* 25 September 2005.

31. Drug Policy Briefing No. 15, *Aerial Spraying Knows No Borders: Ecuador Brings International Case over Aerial Spraying* (Amsterdam: Transnational Institute, September 2005), p. 3.

32. Rich Vecchio, "Peru Court Rules Against Coca Expansion," Associated Press, 28 September 2005.

33. Patricia Rondon Espin, "Venezuela Leader Accuses DEA of Espionage," Associated Press, 7 August 2005.

34. U.S. Department of State, Bureau for International Narcotics and Law Enforcement Affairs, *Statement of Justification: Venezuela,* 15 September 2005.

35. Ibid.

36. Quoted in David Adams and Phil Gunson, "Venezuela-U.S. Division Runs Deep," *St. Petersburg Times,* 17 September 2005.

37. Reported by Jim Schultz, "Bush Brings the False Intelligence Game to South America," *Democracy Center On-Line,* vol. 66, 24 August 2005.

38. Ibid.

39. According to former SouthCom commander General James Hill, "If radicals con-

tinue to hijack the indigenous movement, we could find ourselves faced with a narco-state that supports the uncontrolled cultivation of coca." Posture statement by General James Hill, p. 5.

40. U.S. Department of State, Bureau for International Narcotics and Law Enforcement Affairs, *Statement of Justification: Venezuela*, 15 September 2005.

41. Ibid.

42. Peter Kornbluh, *Cuba, Counternarcotics, and Collaboration: A Security Issue in U.S.-Cuban Relations* (Washington, DC: Caribbean Project, Center for Latin American Studies, Georgetown University, December 2000), p. 10.

43. Interview with Ambassador John Dew, 22 June 2005.

44. Interviews by author in Havana, 23–25 June 2005.

5. Promoting Polyarchy in Latin America:
The Oxymoron of "Market Democracy"

William I. Robinson

1. Cited in Seymour M. Hersh, "The Price of Power: Kissinger, Nixon, and Chile," *Atlantic Monthly*, December 1982, p. 35.

2. For my theory of global capitalism and discussion of this transnational elite, see William I. Robinson, *A Theory of Global Capitalism: Production, Class, and State in a Transnational World* (Baltimore: Johns Hopkins University Press, 2004). This chapter necessarily simplifies complex arguments, which are developed more fully in William I. Robinson, *Promoting Polyarchy: Globalization, U.S. Intervention, and Hegemony* (Cambridge and New York: Cambridge University Press, 1996); William I. Robinson, "Globalization, the World System, and 'Democracy Promotion' in U.S. Foreign Policy," *Theory and Society* 23 (1990): 616–83; William I. Robinson, "Promoting Capitalist Polyarchy: The Case of Latin America," in *American Democracy Promotion: Impulses, Strategies and Impacts,* ed. Michael Cox, G. John Ikenberry, and Takashi Inoguchi (New York: Oxford University Press, 2000).

3. See John Williamson, "Democracy and the 'Washington Consensus,' " *World Development* 21, no. 8 (1993): 1329–36.

4. Gaetano Mosca, *The Ruling Class* (New York: McGraw Hill, 1965), p. 51.

5. Joseph A. Schumpeter, *Capitalism, Socialism and Democracy* (New York: Harper and Row, 1942), p. 285. See also Robert A. Dahl, *Polyarchy: Participation and Opposition* (New Haven, CT: Yale University Press, 1971); Peter Bachrach, *The Theory of Democratic Elitism: A Critique* (Lanham, MD: University of America Press, 1980); Robinson, *Promoting Polyarchy*, pp. 41–72.

6. See Henry Kissinger and Cyrus Vance, "Bipartisan Objectives for American Foreign Policy," *Foreign Affairs* 66, no. 5 (1988): 119.

7. In addition to Robinson, *Promoting Polyarchy*, see Joan M. Nelson and Stephanie Eglington, *Global Goals, Contentious Means: Issues of Multiple Conditionality* (Washington, DC: Overseas Development Council, 1993); Olav Stokke, *Aid and Political Conditionality* (London: Franck Cass, EADI Book Series 16, 1995).

8. On this point, see Robinson, *A Theory of Global Capitalism;* William I. Robinson, "Gramsci and Globalization: From Nation-State to Transnational Hegemony," *Critical Review of International Social and Political Philosophy* 8, no. 4 (2005): 1–16.

9. For early analyses of this reorganization, see, e.g., Albert Fishlow, Carlos F. Diaz-Alejandro, Richard R. Fagen, and Roger D. Hansen, *Rich and Poor Nations in the World Economy* (New York: McGraw Hill, 1978); Robert W. Cox, "Ideologies and the New International Economic Order: Reflections on Some Recent Literature," *International Organization* 33, no. 2 (1979): 257–302. See also Robinson, *A Theory of Global Capitalism*.

10. On this neoliberal restructuring around the world, see *Restructuring Hegemony in the Global Political Economy: The Rise of Transnational Neo-liberalism in the 1980s*, ed. Henk Overbeek (London: Routledge, 1993). On transnational state apparatuses, see Robinson, *A Theory of Global Capitalism*.

11. Agency for International Development, "The Democracy Initiative," Washington, DC, December 1990.

12. See, e.g., Thomas Carothers, *Aiding Democracy Abroad: The Learning Curve* (Washington, DC: Carnegie Endowment for International Peace, 1999); Larry Diamond, "Promoting Democracy in the 1990s: Actors, Instruments, Issues, and Imperatives," in *Report of the Carnegie Commission on Preventing Deadly Conflict* (New York: Carnegie Corporation of New York, 1995).

13. The emergence of new transnational fractions in Latin America is discussed in William I. Robinson, *Transnational Conflicts: Central America, Social Change, and Globalization* (London: Verso, 2003).

14. For discussion of this new model of development and its social implications, see Duncan Green, *Silent Revolution: The Rise of Market Economics in Latin America* (London: Cassell, 1995); Robinson, *Transnational Conflicts*.

15. On Chile and Haiti, see Robinson, *Promoting Polyarchy*. On Nicaragua, see *Promoting Polyarchy;* and William I. Robinson, *A Faustian Bargain: U.S. Intervention in the Nicaraguan Elections and American Foreign Policy in the Post-Cold War Era* (Boulder, CO: Westview Press, 1992). On Panama, see John Dinges, *Our Man in Panama* (New York: Random House, 1991 edition); Philip Wheaton, *Panama Invaded* (Trenton: Red Sea Press, 1992); and John Weeks and Phil Gunson, *Panama: Made in the USA* (London: Latin America Bureau, 1991). On Mexico, see, among other sources, "The Wars Within: Counterinsurgency in Chiapas and Colombia," *NACLA Report on the Americas* 31, no. 5 (March/April 1998); "Contesting Mexico," *NACLA Report on the Americas* 30, no. 4 (January/February 1997); and Tom

Barry, *Zapata's Revenge* (Boston: South End Press, 1995). On Venezuela, see William I. Robinson, "Nuevas Modalidades de Intervención Norteamerica en el Marco de la Globalization: La 'Promoción de la Democracia' y el Caso de Venezuela," *Revista Venezolana de Economía y Ciencias Sociales* (Caracas: Universidad Central de Venezuela, on press). On Bolivia, see Reed Lindsay, "Exporting Gas and Importing Democracy in Bolivia," *NACLA Report on the Americas* 39, no. 3 (November/December 2005): 5–11.

16. Lindsay, "Exporting Gas," p. 6.

17. See, e.g., Larry Diamond, Juan J. Linz, and Seymour Martin Lipset, *Democracy in Developing Countries: Latin America* (Boulder, CO: Lynne Rienner, 1989). In this landmark study funded by the AID, considered the basic primer in this literature, the authors state: "We use the term democracy in this study to signify a political system, separate and apart from the economic and social system. . . . Indeed, a distinctive aspect of our approach is to insist that issues of so-called economic and social democracy be separated from the question of governmental structure" (p. xvi). See also the U.S.-government-funded *Journal of Democracy* 5, no. 4 (October 1994) special issue, "Economic Reform and Democracy."

18. See, e.g., Larry Diamond and Mark F. Plattner, eds., *The Global Resurgence of Democracy* (Baltimore: Johns Hopkins University Press, 1993).

19. For this and related data, see William I. Robinson, "Global Crisis and Latin America," *Bulletin of Latin American Research* 23, no. 2 (2004): 135–53.

20. See Comisión Económica para América Latina (CEPAL), *Panorama Social de América Latina* (Santiago, Chile: CEPAL/United Nations, various annual reports).

21. Green, *Silent Revolution;* John Walton and David Seddon, *Free Markets and Food Riots: The Politics of Global Adjustment* (Oxford: Blackwell, 1994).

22. Antonio Gramsci, *Selections from the Prison Notebooks* (New York: International Publishers, 1971).

23. See "The Wars Within: Counterinsurgency in Chiapas and Colombia," *NACLA Report on the Americas* 31, no. 5 (March/April 1998).

6. Latin America: Persistent Inequality and Recent Transformations

Luis Reygadas

1. David de Ferranti, Guillermo E. Perry, Francisco Ferreira, and Michael Walton, *Inequality in Latin America and the Caribbean: Breaking with History?* (Washington, DC: World Bank, 2004), p. 1.

2. United Nations Development Program (UNDP), *Human Development Report 2005* (New York: Oxford University Press, 2005).

3. Ferranti et al., *Inequality in Latin America*, p. 1.

4. Miguel Szekely and Marianne Hilgert, W*hat's Behind the Inequality We Measure? An Investigation Using Latin American Data*, Luxembourg Income Study, Working Paper No. 234, Syracuse NY, 1999, p. 40.

5. Jeremy Adelman and Eric Hershberg, "Paradoxical Inequalities: Social Science, Social Forces and Public Policies in Latin America," unpublished manuscript, Princeton Institute for Regional Studies, Princeton, NJ, 2004; Paul Gootenberg, "Desigualdades persistentes en América Latina," *Alteridades* 14, no. 28 (2004): 9–19; Kelly Hoffman and Miguel Centeno, "The Lopsided Continent: Inequality in Latin America," *Annual Review of Sociology* 29 (2003): 363–90; Terry Karl, *The Vicious Circle of Inequality in Latin America*, Instituto Juan March, Estudio 2002/177, Madrid, 2002; Alejandro Portes and Kelly Hoffman, "Latin American Class Structures: Their Composition and Change During the Neoliberal Era," *Latin American Research Review* 38, no. 1 (2003): 41–82.

6. María del Carmen Feijoó, *Nuevo país, nueva pobreza* (Buenos Aires: Fondo de Cultura Económica, 2003); United Nations, *The Inequality Predicament: Report on the World Social Situation* (New York: United Nations Department of Economic and Social Affairs, 2005); Karl, *The Vicious Circle of Inequality in Latin America*, p. 6.

7. Sarah Hamilton and Edward Fischer, "Non-traditional Agricultural Exports in Highland Guatemala: Understandings of Risk and Perceptions of Change," *Latin American Research Review* 38, no. 2 (2003): 82–110.

8. José Hernández Laos and Jorge Velázquez, *Globalización, desigualdad y pobreza. Lecciones de la experiencia mexicana* (Mexico City: UAM-Plaza y Valdéz, 2003), p. 91.

9. Ibid.

10. Portes and Hoffman, "Latin American Class Structures," p. 55.

11. Pablo González Casanova, "La explotación global," in *Globalidad: una mirada alternativa*, coord. Ricado Valero (Mexico City: Porrúa, 1999), pp. 89–93.

12. Joseph Stiglitz, *Globalization and Its Discontents* (London: Allen Lane/Penguin Press, 2002), pp. 198–99.

13. Hector Schamis, *Reforming the State: The Politics of Privatization in Latin America and Europe* (Ann Arbor: University of Michigan Press, 2002), pp. 35, 57 and 61–64.

14. UNDP, *Human Development Report 2005*.

15. Sebastián Etchemendy, "Construir coaliciones reformistas: la política de las compensaciones en el camino argentino hacia la liberalización económica," *Desarrollo Económico. Revista de Ciencias Sociales* 40, no. 160 (2001): 675–706.

16. Schamis, *Reforming the State*, pp. 120–21.

17. Victor Tokman, *Una voz en el camino. Empleo y equidad en América Latina: 40 años de búsqueda* (Santiago: Fondo de Cultura Económica, 2004), p. 131.

18. Juan Pablo Pérez Sáinz and Minor Mora, "De la oportunidad del empleo formal

al riesgo de exclusión laboral. Desigualdades estructurales y dinámicas en los mercados latinoamericanos de trabajo," *Alteridades* 14, no. 28 (2004): 37–49, p. 42; Tokman, *Una voz en el camino*, p. 185.

19. Comisión Económica para América Latina (CEPAL), *Panorama Social de América Latina*, (Santiago, Chile: CEPAL/United Nations, 2001).

20. Pérez Sáinz and Mora, "De la oportunidad," pp. 43–44.

21. Graciela Bensusán and Luis Reygadas, "Relaciones laborales en Chihuahua: un caso de abatimiento artificial de los salarios," *Revista Mexicana de Sociología*, no. 2. (2000).

22. Rubén Katzman and Guillermo Wormald, eds., *Trabajo y ciudadanía. Los cambiantes rostros de la integración y la exclusión social en cuatro áreas metropolitanas de América Latina* (Montevideo: Errandonea, 2002), pp. 46–49.

23. Exito Exportador Web site, www.exitoexportador.com.

24. INEGI, *Módulo Nacional de Computación* (Mexico City: Instituto Nacional de Estadística, Geografía e Informática, Encuesta Nacional de Ingresos y Gastos de los Hogares, 2002).

25. Juan Luis Londoño and Miguel Szekely, "Persistent Poverty and Excess Inequality: Latin America 1970–1995," *Journal of Applied Economics* 3 (2000): 93–134.

26. Adelman and Hershberg, "Paradoxical Inequalities."

27. Miguel Szekely and Marianne Hilgert, *The 1990s in Latin America: Another Decade of Persistent Inequality*, Luxembourg Income Study, Working Paper No. 235, Syracuse, NY, 1999, pp. 5–7.

7. A Table to Eat On: The Meaning and Measurement of Poverty in Latin America

Araceli Damián and Julio Boltvinik

1. For a detailed explanation of this method, see Julio Boltvinik, "Anexo metodológico," in Julio Boltvinik and Enrique Hernández-Laos, *Pobreza y distribución del ingreso en México* (Mexico City: Siglo XXI Editores, 1999), pp. 313–50.

2. Evelyne Huber compares the transformations of the welfare state which took place as the process of globalization was advancing in recent decades in Western Europe and Latin America, and notes five fundamental differences: (1) the greater degree of change in the Latin American as compared to the European economies (which were previously highly integrated into international markets); (2) that democratic institutions and internal forces in Europe supported social policies guided by the principles of universality and solidarity, while in Latin America such institutions were weaker; (3) that political parties in Latin America are much weaker (above all leftist and social democracy parties); (4) the weak-

ness of Latin American labor unions, which in general have been co-opted by political parties that have carried out neoliberal reforms; and (5) that the level of debt in these European countries was low, which placed them in a stronger position to design their own austerity policies, rather than be subjected to the remedy applied by international organizations. See Evelyne Huber, "Globalización y desarrollo de políticas sociales en Latinoamérica," in *La pobreza en México y el mundo,* ed. Julio Boltvinik and Araceli Damián (Mexico City: Siglo XXI Editores, 2004), pp. 200–39.

3. For a critique of the changes in economic policy in Latin America, see Joseph Stiglitz, "El rumbo de las reformas. Hacia una nueva agenda para América Latina," *Revista de la CEPAL (CEPAL Review),* August 2003, pp. 7–40.

4. ECLAC notes that this lack of comparability is the result of: (1) changes made in design of the 2002 survey, in which the size of the sample was almost doubled (from 10,000 to 17,000 households); (2) a change in the criteria for selecting households in the sampling procedure; and (3) changes in the questionnaire, above all in the questions on income. Comisión Económica para América Latina (CEPAL), *Panorama Social de América Latina* (Santiago, Chile: United Nations/ CEPAL, 2003), p. 58.

5. ECLAC (ibid.) states: "It becomes obvious that the mentioned factors could have an important effect in the outcomes of poverty and income distribution. To illustrate, if the size of lowest-income (rural) households had evolved (in 2002), as expected—for example, a decline of two-tenths of the 2000 value (5.9 people)— the incidence of extreme poverty would have been about 18%, a higher number than the estimates derived from the data of ENIGH 2002." But this organization continued to use the data derived from ENIGH 2002, and rural poverty in Mexico was calculated at 12.6 percent.

6. This method has also been used, although with some differences with respect to ECLAC's method, by the U.S. government since the 1960s and by the current (2000–2006) Mexican government.

7. Insofar as the income of households grows, the proportion of their spending on food declines. For example, in Mexico in 2002, the poorest 10 percent of urban households spent 40.7 percent of their total expenditures on food, while the richest 10 percent only spent 17 percent on food. The NFB method has been criticized due to the instability of the Engel Coefficient. Aldi J.M. Hagenaars notes that the poverty line is extremely sensitive to the exact value of the Engel Coefficient used. Studies of the Engel Coefficient show that the estimated values can vary considerably among different surveys. See Aldi J.M. Hagenaars, *The Perception of Poverty* (Amsterdam: North-Holland, 1986). Mollie Orshansky, the creator of the official method of poverty measurement in the United States, found values between 0.25 and 0.33 in two surveys of the U.S. population.

8. Óscar Altimir, "La dimensión de la pobreza en América Latina," *Cuadernos de la CEPAL*, no. 27 (1979).

9. CEPAL, *Panorama Social de América Latina*, 2003.

10. See Julio Boltvinik, "El método de la medición integrada de la pobreza. Una propuesta para su desarrollo," *Comercio Exterior* 42, no. 4 (April 1992): 354–65; "Poverty Measurement and Alternative Indicators of Development," in *Poverty Monitoring: An International Concern*, ed. Rolph Van der Hoeven and Richard Anker (New York: St. Martin's Press, 1994), pp. 57–83; "Anexo metodológico," in Julio Boltvinik and Enrique Hernández-Laos, *Pobreza y distribución del ingreso en México* (Mexico City: Siglo XXI Editores, 1999), pp. 313–50; and *Ampliar la mirada. Un nuevo enfoque de la pobreza y el florecimiento humano*, PhD diss., Centro de Investigación y Estudios Avanzados de Occidente (CIESAS), Guadalajara, Mexico, 2005.

11. Ibid.

12. Ibid.

13. As the weights of the different UBN components are the relative social costs of satisfying each group of needs, the combined index of the UBN dimension (as handled in IPMM) provides a measure of the effort required to eliminate this dimension of poverty.

14. Boltvinik, 1992, 1994, 1999, 2005.

15. Household income and expenditure surveys (as all household surveys) generally underestimate income due to, on the one hand, the real difficulty of interviewing very rich people, who tend to reject any type of survey, but particularly those that have to do with income. On the other hand, problems also exist with the sampling design. Households that are selected for the surveys are considered representative of other households with similar income and expenditure patterns. In this way, by extrapolating the sample to the total population, each household interviewed is considered a representative of thousands of households. The problem with the very rich is that they don't represent anyone, nor can they be represented by anyone else. They are truly unique cases. If this is correct, the very rich should be selected in a sample with a probability equivalent to 1—i.e., with certainty. Finally, people who are interviewed tend to under-declare income and expenditure. This understatement is especially acute in countries where a very high proportion of the population evades taxes and fears that the survey can have some link with revenue authorities.

16. The source is the World Bank, *Global Economic Prospects and the Developing Countries* (Washington, DC: World Bank, 2000). However, the bank built this series based on different papers by Miguel Szekely and Nora Lustig. These authors have sometimes used data adjusted to national accounts, so it is very likely that the series is a mixture of data with and without adjustments.

17. Coordinación Nacional del Plan Nacional de Zonas Deprimidas y Grupos Marginados (Coplamar), *Macroeconomía de las necesidades esenciales en México, situación actual y perspectivas al año 2000*, Serie Necesidades Esenciales en México, 2nd ed. (Mexico City: Siglo XXI Editores, 1983).

18. ECLAC, in its 2003 *Panorama social de América Latina*, points to a few problems of comparability of the 2002 ENIGH. Its warnings coincide with those found by several specialists in Mexico (including the Technical Committee in charge of the "official" methodology for the measurement of poverty): (1) The increase of the sample size and the change in the sampling framework changed the quality of the information collected, which can modify the trends in the measurement of poverty. (2) The questionnaire underwent changes, but above all it added more questions designed to collect information about household income. Significantly, the sources of income captured by the new questions doubled in the rural poorest decile (from 8 percent in 2000 to 16 percent in 2002). ECLAC expressed its surprise at the growth of income among the lowest two deciles: by 17 percent in their work-related income and by 20 percent in their total income. (3) Many households ceased to be classified as poor due to the growth in their virtual household income in the form of imputed rent for self-owned dwelling. (4) A fall in the size of the household was observed among the poorest rural deciles (6 percent and 18 percent in the poorest two deciles), which contributed to the decline in measured poverty, since the government method is based on household income per person. CEPAL calculated that if household size in rural areas had behaved as expected, indigence would not have fallen from 15.2 percent to 12.6 percent, but would have risen to 18.6 percent. (5) The evolution of several variables captured by the survey did not correspond with the information derived from other sources of information. This is especially important in respect to income transfers. For example, in the survey, government transfers to support the countryside (Procampo) grew by 131 percent, in acute contrast with administrative data, which showed a reduction of 2 percent; and income from the anti-poverty program, *Oportunidades*, grew twice as much as what was reported in the administrative data. (6) The number of people employed according to the ENIGH grew by 1.3 million per year between 2000 and 2002, in sharp contrast with the 500,000 reported by the specialized National Employment Survey. In 2004, the ENIGH underwent new modifications that prevent the comparability of the 2002 and 2004 surveys.

19. The data for 1981, when there was no ENIGH, have been estimated in all the cases by Boltvinik.

20. The data of the IPMM for 1984 is adjusted to national accounts, while that of 2002 is not. Nevertheless, we suppose that the adjustment will show a similar difference to that which we found between the adjusted and non-adjusted data of

1998, a year in which we have adjusted data. Poverty adjusted to national accounts in 1998 was 75.7 percent, compared to 80.3 percent without adjustment. Since economic conditions in 1998 and 2000 were very similar, poverty with adjusted data should be located very close to the level of 1998 and, therefore, higher than in 1984.

21. Boltvinik, 1992, 1994, 1999, 2005.
22. See, for example, Maira Buvinic, Nadia Youssef, and Barbara Von Elm, *Women-headed Households: The Ignored Factor in Development Planning*, report prepared for the U.S. Agency for International Development, Washington, DC, International Center for Research on Women, 1978.
23. See, for example, Mercedes Barquet, "Condiciones de género sobre la pobreza de las mujeres," in Javier Alatorre, Gloria Careaga, Clara Jusidman, Vania Salles, Cecialia Talamante, and John Townsend (Interdisciplinary Group on Women, Work and Poverty), *Las mujeres en la pobreza* (Mexico City: El Colegio de México, 1994), pp. 73–89.
24. UNIFEM, *¿Cuánto cuesta la pobreza de las mujeres? Una perspectiva de América Latina y el Caribe* (Mexico City: UNIFEM, 1995).
25. CEPAL, *Panorama Social de América Latina*, 1995.
26. See Irma Arriagada, *Políticas sociales, familia y trabajo en la América Latina de fin de siglo*, Santiago de Chile, Naciones Unidas, CEPAL, Serie Política Sociales, 1997, p. 21; and Cinthia B. Lloyd, "Household Structure and Poverty: What Are the Connections?" in *Population and Poverty in the Developing World*, ed. Livi-Bacci and G. de Santis (Oxford: Clarendon Press, 1998), pp. 84–102.
27. Arriagada, *Políticas sociales*, p. 17.
28. Lloyd, "Household Structure and Poverty," p. 95.
29. Ibid.
30. CEPAL, *Panorama Social de América Latina*, 2001, pp. 51–54.
31. CEPAL, *Panorama Social de América Latina*, 2002, pp. 198–99.
32. The countries with a femininity ratio of greater than 100 percent in all areas were Bolivia, Chile, Colombia, Costa Rica, Ecuador, El Salvador, Guatemala, Honduras, Mexico, Panama, the Dominican Republic, Uruguay, and Venezuela. Those with a ratio of over 100 percent in either urban or rural areas were Brazil, Honduras, Nicaragua, and Paraguay. Those with a ratio of less than 100 percent were Argentina and Uruguay. Ibid.
33. Femininity poverty index = (poor women/poor men)/(total women/total men).
34. One possible hypothesis is that the poor men working in the cities and other countries contribute less to their households than those who remain in the household.
35. We used information about the percentage of poverty in total households, since ECLAC does not provide information on those headed by men.

36. CEPAL, *Panorama Social de América Latina,* 2001, table 1.6, p. 53.
37. If we consider only the salaried population, the biggest difference was present in Bolivia, where female wages represent 60 percent of male wages, and the least difference was observed in Panama, where this indicator was 80 percent.
38. The following evidence comes from tables on average income of the economically active male and female population developed by ECLAC (CEPAL, *Panorama Social de América Latina,* 2004, tables 7.1 and 7.2).
39. Argentina, Brazil, Panama, Uruguay, and Venezuela.
40. In urban areas in Bolivia, Guatemala, and Mexico, women between the ages of fifteen and twenty-four had studied on average 10.2, 7.5, and 10 years, respectively, and men 10.5, 7.6, and 10.2 years. On the other hand, in rural areas women had studied 5.6, 3.1, and 7.5 years on average in Bolivia, Guatemala, and Mexico, respectively, while men had studied 6.9, 4.1, and 8.1 years. CEPAL, *Panorama Social de América Latina,* 2001, pp. 258–59.
41. See Araceli Damián, "La pobreza de tiempo: conceptos y métodos para su medición," in Boltvinik and Damián, eds., *La pobreza en México,* pp. 482–518.
42. Agustín Escobar Latapí, "La evaluación cualitativa del programa de desarrollo humano Oportunidades, 2001–2002 (expansión a pequeñas ciudades). Reflexiones y resultados," in Boltvinik and Damián, eds., *La pobreza en México,* pp. 364–408.

8. Crime and Citizen Security in Latin America

Mark Ungar

1. The Health Situation Analysis Program of the Pan American Health Organization, 1997.
2. M. Búvenic and Andrew Morrison, "Notas Técnicas Sobre la Violencia," Inter-American Development Bank, Washington, DC, 1999.
3. J.M. Cruz, A. Trigueros Arguello, and F. González, "El crimen violento en El Salvador: Factores sociales y económicos asociados," IUDOP, San Salvador, 2000. Homicide rose by 379 percent in Peru in the 1990s.
4. In J.L. Londoño, A. Gaviria, and R. Guerrero, eds., *Asalto al Desarrollo: Violencia en América Latina* (Washington, DC: Inter-American Development Bank, 2000).
5. "Inequality in Latin America and the Caribbean: Breaking with History?" World Bank, October 2003.
6. Indigenous men in Latin America earn 35 to 65 percent less than white men, for example, and those of African descent in Brazil earn about 45 percent less than whites. Ibid.
7. Homicide is the second-leading cause of death for that age group in the region's

largest countries. K. Weaver and M. Maddaleno, "Youth Violence in Latin America: Current Situation and Violence Prevention Strategies," *Revista Panamericana de Salud/Pan American Journal of Public Health* 5, no. 4–5 (April/May 1999): 338–43.

8. World Health Organization, "Injury: A Leading Cause of the Global Burden of Disease" (Geneva: WHO, 1999).

9. R. Briceño-León, A. Camardiel, and O. Avila, "Violencia y Actitudes de Apoyo a la Violencia en Caracas," *Fermentum* 9, no. 26 (September/December 1999): 325–35.

10. R.G. Concha-Eastman, "An Epidemiological Approach for the Prevention of Urban Violence: The Case of Cali, Colombia," *Journal of Health and Population in Developing Countries* 4, no. 1 (2001).

11. World Bank Department of Finance, Private Sector and Infrastructure, Latin American Region, *A Resource Guide for Municipalities: Community Based Crime and Violence Prevention in Urban Latin America*, 2003.

12. H. Velasquez, *La Seguridad Ciudadana en Entornos Urbanos Complejos*, Alcaldía Mayor de Bogotá, 2002.

13. George Kelling and Catherine Coles, *Fixing Broken Windows* (New York: Touchstone, 1996).

14. Teresa Borden, "El Salvador Racked by Gangs," Cox News Service, 19 January 2005.

15. Author interview, *defensor adjunto* Samuel Abad Yupanqui, 20 June 2001, Lima, Peru.

16. Author interview, Escuela de Altos Estudios Policiales, Policía Nacional de Perú, 18 June 2001.

17. Benjamin Mendez Bahena, Juan Carlos Hernand Esquival, and Gerogine Isunza Vizuet, "Seguridad Pública y Percepción Ciudadana: Estudio de caso en quince colonias del Distrito Federal" in Fernando Carrion, *Seguridad Ciudadana: Espejismo o Realidad?* (Quito: FLACSO, OPS.PMS, June 2002), pp. 141–66.

18. Author interview with the commissioner, subcommissioner, and two subcommissioned officers of Comisaría 32 of the Policía Federal Argentina, 25 May 2004; and with police commissioners in La Rioja, August 2005.

19. Susana Rotker, "Cities Written by Violence," in Susana Rotker, *Citizens of Fear: Urban Violence in Latin America* (New Brunswick, NJ: Rutgers University Press, 2002).

20. M. Rubio, "El desbordamiento de la violence en Colombia," in Londoño, Gaviria and Guerrero, *Asalto al Desarrollo*.

21. World Values Survey, www.worldvaluessurvey.org/statistics/index.html.

22. "Memoria y Cuenta del Consejo de la Judicatura, Dirección de Planificación, Consejo de la Judicatura." This is the annual self-published report of the *Consejo*

de la Judicatura (national Judicial Council). As of 1994, the council estimated a need for an additional 100 defenders in addition to the 158 then serving.

23. Ximena Sierralta Patron, "Cárceles en Crisis: el Problema más explosivo de América Latina. El caso de Perú," report for the 2003–6 Project *Carceles en Crisis* of the Ford Foundation and Latin American Studies Association.

24. Julita Lemgruber, "The Enigma of Overcrowding," in *Justicia Encarcelada*, ed. Barbara J. Fraser and Elsa Chanduví Jaña (Lima, Perú: Noticias Aliadas/ Latinamerica Press, 2001). Free legal aid centers do not make up for such inadequacies.

25. Author interview, Víctor Parelló, northern region human rights commissioner, 20 February 2004.

26. Author interview, Security Minister Óscar Álvarez, Tegucigalpa, 18 July 2003.

27. Author interview, National Human Rights Commissioner Ramón Custodio, 4 July 2005.

28. Julieta Castellanos, "El Tortuoso Camino de la Reforma Policial," *El Heraldo*, 8 October 2002.

29. *La Prensa*, Tegucigalpa, 17 July 2003; and Casa Alianza, at www.casa-alianza.org/ EN/about/offices/honduras/.

30. Author interview, former UAI Chief Sub-Comisionada María Luisa Borjas, Tegucigalpa, 18 July 2003.

31. Author interview, Human Rights Prosecutor Aída Estella Romero, 22 July 2003. In response to these charges, the security minister accused Dr. Romero of acting "subjectively and with suspicion" against the police. "Álvarez molesto con fiscalía de Derechos Humanos," *La Prensa*, 26 February 2004, p. 14.

32. Author interview, Human Rights Commissioner Ramón Custodio, 4 July 2005; author interview, Gustavo Zelaya, legal coordinator of Casa Alianza, who served on a commission investigating the killings, June 2005.

33. The barrio of Choloma had nine murders in January 2002 but only four per month in the first four months of 2003, and seventeen robberies in January 2002 but none in 2003's first four months. Sources: meeting of the residents' community policing committee, Choloma, 19 February 2004; "Presidente Maduro inaugura programa 'Comunidad Segura' en Choloma, Cortés," 3 May 2003, www.casa presidencial.hn/seguridad.

34. Author interview, Carlos Chincilla, executive director, Comunidad Más Segura, Tegucigalpa, 22 July 2003.

35. Author interview, La Ceiba, Honduras, 25 February 2004.

36. Author interview, Eduardo Villanueva, Fiscal de la Niñez, Tegucigalpa, 15 July 2003. Walter Menjivar Mendoza, the head prosecutor for the northern region (author interview, San Pedro Sula, 26 February 2004) agrees that vigilantism has become uncontrollable, but doesn't want to estimate the number of cases.

37. Juan Ramón Quintana, "Bolivia: militares y policías Fuego cruzado en democracia" (La Paz: Observatorio Democracia y Seguridad, 2004).

38. The ministry's budget increased by 56 percent in nominal terms between 2000 and 2004. Sources: Contaduría General del Estado—Área de Estadísticas Fiscales; "The Budget for State Security in Bolivia 2004," Fundación Libertad, Democracia y Desarrollo, Santa Cruz, April 2004, pp. 11–14.

39. Author interview, Coronel Jaime Gutiérrez, director of human rights, National Police, 13 July 2000.

40. An example is Law 1008 of 1988, which undermines due process by prohibiting pretrial release.

41. Most of the 150 killings by police since 1990 have been part of the anti-coca operation. Juan R. Quintana, "Bolivia: militares y policía—Fuego cruzado en democracia," unpublished manuscript (La Paz: Observatio Democracia y Seguridad, 2004).

42. Author interview, Ana María Romero de Campero, defensor nacional of Bolivia, 12 July 2000.

43. In 2004, the TDS processed 70 percent more officials than in 2003—a jump from 550 to 920 cases. The time in which complaints are processed has dropped from seven to ten years down to ten days.

44. Author interview, William A. Alave, Fiscal de Materia, 17 December 2004.

45. Author interview, Gloria Eyzaguirre, Police Reform Commission, 22 December 2004.

46. "El escándalo no cesa en la Policía, revelan sueldos fantasmas," *La Razón*, 24 September 2004.

47. Movimiento Autonomista: Nación Cambia, "Policía y Seguridad Ciudadana," www.nacioncamba.net.

48. Author interview, former vice president Luis Ossico Sanjinés, 16 December 2004.

49. According to the Police Reform Commission (author interviews, December 2004), laws on state management, administration, and finances are not applied to the police.

50. Instituto Nacional de Estadística y Censos (INDEC); *Registro Nacional de Reincidencia y Estadística Criminal* 38 (Buenos Aires: Ministerio de Justicia de la Nación, 2000).

51. The official, Aldo Rico, is a former military official who led a military uprising in the 1980s and said that "it is necessary to kill [delinquents] in the street without any doubt and without having pity." "El carapintada por la boca muere," *Página/12*, 10 March 1998, p. 12.

52. Author interviews, Mayor Rubén Miranda, June 2004 and August 2005.

9. The Politics of Memory, the Languages of Human Rights

Katherine Hite

1. John Borneman, "Reconciliation after Ethnic Cleansing: Listening, Retribution, Affiliation," *Public Culture* 14, no. 2 (Spring 2002): 281–304.

2. Alex Wilde, "Irruptions of Memory: Expressive Politics in Chile's Transition to Democracy," *Journal of Latin American Studies* 31, no. 2 (1999): 473–500.

3. Richard Wilson, *The Politics of Truth and Reconciliation in South Africa: Legitimizing the Post-Apartheid State* (Cambridge: Cambridge University Press, 2001), pp. 17–20.

4. *Report of the Chilean National Commission on Truth and Reconciliation*, trans. Phillip E. Berryman (Notre Dame, IN: Center for Civil and Human Rights, Notre Dame Law School, 1993), vol. I, pp. 48–49.

5. Recounted by the director of Human Rights Watch-Americas Division José Miguel Vivanco to Priscilla Hayner, cited in Hayner's study of truth commissions around the world, *Unspeakable Truths: Confronting State Terror and Atrocity* (New York: Routledge, 2001), p. 86.

6. Marcie Mersky, "History as an Instrument of Social Reparation: Reflections on an Experience in Guatemala," *The Just Word* V, no. 1 (Spring 2000): 14.

7. Rachel Sieder, "War, Peace, and Memory Politics in Central America," in *The Politics of Memory: Transitional Justice in Democratizing Societies,* ed. Alexandra Barahona de Brito, Carmen Gonzalez-Enriquez, and Paloma Aguilar (Oxford: Oxford University Press, 2001), pp. 164–65; Historical Clarification Commission.

8. *Final Report of the Truth and Reconciliation Commission: Summary of Recommendations Section, Volume IX,* trans. International Center for Transitional Justice, 2003, available at www.cverdad.org.pe.

9. See, for example, "Francisco Diez Canseco: Ex comisionados usaron políticamente a la CVR," *La Primera* (Lima), 5 May 2005.

10. The CVR provided a detailed explanation of the methodology used to estimate the figure and delivered approximately 20,000 fully documented individual cases to the Peruvian government. For a useful presentation of the methodology, see Patrick Ball, Jana Asher, David Sulmont, and Daniel Manrique, "How Many Peruvians Have Died? An Estimate of the Total Number of Victims Killed or Disappeared in the Armed Internal Conflict Between 1980 and 2000" (Washington, DC: American Academy for the Advancement of Science, 28 August 2003), www.aprodeh.org.pe/sem_verdad/otros_doc.htm#metodologia (accessed 25 September 2005).

11. See Martín Tanaka, "Documento de discusión para el taller 'Democracia, ciudadanía y partidos politicos," Instituto de Estudios Peruanos, 9 September 2004.

12. On the power of military prerogatives in democratization processes, see Alfred

Stepan, *Rethinking Military Politics: Brazil and the Southern Cone* (Princeton, NJ: Princeton University Press, 1988).

13. See, for example, Joaquín M. Chavez, "An Anatomy of Violence in El Salvador," *NACLA Report on the Americas* 37, no. 6 (May/June 2004): 31–37.

14. Carlos Nino, *Radical Evil on Trial* (New Haven, CT: Yale University Press, 1996), p. 104.

15. María Elena Castillo, "En peligro testigo de graves violaciones a DDHH," *La República* (Lima), 13 July 2005.

16. Amnesty International, "Guatemala: Deep Cause for Concern," 1 April 2003.

17. Scilingo's confession is reproduced in Horacio Verbitsky, *El vuelo* (Buenos Aires: Planeta, 1995). For a psychoanalytic analysis of Argentina's memory discourses, see Antonius C.G.M. Robben, "How Traumatized Societies Remember: The Aftermath of Argentina's Dirty War," *Cultural Critique* 59 (Winter 2005): 120–64.

18. Kimberly Theidon, "Intimate Enemies: Towards a Social Psychology of Reconciliation," in *Psychological Approaches to Dealing with Conflict and War*, ed. Mari Fitzduff and Chris E. Stout (Westport, CT: Praeger Press, forthcoming).

19. Ibid.

20. Oscar Valderrama López, "Alan García: 'Al acusar a FFAA se cae en juego del senderismo,'" *La Razón*, 15 July 2005, posted on the Asociación Pro-Derechos Humanos (APRODEH) Web site: www.aprodeh.org.pe/servicio/c_infoaprodeh .htm (accessed 15 July 2005).

21. Ibid.

22. Ponciano del Pino, "Uchuraccay: Memoria y representación de la violencia política en los Andes," in *Jamás tan cerca arremetió lo lejos: memoria y violencia en el Perú*, ed. Carlos Iván Degregori (Lima: Instituto de Estudios Peruanos and the Social Science Research Center, 2003), pp. 49–93.

23. Ibid., pp. 86–87.

24. On the notion of "layers of memory," see Elizabeth Jelin and Susana G. Kaufman, "Layers of Memories: Twenty Years After in Argentina," in *The Politics of War Memory and Commemoration*, ed. T.G. Ashplant, Graham Dawson, and Michael Roper (New York: Routledge, 2000), pp. 89–110. See also Jelin, *State Repression and the Labors of Memory* (Minneapolis: University of Minnesota Press, 2003).

10. Give or Take Ten Million: The Paradoxes of Migration to the United States

Judith Adler Hellman

1. See Jeffrey S. Passel, "Estimates of the Size and Characteristics of the Undocumented Population," *Pew Hispanic Center Report*, 21 March 2005; and Leigh Bin-

ford, "A Generation of Migrants: Where They Leave, Where They End Up," *NACLA Report on the Americas* 39, no. 1 (July/August 2005): 32.

2. Jean Papail and Fermina Robles Sotelo, "Inserción laboral de los migrantes urbanos de la región centro occidental de México en la economía estadounidense," in *Insercióín Laboral y Estatus Social de los Migrantes Mexicanos y Latinos en Estados Unidos*, ed. Elaine Levine (México: Universidad Nacional Autonoma de México, Centro de investigacioines sobre América del Norte, 2004), pp. 33–48, cited in Binford, "A Generation of Migrants," p. 33.

3. Personal communication with Nancy Churchill. Also see Nancy Churchill Conner, "Trabajadoras domésticas y migración internacional: Cambios en la vida cotidiana en Santo Tomás Chautla," in *La Economia politica de la migracion internacional en Puebla y Veracruz: Siete estudios de caso*, ed. Leigh Binford (Puebla, Mexico: Benemérita Universidad Autónoma de Puebla, 2004), pp. 277, 290–92.

4. Wayne A. Cornelius, "The Embeddedness of Demand for Mexican Immigrant Labor: New Evidence from California," in *Crossings: Mexican Immigration in Interdisciplinary Perspective*, ed. Marcelo M. Suarez-Orozco (Boston: David Rockefeller Center Series on Latin American Studies, Harvard University, 1998), p. 126.

5. Ibid.

6. Jorge A. Bustamante, "La migración de los indocumentados," *El Cotidiano*, Número especial 1, 1987, pp. 13–29.

7. Rodolfo Garcia Zamora, "Economic Challenges for Mexican Hometown Associations in the United States: Federations of Zacatecan Associations," unpublished paper, p. 16.   Also see Rodolfo Garcia Zamora, *Migración, remesas y desarrollo local*, Doctorado en Estudios del Desarrollo, UAZ, Zacatecas, 2003.

8. The Mexican states with the highest proportion of population that migrates are Durango, Guanajuato, Guerrero, Jalisco, Michoacán, Oaxaca, San Luis Potosí, and Zacatecas.

9. Zamora, "Economic Challenges."

10. "Declaration of Cuernavaca, 2005," p. 3, published in Spanish in *La Jornada*, 5 June 2005, meme.phpwebhosting.com/~migracion/modules/noticias/declaration_of_cuernavaca.pdf.

11. Wayne A. Cornelius, "Death at the Border: The Efficacy and 'Unintended' Consequences of U.S. Immigration Control Policy, 1993–2000," Center for Comparative Immigration Studies Working Paper No. 27, November 2000; and Wayne A. Cornelius, "Controlling 'Unwanted' Immigration: Lessons from the United States, 1993–2004," *Journal of Ethnic and Migration Studies* 31, no. 2 (April 2005).

12. Ibid., p. 6.

13. "Special Report: American Immigration," *The Economist*, 12 March 2005, pp. 28–29.

14. Philip Martin, ed., *Migration News* 8, no. 11 (November 2001): 1.

15. Joe Hill, the legendary labor organizer of the International Workers of the World (the Wobblies), was shot dead by thugs hired to suppress the strike he led. Folk singer Woody Guthrie claimed that Joe never died and would reappear regularly: "Wherever workers organize, it's there you'll see Joe Hill."

11. The Left in South America and the Resurgence of National-Popular Regimes

Carlos M. Vilas

1. Alfio Mastropaolo, "Izquierda," in *Diccionario de política,* ed. Norberto Bobbio and Nicola Matteucci (México: Siglo XXI, 1985), vol. 1, pp. 862–63.
2. Norberto Bobbio, *Derecha e izquierda: Razones y significados de una distinción política* (Madrid: Taurus, 1995).
3. Alejandro Portes and Kelly Hoffman, "Latin American Class Structures: Their Composition and Change during the Neoliberal Era," *Latin American Research Review* 38, no. 1 (2003): 41–82.
4. See, for example, Nancy Birdsall et al., "La desigualdad como limitación del crecimiento en América Latina," *Gestión y política pública* 5, no. 1 (1996): 29–75; Inter-American Development Bank, "América Latina frente a la desigualdad: Progreso económico y social de América Latina," 1998–1999; World Bank, *Attacking Poverty: World Development Report 2000/2001* (Washington, DC: World Bank, 2001); and David De Ferranti et al., *Inequality in Latin America: Breaking With History?* (Washington, DC: World Bank, 2004).
5. I am using the term "national-popular" as conceived of by Germani (Gino Germani, "Democracia representativa y clases populares," in Alain Touraine and Gino Germani, *América del Sur: un proletariado nuevo* [Barcelona: Nova Terra, 1965]).
6. Several factors push for this turnaround, which I have discussed in previous works. See Carlos M. Vilas, "La izquierda latinoamericana: búsquedas y desafíos," *Nueva Sociedad* 157 (1998): 64–74; and "Are There Left Alternatives? A Discussion From Latin America," in *Are There Alternatives?: Socialist Register 1996,* ed. Leo Panitch (London: Merlin Press, 1996), pp. 264–85.
7. Economic Commission on Latin America and the Caribbean Annual Reports, 1998, 2003.
8. In 1998 the richest 5 percent of the Latin American population received a share of income twice as high as the comparable group in OECD countries, while the poorest 30 percent survived on 7.5 percent of the total, 60 percent of the income share of the comparable group in advanced countries. See Portes and Hoffman, "Latin American Class Structures."

9. The polls taken by the organization Latinobarómetro register a decrease in support for democracy. In 2001 only 48 percent of those interviewed expressed a preference for democracy (defined as the realization of regular, clean and transparent elections) versus authoritarianism. The degree of satisfaction with democracy declined from 41 percent in 1997 to 37 percent in 1998–2000 and 25 percent in 2001. In 2002 the index rose to 32 percent but declined to 38 percent in 2003. See www.latinobarometro.org.

10. See Walter Alarcón, "La democracia en la mentalidad y prácticas populares," in W. Alarcón et al., *¿De qué democracia hablamos?* (Lima: DESCO, 1992), pp. 9–47; Carlos Franco, "Visión de la democracia y crisis del regimen," *Nueva Sociedad* 128 (1993): 50–61; Carlos M. Vilas, "Pobreza, desigualdad social y sustentabilidad democrática: El ciclo corto de la crisis argentina," *Revista Mexicana de Sociología* 57, no. 2 (2005): 229–69.

11. Anthony Lake, *From Containment to Enlargement* (Washington, DC: Johns Hopkins University School of Advanced International Studies, 1993).

12. Joseph Stiglitz, "Más instrumentos y metas más amplias para el desarrollo: Hacia el consenso post-Washington," *Desarrollo Económico* 151 (1998): 691–722.

13. Carlos M. Vilas, "La sociología política latinoamericana y el 'caso' Chávez: Entre la sorpresa y el déjà vu," *Revista Venezolana de Economía y Ciencias Sociales* 7, no. 2 (2001): 129–45.

14. Hugo Fazio, *Mapa actual de la extrema riqueza en Chile* (Santiago: LOM-ARCIS, 1997); Portes and Hoffman, "Latin American Class Structures."

15. Luis Lander, "La insurrección de los gerentes: Pdvsa y el gobierno de Chávez," *Revista Venezolana de Economía y Ciencias Sociales* 10, no. 2 (2004): 13–32; Bernard Mommer, "Petróleo subversive," in *La política venezolana en la época de Chávez*, ed. Steve Ellner and Daniel Hellinger (Caracas: Nueva Sociedad, 2003), pp. 167–85; Patricia Márquez, "¿Por qué la gente votó por Hugo Chávez?," in Ellner and Hellinger, *La política venezolana*, pp. 253–72; and Vilas, "La sociología política latinoamericana."

16. Fernando H. Cardoso, "La versión brasileña del sueño americano," *Clarín* (Buenos Aires), 20 February 2005, p. 30.

17. Vilas, "Pobreza."

18. *El País* (Montevideo), 4 March 2005.

19. Speech made before the Legislative Assembly, 25 May 2003, www.eldia.com.ar/discurso-kirchner/.

20. Regarding foreign involvement in the coup of April, see Heather Busby et al., "US Works Closely with Coup Leaders," Resource Center of the Americas, May 2002, www.americas.org/item_227; Christopher Marquis, "Estados Unidos financió a grupos opositores a Chávez," *Clarín* (Buenos Aires), 26 April 2002, p. 10; the declarations of former President Andrés Pérez in *Clarín* (Buenos Aires)

and *El Tiempo* (Bogota), both on 23 August 2004, p. 23; also Agence France Press, "Carlos Andrés Pérez: Sólo queda la violencia para tumbar a Chávez," interview with Radio Caracol (Bogotá), Geneva, 2004, www.rnv.gov.ve/noticias/index .php?act=st&f=2&t=7931/. On the escalation of rhetoric and the declarations of the chairman of the Joint Chiefs of Staff comparing Venezuela with Iraq before the U.S. invasion: *La Nación* (Buenos Aires), 13 April 2005.

21. Condoleezza Rice, "Secretary of State Condoleezza Rice at the Post," 2005 March 25, www.washingtonpost.com/ac2/wp-dyn/A2015–2005Mar25; General James T. Hill, "Statement of General James Hill before the Armed Forces Commission of the House of Representatives," 2004 March 24, usinfo.state.gov/espanol/ 04032904.html; and Hill, "Statement Before the House Armed Service Committee, U.S. House of Representatives, on the State of Special Operation Forces," 2003 March 12.

22. Hugo Alconada Mon, "El eje del mal en América Latina," *La Nación* (Buenos Aires), 2005 April 10.

23. Kenneth Roberts, "Polarización social y resurgimiento del populismo en Venezuela," in Ellner and Hellinger, *La política venezolana*, pp. 75–95; Steve Ellner, "Venezuela imprevisible: Populismo radical y globalización," *Nueva Sociedad* 183 (2003): 11–26; and Ellner, "Hugo Chávez y Alberto Fujimori: Análisis comparativo de dos variantes de populismo," *Revista Venezolana de Economía y Ciencias Sociales* 10, no. 1 (2004): 13–37.

24. Carlos M. Vilas, "¿Populismos reciclados o neoliberalismo a secas? El mito del 'neopopulismo latinoamericano,'" *Revista Venezolana de Economía y Ciencias Sociales* 9, no. 3 (2003): 13–36.

12. De Protesta a Propuesta: The Contributions and Challenges of Latin American Feminism

Norma Chinchilla and Liesl Haas

1. Julieta Kirkwood, "Feminismo y participación politica en Chile," in *La Otra Mitad de Chile*, ed. Maria Angelica Meza (Santiago, Chile: CESOC, 1986), p. 69. Latin America and Latin American as used throughout this discussion include the countries of the Caribbean.

2. Sonia E. Alvarez, Elisabeth Jay Friedman, Ericka Beckman, et al., "Encountering Latin American and Caribbean Feminisms," *Signs: Journal of Women in Culture and Society* 28, no. 2 (2003).

3. "Second wave" feminism, as used here, refers to feminist movements that emerged in the 1970s, based on ideas about the unity of production and repro-

duction, politicizing what society defines as "personal" or belonging to the domestic sphere, and the right of women to control their bodies.

4. Liesl Haas, "The Catholic Church in Chile: New Political Alliances," *Latin American Religion in Motion,* ed. Christian Smith and Joshua Prokopy (New York: Routledge, 1999).

5. Liesl Haas, "Changing the System from Within? Feminist Participation in the Worker's Party in Brazil, 1989–1995," in *Radical Women in Latin America: Right and Left,* ed. Victoria Gonzalez and Karen Kampwirth (University Park: Pennsylvania State University Press, 2001).

6. In 1989, the military government in Chile criminalized all abortions, even those necessary to save a woman's life.

7. Haas interview with Isabel Duque of ISIS international, Santiago, Chile, July 2001.

8. A bill currently pending in the Costa Rican parliament would transform the National Center into the National Women's Institute, an independent government ministry.

9. Nancy Saporta Sternbach, Marysa Navarro-Arangueren, Patricia Churchryk, and Sonia Alvarez, "Feminisms in Latin America: From Bogotá to San Bernardo," *Signs: Journal of Women in Culture and Society* 17, no. 2 (1992): 393–434.

10. Susan Franceschet, "Global Trends and Domestic Responses: Explaining Differences in Gender Politics in Argentina and Chile," paper presented at the Conference on Transnational Dimensions of Democratization in the Americas: New Directions in Research, Mount Allison University, June 24–26, 2005.

11. Jean Franco, "Defrocking the Vatican: Feminism's Secular Project," in *Politics of Culture, Culture of Politics: Re-Visioning Latin American Social Movements,* ed. Sonia Alvarez, Arturo Escobar, and Evelina Dagnino (Boulder, CO: Westview Press, 1998), 278–89.

13. Negotiating Multicultural Citizenship and Ethnic Politics in 21st Century Latin America

Shane Greene

I would like to thank Steve Scott, Jordan Lauhon, and Mike Cepek for reading and reacting to parts of this chapter. Eric Hershberg and Fred Rosen were tremendously helpful with editorial patience and encouragement. I should also extend a special word of thanks to Jean Rahier, who provided me with the opportunity in the first place.

1. For a more extensive analysis of Toledo's borrowing of an Inca image and its implications for Peru's turn toward a multicultural model, see Shane Greene, "Get-

ting over the Andes: The Geo-Eco-Politics of Indigenous Movements in Peru's 21st Century Inca Empire," *Journal of Latin American Studies* 38, no. 2 (2006).

2. Cecilia Méndez, "Incas sí, indios no: Notes on Peruvian Creole Nationalism and its Contemporary Crisis," *Journal of Latin American Studies* 28 (1996): 197-225.

3. See Margaret Keck and Kathryn Sikkink, *Activists Beyond Borders* (Ithaca, NY: Cornell University Press, 1998); Sonia Alvarez, Evelina Dagnino, and Arturo Escobar, *Culture of Politics/Politics of Cultures* (Boulder, CO: Westview Press, 1998); Alison Brysk, *From Tribal Village to Global Village* (Palo Alto, CA: Stanford University Press, 2000); Kay Warren and Jean Jackson, *Indigenous Movements, Self-Representation, and the State in Latin America* (Austin: University of Texas Press, 2002).

4. Donna Lee Van Cott, *The Friendly Liquidation of the Past: The Politics of Diversity in Latin America* (Pittsburgh: University of Pittsburgh, 2000).

5. For a possible exception to this rule, see Marisol de la Cadena, *Indigenous Mestizos* (Durham, NC: Duke University Press, 2000).

6. Brysk, *From Tribal Village*.

7. See Peter Wade, *Race and Ethnicity in Latin America* (London: Pluto Press, 1997); and Juliet Hooker, "Indigenous Inclusion/Black Exclusion: Race, Ethnicity, and Multicultural Citizenship in Latin America," *Journal of Latin American Studies* 37, no. 2 (2005): 285-310.

8. See Louise Silberling, "Displacement and Quilombos in Alcântara, Brazil: Modernity, Identity, and Place," *International Social Science Journal* 55, no. 175 (2003): 145-56.

9. Quoted in Peter Wade, "The Cultural Politics of Blackness in Colombia," *American Ethnologist* 22, no. 2 (1995): 341-57, p. 348.

10. Charles Hale, "Does Multiculturalism Menace?: Governance, Cultural Rights and the Politics of Identity in Guatemala," *Journal of Latin American Studies* 34, no. 3 (2002): 485-524.

11. For more about CONAIE and Pachakutik, see Donna Lee Van Cott, *From Movements to Parties in Latin America* (Cambridge: Cambridge University Press, 2005).

12. My translation from "Luis Macas: 'Volver a lo Nuestro,'" *BBCMundo.com*, 16 September 2005, news8.thdo.bbc.co.uk/hi/spanish/latin_america/newsid_4749000/4749969.stm (accessed 30 December 2005).

13. Juan Forero, "Elections Could Tilt Latin America Further to the Left," *New York Times*, 10 December 2005.

14. My translation from "Ley # 1551: Ley de Participación Popular," www.fps.gov.bo/legal/ley_pdf/ley1551.pdf (accessed 30 December 2005).

15. For more on Bolivian unrest, see Forest Hylton and Sinclair Thomson, "The Roots of Rebellion I: Insurgent Bolivia," *NACLA Report on the Americas* 38, no. 3 (November/December 2004).

16. Clifford Krauss, "Man in the News: Peru's New Leader, an 'Indian Rebel with a Cause,' " *New York Times,* 5 June 2001, p. A3.

17. Xavier Albó, "Ethnic Identity and Politics in the Central Andes," in *Politics in the Andes,* ed. Jo-Marie Burt and Philip Mauceri (Pittsburgh: University of Pittsburgh Press, 2004); Kay Warren and Jean Jackson, eds., *Indigenous Movements, Self-Representation, and the State in Latin America* (Austin: University of Texas Press, 2002); Deborah Yashar, *Contesting Citizenship in Latin America: Indigenous Movements and the Post-Liberal Challenge* (Cambridge: Cambridge University Press, 2005).

18. Carlos Degregori, "Movimientos étnicos, democracía, y nación en Perú y Bolivia," in *La construcción de la nación y la representación ciudadana en México, Guatemala, Perú, Ecuador, y Bolivia,* ed. C. Dary (Guatemala: FLACSO, 1998); de la Cadena, *Indigenous Mestizos.*

19. Beth Conklin and Laura Graham, "The Shifting Middle Ground: Amazonian Indians and Eco-Politics," *American Anthropologist* 97, no. 4 (1995), pp. 695–710; Richard Smith, "Las Políticas de la Diversidad: COICA y las Federaciones Etnicas de la Amazonia," in *Pueblos Indios, Soberanía y Globalismo,* ed. Stefano Varese (Quito: Abya Yala, 1996), pp. 81–125; Andrew Gray, "Development Policy-Development Protest: The World Bank, Indigenous Peoples, and NGOs," in *The Struggle for Accountability: The World Bank, NGOs, and Grassroots Movements,* ed. Jonathan A. Fox and L. David Brown (Cambridge, MA: MIT Press, 1998).

20. See Shane Greene, "Indigenous People Incorporated? Culture as Politics, Culture as Property in Pharmaceutical Bioprospecting," *Current Anthropology* 45, no. 2 (2004): 211–37.

21. See Richard Chase Smith, "Las Políticas de la diversidad: COICA y las federaciones étnicas de la Amazonia," in Varese, *Pueblos indios.*

22. See Greene, "Getting over the Andes."

23. Congreso de la República, "Ley del Instituto Nacional de Pueblos Andinos, Amazónicos y Afroperuano," www2.congreso.gob.pe/sicr/RelatAgenda/proapro.nsf/ProyectosAprobadosPortal/E9F5F4BEA9BA905005256F70006A5 2B3 (accessed 27 December 2005).

14. Labor and the Challenge of Cross-Border, Cross-Sector Alliances

Mark Anner

This chapter draws on an article published with Peter Evans, "Building Bridges Across a Double-Divide: Alliances Between U.S. and Latin American Labor and NGOs," *Development in Practice* 14, no. 1 and 2 (February 2004): 34–47.

1. Statement issued at the Fourth Hemispheric Conference against the FTAA, Havana, Cuba, 30 April 2005, www.asc-hsa.org.

2. Åke Wedin, *La 'Solidaridad' Sindical Internacional y Sus Víctimas: Tres Estudios de Casos Latinoamericanos* (Göteborg: Instituto de Estudios Latinoamericanos de Estocolmo, 1991); Beth Sims, *Workers of the World Undermined: American Labor's Role in U.S. Foreign Policy* (Boston, MA: South End Press, 1992).

3. Ruth Berins Collier and David Collier, *Shaping the Political Arena: Critical Junctures, the Labor Movement, and Regime Dynamics in Latin America* (Princeton, NJ: Princeton University Press, 1991); Francisco Zapata, *Autonomía y Subordinación en el Sindicalismo Latinoamericano* (Mexico City: Fondo de Cultura Económica, 1993).

4. Kim Voss and Rachel Sherman, "Breaking the Iron Law of Oligarchy: Union Revitalization in the American Labor Movement," *American Journal of Sociology* 106, no. 2 (2000): 303.

5. Peter Evans, "Fighting Marginalization with Transnational Networks: Counter-Hegemonic Globalization," *Contemporary Sociology* 29, no. 1 (2000): 230.

6. This section draws on chapters two and four of my dissertation: Mark Anner, "Between Solidarity and Fragmentation: Labor Responses to Globalization in the Americas," unpublished dissertation, Department of Government, Cornell University, Ithaca, NY, 2004.

7. The Union of Needletrades, Industrial and Textile Employees (UNITE) formed in 1995 by the merger of the International Ladies' Garment Workers' Union (ILGWU) and the Amalgamated Clothing and Textile Workers' Union (ACTWU).

8. Henry J. Frundt, *Trade Conditions and Labor Rights: U.S. Initiatives, Dominican and Central American Responses* (Gainesville: University Press of Florida, 1998).

9. U.S./LEAP, "A year after winning legal recognition, STEYY announced on December 10, 2001 that it signed its first contract," January 2003, www.usleap.org/Maquilas/PastMaquilaCampaigns.html (accessed 27 July 2003).

10. UNITE also merged with the Hotel Employees and Restaurant Employees union (HERE) to form UNITE HERE.

11. The top leadership of the AFL-CIO dominates its board of trustees, and the AFL-CIO also contributes small amounts of funding. Yet most funding comes from government funding through the U.S. Agency for International Development and a yearly core grant from the National Endowment for Democracy. ACILS maintains a network of twenty-eight offices, with a total full-time staff of about 160 people, in all regions of the Global South and transitional economies.

12. To my knowledge, the Canadians were the first to ensure that their Web site was fully bilingual so that Southern as well as Northern activists could benefit from their information and analysis.

13. Author interview with Marina Ríos, coordinator, Melida Anaya Montes Women's Movement (MAM), San Salvador, El Salvador, 19 July 2001.

14. The group eventually disbanded after a leadership dispute, although this did not involve a division between NGOs and unions.

15. Author's interviews.

16. Margaret E. Keck and Kathryn Sikkink, *Activists Beyond Borders: Advocacy Networks in International Politics* (Ithaca, NY: Cornell University Press, 1998).

17. The organization is better known in the region by its Spanish name, the Alianza Social Continental (ASC).

18. "Alternatives for America: General Principles," www.web.net/comfront/alts4 americas/eng/01-general-e.html (accessed 20 October 2005). This is the second draft of the 1998 document.

19. Maria Lorena Cook, "Regional Integration and Transnational Politics: Popular Sector Strategies in the NAFTA Era," in *The New Politics of Inequality in Latin America: Rethinking Participation and Representation,* ed. Douglas A. Chalmers, Carlos M. Vilas, Katherine Hite, Scott B. Martin, Kerianne Piester, and Monique Segarra (New York: Oxford University Press, 1997), pp. 516–40.

20. ORIT represents 45 million workers in thirty-three labor centers in the Americas.

21. Héctor De la Cueva, "Crisis y Recomposición Sindical Internacional," *Nueva Sociedad* 166 (2000): 111–22.

22. Interview with author, Buenos Aires, May 2002.

23. Alianza Social Continental, "III Cumbre de los Pueblos," www.asc-hsa.org/article .php3?id_article=276 (accessed 20 October 2005).

Contributors

Mark Anner is an assistant professor of labor studies and industrial relations and political science at the Pennsylvania State University in University Park. Prior to earning his PhD in government at Cornell University, Mark lived in Latin America for ten years, where he worked with labor unions.

Julio Boltvinik is a research professor at the Center for Sociological Studies, Colegio de México. He is currently a federal deputy in the Mexican Congress, representing the Party of the Democratic Revolution. He has published widely on questions of poverty in Latin America, and is the author of *Ampliar la mirada: Un nuevo enfoque de la pobreza y el florecimiento humano.*

Norma Chinchilla is a professor of sociology and women's studies at California State University, Long Beach. She has published numerous articles on women's movements in Latin America and, with Nora Hamilton, co-authored *Seeking Community in a Global City: Guatemalans and Salvadorans in Los Angeles.*

Araceli Damián is a research professor at the Center for Demographic, Urban and Environmental Studies, Colegio de México. She is the co-editor, with Julio Boltvinik, of *La pobreza en México y el mundo.*

Paul W. Drake is the dean of social science and the Institute of the Americas Professor of Political Science and History at the University of California, San Diego. A past president of the Latin American Studies Association, Drake is the author of three award-winning books—*Socialism and Populism in Chile,*

The Money Doctor in the Andes, and *Labor Movements and Dictatorships*—and the editor or co-editor of seven anthologies. He has also published over fifty articles on Latin America.

Shane Greene is an assistant professor of anthropology at Indiana University. His work on indigenous movements and ethnic politics in Peru has appeared in *American Ethnologist, Current Anthropology,* the *Journal of Latin American Studies,* and *NACLA Report on the Americas.* He is currently working on a book titled *Customizing Indigeneity: Paths to a Cultural Politics in Peru.*

Liesl Haas is an assistant professor of political science at California State University, Long Beach. Her research interests include comparative political institutions, women and politics, and religion and politics. Her most recent publication (co-authored with Merike H. Blofield) is "Defining a Democracy: Reforming the Laws on Women's Rights in Chile, 1990–2002," *Latin American Politics and Society* 47, no. 3 (2005): 35–68.

Judith Adler Hellman is a professor of political and social science at York University. She is the author of *Mexico in Crisis, Journeys Among Women,* and *Mexican Lives,* and is currently writing a book on Mexican migration to the United States to be published by The New Press.

Eric Hershberg is a professor of political science and the director of Latin American studies at Simon Fraser University in Vancouver. A senior adviser at the Social Science Research Council, he also chairs NACLA's board of directors and has published extensively on Latin American affairs. He is co-editor, with Paul W. Drake, of *State and Society in Conflict: Comparative Perspectives on Andean Crises* and, with Felipe Aguero, of *Memorias militares: Visiones en disputa en dictadura y democracia.*

Katherine Hite is an associate professor of political science at Vassar College and the author of *When the Romance Ended: Leaders of the Chilean Left, 1968–1998.* She co-edited *The New Politics of Inequality in Latin America: Rethinking Participation and Representation* (with Douglas Chalmers, et al.) and

Authoritarian Legacies and Democracy in Latin America and Southern Europe (with Paola Cesarini).

Luis Reygadas is a professor in the department of anthropology, Universidad Autónoma Metropolitana Iztapalapa, Mexico. He was a Rockefeller Fellow in the Persistent Inequalities in Latin America program at the State University of New York at Stony Brook. His most recent books are *Globalización económica y Distrito Federal: Estrategias desde el ámbito local* and *Ensamblando Culturas: Diversidad y conflicto en la globalización de la industria*.

William I. Robinson is a professor of sociology, global studies, and Latin American studies at the University of California-Santa Barbara. His most recent books are *Critical Globalization Studies* (with Richard Appelbaum), *A Theory of Global Capitalism*, and *Transnational Conflicts: Central America, Social Change, and Globalization*. He was formerly an investigative journalist in Latin America and a consultant for the Nicaraguan government.

Fred Rosen is a political columnist for the Mexico edition of the *Miami Herald*, a contributing editor of *NACLA Report on the Americas*, and a former director of NACLA. His essays and reporting on Latin America have appeared in *Foreign Policy in Focus, In These Times*, and the Mexican papers *La Jornada* and *El Financiero*. He is co-editor of *Free Trade and Economic Restructuring in Latin America*.

Lars Schoultz is William Rand Kenan, Jr., Professor of Political Science at the University of North Carolina at Chapel Hill. A former president of the Latin American Studies Association, he is the author of *Human Rights and United States Policy toward Latin America, The Populist Challenge: Argentine Electoral Behavior in the Postwar Era, National Security and United States Policy toward Latin America*, and *Beneath the United States: A History of U.S. Policy toward Latin America*.

Mark Ungar is an associate professor of political science at Brooklyn College, City University of New York. He also works with NGOs and governments on police reform in Latin America. Ungar is the author of *Elusive Reform: Democracy and the Rule of Law in Latin America.*

Carlos Vilas is a postgraduate professor of government and public policy at the National University of Lanús in Buenos Aires. The author of nineteen books, he is currently the director of the Tripartite Group of Health Services (Etoss) in the Argentine national government.

Coletta A. Youngers is a consultant and senior fellow at the Washington Office on Latin America (WOLA). An analyst of human rights, political developments, and U.S. policy in the Andean region of Latin America, she is the co-editor of *Drugs and Democracy in Latin America: The Impact of U.S. Policy* and *Violencia Política y Sociedad Civil en el Perú: Historia de la Coordinadora Nacional de Derechos Humanos.*

Index